Living Chinese Philosophy

SUNY series in Chinese Philosophy and Culture
―――――――
Roger T. Ames, editor

Living Chinese Philosophy

Zoetology as First Philosophy

Roger T. Ames

SUNY
PRESS

Cover: The familiar expression "ceaseless procreating" (*shengshengbuyi* 生生不已) is used to capture zoetology or "the art of living" as a first philosophy. Calligraphy is by the scholar-artist Ni Peimin.

Published by State University of New York Press, Albany

For information, contact State University of New York Press, Albany, NY
www.sunypress.edu

Library of Congress Cataloging-in-Publication Data

Name: Ames, Roger T., author.
Title: Living Chinese philosophy : zoetology as first philosophy / Roger T. Ames.
Description: Albany : State University of New York Press, [2024] | Series: SUNY series in Chinese Philosophy and Culture | Includes bibliographical references and index.
Identifiers: ISBN 9781438499536 (hardcover : alk. paper) | ISBN 9781438499543 (ebook)
Further information is available at the Library of Congress.

Contents

Introduction

Rehearsing the Argument

In this introduction, let me try to lift the architecture of this monograph to the surface, and to anticipate for the reader how the argument will unfold. The starting point is the pragmatic assumption that all problems arise out of and must be responded to within the context of the practical activity taking place in our immediate experience. Again, given this primacy of practice, the purpose of theorizing, as itself an intrinsic feature of practical activity, is meliorative in the sense of being an attempt to make both the form and the performance of these same practices more intelligent and productive. The mutual entailment of the subjective and objective, self and world, theory and practice as aspects within immediate experience is indicative of the fact that a proper understanding of experience itself is resistant to exclusive, dualistic categories of any kind.

My next step then is to first ask and then to try and answer the question: How can those of us who do philosophy of culture make responsible and productive cultural comparisons? To this end, I lay out what I call the method of comparative cultural hermeneutics. Accepting the inseparability of the subjective and objective aspects of our immediate experience, we must allow that it is this same experience and nothing else that is our ultimate reality; all experience is equally real. That is, contra the equation between knowledge and reality in classical Greek epistemology, coming to know something makes it no more real than the degree to which we actually do know it, and the faltering steps it takes us to get there.

Given the irrevocable continuity between the subjective and the objective in the human experience, all additional meaning that makes experience more intelligent arises between what one encounters in the world as novel experience and the responsiveness to it that is projected out of one's own continuing narrative. Thus, for the method of comparative cultural hermeneutics, the turning of the hermeneutical circle begins in the ongoing attempt to interpret and understand what we do not know. But given the subjectivity of the interpreter that is integral to our hermeneutical sensibilities, in reading and understanding a text we necessarily begin from projected "fore-meanings" that are heavily colored by our own worldview and our purposes in engaging the text. In the case of making comparisons between and among cultures, the encounter with an alternative philosophical tradition requires that we respect its alterity and, at the same time, that in the interpretive process we take advantage of the deepening contrast this alterity provides in identifying and coming to understand the assumptions that we ourselves are bringing to the interrogation.

When from a room brightly lit by our own cultural understanding we look through a window into the darkness of what we do not yet know, the window becomes a mirror, and we see ourselves. On the one hand, there is the persistent danger of a reductionism in which the cultural other is converted into what is familiar within our own cultural narratives. At the same time, however, in the seeing of ourselves, to the extent to which we are able to secure an increasingly self-conscious awareness of our own assumptions and purposes in the inquiry, this awareness enables us to establish an instructive contrast between our past ways of thinking and living, and the additional meaning that is won as we try to make sense of the novel experience. In just this way, the engagement with an alternative philosophical tradition is symbiotic; it provides incrementally new insight into both ourselves and into the other philosophical tradition as we come to experience a fusing of our cultural horizons.

With this method of comparative cultural hermeneutics in hand, I then bring it to bear on what I take to be a fundamental distinction between Greek ontological thinking and what I have termed Confucian "zoetological" thinking, a "first philosophy" distinction that has far-reaching implications for the understanding of both traditions. The classical Greeks give us a substance ontology grounded in "being qua being" or "being per se." In so doing, they posit a self-sufficiency of being-in-itself as it constitutes the identity of any particular thing, with the human "being" being a clear example. It is this "being" that guarantees the identity of a permanent and unchanging subject as a substratum for the human experience, where the "being" itself cannot be relinquished while at the same time remaining the same in kind. This "sub-stance" of independent things necessarily persists through change, entailing as it does the combination of *eidos* as the formal cause (the essential, reduplicative characteristic that makes things what they are) and *telos* as the final cause (the design and purpose that draws a thing to its given end). This substratum or essence is defining of the "what-it-means-to-be-a-thing-of-this-kind," and it includes the existential purpose of any particular thing. Ontology, in providing the strict identity necessary for something to be this and not that, deals in a taxonomy of closed, exclusive boundaries that would isolate things both as things in themselves and as categories of things. Hence, such strict identity in ontological thinking enables the exclusionary principle of noncontradiction that insists that something cannot be at once A and not-A. Such conceptual and classificatory thinking with its promise to reveal to us "what is what" can be fairly described as categorical in the sense of categorizing things in a way that is definite, explicit, and unequivocal.

In the *Yijing* 易經 or *Book of Changes* we find a vocabulary that stands in stark contrast to this substance ontology and its persistent common sense. The alternative cosmological assumptions entail a way of thinking that begins from "living" (*sheng* 生) rather than "being" (*on* or *ousia*), providing the interpretive context for the Confucian canons by locating them within a holistic, organic, and ecological worldview. To be clear, just as there is no exclusivity in the distinction between subjectivity and objectivity, or between the existential and the phenomenal, this understanding of immediate experience as an unbounded ecology is hylozoistic in the sense that there can be no categorical distinction between the animate and the inanimate, between matter and life. The claim in the *Book of Changes* that "procreativity is itself the meaning of change" makes the point that in a vital cosmology that will not brook dualistic categories, we must resist the suppressed assumption that some final boundary can be drawn between what is living and what is not.[1]

To establish a meaningful contrast with the fundamental Greek ontological assumptions that give us "the science of being," I have borrowed the Greek notion of *zoe* or "life" and created the neologism "zoetology" or, in Chinese, *shengshenglun* 生生論 as "the art of living." This cosmology is grounded in "living" (*sheng* 生) as the motive and existential force that enables change, where the ongoing transformation of things is driven by the

---

1. Roger T. Ames, *A Sourcebook in Classical Confucian Philosophy* (Albany: State University of New York Press, 2023), 103: 富有之謂大業, 日新之謂盛德. 生生之謂易: It is because of the proper way's sheer abundance that we call it "the grand workings"; it is because of its daily renewal that we call it "copious virtuosity"; it is because of its ceaseless procreating that we call it "the changes" (*yi* 易).

very nature of life itself to optimize the available conditions for continuing growth. Zoetology gives us a world of boundless "becomings," that is, a contrast between ontologically isolatable "things" that *are* and interpenetrating "events" that *are happening*; a contrast between an ontological conception of discrete human "beings," for example, and a vital, processual, and narrative conception of what I have called human "becomings."[2]

The philosophical term "ontology" is most frequently translated into modern Chinese as *bentilun* 本體論. This specific correlation of terms is the culture's best attempt to express a sense of what is most basic in the human experience, a "first philosophy," with the conventional suffix *lun* 論 giving us the "subject of discussion or study," or "-ology." But even in the formulation of this translated term, when it is taken literally it reveals the suppressed assumption that in the Confucian worldview it is "life" rather than "being" that is perceived as referencing what is most basic and pervasive. That is, both of the terms *ben* 本 as "setting root, root, trunk" and *ti* 體 as "setting root, rhizome, forming, embodying, body, unit" are alluding to the continuing process of vital growth in the life experience. Again, this semantically cognate relationship between these two terms *ben* and *ti* is made explicit in what is commonly used as the simplified form of the traditional character *ti* 體 as *ti* 体, in which the graph includes the character for "root" (*ben* 本) itself.[3]

I would argue that an understanding of zoetology as "the art of living" in expressing what is most basic in the Confucian cosmology is essential to an explanation of the assumed coincidence that obtains among all of the various dimensions of the human experience in Confucian philosophy: aesthetics, education, family life, morality, politics, religion, and so on. That is, all that is beautiful, intelligent, loving, good, just, and sacred in the human experience returns us to nothing more than those modalities of human conduct that strengthen the root and conduce to growth in all of our familial, communal, cultural, and ecological relations.

At the same time, the kind of contrast I am arguing for between onto-logical and zoetological thinking, expressed in different terms by different

---

2. See Roger T. Ames, *Human Becomings: Theorizing Persons for Confucian Role Ethics* (Albany: State University of New York Press, 2021).

3. For more on the *ti* body, see Deborah Sommer, "Boundaries of the *Ti* Body," in *Star Gazing, Fire Phasing, and Healing in China: Essays in Honor of Nathan Sivin*, ed. Michael Nylan, Henry Rosemont Jr., and Li Waiyee, special issue of *Asia Major*, 3rd series, 21, part 1 (2008).

philosophers of culture, has prompted many historians and philosophers, too, to recoil from such thick generalizations as nothing more than an orientalism that would essentialize cultural traditions and, in so doing, make such cultures discrete and incommensurable. Indeed, those of us who would deploy such distinctions have been roundly accused of being "essentialists" of the first order.[4] Preemptively then, and in defense of my comparative cultural hermeneutics as method, I reference two earlier comparative philosophers, G. W. Leibniz and Qian Mu. Taking them as examples of philosophers of culture, I make an earnest attempt to unload the essentialism charge that is so persistently leveled against those of us who would appeal to thick cultural generalizations.

One of the far-reaching implications of ontological thinking is that introducing a disparity between what is real and what is less so generates a proliferation of dualisms as its basic philosophical vocabulary: reality and appearance, subject and object, theory and practice, reason and emotion, soul and body, knowledge and opinion, true and false, good and evil, self and world, and so on. When these same terms are carried over into the province of zoetological thinking, rather than remaining as exclusive dualisms, they become aspectual terms such as right and left or *yin* 陰 and *yang* 陽, and thus become mutually entailing, correlative categories that require each other for their explanation. Contra the assumptions underlying the exclusiveness of dualistic thinking, all experience has both a subjective and an objective aspect, and theorizing becomes an intrinsic and inseparable feature of practical activity. Importantly, assumptions that would posit the primacy of some erstwhile "objective," independent, universal, and unchanging principles, or that would enable the logic of categorical knowing, or that would affirm a mind-independent world, or that would promise us an unconditional truth, have no purchase within this zoetological worldview.

One of my hobbyhorses in advocating for a better understanding of Confucian philosophy has been the exhortation that we commentators must strive to take the tradition on its own terms. But doesn't such an appeal rest upon the suppressed premise of an exclusive and isolating understanding

---

4. In recent times, such a criticism has been directed at myself and my own collaborators D. C. Lau, David L. Hall, and Henry Rosemont, as well as at the comparative work of Marcel Granet, Joseph Needham, Fritz Mote, K. C. Chang, Tang Junyi, Fei Xiaotong, and many others who like us insist that there is no option but to find an explanatory vocabulary that would allow us to locate other philosophical traditions within their own interpretive contexts.

of objectivity? From an ontological perspective, taking the tradition on its own terms would mean that we must commit ourselves to giving an objective account of Confucian philosophy without distorting it by introducing subjective values and alternative cultural importances that are not its own. Using a zoetological perspective to reconceive this same charge of respecting the integrity of Confucian philosophy, however, requires us to abandon any naïve assumptions we might have about an independent "view-from-nowhere" objectivity, and to instead apply our method of comparative cultural hermeneutics. This would mean that our engagement with Confucian philosophy must necessarily include the perspective of our own narrative; we must certainly strive with imagination to allow the Confucian tradition the space to provide us with as full an account of itself as we can. But rather than stopping at Confucian philosophy being "objective" in the sense of standing independent of our assumptions, we have to acknowledge that in our self-conscious engagement with it, we are viewing it from a perspective not its own. While there is always the danger of compromising the integrity of Confucian philosophy, at the same time there is also the opportunity for us to learn and to appropriate from this Confucian tradition in shaping our own world-making "objectives." For an essentialist conception of Confucian philosophy, such an external perspective might be discounted as a source of revision if not distortion, but alternative perspectives can also provide what has been a living, eclectic tradition with an opportunity for expansive growth within the context of world philosophy.

Having summarized some of the implications of ontology, I then allow the canons of the classical Greek tradition—first Parmenides and then Plato and Aristotle—to present their own arguments on behalf of ontological thinking. We only have fragmentary sections of Parmenides's poem *On Nature*, but the reach and influence of his ontological intuition that "only Being is" for the subsequent trajectory of the Western philosophical narrative in its metaphysics, epistemology, logic, ethics, political philosophy, philosophy of religion, and so on, cannot be overstated. Again, in many ways the evolution of Plato's "Theory of Forms" from the early dialogues to his later writings continues the logic of this Parmenidean intuition as an explanation of what really *is*, and the philosophical journey we need to embark upon to come to know it. This ontological thinking has become foundational in both Western philosophy and theology to the extent that A. N. Whitehead, in service to his own thick generalizations, famously claims that "the safest general characterization of the European philosophical tradition is that it consists of a series of footnotes to Plato."[5] Although this statement illustrates all too well what John Dewey has impatiently criticized as Whitehead's "excessive piety toward those historic philosophers from whom he has derived valuable suggestions,"[6] still Whitehead's basic point is well made: the ideas of Plato (and he should include Parmenides and Aristotle as well) were formative, persistent, and indeed even now retain a real relevance for understanding the trajectory of contemporary Western culture in its sustained critique of this old way of thinking.

We next turn to Aristotle's contribution to ontological thinking, beginning at the beginning with his categories. In the *Categories*, Aristotle rehearses what he takes to be those questions that need to be asked to provide us with an exhaustive knowledge of something by giving it a full predication or description, using as he does "the man in the market-place" as his specific example. Although Aristotle is critical of Plato's transcendentalism, his four causes in fact relocate and continue Plato's notions of *eidos* as the reduplicated, essential, and unchanging formal cause of things and *telos* as the design and purpose that draws them to their final end. Aristotle in the *Metaphysics* just as Plato in the *Timaeus* provides a kind of theological account of cosmic order, where Aristotle's concept of *theoria* as the highest stage of knowledge, far from reducing the human *nous* or intellect to the status of a mere external spectator, in fact credits the active *nous* with momentary experiences of what for the Prime Mover is an eternity of "thinking thinking itself," in which being, thinking, and the object of thought are one and the same.[7]

As I cite selected passages from translations of these original Greek texts, I again have recourse to my method of comparative cultural hermeneutics by interrupting these citations with what I call my own "anticipations" that are prompted by some associative or usually contrastive analogies I find in the Confucian tradition. The textual citations are substantial in order to allow the Greek tradition to speak on its own terms, while my punctuating

---

5. A. N. Whitehead, *Process and Reality: An Essay in Cosmology*, corrected 2nd ed., ed. David Ray Griffin and Donald Sherburne (New York: Free Press, 1979), 39.

6. Paul Schlipp, *The Philosophy of Alfred North Whitehead* (New York: Tudor, 1941), 659–660.

7. This logical assumption that the thought and reality must be the same is already present in Parmenides when he states: "For thou canst not know what is not—that is impossible—nor utter it; for it is the same thing that can be thought and that can be."

"anticipations" are reflections on what I deem to be some significant point being made by the Greek philosophers that provides an opportunity for a conversation with alternative assumptions implicit within the Confucian philosophical narrative.

With the Greek texts themselves speaking on behalf of ontology and having thus brought their ontological assumptions into clearer focus, I then turn to Confucian zoetology. Again wanting to allow the original texts to speak for themselves, I excerpt relevant passages from the "Great Commentary" (*Dazhuan* 大傳) to the *Book of Changes* that during this formative period in Chinese culture attempts to make explicit the cosmological assumptions ambient as the persistent intellectual environment in which the various philosophical lineages flourished. Using the language of the *Changes* itself that would construe the continuing process of cultural evolution in terms of "continuity in change" (*biantong* 變通), I argue that this always evolving and yet persistent worldview has over the centuries provided the interpretive context for not only China's indigenous philosophical developments but also for the Confucian engagement with waves of Western learning that begins with Buddhism in the third century CE and then continues down to the present day. In this early cosmology, "change" (*yi* 易) is real, and it is defined explicitly as the generative "procreativity" (*shengsheng* 生生) that animates all experience—that is, the ongoing production of life itself. My argument is that zoetological thinking in this tradition has produced alternative ways of understanding the most basic of our cultural assumptions: that is, an alternative, relational understanding of persons as interdependent human "becomings" rather than as discrete human "beings"; of in situ or situated creativity as the source of meaning rather than meaning being derived from some independent creatio ex nihilo cause; of a generative logic and a *ziran* or "self-so-ing" ecological causality as Confucianism's "own causality and its own logic";[8] of an achieved, optimizing symbiosis rather than a predetermined teleology as the motive force; of the art of living that seeks a musicality in the human experience rather than a quest for certainty; of a family- rather than a God-centered religiousness, and so on.

In the final chapter of this monograph, I argue that the distinction I am making between ontological and zoetological thinking has immediate resonances within the narrative of contemporary Chinese philosophy itself. To this end, I have summarized some of the recent publications of

---

8. Joseph Needham, *Science and Civilisation in China*, vol. 2 (Cambridge: Cambridge University Press, 1956), 280.

four contemporary Chinese comparative philosophers in which they, in their own very different terms, have outlined productive distinctions that I believe are consistent with the contrast I am making herein between ontology and zoetology. I begin with Zheng Kai 鄭開 and the interpretive problem he has described explicitly as "misplaced ontology" (本體論誤置). Zheng rehearses research in Chinese philosophy in the twentieth century as it has been pursued by some of China's most distinguished philosophers, in which they appeal to the language of ontology (本體論) to characterize their own tradition. In their various attempts to qualify Western ontology in explanation of what is basic as first philosophy in the Chinese philosophical tradition, Zheng Kai argues that they cannot help but elide the distinction between Greek ontology and an alternative Confucian process cosmology, introducing equivocations that largely obscure rather than illuminate the differences. Zheng insists that in doing research on Chinese philosophy, we have to begin not with ontology but by asking: What is it that has been taken to be most basic within this tradition itself in its alternative account of the human experience—that is, its own *benti* 本體 or first philosophy? And Zheng's answer is a distinctively Chinese *xinxing* theory (*xinxinglun* 心性論) that emerges in the middle of the Warring States period with the writings of Zhuangzi and Mencius and that then sets a trajectory for the evolution of Chinese philosophy down through to the neo-Confucian thinkers of the Song and Ming dynasties and beyond.

In contrast to the focus on epistemology that comes with Greek ontological thinking, *xinxing* theory appeals to a regimen of personal cultivation that enables persons to make the most out of the heartmind (*jinxin* 盡心) as it is grounded in what is most basic in the natural propensities of human beings (*xing* 性). Tracing the origins of this *xinxing* theory back to the Zisizi tradition that emerges in the historical interval between Confucius and Mencius, Zheng shows how the later elaboration of the notion of *cheng* 誠—"sincerity," "integrity," "creative resolve"—as a cosmic force in the evolving SiMeng school is key for understanding *xinxing* theory.

Inspired by Zheng Kai's setting the problem of "misplaced ontology" and his appeal to the notion of *cheng* 誠 as it functions to clarify *xinxing* theory's own understanding both of what is most basic and what are the heights of human flourishing, I join him in common cause in trying to bring this complex idea, *cheng*, into clearer focus. *Cheng*, as it has been interpreted in both the Chinese and Western commentary on the SiMeng lineage and on *Focusing the Familiar* (*Zhongyong* 中庸) in particular, is associated with cosmic "creativity." Importantly, the only kind of "creativity" that is relevant in this one-world process cosmology is creatio in situ: that is, the co-creativity and growth in meaning that takes place in the relationship between particulars and their contextualizing others.

Zhu Xi 朱熹 like many other commentators in the tradition offers a generative understanding of *cheng*, glossing it as it appears in the *Zhongyong* 中庸 as 真實不妄 that we might translate as "the genuine and undeflected process of coming to fruition." For Zheng Kai, *cheng* is the quality of coalescence that humans are able to cultivate in their relations with the contents of their world and, in so doing, to thereby reconcile all erstwhile dualisms such as subject and object, self and other, human and *tian*, *benti* or what is most basic and its consummating fruition, and so on. Real depth achieved in this coalescence is captured in Mencius's rhetorical question: "Is there any enjoyment greater than, with the myriad things of the world all implicated here in me, turning personally inward and finding resolution (*cheng*) with them all?"[9]

The second contemporary philosopher I summarize and then engage is Zhang Xianglong 張祥龍 with the stimulating distinction he draws between "imagistic thinking" (*xiangsiwei* 象思維) and "conceptual thinking" (*gainiansiwei* 概念思維). Zhang rehearses the history of *gainian* 概念 as a Chinese term that was coined in the second half of the nineteenth century to translate the Western notion of "concept." The history of the English term "concept" itself takes us back to the taxonomical and categorical "A or not-A thinking" of classical Greek ontology that abstracts and detemporalizes some reduplicated, essential form or idea (*eidos*) from the particular instances of things. Such higher-order conceptual thinking gives privilege to formal definition and theoretical explanation, dealing in a currency of abstract universals that retrospectively hypostasize and thus make stable those objects of thinking that would rationalize the human experience. Most noteworthy in Zhang's characterization of this kind of thinking is that, in purporting to constitute the unchanging logic that provides access to a given, transcendent reality, conceptual thinking is not generative in the sense of its being able to produce new meaning.

For Zhang, imagistic thinking is different. Change and growth is real. Drawing upon the process cosmology and the language of images made explicit in the *Book of Changes*, Zhang argues that this way of thinking begins from the strains, tensions, and conjunctions that reside within dyadic *yinyang* images as they themselves are the source of growth and change.

---

9. *Mencius* 孟子 7A4: 萬物皆備於我矣. 反身而誠, 樂莫大焉.

We might recall that the *Changes* provides its own denotative definition of change when it states explicitly that "procreativity is itself the meaning of change."[10] Thus, both the changing faculties and the objects of human knowledge reside within a vital cosmology that takes the life and growth of organisms within their environing conditions as what is most basic. Imagistic thinking functions within the holistic context of immediate experience in which doer, doing, and what is done are all coterminous and mutually entailing. Such thinking is nonobjectifying in the sense that it does not hypostatize what are always transforming events that share overlapping, shifting horizons rather than exclusive boundaries.

It is the function of conjured images to introduce adjustments in experience that restore equilibrium and balance to it. Images are radically temporal in the sense that, rising and falling, living and dying, they resist finality or definition. Restating Martin Heidegger's claim that "language is the house of being," Zhang sees imagistic thinking and its capacity to produce meaning expressed through the medium of language to be a vital source of the situated creativity that locates humankind as "language animals" squarely in their "house of becoming."

I respond to Zhang Xianglong from the perspective of the Western philosophical narrative that from early times has appealed to a distinction between philosophy and rhetoric, between the literal and the metaphorical, between the universal and the particular. As a way of further clarifying Zhang's distinction between concept and image for a Western philosophical narrative that has in important degree favored the conceptual and theoretical over imagistic thinking, I search the classical Chinese philosophical canons and commentaries in an attempt to bring the less familiar notion of "image" (*xiang* 象) into clearer focus. Even though metaphorical language has always functioned as an important source of meaning in the tradition, it is only recently in our narrative with philosophers such as J. L. Austin, Ludwig Wittgenstein, Stephen Pepper, George Lakoff, and Mark Johnson that we have arrived at a sustained reflection upon the power of metaphor as the motor of meaning in the structure of our thinking, and in the performative functions that language accomplishes.

As early as the third century in the Chinese narrative, Wang Bi 王弼 in his commentary on the *Book of Changes* appeals to Daoist intuitions in outlining the nonfoundational and nonreferential function of the symbiotic sequencing of image (*xiang* 象), language (*yan* 言), and meaning (*yi* 意), with

---

10. 生生之謂易.

each of these phases giving rise to the other two. There is a trade-off that follows from this distinction. Conceptual thinking in its appeal to necessity and formal definition provides a clarity and precision made possible through the rationalization of the human experience. On the other hand, imagistic thinking as the ongoing and open-ended process of making suggestive correlations among available possibilities is at best vague and allusive, but at the same time, it generates additional meaning.

A third prominent voice in contemporary comparative philosophy is Zhao Tingyang 趙汀陽, who begins by indicting the discipline of philosophy from start to finish for its utter failing to provide an ontology that is consistent with the lived human experience. Zhang makes a distinction between a metaphysics of "things" that has explanatory force for the world of science and logic, and what he calls a metaphysics of *facta* (*shi* 事) that can speak to the "doings" and the "makings" that are constitutive of lives lived in the world. In Zhao's revisionist "ontology," he challenges Descartes's radical subjectivity and its foundational dualism as it is captured in the *cogito* and gives priority to the wholeness of experience and the world-making that it produces as it is expressed through his alternative to Descartes—*facio ergo sum*: "I do therefore I am."

Again, beginning from the irreducibly relational nature of the human experience, Zhao privileges "coexistence" (*gongzai* 共在) over mere existence (*cunzai* 存在) with the immediate consequence that this new ontology spills over into ethics, and social and political philosophy. In the transition from an ontology of "is" to one of "doing," when we acknowledge that we are choosing to do "this" rather than "that," the gap between what "is" and what we "ought" to do closes, and fact and value thus find reconciliation. Given that this doctrine of coexistence leads humankind into a recognition of their shared future, it stands as a stark alternative to the disenchantment of the human experience that is the byproduct of an ideology of foundational individualism. For Zhao, individualism is an ontological mistake that leads him ultimately to the poignant observation that "no one can be happy by himself."

I find important corroboration for my ontology and zoetology distinction in the fact that Zhao, in his more recent publications, sets up a contrast between classical Greek ontology and an alternative Confucian "creatiology" (*chuangshilun* 創世論) that resonates closely with my own attempts to clarify what I mean by zoetology. One salient feature of Zhao's formulation of his "world-making" ontology is that, although he certainly draws important insights from the Confucian philosophical tradition, he takes as his purview world philosophy broadly construed and speaks to its needs in an inclusive way. Given that Confucian philosophy begins from the lifeworld with its wholeness of experience, these commitments make the formulation of its own ontology an aestheticism that aspires to a human historicity in which the quality of humankind's "doings," "makings," and "actings" conduce ultimately to its full participation in a cosmic musicality.

In my own response to Zhao Tingyang, I try to show how his formulation of this alternative ontology serves as the ground for, and can be correlated with, his further thinking about China as a history, a state, and a civilization that informs his interpretation of the emergence of Chinese culture and its basic values. We are able to lift the logic of Zhao's ontology to the surface by beginning from the cluster of terms he appropriates from the canonical texts, then next move to the abstract terms he introduces in expressing this ontology as a metaphilosophy, and then finally correlate this language with the terms and the metaphors he appeals to in telling the story of China.

Zhao, in formulating his revisionist ontology, appeals first to the standard vocabulary of the *Book of Changes* and other canonical texts: "procreativity" (*shengsheng* 生生), "persistence in change" (*biantong* 變通), "superlative harmony" (*he* 和), "focusing the familiar" (*zhongyong* 中庸), and so on. In building his argument by appealing to these classical texts, he is able to lay a foundation that carries with it the authority of the tradition itself.

The next step for Zhao is to set up a contrast between this vocabulary and the dualistic ontologies expressed in traditional Western philosophers from the classical Greeks through Descartes. Qualifying the assumptions of traditional ontology with the attempts by philosophers such as Giambattista Vico and Martin Heidegger to overcome this entrenched way of thinking, he constructs a new vocabulary for his alternative metaphysics. Contrasting the Greek language of "being" (*cunzai* 存在) with familiar and yet abstract terms such as "doing" (*shi* 事), "making" (*zuo* 作), "coexisting" (*gongsheng* 共生), "setting the root" (*zhagen* 扎根), "growth" (*shengzhang* 生長), and so on, he is able to give expression to an alternative vision of what is most basic in Confucian "world-making" that he then calls "creatiology" (*chuangshilun* 創世論). At the heart of his new ontology is not only the fact of the radical contextuality of all change, life, and growth but also a recognition that the nature of life itself, through mutual accommodation between organism and environment, is to seek to optimize its conditions for growth.

I then apply this unbounded, holistic ecological sensibility—that is, rootedness, life, growth, historicity, emergence, hybridity, an optimizing symbiosis, and so on—to Zhao Tingyang's concrete project of answering the question: Where did China come from? In giving his "whirlpool" account of a Chinese "world-making," Zhao creates yet another cluster of terms needed to tell the story of China as *tianxia* or "All under Heaven." The unboundedness and holistic vision of "taking the world as a world" (*yitianxiaguantianxia* 以天下觀天下) is captured in the language of "no outside" (*wuwai* 無外) and "internality" (*neibuxing* 內部性); the need for "setting the root" and "growth" becomes "transitivity" (*chuandi* 傳遞) and "historicity" (*lishixing* 歷史性); the move from existence to coexistence becomes "compatibility" (*xiehe* 協和) and "relational rationality" (*guanxilixing* 關係理性); and so on.

Zhao's concrete example of the Confucian aspiration to establish an unbounded planetary order can be extended to provide us with a clearer understanding of some of the major themes that have defined Confucian values across the centuries: that is, *he* 和 not as "harmony" but as an "optimizing symbiosis"; *ru* 儒 not "Confucians" but as "a social stratum of intergenerational transmitters of a living literati culture"; *xiao* 孝 not as "ancestor worship" but as the "feelings of family reverence that allow each succeeding generation to embody the continuing civilization and build its own connector to the next"; *dao* 道 not as a monism or universalism but as a generative "one is many, many one" pluralism (*yiduobufen* 一多不分) with the many being imbricated in the one, and the one being constituted by the many.

A fourth contemporary scholar who has made an important contribution to rethinking ontology in a way that would make it consistent with Confucian cosmology is Sun Xiangchen 孫向晨. Sun in his revisionist ontology, like Zhao Tingyang, begins from an appreciation of Heidegger's formidable challenge to traditional Greek ontology. And yet at the same time, from Sun's own awareness of the important implications of "family reverence" (*xiao* 孝) in Confucian philosophy and the sense of "rootedness" and intergenerational growth (*shengsheng* 生生) that it carries with it, he has become cognizant of several of Heidegger's blind spots and omissions. Sun exposes a failure on the part of Heidegger to do justice to the irreducibly social and radically temporal dimensions of his own contextualizing "thereness" of *Dasein* that he calls "being-in-the-world."

Indeed, Sun Xiangchen in his appeal to "family reverence" (*xiao*) as the ontological structure of "generationality" retrofits the Heideggerian understanding of this term *Dasein* from "being-in-the-world" to a Confucian "being-between-the-generations," thus redefining *Mitsein* or "being with" in a way that resolves the persistent problem of Heidegger's *Dasein* being read in an individualistic way. While Heidegger is certainly a disrupter of the first order in challenging the categorical and decontextualizing force of traditional ontology, he is still himself a philosopher within a narrative where its languages and its common sense pull him in the direction of hypostasizing the eventfulness of the human experience and thereby neglecting its radical transitivity, relationality, and temporality.

Another implication of "family reverence" (*xiao*) as the prime moral imperative in Confucian philosophy is the centrality of "body" as the flesh and blood conduit through which a living cultural tradition is quite literally "embodied" in its continuing intergenerational transmission. There is a genealogical continuity of an existential, social, and cultural body that locates us between the past and the future, and that cannot be separated from the lineage of ancestors, parents, and children in which progenitors live on in their progeny. At the end of the day, the higher order, complex and organically related table of Confucian values are themselves all grounded in and derived from what is primal in the human experience—that is, "family feeling" or "devotion to kinship" (*qinqin* 親親).

Sun Xiangchen is keen to allow the canonical texts to speak for themselves in constructing the compelling argument that "family" as a human institution, all but ignored by Heidegger, is in fact the existential structure of *Dasein*. Indeed, Sun takes the primal status of "devotion to kinship" (*qinqin*) a huge step further, arguing that we can extrapolate from the Confucian case where such family feeling is the ground of the second order moral vocabulary to extend its relevance to humanity as a whole. That is, "devotion to kinship" (*qinqin*) can be universalized as those primordial kinship feelings that are the substance of an unbounded moral consciousness in the human experience in its broadest and most inclusive sense.

A theme in Sun's critique of Heidegger about the face-to-face relational context that he then extends to other major contemporary figures such Martin Buber and Emmanuel Levinas, and that has become the direction of Sun's own most recent, groundbreaking work, is philosophy of family. For the most part, the Western philosophical narrative has privileged the synchronic over the diachronic and, in relations, the impartial over the partial. In so doing, it has also largely excluded the intimacy of family from its crucial role in the education and moral life of human beings. Heidegger describes *Dasein*'s ontological "homelessness" as the anxiety that comes with a lack of subjective control over our own narratives as we are simply "thrown into the world." Sun argues that Confucianism counters such existential angst by its deep appreciation of the role of "being-born-into-the-family" and the consequent warmth, intimacy, and joy to be found in such family bonds. Indeed, for Sun, the sense of joy that is omnipresent in the classical Confucian texts has not been sufficiently appreciated as feelings that are pervasive in both the moral and religious consciousness.

Sun goes on to develop a distinctively Confucian understanding of a family-centered religiousness. Heidegger makes much of *Dasein*'s "being-toward-death" in which the inevitability of death and human finitude has a profound impact on the entire existential project. Where Sun again finds Heidegger wanting is in his failure to develop an appreciation of the relationship between the living and the dead, offering a Confucian alternative to fill this lacuna that we might call "being-toward-life." While Heidegger invests a great deal of concern in his "authentic and inauthentic" distinction, Sun sees the "teaching and learning" (*xue* 學) that is the substance of a continuing and vital cultural tradition to be the ontological framework within which each generation through the emulation of those who have come before achieves its own identity. One cannot overstate the deep and persistent influence that, from earliest times, the institution of ancestral sacrifice has had on the life of this Confucian, family-centered religiousness. These sacrifices are the continuity between the human and spiritual worlds in which the solemn reverence and sincerity expressed in embodied ritual practices conjure forth the spiritual world of the ancestors and make it present to the living.

In rehearsing the important contributions of these four contemporary philosophers, I begin from Zheng Kai's argument that in the Confucian philosophical narrative the notion of *cheng* 誠 as it has been developed in the SiMeng lineage has profound explanatory force in our grasp of *xinxing* theory (*xinxinglun* 心性論) as an alternative first philosophy. In my response to Zheng, I survey the canonical texts and try to bring additional clarity to this crucial but in some ways recondite term *cheng*. Again responding to Zhang Xianglong's contrast between imagistic and conceptual thinking, I have tried to extend his important insight by surveying the meaning and function of the notion of "image" (*xiang* 象) as it is appealed to in the Confucian canons. Similarly, in my response to Sun Xiangchen's engagement with Heidegger and his alternative understanding of *Dasein* as "being-between-the-generations" rather than "being-in-the-world," I have thought it prudent to expand upon three themes that are more or less omitted in Heidegger and yet are central to Sun's argument.

First, for Western readers the history and the meaning of "family reverence" (*xiao* 孝) as the prime moral imperative in Confucian philosophy needs further explication. Because the institution of family has had little relevance in the Western philosophical narrative, *xiao* is not a familiar idea, and where it is referenced, it is often undervalued if not misunderstood. Second, integral to *xiao* as the intergenerational transmission of a living cultural tradition is a fuller understanding of how the complex notion of body as "embodying" functions to perpetuate the civilization. Third, an extension of this somatic dimension of *xiao* is a cognizance of how the institution of ancestral sacrifice has grounded the civilizing of experience in early China, ritualizing and aestheticizing its characteristic ways of living and thinking.

In expanding upon "family reverence" (*xiao*) as a technical term, I begin from defining it through its etymology and its central place in the Confucian canons, thereby underscoring Sun Xiangchen's claim that it serves as a primal value in the tradition. The example I appeal to is the intimate relationship between *xiao* and "consummate conduct" (*ren* 仁), with the *ren* habitude being rooted in and growing out of *xiao* family feelings.

I then offer three clarifications necessary to get past common misinterpretations of *xiao*. The ideal of *xiao*, far from being unilateral and impositional as an imperative for blind obedience, is in fact resolutely collateral, functioning in both directions. That is, *xiao* is the bilateral relationship between the elder and younger generations. Ideally, where the elders are entitled to attentiveness and respect from their progeny, the progeny derive pleasure in deferring to those who, through the process of emulating their seniors, have enabled the continuing construction of their own personal and cultural identities. Important in this relationship is not only the progeny's sense of duty but the stern imperative for the younger generation to remonstrate (*jian* 諫) with their elders when they deem that these seniors have strayed from their moral compass.

A second clarification with respect to *xiao* is that, while it is rooted in familial roles and relations, this is only its beginnings. *Xiao* has immediate relevance to the structure and function of all dimensions of the human experience. The assumption is that social, political, moral, religious, aesthetic, and indeed cosmic order are derived from devotion to kinship not only as what is most basic in human feelings but also as what is most intense and close to the bone.

And a third clarification is that *xiao* challenges the uncritical celebration of simple equality and the rejection of all hierarchies as assumptions that are inconsistent with the everyday life of human beings. There is a reconciliation of this tension between hierarchy and equality in the affordances available through acknowledging the value of relational equity as a continuing source of diversity. Appropriate differences that define both roles and different stages in the career of the human being are accommodated through relational diversity, while at the same time serving to keep the specter of coercion that attends imposed homogenization at bay.

Given the centrality of family (*jia* 家) in all dimensions of Confucian philosophy, this enduring institution can be used as a heuristic to give an account of Confucian civilization from earliest times to the present day. The ultimate source of the written language and much of the Confucian moral vocabulary is derived from the practices of ancestral sacrifices, from ritual propriety (*li* 禮) that gives everyone a place to stand to a sense of appropriateness (*yi* 義) that provides guidance for everyone in what to say and do. The lettered classes in the inheritance and transmission of the culture are the "literati family" (*rujia* 儒家) who provide the tradition with its orthodoxy (*daotong* 道統). This elite stratum of society models the shared family values (*xiaodao* 孝道) that provide structure for the inclusive social and political order, and it derives its authority from the deference paid to it from within the family lineages (*jiazu* 家族) that constitute its community, and that are the substance of its continuing identity as a uniquely cultured people (*minzu* 民族).

Having formulated a method for making cultural comparisons that allows traditions to speak on their own terms, I have then applied this comparative cultural hermeneutics to two different conceptions of first philosophy: the more familiar Greek ontological thinking and the alternative zoetological thinking that has been both persistent and dominant in Chinese cosmology, and that has also more recently become mainstream in the postmodern Western philosophical narrative. In attempting to bring further authority to my argument for the important implications of this distinction, I have appealed to the voices of these four contemporary Chinese comparative philosophers, who I believe are, in their own language, formulating a comparison that has an affinity with my own.

Chapter 1

Comparative Cultural Hermeneutics as Method

Taking Advantage of Our Gadamerian Prejudices

As a self-confessed philosopher of culture, I take it as my task to identify, excavate, and articulate generalizations that would distinguish and thus provide insight into different cultural narratives. It is only in being cognizant of these uncommon cultural assumptions that, in some degree at least, we are able to respect fundamental differences and locate the philosophical discussion somewhere between the alternative worldviews. Just as with the watershed of the Western cultural narrative that we would associate with Plato and Aristotle and Hellenistic culture, certain enduring commitments were made explicit in the formative period of Chinese philosophy that are more persistent than others, and that allow us to make useful generalizations about the evolution of this continuing tradition. According to a central precept in the *Yijing* 易經 or *Book of Changes*, we must anticipate "continuities in change" and "change within continuity" (*biantong* 變通).

In insisting upon the central role that language plays in constituting the human experience, Charles Taylor has called humankind "the language animal."[1] If we acknowledge the power that entrenched and constitutive linguistic propensities woven into our human forms of life and our "webs of interlocution" might have in shaping the philosophy of grammar of any given population, it might occasion a reconsideration of our usual way of thinking about the originality of our own great philosophers.[2] Without

---

1. Charles Taylor, *The Language Animal: The Full Shape of the Human Linguistic Capacity* (Cambridge, MA: Harvard University Press, 2016).

2. Charles Taylor, *Sources of the Self: The Making of the Modern Identity* (Cambridge MA: Harvard University Press, 1989), 36.

slighting the defining influence they have had on their respective traditions, we might ask to what extent in the history of thought are a Plato and an Aristotle and indeed a Confucius, too, constructing their philosophical precepts out of whole cloth, and to what extent are they—with penetrating insight, certainly—only making explicit what is largely already implicated in the structure and function of the languages they have inherited from the intergenerational transmission of a living tradition? In what degree are they cultural archaeologists in the business of "recovering" and laying bare the legacy of a hard-won "common sense" bequeathed to them by the best of those who have come before? And at our own historical moment what method of inquiry can we deploy that will enable us to make responsible comparisons between one of these cultural traditions, as it has been sedimented in its language, and another?

A familiar way of thinking about "methodologies" that we associate with rational, systematic philosophies is that they are the formal principles or theoretical procedures of inquiry employed in a particular field or discipline. For example, in philosophy, we might speak of Socratic dialectics or Cartesian rational skepticism as methodologies, and of analytic, logical, and phenomenological methodologies among many others. The term "methodology" itself suggests the familiar theory/practice dichotomy by formalizing the method and establishing the principles of explanation prior to their application.

In looking for a starting point and formulating my own method for doing comparative philosophy, I appeal to John Dewey's postulate of immediate empiricism and the primacy he gives to practice. Dewey observes that "there is, then, from the empiricists' point of view, no need to search for some aboriginal *that* to which all successive experiences are attached, and which is somehow thereby undergoing continuous change. Experience is always of *thats*; and the most comprehensive and inclusive experience of the universe that the philosopher himself can obtain is the experience of a characteristic *that*."[3] As Dewey's alternative to starting from abstract philosophical concepts and theories, he is arguing that all of our terms of art must be understood as the "thats" of specifically experienced meanings. For Dewey, the root paralogism or illogic in all idealisms is the equation posited between knowledge and reality that arises from the ontological dualisms of Being and Nonbeing, reality and mere appearance. Indeed, for

---

3. John Dewey, *The Middle Works of John Dewey, 1899–1924*, edited by Jo Ann Boydston (Carbondale: Southern Illinois University Press, 1977), vol. 3, 165.

Dewey knowing is only one kind of experience that is properly served by the "reals" of all the other *thats* as they lead us toward the true worth of intelligent practice. As a philosophical method then, Dewey's empiricism requires that since all human problems arise within the "hadness" of immediate experience as it is had by specific persons in the world, the resolution to these problems must be sought through theorizing this same experience in our best efforts to make its outcomes more productive and intelligent. "Hadness" for Dewey is not some claim to "pure" or "primordial" experience but simply what experience *is* as it is *had* by those persons experiencing it. In formulating this method, Dewey begins by asserting that "immediate empiricism postulates that things—anything, everything, in the ordinary or non-technical use of the term 'thing'—are what they are experienced as. . . . If you wish to find out what subjective, objective, physical, mental, cosmic, psychic, cause, substance, purpose, activity, evil, being, quality—any philosophic term, in short—means, go to experience and see what the thing is experienced *as*."[4] Dewey's method provides us with a way of ascertaining what the language we use actually means, and it precludes the dualisms that usually follow in the wake of deploying abstract and thus decontextualizing terms such as reality, rationality, objectivity, justice, and indeed methodology itself. And corollary to Dewey's immediate empiricism is a recognition of the fact that experience itself is always a vital, continuous, collaborative, and unbounded affair. Thus, his "hadness," far from precluding a robust subjective aspect, insists upon it.

Before Dewey formulated his postulate of immediate empiricism, William James had earlier offered his own version of a similar idea that probably inspired Dewey, referring to it as a "radical empiricism": "To be radical, an empiricism must neither admit into its constructions any element that is not directly experienced, nor exclude from them any element that is directly experienced. For such a philosophy, *the relations that connect experiences must themselves be experienced relations, and any kind of relation experienced must be accounted as 'real' as anything else in the system*" (italics original).[5] And more recently, yet another advocate of a pragmatic approach to philosophy, Hilary Putnam, brings additional clarity to this postulate of immediate empiricism by not only rejecting "view-from-nowhere" objectivism, but by further underscoring the fact that the subjective dimension of experience is

---

4. Dewey, *Middle Works*, vol. 3, 158, 165.

5. William James, *The Works of William James*, vol. 3: *Essays in Radical Pragmatism* (Cambridge, MA: Harvard University Press, 1976), 22.

always integral to what the world really is. Putnam insists that "elements of what we call 'language' or 'mind' *penetrate so deeply into what we call 'reality' that the very project of representing ourselves as being 'mappers' of something 'language-independent' is fatally compromised from the start.* Like Relativism, but in a different way, Realism is an impossible attempt to view the world from Nowhere" (italics original).[6] Putnam will not admit of any understanding of the real world that cleaves it off from its human participation and that does not accept our experience of it as what the world *really* is. He is making this same point regarding the holistic and inclusive nature of experience when he insists: "The heart of pragmatism, it seems to me—of James' and Dewey's pragmatism if not of Peirce's—was the supremacy of the agent point of view. If we find that we must take a certain point of view, use a certain 'conceptual system,' when engaged in a practical activity, in the widest sense of practical activity, then we must not simultaneously advance the claim that it is not really 'the way things are in themselves.' "[7]

When we carry Dewey's postulate of immediate empiricism over to the task of interpreting another philosophical tradition, we can perhaps best resist cultural reductionism and allow the other culture to speak on its own terms by employing a comparative cultural hermeneutics as our method of inquiry. The starting point of hermeneutics is an acknowledgment of the interpretive interdependence of the subjective and objective structures of meaning within the experience from which understanding is to be gained. Hans-Georg Gadamer insists that "understanding is not a method which the inquiring consciousness applies to an object it chooses and so turns it into objective knowledge; rather, being situated within an event of tradition . . . is a prior condition of understanding. *Understanding proves to be an event*" (italics original).[8] Understanding as an "event" begins with interpreters reading a text from the perspective of their own worldview and thus produces what Gadamer calls "fore-meaning," where

> whoever is trying to understand a text, always engages in project-
> ing (*Entwerfen*): he/she projects a meaning for the text as soon
> as some initial meaning comes to the fore. That initial meaning,

---

6. Hilary Putnam, *Realism with a Human Face* (Cambridge, MA: Harvard University Press, 1990), 28.

7. Hilary Putnam, *The Many Faces of Realism* (La Salle, IL: Open Court, 1987), 83.

8. Hans-Georg Gadamer, *Truth and Method*, 2nd ed., trans. Joel Weinsheimer and Donald G. Marshall (New York: Crossroad, 1997), 309.

however, emerges only because the text is read with certain expectations regarding its meaning. . . . We are not expected to jettison all our "fore-meanings" concerning its content. All that is asked is that we remain open to the intrinsic lesson of the text. . . . That is why a hermeneutically trained person must be, from the start, sensitive and receptive to the text's alterity or difference (*Andersheit*).[9]

It is in this spirit of understanding as an event that begins from one's own "fore-meanings" that Gadamer uses the term "prejudices" (*Vorurteil*), not as blind biases but, on the contrary, as a way of acknowledging that a deliberate cognizance of our own prejudgments facilitates rather than obstructs our access and insight into something we do not know. These prejudgments are not only our presuppositions but also our projective interests and concerns in undertaking the inquiry. For Gadamer, the hermeneutical circle within which understanding is always situated requires of us that we continually strive to be aware of what we carry over into our new experience, since critical attention to our own assumptions and purposes can serve to positively condition the depth and quality of our interpretation of what it is we encounter.[10]

We can perhaps take this understanding of interpretation one step further by referencing J. L. Austin who remarks that "the world must exhibit (we must observe) similarities and dissimilarities (there could not be one without the other): if everything were either absolutely indistinguishable from anything else or completely unlike anything else, there would be nothing to say."[11] We might read Austin as insisting that analogical correlations that appeal to either similarities or differences can be productive or otherwise to the extent that they are a source of increased meaning. Where this is relevant to our comparative cultural hermeneutics is that the real "distance" between deeply different cultural traditions is most likely to provide us with a wealth of "dissimilarities" that allow for more expansive correlations and thus give us something new and important to say. We need only to reflect, for example, on how the hundreds of translations and interpretations of the

---

9. Gadamer, *Truth and Method*, 267–269.

10. See Jeff Malpas, "Hans-Georg Gadamer," in *The Stanford Encyclopedia of Philosophy* (Fall 2018 edition), ed. Edward N. Zalta, https://plato.stanford.edu/archives/fall2018/entries/gadamer/.

11. J. L. Austin, *Philosophical Papers* (Oxford: Oxford University Press, 1961), 89–90.

Daodejing over the past few centuries with all of their different philosophical perspectives have extended the meaning of this protean text and elevated its status to the highest echelons within world literature.

To be clear, the claim here is that a comparative cultural hermeneutics has the potential to inspire a greater degree of insight than simply working within either tradition separately, because the analogical associations and contrasts that emerge in the challenging process of working between traditions are productive of a greater quantum of meaning and a more robust quality of understanding. Indeed, fundamental differences when used properly can be activated to make a difference, and they can serve the interests of clearer understanding on both sides.

Comparative Cultural Hermeneutics as Analogical Thinking

With the term "interpretation" itself meaning literally "a go-between negotiation," it can be argued that all meaningful interpretation of experience emerges analogically through establishing and aggregating a pattern of truly productive correlations between what we already know and what we would know. In interpreting a bump in the night, we immediately look for correlations in our past experience for explanation. Analogize we must, but at the same time, we might also want to allow that not all analogies are equally apposite. As has become apparent in the troubled history of how Chinese philosophy has been translated and thus "carried over" into the Western academy, poorly chosen comparisons can become an entrenched and persisting source of distortion and of the cultural condescension that often comes with it. A heavy-handed and impositional "Christian," "Heideggerian," and yes "pragmatic" or "Whiteheadian" reading of Chinese philosophy as well, betrays the reader by distorting both the Chinese tradition and the Western analog in the comparison. As inescapably correlative thinkers, we need to be analogically retail and piecemeal rather than working in whole cloth. While a careful comparison of Heidegger's *Dasein* and the *Daodejing*'s 道德經 use of "insistent particularity" (*de* 德) as an embedded event might be profitable, a wholesale "Heideggerian reading" of the *Daodejing* betrays not only both Heidegger and Laozi but also the credulity of the unwitting reader who is being offered such an interpretation.

Analogies can be productive of both associations and contrasts, and we can learn much from both. To take an example, *Focusing the Familiar*

(*Zhongyong* 中庸) was hugely influential as a singularly important fascicle in the *Record of Rites* (*Liji* 禮記) and was later canonized a second time as one of the Confucian *Four Books.* This canonical text argues that the best of human beings have both the capacity and the responsibility to be co-creators with the heavens and the earth. In seeking to interpret this text, we might find an associative analogy in the work of A. N. Whitehead with his concern to reinstate "creativity" as an important human value. For Whitehead, claims about perfection and thus the aseity (or self-sufficiency) of God in traditional theology precludes any interesting or coherent sense of human creativity. Following Whitehead's sustained critique of conventional ways of thinking about creativity, the word "creativity" itself becomes an individual entry in a 1971 supplement to *The Oxford English Dictionary* with two of the three references being to Whitehead's own *Religion in the Making.*[12] At the same time, however, we can find a contrastive analogy when the same Whitehead invokes the primordial nature of God and the Eternal Objects that are sustained in His thinking. Indeed, the long shadow of Aristotelian metaphysics and the teleological function of his Unmoved Mover sets a real limit on the relevance of these aspects of Whitehead's philosophy for classical Chinese process cosmology.

Aristotle's teleology, his substance ontology and the categorical thinking it promotes, and his reliance upon logic as *the* demonstrable method that will secure us truth certainly serve as contrastive analogies with Chinese process cosmology. After all, such a process cosmology abjures fixed beginnings and ends, precludes any notion of strict formal identity, and will not yield up the principle of noncontradiction as enabling of erstwhile apodictic knowledge. On the other hand, Aristotle's resistance to Platonic abstraction in promoting an aggregating practical wisdom correlates rather productively with one of the central issues in classical Confucian moral philosophy. That is, although Aristotle's *theoria* as the highest level of knowledge has no counterpart in the Confucian theory of knowledge, *phronesis* with its commitment to the cultivation of excellent habits (*hexis*) in the practical affairs of everyday living has some immediate resonance with the ubiquitous Confucian assumptions that "knowing and doing are inseparable and mutually entailing" (*zhixingheyi* 知行合一) and that "forming and functioning have a shared source" (*tiyongyiyuan* 體用一源).

---

12. See the review of John Berthrong, *Concerning Creativity: A Comparison of Whitehead, Neville, and Chu Hsi,* Albany: State University of New York Press, 1998, by David L. Hall in the *American Journal of Theology and Philosophy* 20, no. 3 (September 1999): 285–292.

To summarize, in our project of cultural interpretation, we are cognizant of the fact that we have no choice but to identify productive correlations whether they be associative or contrastive analogies. And we do best to deploy such analogies modestly at a retail rather than at a wholesale scale. With some effort and imagination, such analogies can be qualified and refined to introduce culturally novel ideas into our own world as a source of enrichment for our own ways of thinking and living. In this process of cultural translation, we do well to be deliberate in the picking and the choosing of our analogies, but at the end of the day, pick and choose we must.

Classical Greek Ontology and Chinese Zoetology: "A Small Stock of Ideas"

As we continue, we will have recourse to invoke the work of two of our most distinguished philosophers of culture in recent Western sinology, Joseph Needham and Nathan Sivin, both of whose approaches can be fairly described as a comparative cultural hermeneutics. While the meticulous Sivin is adamant in exhorting us to resist "either-or" simplicity in our cultural comparisons, at the same time he has also observed that "man's prodigious creativity seems to be based on the permutations and recastings of a rather small stock of ideas."[13] If such be the case, how then do we get at this "rather small stock of ideas" that might allow for the mapping out of the subsequent permutations and recastings of these same ideas? Where in our ways of thinking as they are rooted in the classical Greek and Chinese worldviews are Austin's similarities and dissimilarities, and what are the respective Gadamerian "prejudices" that set these traditions apart? From where in their deepest cultural strata can we excavate their uncommon assumptions as those prejudgments that have their beginnings in the self-understanding of the always situated human experience?

Sivin has made a singularly important contribution in his efforts to distinguish Greek and Chinese cosmological assumptions both in his own substantial oeuvre and in his work with the Cambridge historian Geoffrey Lloyd.[14] On the one hand Sivin insists that cultures are too subtle and

---

13. Nathan Sivin, foreword to Manfred Porkert, *The Theoretical Foundations of Chinese Medicine* (Cambridge, MA: MIT Press, 1974), xi.

14. Geoffrey Lloyd and Nathan Sivin, *The Way and the Word: Science and Medicine in Early China and Greece* (New Haven: Yale University Press, 2002).

complex to allow for overly heavy-handed assertions, and he has prudently cautioned us against wholesale "rather than" approaches to cultural comparisons.[15] With just such a caution in mind, in his essay "Comparing Greek and Chinese Philosophy and Science," Sivin still makes some fundamental generalizations that establish a framework and a helpful vocabulary for both associative and contrastive analogies. Indeed, in this regard, Sivin's work, while yielding substantial historical dividends, has important implications for philosophical interpretation as well.[16] For example, Sivin is consonant with his fellow sinologists in asserting that the reality/appearance distinction prevalent in early Greek philosophy "has no counterpart in China."[17] The philosophical "permutations" or implications of the claim that the ontological disparity entailed by the reality/appearance distinction has little relevance for early Chinese cosmology are numerous and profound. And Sivin himself identifies several of these implications in his summary reflections on a comparison between Greek and Chinese philosophy.

For starters, Sivin registers the relative absence of logic as a privileged field of study in early China while at the same time noting the pervasive importance of semantics and pragmatics in the evolving Chinese cultural narrative. This contrast between logic and pragmatics is another way of saying that the Chinese tradition does not privilege some fixed formal aspect—in this case, logic as that "form" of thinking that demonstrates necessary truths—as being more "real" than what is otherwise in flux (that is, meaning as something done). Relatedly, Sivin's observation regarding the ubiquitousness in the Chinese tradition of variations on the "using names properly" theme (*zhengming* 正名) suggests that the function of language used in a Chinese processual cosmology must itself reflect the flux and flow of that cosmos.[18] In this cosmology it is certainly the task of the lettered

---

15. Nathan Sivin, *Medicine, Philosophy and Religion in Ancient China: Researches and Reflections* (Aldershot, UK: Variorum, 1995), viii.

16. See Roger T. Ames, "What Ever Happened to Wisdom? Confucian Philosophy of Process and 'Human Becomings,'" in *Star Gazing, Fire Phasing, and Healing in China: Essays in Honor of Nathan Sivin*, ed. Michael Nylan, Henry Rosemont Jr., and Li Waiyee, special issue of *Asia Major*, 3rd series, 21, part 1 (2008).

17. Sivin, *Medicine, Philosophy and Religion in Ancient China*, Section I, 3.

18. Han Feizi appeals to the notion of "accountability" (*xingming* 形名)—that is, the relationship between what is claimed and what is subsequently accomplished—as a precept in his political philosophy. John Makeham interprets the exposition of what he translates as "name and actuality" (*mingshi* 名實) as being the main theme of Xu Gan 徐幹 (170–217) in his *Zhonglun* 中論. See *Name and Actuality in Early Chinese Thought*

classes to stipulate standard meanings for terms that can be used to effect and sustain social and political order. At the same time, however, they must accept the processual, fluid, and hence provisional if not arbitrary character of a language that does not appeal to some ostensive literal ground as a guarantee of some underlying reality.

Sivin makes another important distinction between the dialectical versus the consensual expectations of philosophical engagement in the classical Greek and Chinese worlds respectively, observing that "Greek culture in the period that concerns us encouraged disagreement and disputation in natural philosophy and science as in every other field; in China the emphasis remained on consensus."[19] The contrast noted here is between Greek dialogue with its assumption that rational analysis will provide access to some exclusive logos, and a Chinese conversation that requires the ongoing negotiation of an inclusive consensus on the best way forward. The epistemic quest for "apodictic" truth drove the Greek dialogue in its search for an absolute and unconditioned quality of knowledge promised by its avatar, mathematics. By contrast, the continuing need to negotiate order within the assumed processual experience of Chinese cosmology had far-reaching ramifications for Chinese philosophy. Such ongoing, inclusive conciliation within the Chinese narrative would explain why achieved consensus in its many forms was regarded as having high value in the classical Chinese world. That is, there is much value invested in the attainment of an inclusive harmony, in the intergenerational reauthorization of a moral orthodoxy, in the continuing commentary on a shared canonical core, in "the art of accommodation" (*jianshu* 兼術) in philosophical deliberation, in the didactic function that the sage has as virtuosic communicator and consolidator, in a recognition of a continuity between humanity and the numinous, in the priority given to reflexive ritual propriety over objective rule or law, in the privileging of appropriate models as an inspiration for proper conduct over an appeal to fixed moral principles, and so on.[20]

(Albany: State University of New York Press, 1994). Versions of this expression *mingshi* are to be found earlier than Xu Gan in School of Names thinkers such as Gongsun Longzi and in the Later Mohist canons, as well as in the *Xunzi*, in the *Chunqiufanlu* 春秋繁露 attributed to Dong Zhongshu 董仲舒 (ca. 179–ca. 104), in the Lunheng 論衡 of Wang Chong 王充 (27–ca. 97), and in the writings of Wang Fu 王符 (85–162).

19. Sivin, *Medicine, Philosophy and Religion in Ancient China*, Section I, 8.

20. Xunzi 荀子 is frequently regarded as the most dialectical of the pre-Qin philosophers, yet he too placed considerable value in the kind of consensus referenced by the expression

In recalling Sivin's "small stock of ideas," one prejudice of the first order that emerges early in the Western philosophical narrative is the commitment to substance ontology with all of its far-reaching implications. Ontology is the branch of metaphysics that seeks to classify and explain the things that exist, with its underlying assumption being that there are substances or essences inherent in things that are available to us as a means of classifying them as this and not that. Ontology privileges "being per se" with its categorical language and its "substance" and "attribute" dualism, giving us substances as property bearers, and those properties that are borne, respectively. Such ontological thinking animates Plato's pursuit of formal, "real" definitions in his quest for certainty (that is, definitions not of words but of what really *is*) and also underlies Aristotle's taxonomical science of knowing "what *is* what." For these classical Greek philosophers, only what is real and is thus true can be the proper object of knowledge, giving us a logic of the changeless. Indeed, such ontological assumptions produce a decidedly categorical way of thinking captured in the principle of noncontradiction that claims something cannot be "A" and "not-A" at the same time.

When we reflect further on Sivin's "rather small stock of ideas," G. W. F. Hegel comes to mind where in his introduction to *The Encyclopedia Logic* he ruminates at great length upon the question: Where does philosophy begin? And in this reverie, he concludes that because philosophy "does not have a beginning in the sense of the other sciences," it must be the case that "the beginning only has a relation to the subject who takes the decision to philosophise."[21] I want to embrace Hegel's concern about the importance of understanding the starting point of our philosophical inquiry, and to heed his injunction to begin from the subjects who take the decision to philosophize. In trying to understand the subject of philosophizing, I will take as my beginning a contrast between a classical Greek ontological conception of the individual human "being" and a classical *Book*

"the art of accommodation" (*jianshu* 兼術) HY 14/5/49. See also David L. Hall and Roger T. Ames, *Thinking from the Han: Self, Truth, and Transcendence in Chinese and Western Culture* (Albany: State University of New York Press, 1998), part 2.

21. G. W. F. Hegel, *The Encyclopedia Logic* (Indianapolis/Cambridge: Hackett, 1991), 41. For Hegel like Confucian philosophy, persons are not facts (like legs) but achievements (like walking) that could not do what they do and become what they are without the structures of the human community. For Hegel, the person as an abstract fact does not do justice to the process of becoming a person. Personhood is an irreducibly social achievement in the sense that identities emerge in and through difference, being at once affirmed by oneself and conferred on one by others.

of Changes process conception of what I will call human "becomings," a contrast between the discrete human being as a noun and interdependent human becomings as gerunds.

The ontological intuition that "only Being is" is at the core of Parmenides's poem *On Nature* and is the basis of the ontology that follows from it. The classical Greeks give us a substance ontology grounded in "being qua being" or "being per se" (*to on he on*) that guarantees a permanent and unchanging essence of the subject as the substratum for the human experience. With the combination of *eidos* (the essential characteristic that makes something this and not that) and *telos* (the design and purpose of a thing) as the formal and final causes of independent things such as human "beings," this "sub-stance" (Gk. *ousia*, L. *substantia* or *essentia*) in "standing firm" necessarily persists through change. In this ontology, "to exist" and "to be" are implicated in one term. The same copula verb "is" (or L. *esse*) that connects the subject with its complement answers the twofold questions of first *why* something exists, that is, its origins and its goal, and *what* it is, its substance. This substratum or essence includes its purpose for being and is defining of the "what-it-means-to-be-a-thing-of-this-kind." In thus setting a closed and exclusive boundary on any particular thing, it provides the strict identity necessary for it to be this, and not that.

The causal question of *why* something exists is thus answered by an appeal to determinative, originative, and indemonstrable first principles (Gk. *arche*, L. *principium*) and provides the metaphysical separation between creator and creature. The question of *what* something *is* is answered by its limitation and definition and provides the ontological distinction between its substance and its accidents, between its real essence and its contingent attributes. In expressing the necessity, self-sufficiency, and independence of things, this substance or essence is both the subject of predication and the object of knowledge. It tells us, as a matter of logical necessity, what is what, and is the source of truth in revealing to us with certainty, what is real and what is not.

What then is zoetological thinking? In the *Book of Changes*, we find a vocabulary that makes explicit cosmological assumptions that stand as a stark alternative to substance ontology and that have prompted me to create the neologism "zoetology" with Greek *zoe-* "life" and *-logia* "discourse" as a new term for this old way of thinking. The introduction of this new term gives us a contrast between "*ont*ology" as "the science of being per se" and "*zoe*tology" that we might translate into modern Chinese as *shengshenglun* 生生論: "the art of living." The starting point in this zoetological cosmology then is that nothing does anything by itself; association is a fact. And further, it is the nature of life that it seeks to optimize the available conditions for its continuing growth, where such growth has a persistent existential and thus intentional aspect. Since the very nature of life is associative and transactional, the vocabulary appealed to in defining Confucian cosmology is irreducibly dyadic and collateral: always multiple, never one. Everything is at once what it is for itself, for its specific context, and for the unsummed totality. Thus there are always correlative *yinyang* 陰陽 aspects within any vital process of change, describing the focal identity that makes something uniquely what it is and, by virtue of the persistent activity within its relations, what it is becoming. Any given thing is internalizing its context in shaping itself, while its contextualizing others in turn are shaped by internalizing it. Important to an understanding of this vocabulary is the gestalt shift from the Greek noun-dominated thinking, with its world of human "beings" and a myriad of essential "things," to the Confucian gerundive assumptions about the always eventful nature of human "becomings" living their lives within their unbounded and interpenetrating natural, social, and cultural ecologies. It is the difference between a leg and walking, between a lung and breathing.

Turning to the human experience specifically, persons are not defined in terms of limitation, self-sufficiency, and independence but ecologically by the vital growth they experience in their intercourse with other persons and their worlds. Given the primacy of lived relationality that gives persons their focal identities, and given the unbounded nature of such relations, any particular person is holographic in existing at the pleasure of everything else. The zoetological question of why such persons exist is explained by the cultivation of their relations to live their roles in family and community productively, and by what they have come to mean for each other. And in zoetological thinking, the necessity entailed in ontology for defining "what is what" is replaced by the correlative possibilities each thing affords everything else for its growth, revision, and redefinition.

But I must hasten to observe that the distinction between ontological and zoetological thinking is not a simple contrast between Chinese and Western philosophy. In the epilogue at the end of this monograph I identity only a few of the many philosophers and thinkers in the countercurrent of the Western philosophical narrative that have challenged ontological thinking. More substantially, the rejection of this substance ontology that begins in earnest in the second half of the nineteenth century becomes a sustained internal critique that, along with it, ushers in a seismic zoetological turn. Indeed, such ontological thinking is precisely what John Dewey is referencing in his deep concern about what he calls *the* philosophical fallacy. Dewey alerts us to our inveterate habit of decontextualizing and essentializing one element within the continuity of experience, and then in our best efforts to overcome this post hoc diremption, of then construing this same element as foundational and causal. For example, in shaping our personal identities in the process of our ongoing narratives, we abstract something called "human nature" or human "being" out of the complexity of this continuing experience, and then we make this abstraction antecedent to and causal of the subsequent process. For Dewey, contrary to this substance thinking "the reality is the growth-process itself. . . . the real existence is the history in its entirety, the history just as what it is. The operations of splitting it up into two parts and then having to unite them again by appeal to causative power are equally arbitrary and gratuitous."[22]

---

22. John Dewey, *The Later Works of John Dewey, 1925–53*, ed. Jo Ann Boydston (Carbondale: Southern Illinois University Press, 1985), vol. 1, 210.

Chapter 2

Unloading the Essentialism Charge

A familiar criticism leveled against those of us who attempt to excavate cultural differences such as ontological and zoetological thinking, and causal and correlative thinking as well, is that in so doing, rather than making responsible and useful cultural comparisons, we are guilty of essentializing these same cultures. A recent example of this charge is Edward Slingerland in *Mind and Body in Early China: Beyond Orientalism and the Myth of Holism.* In this monograph, Slingerland characterizes me (and many other contemporary students of Chinese philosophy) in our interpretations of early Chinese cosmology and theory of knowledge as purveyors of "the myth of holism." Slingerland would have it that I in positing a "strong" holist position hold "that, for the early Chinese (or 'the Chinese' or even the 'East' more generally), there exists no qualitative distinction at all between anything we could call *mind* and the physical body or other organs of the body."[1] As putative "postmodern neo-Orientalists," we all believe that "holistic" Chinese philosophers were incapable of making any such distinctions, and further we would all claim on the basis of this same strong holism that our different cultural traditions are monolithic and incommensurable.[2]

---

1. Edward Slingerland, "Body and Mind in Early China: An Integrated Humanities–Science Approach," *Journal of the American Academy of Religions* 81, no. 1 (2013): 4. This essay was preliminary to the later monograph cited in note 2 in this chapter.

2. Edward Slingerland, *Mind and Body in Early China: Beyond Orientalism and the Myth of Holism* (Oxford: Oxford University Press, 2019). I am entirely sympathetic with Jim Behuniak's critical review of this book in *Dao: A Journal of Comparative Philosophy* 18 (2019): 305–312, in which he defends me and a legion of other contemporaries against Slingerland's rather wanton and gratuitous caricatures, ascribing to us positions that we

Of course, as early as 1987 in *Thinking Through Confucius*, David Hall and I in offering a clear distinction between mind and body in the Chinese tradition were keen to distinguish ontological dualism from correlative polarity, the difference between the Platonic-cum-Cartesian mind/body dualism and the correlative and mutually entailing, "aspectual" relationship between mind and body (*xinshen* 心身) pervasive in Confucian cosmology. We state explicitly that "in the polar metaphysics of the classical Chinese tradition, the correlative relationship between the psychical and the somatic militated against the emergence of a mind/body problem. It is not that the Chinese thinkers were able to reconcile this dichotomy; rather it never emerged as a problem. Because body and mind were not regarded as *essentially* different kinds of existence, they did not generate different sets of terminologies necessary to describe them" (italics added).[3] Simply put, ontological disparity and the dualisms that follow from it have no purchase in a tradition that does not have Greek ontology. And this position that we stipulated with respect to the correlative *yinyang* relationship between mind and body has not changed, where *yinyang* is itself the meaning of qualitative distinction in Chinese cosmology. Our argument is that in the Confucian tradition, mind and body rather than being ontologically and thus essentially different in kind are two nonanalytic and yet importantly different aspects of the same phenomenon. When we reflect on a Hawaiian sunset with the red sky, the rolling surf, and our deep appreciation of the event, all of these features are mutually imbricated yet importantly different aspects of the same thing, and each of them add an important dimension of complexity to the experience that makes it what it is. Stated another way, we would appeal to the New Confucian philosopher Tang Junyi's 唐君毅 cosmological postulate of "the inseparability of the one and the many" (*yiduobufenguan* 一多不分觀) to assert that persons are one and many at the same time, where mind and body like self and other or subjective and objective are inseparable as two different aspects of same thing.[4] In fact, in the second half of the nineteenth century in the wake of the zoetological turn in the Western philosophical narrative that for the most part has sought to repudiate ontological thinking, many contemporary Western philosophers

---

simply do not hold. See also the subsequent exchange between Slingerland and Behuniak in *Dao* 18, no. 3 (2019): 485–488 and 489–491.

3. David L. Hall and Roger T. Ames, *Thinking Through Confucius* (Albany: State University of New York Press, 1987), 20.

4. Tang Junyi, *Complete Works* 唐君毅全集 (Taipei: Xuesheng shuju, 1991), vol. 11, 16–17.

from James, Dewey, and George Herbert Mead to Charles Taylor and Mark Johnson abjure mind/body dualism and describe the relationship between mind and body in a similar, correlative way.

But Slingerland is not alone in proffering such strident and undocumented characterizations. Indeed, he has been encouraged by some other interpreters of Chinese philosophy who, presumably to avoid essentializing themselves, would go so far as to recommend that in discussing Chinese culture, we would do well to forswear generalizations altogether. Paul Goldin and Michael Puett, for example, have indicted me and my collaborators as offering what Goldin again calls "an updated Orientalism." For Puett, not only David Hall and I but many of our distinguished precursors such as Marcel Granet, Fritz Mote, Joseph Needham, Angus Graham, and K. C. Chang are all "cultural essentialists" in our best attempts to articulate an interpretive context for understanding Chinese culture. Goldin charges us and these same fellow travelers with presenting "China as a reified foil to a reified West, an antipodal domain exemplifying antithetic mores and modes of thought."[5]

Contra Puett and Goldin, what we and this cohort of alleged "cultural essentialists" in fact share in common is the belief that there is a distinctive yet always evolving way of thinking that needs to be taken into account in understanding an unbounded and holistic Chinese cosmology. Further, we assert that this dynamic Chinese cosmology posits a world that is naturalistic, autogenerative, and self-construing without appeal to some causal metaphysical principle as its external and unilateral source of order. We and the other commentators who share this concern for interpretive context are self-consciously historicist in tracing the evolution of this Chinese worldview through the corpus of canonical texts and are again historicist in our understanding of its application to and elaboration in different dimensions of the Chinese experience, including the cosmology as it comes to be made explicit in the various Han dynasty taxonomies.

To appreciate what is philosophically at issue in this debate, we need to maintain a clear distinction between the ahistorical implications of rational or logical thinking that is analytical and that seeks closure in patterns of fixed regularity, and the historical entailments of correlative thinking that is synthetic, and that seeks open-ended, aesthetic disclosure in ad hoc unities constituted by unique details. This distinction is captured in the

---

5. Paul R. Goldin, "The Myth That China Has No Creation Myth," *Monumenta Serica* 56 (2008): 3.

difference Whitehead asserts in defining a logical and an aesthetic order, where the former as an act of closure has universalistic pretensions, while the latter as an act of disclosure is radically historicist.[6] While traditional logic requires a notion of strict ontological identity as the ground for its formal essentialism, art only allows for analogical relations among unique and always particular details.

Puett rehearses the distinction we make between the aesthetic and rational sensibilities that we also refer to as the difference between first and second problematic thinking, and between analogical and causal thinking as well. In so doing, he would allow that through such distinctions, Hall and Ames like Granet before them "attempt to illumine the contrasting assumptions shaping classical Chinese and Western culture."[7] True enough. And that, like Graham, they "see each of these ways of thinking as existing to some degree in both Chinese and Western cultures, and . . . are thus able to argue that Chinese thought is something that can be fully assimilated into contemporary Western thinking."[8] Again confirmed.

With Puett describing all of us in such historicist and inclusive terms, I cannot understand his characterizing this lineage of scholarship, committed as it is to providing an evolving interpretive context for the classical Chinese canons, as advocating for a "cultural-essentialist mode of interpretation."[9] Essentialism on my reading is typically understood as a universalistic claim stating that certain properties possessed by a given population are defining of that culture and, at the same time, are exclusive to them. Such properties are thus not dependent upon contingencies of context and, being exclusively theirs and no one else's, bring along with them a pernicious relativism and thus an incommensurability in their relations with other cultures. But as described by Puett himself, the account being given by us and these other interpreters, rather than being an essentialism, is in fact radically historicist as a mutually open-ended, overlapping, and inclusive pluralism. And given that our characterization of Chinese culture anticipates a productive dialogue among what are importantly different cultural narratives, I would

---

6. Whitehead, *Modes of Thought* (New York: Free Press, 1938), 60–63.

7. Michael Puett, *To Become a God: Cosmology, Sacrifice, and Self-Divinization in Early China* (Cambridge, MA: Harvard University Asia Center, 2002), 17.

8. Puett, *To Become a God*, 18.

9. For a fuller discussion of Puett's distinction between the essentialist and evolutionary paradigms, see Roger T. Ames, *Confucian Role Ethics: A Vocabulary* (Albany: State University of New York Press, 2020 [rpt.]), 24–30.

in fact describe it as "evolutionary" in the best syncretic and meliorative sense of that term.

Equally curious is that Puett describes yet another group of prominent interpreters of Chinese culture as belonging to the "evolutionary paradigm"—Max Weber, Fung Yu-lan, Karl Jaspers, and Heiner Roetz. On Puett's reading, these scholars share in common a commitment to taking a kind of universal rationality as the gold standard, and then they attempt to weigh and measure the development of Chinese culture against it. Ultimately these interpreters either assert that China like Europe has evidenced the transition from the proto-rational to the rational stage, or they dispute such a claim. Philosophers who would advocate this understanding of culture as a universal history emphasize the emergence of a common consciousness among cultures rather than the growth of assumptions that would make these cultures distinctive. Indeed, when as we find in Jaspers that both the "origins" and the "goal" of history are already predetermined, one wonders in what possible sense such a thesis can be described in any meaningful way as "evolutionary"?

Returning to Goldin, as his alternative to our alleged "Orientalism," he would argue categorically that "if there is one valid generalization about China, it is that China defies generalization. Chinese civilization is simply too huge, too diverse, and too old for neat maxims."[10] And again for Puett, "all of these interpretive strategies—reading in terms of schools, essentialized definitions of culture, evolutionary frameworks—have the consequence of erasing the unique power that particular claims had at the time."[11] Explicitly rejecting our self-consciously interpretive strategies, Puett's alternative recommendation is that "we should instead work towards a more nuanced approach in which we make no *a priori* assumptions regarding single statements made in single texts and the significance of any individual claims."[12] I think the best we can make of Goldin and Puett, if not Slingerland as well, is that while aspiring to some ostensive interpretive objectivity, they are in fact advocating for nothing short of a naïve realism that fails to acknowledge the profoundly subjective coloration of all interpretative experience. At the same time and quite ironically, in advancing these same claims to objectivity, they are essentializing their own realist way of thinking as the one and only way to deal with cultural differences.

---

10. Goldin, "The Myth That China Has No Creation Myth," 21.

11. Puett, *To Become a God*, 25.

12. Puett, *To Become a God*, 24–25.

Two Philosophers of Culture: Leibniz and Qian Mu 錢穆

In this attempt to unload the essentialism charge, I want to appeal to two historical examples of distinguished philosophers of culture—one from Europe and one from China—who were themselves ready and willing to risk thick generalizations. In the preface to his *Novissima Sinica* or "News from China" written over the period of 1697–1699, an astute and penetrating G. W. Leibniz offers a synoptic comparison between the profound cultural achievements of both Europe and China as the then-current arbiters of high civilization on the planet. Leibniz argues that, in the specifically theoretical disciplines such as mathematics, logic, metaphysics, and by implication, theology, there is a clear European superiority over China. Indeed, for Leibniz, Europeans "excel by far in the understanding of concepts which are abstracted by the mind from the material."[13] Europeans own the theoretical sciences and surpass the Chinese in those rational tools of the intellect that promise us demonstrable truth; in this respect, the Chinese instead struggle with a kind of empirical geometry owned by most artisans.

In contrast to this European advantage in the highly abstract and theoretical disciplines, Leibniz insists that Chinese culture excels in the various pursuits of civil philosophy. Indeed, Chinese "civilization" has set a standard in ethics, social philosophy, and politics that Leibniz deems far superior to that found in Europe. In Leibniz's own words:

> But who would have believed that there is on earth a people who, though we are in our view so very advanced in every branch of behavior, still surpass us in comprehending the precepts of civil life? Yet now we find this to be so among the Chinese, as we learn to know them better. And so if we are their equals in the industrial arts, and ahead of them in contemplative sciences, certainly they surpass us (though it is almost shameful to confess this) in practical philosophy, that is, in the precepts of ethics and politics adapted to the present life and use of mortals.[14]

In the details that emerge in Leibniz's generalizations regarding Chinese family and community life, we can actually discern his grasp of the seminal

---

13. Gottfried Wilhelm Leibniz, *Writings on China*, trans. Daniel J. Cook and Henry Rosemont Jr. (La Salle, IL: Open Court, 1994), 46.

14. Leibniz, *Writings on China*, 46–47.

and peculiar cluster of terms that are defining of Confucian ethical and political philosophy: that is, *xiao* 孝 as the intergenerational embodiment and transmission of the cultural tradition through patterns of deference in lived familial relations, and following from this prime moral imperative, *li* 禮 as aspiring to an achieved propriety in our family-centered roles and relations, *yi* 義 as seeking after an optimizing appropriateness and decorum in our roles and relations, *he* 和 as the unrelenting pursuit of an optimizing symbiosis within the diversity of our familial, communal, political, and cosmic roles and relations, and so on. It is precisely in just such terms that Leibniz describes the China of his day, saying that

> it is difficult to describe how beautifully all the laws of the Chinese, in contrast to those of other peoples, are directed to the achievement of public tranquility and the establishment of social order, so that men shall be disrupted in their relations as little as possible. . . . Certainly the Chinese above all others have attained a higher standard. In a vast multitude of men they have virtually accomplished more than the founders of religious orders among us have achieved within their own narrow ranks. . . . Moreover, there is among equals, or those having little obligation to one another, a marvelous respect, and an established order of duties.[15]

What is clear in Leibniz's account is an important distinction between the abstract theoretical, conceptual, and categorical thinking associated with ontology that he would ascribe to the European tradition, and the concrete historical, empirical, and aesthetic patterns of correlation and deference needed to effect and sustain ethical and sociopolitical order he attributes to the Chinese that I would associate with zoetological thinking.

Considering the dearth of information on China available to Leibniz in his own time, this comparative philosopher with his own decidedly formalist and universalistic proclivities—that is, Leibniz's advocacy for an ecumenicalism, a universal language, his *characteristica universalis* for mechanical calculation, a universal calculus, a world government, a shared biblical history, and so on—is often misread as simply using the high culture of China to corroborate his own European universal indices. But in advancing his own generalizations about European and Chinese values, Leibniz is in fact a surprisingly keen and honest observer of their cultural continuities

---

15. Leibniz, *Writings on China*, 47.

and differences. Leibniz saw and registered a clear contrast between the value invested in the abstract, theoretical disciplines in the European academy that are in search of axiomatic-deductive demonstration, and the more aesthetic and pragmatic applications of the Chinese tradition—a distinction that broadly distinguishes a European confidence in the dividends of the rational sciences from those alternative rewards that can be derived from virtuosity in the Chinese art of living in family and community.

In fact, it was more than a fundamental sympathy and respect for Chinese culture that led Leibniz to defend Matteo Ricci's advocacy of an accommodationist Christianity in the long-simmering Rites Controversy in Rome as it came to a boil toward the end of Leibniz's own life. Leibniz's commitment to accommodationism was clearly based on his conviction that Europe had much to learn from China. For him, the precepts of any universal civil philosophy that would seek to construct a framework for optimizing the social, political, and indeed religious life of human beings in community would do well to take into account the substantial accomplishments that Chinese culture had accrued in this same effort.

The twentieth-century "New Confucian" (*xinruxuejia* 新儒學家) Qian Mu 錢穆 is a second example of a distinguished philosopher of culture who was again willing to appeal to thick generalizations. He attempted to provide a corrective on the key Confucian philosophical terms that had been compromised by the missionary translators and interpreters in their conversion of these same terms to the language of Christianity. Qian is adamant that this vocabulary expressing the unique and complex Confucian vision of a moral life simply has no counterpart in other languages.[16] His point in making this claim is not to argue for interpretive incommensurability, cultural purism, or Chinese superiority. On the contrary, he would allow that with sufficient exposition made through thick generalizations (the ambitious objective of such philosophers of culture), the Confucian world can in important degree be understood, expanded upon, and further "appreciated" (with all of the implications of this term) by those from without. Qian Mu's claim is on behalf of the uniqueness and the value of a tradition that has defined its terms of art over millennia through the lived experience of its people and is simply anticipating the real difficulty that must be faced in attempting to capture this complex and organically related vocabulary in other languages. What Qian is insisting upon is that any attempt to conceptualize this

_____

16. Jerry Dennerline, *Qian Mu and the World of Seven Mansions* (New Haven: Yale University Press, 1988), 9.

Confucian tradition must begin from the concrete values and practices that over time evolved as the defining narrative of a particular population. And to take Qian's observations one step further, the fact is that the argument for historical sedimentation he is making on behalf of Confucian language and culture could in principle be transposed to the reception of any other culture in any other academy as well.

In service to the value of such cross-cultural understanding, I want to contest the resistance among some contemporary scholars to accept the kind of thick cultural generalizations being made by both Leibniz and Qian Mu that I believe are necessary if we are to respect the rich differences that obtain among traditions, and if we are to avoid as best we can an impoverishing cultural reductionism. I would posit that the canopy of an always emerging cultural vocabulary is itself rooted in and grows out of a deep and relatively stable soil of unannounced assumptions sedimented over succeeding generations into the language, the cultural habits, and the life forms of a living tradition. And further, I would argue that to fail to acknowledge the fundamental character of cultural difference as an erstwhile safeguard against the sins of "essentialism" is not itself innocent. Indeed, ironically, as we have seen with Puett, Goldin, and Slingerland, this antipathy to cultural generalizations leads to the uncritical essentializing of their own contingent cultural assumptions and to the willy-nilly insinuating of these same presuppositions into their interpretation of the ways of thinking and living of other peoples.

One might also argue that the bugbear of "essentializing" itself, like any corollary of "universalism," is largely a culturally specific deformation. Essentialism itself arises from classical Greek ontology as "the self-sufficiency of being" and from the appeal to strict identity or essences as the principle of individuation. It is this very notion of "essences" (*eidos*) that grounds Platonic idealism and his search for formal, real definitions of what something *is* as the source of knowledge. Such an essentialism is also the basis of the Aristotelian logic of knowing with its categorical "A or not-A" principle of noncontradiction, and his doctrine of species (*eidos*) as immutable natural kinds. We can only "essentialize" if we are predisposed to believe there are such things as "essences," an ontological way of thinking about the world as being constituted by essences and attributes that did not recommend itself to the formative, analogizing thinkers of classical China. Indeed, in zoetological thinking as a radical empiricism that gives primacy to vital relationality, always unique things and always particular cultural traditions are continuous with other things and other traditions, and they thus cannot be understood independent of their contexts.

The Value of Thick Cultural Generalizations

I certainly find common cause with the internal critique of substance ontology as it is currently being waged within the Western philosophical narrative. But while rejecting ontological thinking that would posit a permanent and unchanging substratum in the human experience as fundamentally fallacious, I would still want to argue that in the absence of such foundationalism, there are still persistent cultural continuities that allow for responsible generalizations. Indeed, a prime example I would argue is the distinction between ontological and zoetological thinking. A point drilled into me by my teachers is that different cultures think differently, and that if we are to come to know them in their differences, then we elide the important distinctions that can be made among them at our own peril. D. C. Lau 劉殿爵, for example, spent his lifetime studying languages—not only English and Chinese, of course, but Greek, Latin, German, and Japanese as well. While doing my PhD under his mentorship at the University of London in the 1970s, we studied Pāli together at a Buddhist vihara in West London and became acquainted with both the people and the mission of the Pāli Text Society. When visiting with Lau in Hong Kong to pursue our collaborative projects long after we had both left London, my gift to him was usually a volume from the Loeb library of Greek and Latin classics. Lau's keen interest in these languages—their grammar and syntax more than the semantics—had nothing to do with some grand self-image of a cosmopolitan polyglot traveling with linguistic facility throughout the world. Indeed, Lau rarely traveled anywhere. Rather he had a strong conviction that different worldviews and ways of thinking are sedimented into our languages and are revealed to us in our best efforts to master them.

The distinguished sinologist Angus Graham, another of my University of London professors, also ascribed unique and evolving categories and conceptual structures to different cultural traditions. In so doing, he challenged the Saussurean structuralist distinction between *langue* (universal and systematic linguistic structures and rules governing all languages) and *parole* (diverse and open-ended speech acts in any of our natural languages).[17] Like many (but not all) of us, Graham was persuaded that different populations

---

17. Saussure uses the analogy of a chess game, where *langue* are the fixed rules that govern the game and *parole* are the actual, varied moves made by different people that come to constitute any particular contest.

located within always changing cultural milieus appeal to importantly different concepts and ways of thinking and living. And Graham spent his long and illustrious career doing his very best to bring some clarity to these differences. In his writings, Graham over the years has consistently warned us that serious equivocations emerge when we elide the distinction between classical Greek ontological commitments and those assumptions grounding a classical Chinese processive, procreative cosmology. Ontology privileges "being per se" and a substance language with its reality and appearance, and essence and attribute dualisms. Process cosmology, on the other hand, gives privilege to "becoming" and the vital, interdependent, correlative categories needed to "speak" process and its eventful content. Graham is quite explicit about the nature of these philosophical differences and their linguistic entailments in observing that "in the Chinese cosmos all things are interdependent, without transcendent principles by which to explain them or a transcendent origin from which they derive. . . . A novelty in this position which greatly impresses me is that it exposes a preconception of Western interpreters that such concepts as *Tian* 'Heaven' and *Dao* 'Way' must have the transcendence of our own ultimate principles; it is hard for us to grasp that even the Way is interdependent with man."[18] As I have argued in positing a comparative cultural hermeneutics as my method, the entertainment of other cultural narratives is always a reflexive exercise. If we acknowledge that the experiencing of other cultures is a matter of mutually shaping stories, then in failing to articulate apposite generalizations, we are at real risk of imposing upon others cultural importances that are not their own. After all, without struggling with imagination to identify, refine, and ultimately defend such characterizations, the default position is an uncritical cultural assimilation. Such cultural reductionism follows from the seemingly respectful and inclusive assumption that we are all the same, a claim that, far from being innocuous, is in fact asserting that "they" are the same as "us." And in the cautionary language of Richard Rorty, such forced redescription is not only condescending but, indeed, can become cruel and humiliating.

My teachers thought that to claim peoples and cultures are either too complex to make the necessary generalizations that allows them their differences, or by default that they are somehow "equal" to us in their ability to think and communicate, might at first blush seem to be liberating. And while

---

18. A. C. Graham, "Replies," in *Chinese Texts and Philosophical Contexts: Essays Dedicated to Angus C. Graham*, ed. Henry Rosemont Jr. (La Salle, IL: Open Court, 1991), 287.

such assurances might be so for some interpreters, I would argue that this assertion is hardly innocent. Why would we assume that, in allowing that other traditions have their own culturally contingent modalities of thinking, we are in fact making the claim that such traditions do not know how to think? Such an assumption would require us to believe that in fact there is only one way of thinking, and that this way of thinking—that is, *our* way of thinking, is the only way. Indeed, the uncritical assumption that other cultures must think the same way that we do is for me the very definition of an ethnocentric essentialism. I would argue that it is precisely the hard work needed to excavate, to recognize, and to appreciate the degree of difference obtaining among cultures in their living and thinking that properly motivates cultural translation in the first place, and that ultimately rewards the effort. Surely, contending that there are culturally contingent modalities of thinking can be pluralistic rather than relativistic, can be accommodating rather than condescending, and can be a source of shared cultural growth rather than contest or diminution. At the very least, if the disciplines in comparative cultural studies are to provide us with the mutual enrichment they promise, we must strive to take other cultures on their own terms and to appreciate fully the differences that obtain among them.

This same point can be made another way. I would argue that the only thing more dangerous than striving to make responsible cultural generalizations is failing to make them. Generalizations do not have to preclude appreciating the richness and complexity of always evolving cultural traditions; in fact, it is generalizations that locate and inform specific cultural details, and provide otherwise sketchy and fragmentary historical developments with their coherence. At the same time, generalizations must not be overdetermined. We must embrace an open, hermeneutical approach that is ready to modify always provisional generalities with the new information that additional detail yields as it is interpreted and factored into the established yet evolving grid of interpretive assumptions in which the event of understanding is taking place.

There are important scholars who are resistant to thick cultural generalizations to whom we must make our arguments. The distinguished comparativist Zhang Longxi 張隆溪, for example, in his equally sincere commitment to pursuing intercultural understanding, is quite critical of those of us (singling out Jacques Gernet as one primary example) who would describe the tension between Christianity and Chinese culture as not only one "of different intellectual traditions" but also "of different mental categories and modes of thought."[19] Zhang becomes impatient when "the cultural difference between the Chinese and the Western is formulated as fundamentally distinct ways of thinking and speaking, as the ability, or lack of it, to express abstract ideas."[20] Earlier we saw that Leibniz quite proudly took the equation between abstract ideas and access to a higher intellectual and spiritual reality to be a distinctively European achievement. In embracing this European metaphysical assumption that what is most abstract is most real and is thus the inspiration for spiritual and theoretical assent, Zhang does not see that in giving abstract ideas such pride of place, he is advocating for decidedly Western ontological prejudices that are absent in the classical Chinese tradition. In fact, as I have argued earlier, for more than a century now within the narrative of Western philosophy itself, there has been a reversal of gravity under the sway of which these speculative, universalistic assumptions that would understand ultimate reality and truth in abstract terms have been under assault. This means perhaps that, in our interpretation of the Confucian tradition, we ought to be wary of ascribing to it an ontological way of thinking that we ourselves have deemed fallacious.

Why then would some scholars choose to characterize philosophers of culture with what they themselves take to be deprecatory terms such as "postmodernists" and "neo-Orientalists"? How did "oriental" as the opposite of "occidental" become a bad word? Edward Said, one of the important founders of decoloniality studies, was committed to the enlightened idea that many different voices should be heard. In his influential book, *Orientalism*, he made the claim that "Oriental studies" in the Western academy, largely for political reasons in service to its own self-image and understanding, has constructed a distorted and condescending description of Middle Eastern cultures as the mirror image of its own cultural importances.[21] In the decades since Said's cautions regarding the projection of "orientalist" misrepresentations into the study and teaching of other cultures were properly acknowledged, the tendency in academic circles has been to steer clear of what has come to be understood as the epistemic injustices that follow from heavy-handed

---

19. See Zhang's "Translating Cultures: China and the West," in *Chinese Thought in a Global Context: A Dialogue between Chinese and Western Philosophical Approaches*, ed. Karl-Heinz Pohl (Leiden: Brill, 1999), 44. He cites Jacques Gernet, *China and the Christian Impact: A Conflict of Cultures*, trans. J. Lloyd (Cambridge: Cambridge University Press, 1985), 8.

20. See Zhang, "Translating Cultures: China and the West," 44.

21. Edward W. Said, *Orientalism* (New York: Pantheon Books, 1978).

"essentialist" constructions of culture that would create an antithetical other as a way of elevating their own values. This cautionary corrective has resulted in valuable efforts to peel back layers of exotic and universalizing veneer that previous generations of scholarship had effectively laid over cultural differences. In thus rejecting the violence of cultural stereotyping, it has in some important degree shone light on the often convoluted and condescending readings of living and changing cultures. In rejecting such crude interpretations, a genuine endeavor has been made in the scholarship to try with imagination to take other complex cultures on their own terms. However, this important attempt to rethink and get past the naïve and monochromatic constructions of cultural others can go too far, running the risk of obscuring the crucial and still vital role played by assaying differences in ways of thinking and living, and acknowledging diverse cultural ideals and how they serve to engender cultural change.

A World Cultural Ecology:
Organically One and Many at the Same Time

But the argument for unloading the essentialism charge against philosophers of culture becomes even more compelling when culture itself is construed ecologically as one and many at the same time. As a consequence of the challenge of new directions in historiographical thinking, over the past several decades the assumption that cultural families develop their distinctive patterns of values, norms, and practices in relative isolation from one another has become markedly less trenchant. Both historians and philosophers have come to recognize significant distortions that attend any unreflective tendencies to compartmentalize the ancient and premodern worlds according to currently prevailing spatial and conceptual divisions and their underlying (often highly political) rationales. In particular, critical assessment is now well established regarding the degree to which persistent prejudices about metageography—especially the "myth of continents"—have shaped and continue to shape representations of history and cultural origins. The classic assertion of "independently originating" European and Asian cultures on either side of the Ural Mountains, for example, is being abandoned in favor of highlighting "Eurasian" characteristics in the complex cultural genealogies of both "West" and "East." Indeed, given that cultures arise interculturally or, better yet, *intra*culturally, as a borderless ecology of cultures having an inside without an outside in wide-ranging, intimate commerce with one another over time, and given that it is ecotones as porous horizons between cultures that are the most fecund sites for growth and change, it would seem that no culture can be properly understood in isolation from its others.

It was thus that, years ago, we asked the question: Given these ecological continuities, is there really more than one culture? Perhaps the best way to understand the vagueness of culture then is to declare that there is *at most* only one culture, highlighting as this claim would an unbounded and unsummed continuity in difference. This understanding of cultural continuity resonates rather closely with the cosmological postulate of "the one is many, many one" (*yiduobufenguan* 一多不分觀) as it is captured in the "focus and field" understanding of *dao* 道 as the continuous, unbounded, and unsummed totality of all orders as they are construed from insistently particular perspectives (*de* 德). If such continuity is the case, one can celebrate the multiplicity of cultures while abjuring the need to introduce any final distinctions among them.[22]

The development and growth of particular cultures certainly takes place through historical interactions among them, resulting either in accommodations of differences as conditions for mutual contribution, or in competition for acknowledged superiority. However, cultures change not only in adaptive response to others and to political, economic, or environmental exigencies but are also animated by an internal impulse as an expression of their own particular aspirations. Cultural change certainly *does* occur morphologically in response to differing circumstantial realities, but it also takes place genealogically as a function of pursuing new or not-yet-actualized ideals. Quite often, this change involves and requires envisioning ways of life distinctively other than those that are near and familiar, revealing with greater or lesser clarity what present cultural realities are not, and do not promise. Said differently, ideals as "ends-in-view"—what Charles Taylor calls "hypergoods"—are also realities that live in history and that, at least in some important degree, have the force of directing the patterns of change.[23]

---

22. See David L. Hall and Roger T. Ames, *Anticipating China: Thinking Through the Narratives of Chinese and Western Culture* (Albany: State University of New York Press, 1995), 175–179.

23. "Hypergoods" is a useful neologism introduced by Charles Taylor in his *Sources of the Self*: "Most of us not only live with many goods but find that we have to rank them, and in some cases, this ranking makes one of them of supreme importance relative to the others. . . . Let me call higher-order goods of this kind "hypergoods," i.e., goods which not only are incomparably more important than others but provide the standpoint from which these must be weighed, judged, decided about" (62–63).

This acknowledgment of the indigenous impulse has as its own corollary the insight that the histories through which cultures narrate their own origins and development are not simply or perhaps not even primarily aimed at accurately depicting a closed past but rather are intended to disclose arcs of change projected into open and yet more or less distinctly anticipated futures. The cliché that history is written by the winners is perhaps better couched in terms of history being written to affirm that what has occurred *amounts to* a victory. Cultural change is inseparable from the process, at some level, of both valorizing and actualizing new (or at least alternative) interpretations of the changes that have occurred. Thus, in trying to glean resources from our past cultural narratives, we must be self-conscious of the fact that our redescriptions of these cultures, while certainly being informed by their past, are also being reformulated to serve our own contemporary and future needs and purposes.

Self-Consciously Interpretive Translation

One area in which we have consistently applied our comparative cultural hermeneutics as a method in our best efforts at the redescription of culture has been in our forays into what we have called "philosophical translations" of the Chinese canons. Over the years I and my several collaborators, rather than beginning from some uncritical assumptions about trying to be literal or objective, have produced what we have professed to be "self-consciously interpretive translations." In describing our translations as self-consciously interpretive, however, we are not in any way allowing that we are recklessly speculative or given to license in our renderings. Nor are we willing to accept the reproach that we are less "literal" and thus more "creative" than other translators. On the contrary, appealing to the comparative cultural hermeneutical method as a caution against objective realism, I would insist that any pretense to a "literal" translation is not only naïve but is itself an "objectivist" prejudice of the first order.

We might begin from the commonplace that just as each generation selects and carries over earlier thinkers and reshapes them in their own image, so too do they in degree reconfigure the classical canons of world philosophy to serve their own needs. Encountering the unsummed richness of the original texts, we as interpreters are ourselves always collaborators from a specific time and place. Such an interface between fundamentally different interpretive contexts is in itself a formula for what all too easily becomes a cultural reductionism. Certainly our too hastily constructed interpretive strategies and overarching theories—"philosophical" or otherwise—when applied in the practice of cultural and textual translation, cannot but put the concrete detail of another tradition at some considerable risk. When Robert Frost remarks that "what is lost in translation is the poetry," I think that he as an artist is quite properly concerned that the project of translation is a literary transaction and in its outcomes makes the text at the very least different, and in many (but not all) cases, makes it less.

Indeed, in order to maximize our efforts in translation, we first and foremost need a commitment to a Heideggerian *Destruktion* that itself was initially controversial and provocative in his recovery of classical Greek terms. That is, we must struggle to retrieve the situated, primordial meanings of the key terminology by excavating and "polishing" them. This process is "conservative" in the archaeological sense of working backward through each stratum of the distortions layered over the terminologies across the ages as an effort to recover their origins. The search is to retrieve as much of the contextualizing detail as possible, and the process is "radical" in the sense of seeking to trace the meanings back to their roots within the landscape of the culture itself. While fully cognizant of our inescapable interpretive limitations, to the extent that we can, we must struggle to allow a text that belongs to another cultural narrative to reveal its poetry—the unmediated, nonreferential bottomlessness of its own particularity.

But in this effort, the image of Jorge Luis Borges's "Funes the Memorious" comes to mind, raising the question to what extent we can actually "think" particularity.[24] We have to ask in what degree is it ever possible to escape our own facticity and read these texts with naïveté and innocence, free from our own cultural assumptions. Clearly, instead of pretending to an impossible objectivity, we need a self-conscious hermeneutical openness in the project of cultural interpretation. That is, beyond the necessary commitment to respect the particularity of the text, we are in need of hermeneutical sensibilities that begin from a self-conscious awareness of our own prejudgments, and that allows for both textual detail and interpretive generalizations in the ongoing and inevitable fusion of horizons.

In fact, when we ask the question: Why do we pursue comparative studies in the first place? my simple answer would be that in the case of philosophy, understanding different traditions provides us with resources for

---

24. In this story, Borges introduces a character who, with perfect memory of every detail of his day, requires fully twenty-four hours to remember twenty-four hours. Such interpretive completeness turns Greek abstraction on its head, precluding any possibility of rising above the detail to reflect upon and think through one's experience.

further philosophizing. If *philosophia* is the pursuit of wisdom, it can be argued that "wisdom" itself emerges analogically through establishing and aggregating a pattern of truly productive correlations between what we already know and what we would know, and then applying these novel associations in what we do. Such correlations are "productive" in that they increase meaning and, to the extent that we are able to optimize these meaningful associations effectively in our practical life situations, provide us with the possibility of actually achieving more intelligent practices.

The Familial Roots of Ecological Language

Wisdom thus understood as a repository of productive correlations has its roots in the practical affairs of the day. The Wittgensteinian scholar Elizabeth Wolgast advocates for an interpretation of social justice that resonates rather closely with Confucian assumptions regarding the primacy of vital relations.[25] In her monograph *The Grammar of Justice*, she has argued that the growth of both our moral language and our practices takes place locally in the grammatical ecologies of our families and communities. Indeed, this term "ecology" itself was coined by the German zoologist Ernst Haeckel in 1866 to describe the "economies" of living forms. The etymology of "ecology" is *eco* from the Greek *oikos*, meaning "household, habitat," and *logia*, meaning "the study of." More generally, ecology for zoetological thinking means our best efforts to understand the vital, interdependent relations that obtain among organisms within their environments and, more specifically, within their family environment. Given the primacy of relationality in this alternative, eventful way of thinking about ostensive "things," I and my collaborators have appealed to a holographic, "focus-field" language as a way of giving expression to such an "eventful" world as well as of distinguishing it from our default ontological world of "things" and its "part-whole" way of thinking.

Resonating with *eco* as "household," the etymology of "focus" is the Latin *focus*, meaning "hearth, fireplace" (figuratively, "home, family"). The familial and thus "familiar" hearth is focal as the nucleus around which life in the home has traditionally taken place. By extension, focus is the area or point of convergence that, resolving as it does into a clear image, allows

---

25. Elizabeth H. Wolgast, *The Grammar of Justice* (Ithaca, NY: Cornell University Press, 1987).

something to be seen distinctly—for example, the focusing of a camera lens. "Field" then is another term that, like focus, has a domestic reference as the agrarian land that is farmed and grazed, and that supplies the family with the raw provisions needed to be further prepared at the fireplace. From this core idea of hearth and home, focus has come to mean the "locus of divergence and convergence" where persons as organisms achieve a focal identity within a "field"—that is, the distinctive, continuing identity of particular persons in family that emerges from what members of the family carry off from the home, and what they are able to bring back to it.

In seeking to grasp and apply this ecological way of thinking, we have to be self-conscious of our own ontologically informed common sense that defaults to construing the furniture of the world as self-sufficient "things" rather than as always open-ended, interpenetrating events. While zoetology is best expressed through an ecologically sensitive vocabulary, one limitation we must acknowledge as we seek to invoke our own holographic, focus-field language is that it seems insufficiently dynamic to capture the complex process of ceaseless growth and change that attends the eventful lives of organisms as they are continuously evolving and transforming within their environments. And again, in making use of the organic metaphor as it is rooted for us in classical Greek ontology, we have to be careful to absolve it of the heavily freighted teleological assumptions that it carries with it.

On the other hand, it is this holographic, focus-field language that is particularly felicitous in clarifying Confucian values where family is the governing cultural metaphor, and where the notion of "family reverence" (*xiao* 孝) is its prime moral imperative. The cluster of modal, associative terms referencing life and growth that constitutes the language of both ecology and Confucian morality become normative when they take the discussion back to achieving a meaningful resolution and a shared flourishing in the roles and relations within the family and community.

Chapter 3

"Taking the Confucian Tradition on Its Own Terms"

A Different Understanding of Objectivity

Returning to Confucian culture in this "many is one, one many" ecological interpretation of culture itself, a rather obvious methodological objection might be raised. In applying the comparative cultural hermeneutics as our method and thus advancing the claim that experience is necessarily a collaboration between what we already know and what we would know, what then could it mean "to take the Chinese philosophical tradition on its own terms" as our stated goal? Recalling Gadamer's hermeneutical circle, is an objectivity that stands free of our own prejudgments and purposes even possible? Indeed, the very question of whether we are able to take Chinese philosophy on its own terms arises because of our default dualistic understanding of objectivity as excluding the subjective. Perhaps in responding to this question of how to best understand the implications of objectivity itself, we might want to return to Dewey's postulate of immediate empiricism and ask: What is "objectivity" in fact experienced *as*?

In asking what is "objectivity experienced *as*," we have to be careful not to overstate the case in the distinction to be made between definition as it functions within ontological and zoetological thinking. Confucian zoetological thinking would certainly abjure the possibility of any "view-from-nowhere" experience of objectivity. At the same time, the need to establish persistent definitions of terms to discipline the arbitrariness and contingency of language in service to clarity and precision has an important role in Confucian thinking, being captured in one of its central doctrines, "using names properly" (*zhengming* 正名), or as translated by Timothy O'Neill, "making words correct."[1]

This notion of *zhengming* has conventionally been translated as "the rectification of names," suggesting that in the relationship between language and conduct, we need to satisfy the stipulated definitions of names and ranks. And this requisite is certainly part of the story. For Confucius, language is retrospective in the sense that effective discourse requires the use of language according to received, operational definitions—for example, the deployment of proper titles and a respect for the entitlements that accompany rank. In the literature, Confucius has a strong commitment to such conventions, and to this extent the idea of "rectification" certainly does have a role to play. Simply put, established conventions provide stability and reinforce the hard-won values that are defining of a persistent cultural identity.

For Confucius, in his commitment to conventions, there is an immediate association between the strict use of political titles and maintaining the integrity of the state. In the *Zuozhuan* commentary on the *Spring and Autumn Annals* it gives an account of a person who, in being rewarded for saving a prominent man's life, declines the offer of a city and asks instead to be allowed to use the dress and accoutrements of a prince. Confucius on hearing of this event denounces it bitterly as a travesty and anticipates what dire consequences will follow from it:

> Confucius on hearing about this said: "What a pity! It would have been better to give him many cities. It is insignias of office and titles alone that cannot be conceded to pretenders—they must be managed by the ruler. Proper titles give rise to confidence (*xin*), and confidence is what protects the insignias of office. It is insignias in which the meaning of ritual propriety is invested, and it is ritual propriety (*li*) that carries appropriate conduct (*yi*) into practice; appropriate conduct is what gives rise to benefit, and it is benefit that brings equanimity to the people. Such things are what structure government, and if you concede them to pretenders, you concede the government along

---

1. Timothy Michael O'Neill, *Ideography and Chinese Language Theory: A History* (Berlin/Boston: Walter de Gruyter, 2016).

with them. If the government is lost, the state will follow, and there can be no stopping its collapse."[2]

A major theme running through the *Analects* is Confucius's insistence that unrelenting attention must be given to retaining a strict correspondence between formal ritual practices and the ranks of office, with the risk of political collapse being the consequence of doing otherwise.[3] More specifically, Confucius is repeatedly chagrined at the powerful Ji family's usurpation of practices and privileges appropriate to the royal house.[4] In this same vein, Xunzi in his later elaboration on Confucius's doctrine of *zhengming* has a deep and abiding respect for the function of language to convey the aggregated social, political, and cosmic order from generation to generation, and to thus provide a civilizational continuity and solidarity.

A past stabilized by the conventional use of language is also important as guidance for new experience. But to understand language as only retrospective reduces it to a symbolic and representational means of mapping an already existing world—that is, to know the world is to find the right name for things. Indeed, language is much more. Because novel experience is always underdetermined and must literally be taken on its own terms, the standard translation of *zhengming* as "rectification of names" is inadequate in failing to include what is perhaps the most important function of language: that is, the prospective, illocutionary and perlocutionary force of language. Language as an activity is a doing and a making. Hence, within the process cosmology that serves as interpretive context for early Confucian philosophy, the doctrine of "using names properly" has to be understood holistically as having both retrospective and prospective reference.

---

2. The *Zuo Commentary to the Spring and Autumn Annals*, Duke Cheng 2: 仲尼聞之曰, 惜也, 不如多與之邑, 唯器與名, 不可以假人, 君之所司也, 名以出信, 信以守器, 器以藏禮, 禮以行義, 義以生利, 利以平民, 政之大節也, 若以假人, 與人政也, 政亡, 則國家從之, 弗可止也已. Cf. James Legge, trans., *The Chinese Classics*, 5 vols. (Hong Kong: University of Hong Kong Press, 1960 [rpt.]), vol. 5, 344. The *Hanshi waizhuan* records a story in which again Confucius in attendance on Ji Sun (see *Analects* 14.36) worries over the appropriate use of names. See D. C. Lau and Chen Fong Ching, *A Concordance to the Hanshiwaizhuan* (Hong Kong: Commercial Press, 1992), 5.34/41/19.

3. See for example *Analects* 3.10, 3.22, 11.6, 11.17.

4. See for example *Analects* 3.1, 3.2, 3.6.

Confucius is expounding upon precisely this point when he explains to his protégé Zilu what he means by this central Confucian precept, "using language properly" (*zhengming* 正名).[5] In this exposition, Confucius uses "names" as "pragmatics" to do the work of an expanding range of different yet organically related modes of discourse on which the flourishing of communal life depends, from language itself to the functioning of the institutions of law and governance. Most importantly, for Confucius, the function of "naming," far from being primarily abstract, theoretical, and referential, has immediate, practical consequences for the quality achieved in the always changing life of the community:

> "Were the Lord of Wei to turn the administration of his state over to you, what would be your first priority?" asked Zilu.
>
> "Without question it would be to ensure that names are used properly (*zhengming*)," replied the Master.
>
> "Really? That is so pedantic," responded Zilu. "What does it mean to use names properly anyway?"
>
> "How can you be so ignorant!" replied Confucius. "Exemplary persons defer on matters they do not understand. When names are not used properly, language will not be used effectively; when language is not used effectively, matters will not be taken care of; when matters are not taken care of, propriety in roles and relations and in the playing of music will not be achieved; when propriety in roles and relations and in the playing of music is not achieved, the application of laws and punishments will not be on the mark; when the application of laws and punishments is not on the mark, the people will not know what to do with themselves. Thus, when exemplary persons put a name to something, it can certainly be spoken, and when spoken it can

---

5. Zilu was one of Confucius's best-known and favorite protégés. Confucius's feelings for Zilu were mixed. On the one hand, he was constantly critical of Zilu's rashness and immodesty, and impatient with his seeming indifference to book learning. On the other hand, Confucius appreciated Zilu's unswerving loyalty and directness—a person who never hesitated in fulfilling his commitments. He was a person of courage and action who was sometimes upbraided by Confucius for being too bold and impetuous. But being nearer Confucius in age, Zilu with his military temper was not one to take criticism without giving it back. With all such complexities and complications taken into account, at the end of the day, Confucius's enormous affection for the irrepressible Zilu comes shining through.

certainly be acted upon. There is nothing careless in the attitude of exemplary persons toward what is said."[6]

In this explanation of *zhengming*, a correlative complementarity obtains between idea and action, reason and experience, theory and praxis. If persons and personal relationships require a constant attuning to be optimally meaningful, it would follow that the media or forms through which these persons are composed, related, and performed—mediums such as language, body, ritual actions, food, and music—also require unrelenting attention.

Zhengming should certainly be understood as remembering and applying standards inherited from the past. But as we see in Confucius's explanation of the social and political implications of *zhengming*, language is importantly performative. There is the need for the community, grounded in the *gravitas* of its traditions, to continue to make productive adjustments and novel correlations within its always evolving social and political structures. A thriving community must continue to reform, reconfigure, and reauthorize its institutions and practices, with the effective use of language having high priority. The "proper" use of language is a continuing redefining of our terms of understanding, explanation, and performance through semantic and phonetic correlations that would enable us to get the most out of an always changing world.

Dao 道 means both "way-making" and "speaking," where these are two aspects of the same activity. The fertility of language lies in speaking a world into being by activating the indeterminacies that are always available in experience and, in so doing, allowing for *ars contextualis*: that is, the omnipresent opportunity for artful recontextualizing. Confucius is himself keenly aware of the performative and perlocutionary power of "relatings" or discourse—that is, the capacity that the activity of language in its broadest sense (*ming* 名) has to shape the community and to command a desired world into being (*ming* 命). For Confucius, "knowing" a world, far from being simply cognitive, is to realize it in the deliberate and constructive sense of "making it real." This correlating process can be understood by reference to the technical term "paronomasia" as a prospective reconstruing of the contextualizing conditions of any situation that would allow something to be called by "another name" and, in so doing, to produce additional meaning.

---

6. *Analects* 13.3: 子路曰: "衛君待子而為政, 子將奚先?" 子曰: "必也正名乎!" 子路曰: "有是哉, 子之迂也! 奚其正?" 子曰: "野哉由也! 君子於其所不知, 蓋闕如也. 名不正, 則言不順; 言不順, 則事不成; 事不成, 則禮樂不興; 禮樂不興, 則刑罰不中; 刑罰不中, 則民無所措手足. 故君子名之必可言也, 言之必可行也. 君子於其言, 無所苟而已矣."

This meaning-producing function of language is an insight being made much of in the contemporary philosophical discourse. For example, Ludwig Wittgenstein posits an understanding of how language functions that resonates with the prospective expectations expressed by Confucius in this passage. Introducing his notions of "language games" and "family resemblances," Wittgenstein like Confucius is keenly aware that language and life are two aspects of the same experience. Wittgenstein challenges realist assumptions that language is somehow separate, and that by mapping it onto the world, it comes to "correspond" to reality in some referential and representational way. Wittgenstein uses the term "language-games" to highlight "the fact that the speaking of language is part of an activity, or a form of life" (*PI* 23), where such games consist "of language and the actions into which it is woven" (*PI* 7). And Wittgenstein has a keen awareness of the underdeterminedness of language, allowing room for the prospective activation of its ambiguities and equivocations that are always available to increase its meaning and effect. Wittgenstein argues that concepts do not need to be clearly defined to be meaningful and to precipitate change in the world. He uses the analogy of "family resemblances" to describe how the same word is used in many different ways without any ultimately final or essential meaning in an effort to underscore the lack of any formal boundaries or reduplicated precision in the different application of one and the same concept. Such an understanding of language highlights the allusiveness and the productive ambiguity that attend the imaginative use of language.

John Dewey too invests enormously in the centrality of language and other modes of communicative discourse (including signs, symbols, gestures, and social institutions) in explaining how the community grows its irreducibly social persons and their mutually imbricated minds: "Through speech a person dramatically identifies himself with potential acts and deeds; he plays many roles, not in successive stages of life but in a contemporaneously enacted drama. Thus mind emerges."[7] For Dewey, mind is "an added property assumed by a feeling creature, when it reaches that organized interaction with other living creatures which is language, communication."[8] Self-conscious identity formation is located within the process of realizing a world. Borrowing the resonant term *xin* 心 from Confucian moral psychology, such "heartminding," like the world within which it is occurring, is *becoming* rather than *being*, and the challenge is always how much shared meaning and enjoyment can be generated in the process. The alternative—that is, for a community to

---

7. Dewey, *Later Works*, vol. 1, 135.

8. Dewey, *Later Works*, vol. 1, 198.

fail to communicate effectively—is for it to wither, leaving it vulnerable to the "mindlessness" of violence and "heartlessness" of atrocities perpetrated by shameless creatures who have failed to become human.

This understanding of the generative function of language is further developed in the work of Charles Taylor who, taking discourse as one of the sources necessary in the shaping of our personal identities, says: "One cannot be a self on one's own. I can only be a self in my relation to certain interlocutors. . . . A self only exists within what I call 'webs of interlocutions.' "[9] In Confucian philosophy there is an appreciation of the important function language has in reinforcing and perpetuating the existing social and political institutions human beings need to live their lives in the most productive way. To this extent, it invests value in the stability of language achieved through stipulated meanings that provide a degree of clarity and precision. But its own appeal to such practices of "formal" definition as they occur within a performative and generative understanding of language stands in rather stark contrast to the expectations we find in the epistemologies of Plato and Aristotle. Plato's search for "real" definitions as those abstract and originative principles around which reality itself is structured is grounded in an ontological disparity that privileges the objective over the subjective and the real over what is only apparent. Again, Aristotle's appeal to formal and reduplicative essences as the ultimate objects of apodictic knowledge is dependent upon the same kind of ontological assumptions as the source of the dualistic vocabulary that is used to express this world.

A Confucian Alternative to the
Objective/Subjective Dualism

The commonplace dictionary understanding of objectivity is that it is the opposite of and excludes subjectivity. Within such a persistent worldview, objectivity is a judgment of the facts of a situation independent of subjective feelings or opinions and, as such, promises to yield up the unvarnished truth. This familiar dualistic way of thinking about objectivity derives from and belongs to realist assumptions that take as their starting point a mind-independent world—that is, the kind of "view-from-nowhere" realism that Hilary Putnam has quite properly rejected. Such a way of thinking about objectivity goes back to Platonic "two-world thinking" that would posit an a priori intelligible world constituted by divine principles available to us

9. Taylor, *Sources of the Self,* 36.

as a basis for taking the weight and measure of everything in the sensible world. With Plato's distinction between *episteme* as true knowledge and *doxa* as mere opinion, and with his doctrine of *anamnesis* or "recollection," our knowledge of the intelligible world is a priori and objective because it is not dependent upon the world of the senses. Indeed, although the sensual world does have the salutary function of reminding us of the a priori objective world that we already know, it is itself merely a poor reflection of the real world.

Isaac Newton in this same persistent realist tradition was certainly an experimental scientist, but more important to his own self-understanding he was a theologian who had authored many religious tracts on a reading of the Bible that he took to be consistent with his science. From his point of view, the ultimate value of science was that it gives us insight into the objective laws of nature and, in so doing, access to the mind of God. With such a realist understanding of objectivity often being referred to in common parlance as "a God's-eye view," Newton's science was also the source of ample religious dividends with respect to truth, beauty, and goodness. The worry here with respect to Newton's understanding of objectivity, however, is that unless we like God who, residing outside of the temporal and spatial world, are indeed Nowhere, we do not have the purchase to understand what such a concept of objectivity actually means. It is certainly not what we experience objectivity *as*.

Again, historically this way of thinking about objectivity gave rise to the "subjective" rationalist and "objective" empiricist dichotomy that persisted in the Western philosophical narrative until Kant's Copernican revolution, in which the sovereignty given to reason by the Enlightenment could be justified by the capacity of reason to critique itself without appeal to any other authority. Kant was able to reconcile the divide between modern science and traditional morality by arguing that the sensible world is constructed by the a priori categories of the human mind, with its understanding being a function of these human cognitive faculties collaborating with the passive reception of sensory matter.

More recently, Dewey with his insistence that we must ask "What is objectivity experienced *as*?" wants to entertain immediate experience without imposing upon such experience abstract assumptions such as the givenness of Kant's a priori mental categories or his notion of impersonal reason. In giving primacy to practice itself, Dewey offers us a revisionist understanding of objectivity that challenges our entrenched dualistic common sense. He insists that "objectivity" in experience is for experience to simply be what *it* is, with its subjective aspect being the "hadness" of this experience for us. As Dewey observes, "If *any* experience, then a *determinate* experience; and this determinateness is the only, and is the adequate, principle of control, or 'objectivity.' The experience may be of the vaguest sort. . . . It is not just vagueness, doubtfulness, confusion, at large or in general. It is *this* vagueness, and no other; absolutely unique, absolutely what *it* is" (italics original).[10]

The zoetological cosmology of the *Book of Changes* begins from just such "suchness" (or perhaps better, "such-ing") and shares with Dewey the primacy he affords immediate, continuous, unbounded, and collaborative experience. There is no "outside" of the "worlding" of which we are an integral aspect.[11] It is thus that Tang Junyi insists that "when Chinese philosophers speak of the world, they are thinking of the world that we are living in. There is no world beyond or outside of the one we are experiencing. . . . They are not referencing '*a* world' or '*the* world,' but are simply saying 'worlding,' where the fact that an article is not placed before 'world as such' is most significant."[12] And the energy of the flux and flow of such "worlding" is integral to the world itself without the need to appeal to some independent, foundational, and causal source. It is "self-so-ingly-so" (*ziraner'ran* 自然而然). Tang observes that, "in the minds of Chinese people, the cosmos has always been nothing more than a continuous stream, a kind of flow; all of the things and events of the cosmos are just a continuing process. And beyond this process there is not some other fixed substratum that supports it."[13]

When we go to the Confucian texts, the sense made of an "objective" standard is not some antecedent, abstract principle that, as an erstwhile substratum outside of this continuing cosmic process, can be applied as a norm to any particular situation exclusive of subjective concerns. Indeed, perhaps it is the ambitiousness of the realist notion of grasping what is objective that in European languages has given the term a seemingly

---

10. Dewey, *Middle Works*, vol. 3, 164.

11. "Worlding" is, literally, *shijie* 世界 or "worlding as time + space," or better perhaps, "as the taking place of the world."

12. Tang Junyi, *Complete Works*, vol. 11, 101–103: 中國哲人言世界, 只想著我們所處的世界. 我們所處的世界以外有無其他的世界 . . . 中國的哲人說世界不說我們的世界是一世界 A World, 亦不說是這世界 This World, 而只是說世界, 天地, World as Such 前而不加冠詞, 實是有非常重大的意義的.

13. Tang Junyi, *Complete Works*, vol. 11, 103: 中国人心目中之宇宙恒只为一种流行, 一种动态; 一切宇宙中之事物均只为一种过程, 此过程以外别无固定之体以为其支持者 (substratum).

derivative meaning of the setting of a goal or purpose for any particular undertaking, thereby giving the undertaking its "objective." It is this aspirational sense of an objectivity that is primary in the Confucian tradition in the sense that in the search for an optimal result, subjective and objective interests are mutually implicated and inseparable. Such an inclusive, holistic understanding of objectivity is suggested by the modern Chinese loanwords borrowed from the translation of "objective" and "subjective" into modern Japanese *kanji* as *zhuguan* 主觀 and *keguan* 客觀: literally, a situation seen from the host's and the guest's points of view respectively. *Zhuke* references the perspectives of host and guest as they defer to each other in service to the best possible outcomes.[14] *Zhu* and *ke* are aspectual terms with the host and guest accommodating each other as their relationship unfolds toward an evolving, desired end. Even though the viewpoints of host and guest are different, rather than being the putatively exclusive, "either/or" of the subjective and objective dualism, "hosting and guesting" (*zhuke* 主客) is an inclusive, correlative dyad that is gerundive in its search for a welcome outcome. When we turn to a zoetological understanding of "objectivity" as it is entailed in "taking Chinese philosophy on its own terms," just as in the case of host and guest, the desired "objective" would be to allow Chinese philosophy full participation in world philosophy as a voice integral to the optimal "growth" of the discourse itself.

This understanding of objectivity as resolutely reflexive in its inclusion of a subjective aspect is necessary if we are to grasp the holistic assumptions behind the Confucian resolution to live the moral life. Such inclusiveness precludes any severe subject/object dichotomy in the moral terms of art. For example, in trying to make the most of any particular situation, high value is given to an inclusive, optimizing sense of appropriateness (*yi* 義) that would seek to take all relevant interests into account, including one's own. In Confucian morality, it is this inclusive, optimizing appropriateness that serves as its objective.

The prominent Confucian value of "consummate conduct" (*ren* 仁) as another example, cannot be understood as "benevolence" in the sense of a Good Samaritan's altruism in which a Jesus-like moral agent does good to his destitute neighbor. A Jewish priest and a Levite not wanting themselves to be inconvenienced pass by one of their own on the roadside who has been beaten and robbed. The Samaritan rising above the schism

---

14. See Lydia H. Liu, *Translingual Practice: Literature, National Culture, and Translated Modernity—China, 1900–1937* (Stanford: Stanford University Press, 1995), appendix 2.

between his people and the Jews to do the right thing, personally bathes the wounds of the injured man and provides him with food and lodging. Behind benevolence as Christian charity is the assumption that there is an objective ethical standard for all people to follow—Jesus's "do unto others as you would have them do unto you." Again, there is the asymmetry that separates the altruistic almsgiver from the needy medicant.

Ren is importantly different. Instead of distinguishing benefactor and beneficiary with the former serving an objective sense of what is right, *ren* takes as its consummatory objective a cultivated depth in the relationship between self and other that enriches the lives of both. The disposition needed for achieving *ren*, rather than being a generosity motivated by mercy or pity, is putting oneself in the place of the other in order to make one's own judgment on what is best for growth in the relationship. Such a holistic, relational ethics is reflexive, requiring deference to both the specific needs of others and concern for one's own interests. Such being the case, particular instances of consummate conduct will always be person and situation specific. This specificity and inclusiveness is made clear in the *Analects* where Confucius, in providing one of his several definitions of *ren*, states that becoming consummate in one's person "is to establish others in seeking to establish oneself, and to promote others in seeking to get there oneself."[15]

Again, the "single thread" that pulls the Confucian doctrines together (*yiyiguanzhi* 一以貫之) is captured in the exhortation to "put oneself in the place of the other" (*shu* 恕) in performing a dramatic rehearsal of possible futures. Having thus determined the best way forward inclusive of self and other in establishing a common objective, one must then "be conscientious" (*zhong* 忠) in exerting one's best effort to bring about the desired outcome. The proper measure (*du* 度) in the quality of such deferential objectivity is to be achieved as an optimizing symbiosis (*gongsheng* 共生) inclusive of all relevant interests. Thinking prospectively, the pursuit of such an "objective" is always local and situational with prior historical instances of achieved "objectivity" being available to us as functional analogies that can inform our present judgments in a productive way.

The zoetological cosmology of the *Book of Changes* that serves as the interpretive context for the Confucian corpus is also shared by the Daoist canons as well. As with the Confucian texts, the one thread that runs through the Daoist texts is the decisive role that deference has in establishing, cultivating, and sustaining relations. The *Daodejing* expresses this

---

15. *Analects* 6.30: 夫仁者, 己欲立而立人, 己欲達而達人.

deferential attitude in its own technical language that David Hall and I in our translation of the *Daodejing* have described as the "*wu* 無-forms."[16] The meaning of the three most familiar of these dispositional *wu*-forms are (1) *wuwei* 無為 as acting noncoercively in accordance with the virtuosity of other things (*de* 德) that allows for optimal coalescence with them (*de* 得), (2) *wuyu* 無欲 as that kind of objectless desiring that does not seek to possess or control its "object," and (3) *wuzhi* 無知 as pursuing a robust understanding of other things that does not overwrite them with preconceived principles or judgments. This cultivated *wu*-form habitude is an attempt to achieve a mirroring relationship with one's environing others that, in deferring to them, allows them to be fully who and what they are in the relationship. Such deference is a precondition for them to be available to us as robust collaborators that have their own integrity and that can be taken on their own terms. These mirroring *wu*-forms with their holistic, reflexive, and inclusive understanding of objectivity seek to make the most of the creative possibilities available in any particular situation.

This mirroring disposition advocated in Daoist philosophy is a form of situated activity that allows other things to be themselves in their unique particularity, in their relationality, and in their transitoriness. It is the things themselves as uniquely particular events with their construal of order emanating from their own particular perspectives that are reflected in the mirroring process. At the same time, the projective illumination provided by the mirror is a function of its reflecting the world from its own particular angle and vantage point. Primacy is thus given to the mirroring situation over any agency that is to be abstracted from it. In the *Huainanzi*, Daoist sages are described in precisely such terms:

> Sages are like mirrors—
> They neither go out to meet things nor see them off,
> And they respond to things without storing anything up.
> Hence in a myriad of transformations they are innocent of harm.[17]

And again, the *Huainanzi* elaborates upon the meaning of such "objectivity" in this mirroring attitude: "It is because the mirroring water in anticipating

---

16. Roger T. Ames and David L. Hall, trans., *Daodejing: Making This Life Significant* (New York: Ballantine, 2003).

17. D. C. Lau and Chen Fong Ching, *A Concordance to the* Huainanzi, 6/51/15: 故聖若鏡, 不將不迎, 應而不藏, 故萬化而無傷.

its encounter with shapes does not equip itself with cleverness and with presuppositions that it cannot but reflect them as they really are: that is, as square, round, bent, and straight."[18] Rules of thumb, habits of action, customs, fixed standards, methodologies, stipulated concepts, presuppositions, categories, commandments, principles, laws of nature, all require us "to go out to meet things" and "to see them off." Having stored up past experience and prioritized things in terms of our own values and standards, we anticipate, recall, and celebrate a world patterned by such discriminations. Sages, however, are described as responding to things "without storing anything up," and mirroring the moment as it is being cast from their own particular point of view without overwriting it with either the conditions of a world passed away, or in anticipation of a world yet to come.

A reading of these *Huainanzi* passages is itself an object lesson in this alternative understanding of objectivity. That is, to interpret these passages as though they are providing an objective description of a particular situation would vitiate the correlative and thus reflexive expectations of the text and its message. The text is by implication counseling us to refrain from treating its own statements as definitive propositions that would deploy its terms of art in a univocal way that would preclude the viewpoint of its reader. In the *Daodejing*'s allusions to sages, for example, in some cases sagacity (*sheng* 聖) is the highest goal of humanity and is thus celebrated as a good thing (chapter 49), but in other cases the same term is used to mean false erudition and thus requires us to excise it and get rid of it (chapter 19). Any literal or expository reading of these *Huainanzi* passages would certainly prompt counterexamples. For example, is it hermeneutically possible for anyone to engage the world "without going out to meet things" and without "sending them off"? In trying to understand this *wu*-form disposition of the sages, we have to resist ontological thinking that would take the characterization of them and their actions as categorical—that is, as a formal definition of what it means to be and act like a sage. What the text is offering us instead is the insight that, generally speaking, the always unique sages in dealing with the world are open-minded, flexible, and accommodating, and as such, do their best to take other things on their own terms without the need to exercise control over them. Enough said.[19]

---

18. D. C. Lau and Chen Fong Ching, *A Concordance to the* Huainanzi, 1/2/13: 夫鏡水之與形接也, 不設智故, 而方圓曲直弗能逃也.

19. The familiar adage "a watched pot never boils" is empirically false, but it solicits the complicity of the listener in making good psychological sense of what it means.

To take Chinese philosophy on its own terms, then, does not mean to decontextualize it and, in so doing, to reify, objectify, detemporalize, and essentialize it. The generosity of the subjective aspect in the hermeneutical circle is itself a resource within a living tradition for continued growth as the subjectivity of persons interacts with their worlds. In our times specifically, taking Chinese philosophy on its own terms means to mirror it and, in so doing, to give it its proper place as an integral voice in the ecology of world philosophy. Such an amplificatory, synergistic process allows us in appreciating its differences to find in Chinese philosophy a resource for our own enrichment. At the same time, Chinese philosophy in thus being included and appreciated as a collaborator in world philosophy achieves a quantum increase in its own worth.

In fact, Confucianism is itself an immediate and concrete historical example of this continuing hermeneutical process. Confucian philosophy has grown and is different as over the centuries it has been engaged and internalized by Korean, Japanese, and Vietnamese cultures, and in our own time it is being further appreciated as it continues on its course to become a strong presence within world philosophy as a whole. I remember vividly when many decades ago my first Chinese philosophy teacher, Lao Sze-kwang 勞思光, in laying down our own shared "objective" as philosophers, would say to say to me, "Roger, we do not want to talk about Chinese philosophy; we want to talk about Chinese philosophy within the context of world philosophy."[20]

Two Alternative Meanings of Objectivity: (1) Truth about a Given Reality or (2) "Trust and Confidence" (*xin* 信) in Our World-Making Objectives (*dao* 道)

This holistic and thus inclusive understanding of objectivity as a shared objective is also a challenge to the conventional way of thinking about philosophy as "the mirror of nature." In Rorty's best efforts to overcome the old epistemology based as it is on a representational theory of perception and a correspondence theory of truth, he occasioned a pivotal turn in the Western philosophical narrative. In the traditional realist representational way of thinking about knowledge acquisition, our experience and the language

---

20. "Roger, 我們要談的不是中國哲學而是世界哲學中的中國哲學."

that reports on it find their truth in mirroring an erstwhile mind-independent and thus objective reality. The perceived relationship between objectivity and truth in this mimetic epistemology has persuaded traditions informed by Greek philosophy that historicity is what "really" happened in a way independent of who it is that is telling the story. Using *logos* as univocal rational explanation to discipline *historia* by cleansing it of both our subjectivity and a fictive and fanciful *mythos*, it provides an exclusive account that has thus sanitized "the story" of what has gone before.

Alternatively, a Confucian theory of knowledge based on a holistic understanding of objectivity means that the "truest view" (*zhenmianmu* 真面目) in the sense of being most trustworthy is the most panoramic engagement with any particular situation—that is, the most comprehensive reading of and full participation in what *is happening*. In this synoptic theory of knowledge, assumptions regarding history give both subjectivity and *mythos* a more positive value. For example, Confucius is at once a historical flesh-and-blood philosopher who lived, taught, and died in the state of Lu and, from the Han dynasty on, became an institutionalized, cultural "god" to be revered with all of the temples, icons, and formal observances appertaining thereto. Confucius has not been celebrated as a purveyor of truth about a given reality but as an exceptional life lived as a teacher of cultural values and habituated dispositions that can be relied upon and thus "trusted" by a living tradition in its own civilizing of the human experience.

These alternative meanings of "objectivity" carry over into different modes of philosophical engagement. In a world of human "beings," the equation between objectivity and what is real gives privilege to the analytic and dialectical mode of engagement. In promising a single truth it allows discrete parties to "protest" in the sense of standing apart from, "objecting" to, and thus dissenting on behalf of this single truth. An alternative mode of discourse available for human "becomings" is captured in the positive and inclusive sense of "protest" we find in the familiar expression, "I protest my innocence." To protest thusly, far from objecting to something, is "to testify on behalf of" and in service to the orchestrating of a shared consensus, to affirm with solemnity the veracity and trustworthiness of one's interpretation of a given situation. Here the guiding assumption is an awareness that our transactions are always relational and reflexive, implicating us in one way or another in whatever depositions we might choose to make. At the same time, it is the common objective that emerges out of an intelligent and inclusive conversation rather than any univocal truth that provides us with our shared way forward.

Angus Graham is making this same point when he develops a contrast between classical Greek dialectical argument and the Confucian valorization of an achieved consensus. Dialectical dispute is characteristic of a people who would ask, "What is the Truth?" while the promotion of a consensus serves the collaborative efforts of those who would ask, "Where is the Way?"[21] Taking Graham's distinction another step, it is significant that the character for *dao* 道 found on the bronzes 道 is not simply a road or "the Way" as it has been conventionally translated into English. *Dao* is reflexive in including within this character a clear graphic representation of a person composed of the human head (*shou* 首) with its coiffured head of hair as found on the oracle bones 首 and on the bronzes 首.[22] Simply put, *dao* is not *the* Way or *His* Way, but it is rather the making of *our* way together, both ancestors and progeny, both whence and whither, as we intentionally and self-consciously forge straight ahead and strive to be "true" in our way-making.

The contrast between truth-seekers and way-seekers then, is between a principled, ontological way of thinking and zoetology's analogical alternative. While principled thinking through a reasoned grasp of *episteme* or "true knowledge" seeks closure, the analogical mode of thinking is the continuing search for the disclosure of additional meaning that emerges through productive correlations. Such disclosure eschews any assumption that there is some final truth to be attained or, for that matter, any finality about the interpretive tools we continue to use. In the classical Chinese language just as the character *you* 有 as "being around and available for shared engagement" does much of the work of the copula verb in conjoining subject and world, perhaps it is the term *xin* 信 as "the credibility of and thus trust in our shared objectives" that comes closest to its alternative construal of the meaning of "truth."

The assumption in this zoetological worldview that "knowing is doing" means that such knowing must be situation specific. Hence, as with many of the classical Chinese expressions, in understanding *xin* 信 as a fiduciary situation we must appreciate the priority of situation over agency, with agents themselves being second-order abstractions from the concrete circumstances. *Xin*, in describing the fiduciary situations of persons living up to their word, goes in both directions. That is, *xin* references both the achieved credibility of the benefactor and, as a consequence of this standing, the concomitant

---

21. See A. C. Graham, *Disputers of the Tao* (La Salle, IL: Open Court, 1989), 3.

22. See Kwan Tze-wan, "Multi-function Character Database," 2014, http://humanum. arts.cuhk.edu.hk/Lexis/lexi-mf/ (西周晚期) CHANT 4469, (甲骨文合集) CHANT 3501C, and (飾奎父鼎西周中期) CHANT 2813.

trust the beneficiary has in this benefactor. For example, a passage in the *Daodejing* reports that "where there is a lack of credibility in a situation, there will be a lack of trust." The same character *xin* has to be translated in the first instance as "credibility" and then in the second as "trust."[23] This same pattern occurs in another passage in the *Daodejing* in which it insists that "to not only treat the credible as credible, but to treat those you do not trust as credible, too, is a quantum gain in credibility."[24] *Xin* thus understood is the ingenuity to discover equitable relationships among people that would allow for those affordances necessary to find consensus in the objectives of our shared undertakings.

With our behavioral objective being a shared broadening of the way, actions are not to be judged primarily in terms of binaries such as right or wrong, good or bad, true or false. The measure for conduct arises from its being reliable not only in the degree of commitment but also in terms of the accountability that comes with being able to actually accomplish what is being proposed. It is because simply being well intentioned is not enough to be *xin* 信 that I usually eschew the conventional translation of *xin* as "trustworthiness." Instead of a term that would seem to favor agency over action, I appeal to the accomplishment language of "living up to one's word" or "making good on one's word." *Xin* requires authentication in practice. In Confucian philosophy, it is this notion of "trust" in a shared objective that does much of the work of "truth." *Xin* points to "true" friends acting "truly" and thus engendering the "trust" necessary for social and political solidarity.

We might reference other such key situational terms that are suggestive of agreement on a shared objective. When we turn to the notion of "good" (*shan* 善), for example, there is an immediate parallel with the fiduciary understanding of "truth" as an achieved "trust" (*xin*) in both persons and the outcomes of our communal activities. In the case of *shan*, it is an irreducibly social and discursive understanding of "good" that is the product of efficacious discourse in its various forms. This discursive understanding of *shan* is made evident in the graph as it is found on the bronzes and in the small seal script 譱 where it is written with at least two and occasionally three "speech" radicals (*yan* 言), prompting philosopher-philologist Kwan Tze-wan 關子尹 to suggest that "this kind of repetition might reflect the fact that when the ancients talked about *shan* they were not referring to 'good' in itself but 'good' as it obtains in the relations among people. In

---

23. *Daodejing* 17: 信不足焉, 有不信.
24. *Daodejing* 49: 信者, 吾信之; 不信者, 吾亦信之; 德信.

thus combining the auspicious sheep and multiple speech components the character gives us the meaning of two persons speaking face-to-face with warmth and fondness."[25]

Although *shan* is conventionally translated as "good," such a rendering has the disadvantage of essentializing and hypostasizing a notion that, as Kwan suggests, is fundamentally relational and processual. That is, *shan* is the quality of a radically contextualized, discursive activity that conduces to welcome outcomes. "Good" is in the first instance "good with," "good to," "good in," "good for," "good at," and thereby only derivatively and abstractly, "good." It is first and foremost a compounding "felicity" or "efficacy" in one's relationships that in the fullness of time can be abstracted from one's habits of conduct to be a summary description of that person. Indeed, *shan* is most concretely imputed to the narrative rather than the person, the shared, efficacious path one's life is taking in one's relations with others (*zhishan zhi dao* 至善之道) as it stands in contrast to the paths of those who are less so. "Good," far from being some remote principle that we can appeal to in adjudicating actions or some character trait that informs our conduct or some idealized goal for activity, is what is actually happening to ongoing experience within a communicating community.[26]

Within the zoetological cosmology made explicit in the *Book of Changes*, absent the external standpoint for asserting objective truths about the world, persons are always reflexively implicated in the way in which they organize and understand their experience of it. And the values of always interested viewers are thus necessarily entailed by any observation they choose to make about this world. As a consequence, saying something about the world is always a matter of selected interest that would valorize

---

25. Kwan Tze-wan, "Database": 善夫吉父鬲 (西周晚期) CHANT 704. 凡此種種, 可能反映古代談《善》都不指獨善, 而指人際關係中的善, 故羊、誩合起來意會二人好言相向(關子尹).

26. This same claim would also hold for Mencius's notion that "human propensities are good" (*renxingshan* 人性善) if instead of reading *xing* as "human nature" in the sense of some universal essence we instead understand it as a narrative understanding of persons: *Mencius* 7A1: 盡其心者, 知其性也. "Those who make the most of their 'embodied thinking and feeling' (*xin*) realize their natural propensities (*xing*)." *Xin* 心 can be parsed at first as the initial, native prosocial conditions available for growth—what Mencius calls the "four inclinations" (*siduan* 四端). Then in "making the most" of this resolute and deliberate *xin* through assiduous cultivation, the consummate *xin* as the product of this cultivation becomes the same referent as *xing* 性. That is, *xing* 性 as is suggested by the graph, is *xin* 心 plus its growth (*sheng* 生). When the process of growth has run its course, there is no equivocation in the shared identity of *xin* and *xing*.

one's attention to this rather than that and reflects something about one's own person and one's perspective on the world. The absence of any wholly abstract basis for making objective statements about our experience means that erstwhile objective definition and simple description are problematic, and further that fact and value are interdependent and mutually entailing. Indeed, the distance between description and prescription is ultimately dependent upon the degree of self-consciousness in what is done. That is, a greater hermeneutical awareness of who one is and of the prejudgments one is bringing to an experience presumably leads to an enhanced awareness of one's own prejudices and thus allows for a more complete appreciation of its object. William James provides some insight here into the inescapability of the subjective point of view when he describes the content of experience as a "full fact": "A conscious field *plus* its object as felt or thought of *plus* an attitude towards the object *plus* the sense of self to whom the attitude belongs . . . is a *full* fact, even though it be an insignificant fact; it is of the *kind* to which all realities whatsoever must belong" (italics original).[27] Consistent with this holistic understanding of a "full fact" is what James criticizes explicitly as "the rationalist fallacy," that is, the inveterate habit of abstracting ideas like "truth," "the good," "reality" (and we might add "objectivity" as well) from "the concretes of experience" and then opposing them to that same experience.[28]

In this early Confucian cosmology, absent the dualistic and decontextualized understanding of *objectivity*, there can only be the flux of passing circumstances. And absent such objectivity, erstwhile objects or "things" dissolve into the flux and flow—that is, into the changefulness of their

---

27. William James, *Varieties of Religious Experience: A Study in Human Nature* (New York: Penguin, 1981), 499. One unresolved incoherence in James is that he wants to hold on to this holistic understanding of experience and at the same time, as a scientist, to assert the possibility and desirability of pure description, of descriptive neutrality that would seek to bracket out subjectivity. Perhaps one way of resolving this issue would be to distinguish phenomenal description from interpretive description. What does it mean to give a good account of something? For James, genius lies with what Emerson called "seeing-into" things and taking them all in—being a good visualizer. Again, perhaps for James such objectivity is just a matter of psychological motivation. Consistent with the way in which the Daoist canons deploy the metaphor of the mirror, to strive to be as neutral as we can in our descriptions in order to get the most out of things does make a difference.

28. William James, *The Works of William James*, vol. 1: *Pragmatism*, ed. Frederick H. Burkhardt (Cambridge, MA: Harvard University Press, 1975), 109.

surround. Indeed, they are not "objects" as such but *events*, continuous and interpenetrating with all other events. What are perceived as persistent "things" that sustain an identity across time from birth, maturation, and eventual decline are in fact horizons of relationships that have relative yet transitory stability within a manifold of constant change. The identity of any "thing" thus conceived, though persistent, is analogic in the sense of being constituted by and a function of the range of its dynamic associations. It is what it is by virtue of its location and its particular role within a boundless pattern of vital relations. We might say that the "where" and the "when" of something is its "what." The language of process is an eventful discourse without discrete objects or erstwhile objective facts, and to speak and hear this language is to experience and be inspired by the flow of things.

And another point to be made arises from the singular role the person of Confucius has played in setting the "objectives" and thus guiding the production of Chinese culture in the broadest sense. Confucius is a prime example of how the subjective transformation of experience, with the effects of this transformation at the same time being fully "squared" with the funded character of experience, comes to serve as the shared cultural objective in realizing a possible world. When the best effort is made to coordinate Confucian values with their empirical context, the inclusive and continuing cultural objective emerges as a force for stability and control. On the other hand, any failure to pursue such coalescence between intentions and world would move Confucian or any other culture in the direction of either sterility or worse, chaos.[29]

While certainly having important theoretical implications, what is compelling about the Confucian project and the zoetological cosmology that grounds it is that it proceeds from a relatively straightforward account of the actual human experience. Rather than appealing to speculative assumptions about fixed, essential natures or supernatural speculations about immortal souls and salvific ends, all of which would take us outside of the world of our empirical experience, the objective of Confucian culture focuses instead on the possibilities for enhancing personal worth available to us here and now through enchanting the ordinary affairs of the day. Confucius by developing his insights around the most basic and enduring aspects of the

---

29. William James offers a stern warning about the consequences of failing to coordinate our intentions with the world: "Woe to him whose beliefs play fast and loose with the order which realities follow in his experience: they will lead him nowhere or else make false connexions." James, *Pragmatism*, 99.

ordinary human experience—that is, personal cultivation in family and communal roles, family reverence, deference to others, propriety achieved in our roles and relations, friendship, a cultivated sense of shame, moral education, a communicating community, a family-centered religiousness, the intergenerational transmission of culture, and so on—has guaranteed the continuing relevance of this accumulating wisdom.

In addition to being focused on such perennial issues, one further characteristic of Confucian philosophy that is certainly present in the person of Confucius himself, and that has made his teachings so resilient in this living tradition, is the porousness and adaptability of his philosophy. In the *Analects*, Confucius is described in the following terms: "There were four things the Master abstained from entirely: He would not conjecture, he would not claim or demand certainty, he was not inflexible, and he was not self-absorbed."[30]

The positive implication of these four abstentions taken in sum is that, for Confucius, living an ethical life is much more than subscribing to a moral catechism or complying with some predetermined set of imperatives. From these strictures, we can infer an overarching, hermeneutical disposition in his own desired habits of action. We can tell that he has a commitment to pragmatic engagement rather than abstract speculation, an attitude of openness and accommodation rather than any need for finality, a willingness to be flexible rather than any intransigence or obstinacy, and a sensitivity and deference to the needs of others rather than any inordinate concern for his own personal advantage. This habituated disposition then is what motivates the virtuosic if not indeed sagacious conduct we associate with the person of Confucius, someone who has served as *the* ultimate role model for an entire cultural tradition. His enduring contribution was simply to strive to take full ownership of the cultural legacy available during his time and place, to seek to embody this culture in living an exemplary life that became a role model for the ages, to adapt this compounding wisdom from the past for the betterment of his own historical moment, and then to recommend to future generations that they continue to do the same.

And what can be said about Confucius as a person can also be said about Confucian culture as a tradition. In the Confucian process cosmology that eschews any strong sense of teleology or idealism, the focus is on making the most of the "very now" rather than anticipating the actualization of some delayed end. As a personal regimen and as a shared cultural objective,

---

30. Ames, *Sourcebook*, 372. *Analects* 9.4: 子絕四: 毋意, 毋必, 毋固, 毋我.

these abstentions locate conduct relationally in what is most immediate in the human experience and focus on shaping a habitual disposition that is most effective in responding concretely to what are always changing circumstances. As a cultural tradition, these abstentions become a focus upon what is most immediate in experience, a commitment to possibility rather than to necessity, flexibility in the face of the inevitability of change, and an openness to syncretism in its relationships with other cultural traditions.

Chapter 4

Classical Greek Ontological Thinking

Substance Ontology and Its Far-Reaching Implications

The oldest extant record of the term "ontology" as Greek *onto-*, "being" or "that which is," and *logia*, "discourse," is in its Latin form *ontologia* as it appears in the writings of two seventeenth-century German philosophers, Jacob Lorhard's *Ogdoas Scholastica* (1606) and Rudolf Gockel's *Lexicon philosophicum* (1613). Like "zoetology," it too is a new term for an old way of thinking, a way of thinking that can be traced back to the classical Greek sources and their most fundamental philosophical concerns. While ontology as "the science of being per se" in its earliest formulation is often associated with Parmenides, it addresses the most basic of philosophical issues such as identity and change, the one and the many, and appearance and reality. These same concerns are certainly there in the works of the Milesian and Pythagorean philosophers as well, taking ontology as causal thinking back to our earliest philosophical records.

With the development of a self-conscious notion of "personality" among the Greeks, we begin to encounter an ethical and religious problem that is focused on the tensions between mind and materiality. Heretofore the uncritical hylozoistic assumption was one of a vitalism in which persons are one with their bodies, but as the exercise of reason and thought itself came increasingly to be identified with the guiding and directing agency of the world, a distinction between "that which orders" and "that which is in need of being ordered" arose. The dualism between soul and body familiar to us from Christian theology (as it was inherited from Pythagoras and Plato) presented a new problem for the early Greek philosophers.

Pythagoras (ca. 570–ca. 475 BCE) conceived of the nature of things as number and the relations among things to be the sort of relations numbers have. And as he conceived the world to be a harmonious order, the relations among things (numbers) were such as to establish harmonies. This means that numerical relationships could be expressed as mathematical ratios. Aristotle in characterizing the Pythagoreans focuses on their assumption that the abstract and quantitative nature of mathematics can serve as the underlying explanation of the whole of reality. He observes that

> the Pythagoreans, as they are called devoted themselves to mathematics; they were the first to advance this study, and having been brought up in it they thought that the principles of it were the principles of all things. Since of these principles numbers are by nature the first, and in numbers they seemed to see many resemblances to the things that exist and come into being—more than in fire and earth and water (such and such a modification of numbers being justice, another being soul and reason, another being opportunity—and similarly all other things being numerically expressible); since, again, they saw that the attributes and the ratios of the musical scales were expressible in numbers; since, then, all other things seemed in their whole nature to be modelled after numbers, and numbers seemed to be the first things in the whole of nature, they supposed the elements of numbers to be the elements of all things.[1]

When we count to ten, we can do it in our minds without the need to appeal to any category of particular things in the world or to the particular things themselves, whether it be apples, or fingers, or minutes. And the numbers remain unaltered by the world. If numbers are things and their relations form patterns by virtue of proportions and ratios, then we have a geometrical vision of the world. It is this vision that underwrites the perfection of the soul vis-à-vis the body. Malleable materiality is ultimately dissolved into the formal and stable patterns or structures established by

---

1. Aristotle, *The Metaphysics*, in *The Complete Works of Aristotle: The Revised Oxford Translation*, ed. Jonathan Barnes (Princeton: Princeton University Press, 1984), 1539, 985b23–34. Used with permission of Princeton University Press; permission conveyed through Copyright Clearance Center, Inc.

numerical order. Further, quantitative exactness is assured, and pleasurable musical harmonies especially are the consequences of reliably exact ratios.

It must be stressed that the Pythagoreans—and Plato who is much influenced by them—were always concerned to maintain the relationship between quantity and quality, between numerical order and the harmonies or values that promote normative human life. Indeed, the Pythagoreans as a profoundly religious community were interested in ordering the relationship between the soul and the body. It is just such a concern over the relationship between quantity and quality that echoes down the centuries to our own times. Indeed, it is only in recent decades with our exponential technological advances that a separation has emerged that would cleave the quantitative off from the qualitative, driving a wedge between value and values, between worth and what is worthwhile, and between economics and social justice.[2]

Parmenides: *On Nature*

Pythagorean dualism of soul and body understood in terms of the numerical character of all things places such thinking on the side of permanence over change. And the ontological and logical claims introduced by Parmenides shortly thereafter (b. ca. 515 BCE) add plausibility to this preference. The surviving portions of Parmenides's work *On Nature* are fragmentary and highly metaphorical, a potent brew of logic and mysticism. It consists of a prologue and two parts, "The Way of Truth" (*Aletheia*) and "The Way of Belief" (*Doxa*). The latter is concerned with a world of becoming, flux, and change, a world admixed of Being and Not-Being. This then is the sensible world in which opposites are said to coexist and to be interdependent.

But it is "The Way of Truth" that has had by far the greatest influence on the evolution of Western philosophy, introducing as it does not only logic, ontology, metaphysics, epistemology, ethics, and philosophy of religion but the idea of a philosophical argument as second problematic thinking. Herein Parmenides examines the implications of an intuition asserted in the form of "only Being is; Not-Being cannot be." This Being is one, eternal, and indivisible. The explicit Parmenidean claim that thought, word, and

---

2. See the introduction to *Value and Values: Economics and Justice in an Age of Global Interdependence*, ed. Roger T. Ames and Peter D. Hershock (Honolulu: University of Hawai'i Press, 2015).

being are one and the same again brings with it the doctrine of a strict rationalism on which most of Greek philosophy measures itself.

Being can have no beginning since that would require that it came into being. But it could not have come into being because only Being is, and therefore there can be no "nothing" from which Being could have come. Further, if Being had parts or elements, and if more than a single Being existed, they would have to be separated by Not-Being—a void, nothing. But if nothing separated beings, then nothing would *be*, and Not-Being cannot be. Further, if there are no parts, then it must be immovable and rest in one place. And Being itself cannot move or be moved since such a change in place requires space, or "nothing," to traverse.

What Parmenides attempts to show is that any belief that would challenge the unity of Being would lead to a logical contradiction expressed as A is both A and not-A. Parmenides again argues that any appeal to the idea of Not-Being as actually existing would lead one into this same sort of contradiction: that is, the "nothing" from which Being might be said to come, or the "nothing" that would be posited as separating beings would then be said to be and not be at the same time.

In these doctrines, we can see the use of logical distinctions probably derived in part from the mathematical speculations and constructions that the Pythagoreans employed in their defense of a fundamental intuition concerning the nature of things. There are some modern critics of Parmenides's intuition that "only Being is; Not-Being cannot be" who appeal to logical arguments to challenge his conviction that "only Being is." They claim that Parmenides has confused the existential and the predicative sense of the verb "to be," that is, that something exists, and that it has certain attributes or characteristics. Indeed, to say something is or is not is qualitatively distinct from saying it is or is not round. Much has been made of this kind of critique of Parmenides, but it hardly touches the insight of Parmenides at all. Parmenides's intuition is of the unity of Being. And he employs logic to defend that intuition. Indeed, logically there can be no distinction between the existential and the predicative senses of the verb "to be" if one affirms the unity of Being. For if we accept the unity of Being, there would be no beings about which we might predicate this or that. Of course, this does not justify Parmenides in his predicating of "oneness," "indivisibility," "immovability," and "eternality" to Being, and doubtless Parmenides would be mildly uncomfortable (or could be made so) by virtue of this fact. Given the nature of Being, there is a proper concern about any literal or expository interpretation of the positive predications that Parmenides makes of Being: for example, when he claims that Being is like "the mass of a well-rounded sphere." While the distinction between the existential and predicative sense of "to be" is a mainstay of our world of Belief, it cannot be applied to the Way of Truth. Indeed, we are forced to accept the limitations of ordinary language with respect to such mystical intuitions.

When we turn to the text of *On Nature*, we find a poetic description of two very different worlds. "The Way of Truth" is in fact a mystical, metaphorical, and poetic argument for the logical infallibility of the unity of Being or "only Being is." Or perhaps stated more succinctly, and to avoid any temptation to assume an "it" as subject, we might just say "is" and that is all. While the noun-centered prejudice of ontological thinking and the many descriptions offered by the text itself ("it is complete on every side, like the mass of a rounded sphere, equally poised from the centre in every direction") might prompt us to conjure forth an extended material object, such a default response on our part is a distraction. First, Parmenides's "is" is normative, associated with "justice," "truth," and "beauty" in its presentation that would distinguish it from a material object. Again, in spite of Parmenides's own lapses, the inappropriateness of our making any predication of the existential "is" requires that we surrender any and all of our dualistic binaries such as subject and object, knower and known, idea and world, self and other, means and end, fact and value, and so on. Parmenides does claim that "thou canst not know what is not—that is impossible—nor utter it; for it is the same thing that can be thought and that can be," and again "the thing that can be thought and that for the sake of which the thought exists is the same; for you cannot find thought without something that is, as to which it is uttered."

In many ways, this early mystical challenge to our commonsense way of parsing experience anticipates the complex and obscure notion of *theoria* or "thought thinking itself" that we find so fundamental in the epistemologies of Plato and Aristotle. But because it confounds our ontological thinking and the logic of strict identity that follows from it, not all commentators would agree that "thought thinking itself" is an acceptable interpretation of Parmenidean "being." For example, John Palmer is adamant that "the incoherence of the claim that thought and being are identical (*esse = intellegere*) does not automatically entail that Parmenides did not mean to advance it, and some interpreters will continue to view as central to the Parmenidean system this nonsensical thesis. That anyone should be willing to do so, however, when there are sound interpretive alternatives available seems remarkable."[3] For Palmer, these "sound interpretive alternatives" would at least, contra *theoria*, include his own logical insight that thinking, thought, and being must be distinct because, "if Parmenidean Being is at once thinking and the object of its own thought, then it already violates the principle of the identity of thinking and being. In so far as it is thought, it is not thinking, so that its being cannot be identical with its activity of thinking but must also consist at least in part in its being such as to be thought."[4] When we turn to reflect on Plato and Aristotle's understanding of *theoria* as some variation on "thinking thinking itself" that seems to be derived from Parmenides, we will find that they too advance what Palmer would dismiss as this same "nonsensical thesis."

In many ways, there are resonances between the poem of Parmenides and Plato's account in the *Symposium* of the ascent of Socrates to experience the principle of Beauty that "exists as itself in accordance with itself, eternal and uniform." In *On Nature*, the description of the goddess who offers her instruction to the man who "shouldst learn all things" is echoed in the *Symposium* story of Diotima leading the young Socrates up out of the sensible world to encounter Beauty-in-Itself. Plato like Parmenides before him struggles and yet must necessarily fail in finding the language adequate to giving an account of what seems to be the same kind of mystical experience.

When we move to "The Way of Belief," Parmenides with his own two-world theory characterizes the thinking of mortals in the correlative and generative terms we associate with zoetological thinking: fire and the rays of the sun, light and night, sun and moon, male and female, Eros as the first of the gods, the birthing female, and so on. Again, what necessarily precludes such an association between the metaphorical language of Parmenides and the analogical thinking of zoetology is his further claim that this is the way of thinking where mortals "go astray from the truth." Plato runs up against this same issue in the *Republic* when he chooses to use the analogy of the sun to provide insight into his own unifying principle of the Good. Just as for Parmenides the generative terms used to describe the "way of belief" offend against the truth of being in itself, so too the generative and life-giving operations of the sun are anathema to the purely "causal" function of the Good. Plato's ontology like Parmenides's before him requires a radical disjunction between the real intelligible world and

---

3. John Palmer, *Parmenides and Presocratic Philosophy* (Oxford: Oxford University Press, 2009), 122.

4. Palmer, *Parmenides and Presocratic Philosophy*, 121.

its illusory shadows in the sensible world. Where the metaphors appealed to in zoetological thinking are correlations productive of additional meaning, the same tropes in the ontological thinking of Parmenides and Plato are at best signposts that direct philosophers in their dialectical ascent to some permanent and unchanging transcendent reality.

Poem of Parmenides: *On Nature*

PROEM

(1)

The car that bears me carried me as far as ever my heart desired, when it had brought me and set me on the renowned way of the goddess, which leads the man who knows through all the towns. On that way was I borne along; for on it did the wise steeds carry me, drawing my car, and maidens showed the way. And the axle, glowing in the socket—for it was urged round by the whirling wheels at each end—gave forth a sound as of a pipe, when the daughters of the Sun, hasting to convey me into the light, threw back their veils from off their faces and left the abode of Night.

There are the gates of the ways of Night and Day, fitted above with a lintel and below with a threshold of stone. They themselves, high in the air, are closed by mighty doors, and Avenging Justice keeps the keys that fit them. Her did the maidens entreat with gentle words and cunningly persuade to unfasten without demur the bolted bars from the gates. Then, when the doors were thrown back, they disclosed a wide opening, when their brazen posts fitted with rivets and nails swung back one after the other. Straight through them, on the broad way, did the maidens guide the horses and the car, and the goddess greeted me kindly, and took my right hand in hers, and spake to me these words:

Welcome, O youth, that comest to my abode on the car that bears thee tended by immortal charioteers! It is no ill chance, but right and justice that has sent thee forth to travel on this way. Far, indeed, does it lie from the beaten track of men! Meet it is that thou shouldst learn all things, as well the unshaken heart of well-rounded truth, as the opinions of mortals in which is no true belief at all. Yet none the less shalt thou learn these things also,—how passing right through all things one should judge the things that seem to be.

But do thou restrain thy thought from this way of inquiry, nor let habit by its much experience force thee to cast upon this way a wandering eye or sounding ear or tongue; but judge by argument the much disputed proof uttered by me. There is only one way left that can be spoken of . . .

I. The Way of Truth

(2)

Look steadfastly with thy mind at things though afar as if they were at hand. Thou canst not cut off what is from holding fast to what is, neither scattering itself abroad in order nor coming together.

(3)

It is all one to me where I begin; for I shall come back again there.

(4, 5)

Come now, I will tell thee—and do thou hearken to my saying and carry it away—the only two ways of search that can be thought of. The first, namely, that *It is*, and that it is impossible for it not to be, is the way of belief, for truth is its companion. The other, namely, that *It is not*, and that it must needs not be,—that, I tell thee, is a path that none can learn of at all. For thou canst not know what is not—that is impossible—nor utter it; for it is the same thing that can be thought and that can be.

(6)

It needs must be that what can be spoken and thought is; for it is possible for it to be, and it is not possible for what is nothing to be. This is what I bid thee ponder. I hold thee back from this first way of inquiry, and from this other also, upon which mortals knowing naught wander two-faced; for helplessness guides the wandering thought in their breasts, so that they are borne along stupefied like men deaf and blind. Undiscerning crowds, who hold that it is and is not the same and not the same, and all things travel in opposite directions!

(7)

For this shall never be proved, that the things that are not are; and do thou restrain thy thought from this way of inquiry.

(8)

One path only is left for us to speak of, namely, that *It is*. In this path are very many tokens that what is is uncreated and indestructible; for it is complete, immovable, and without end. Nor was it ever, nor will it be; for now *it is*, all at once, a continuous one. For what kind of origin for it wilt thou look for? In what way and from what source could it have drawn its increase? . . . I shall not let thee say nor think that it came from what is not; for it can neither be thought nor uttered that anything is not. And, if it came from nothing, what need could have made it arise later rather than sooner? Therefore must it either be altogether or be not at all. Nor will the force of truth suffer aught to arise besides itself from that which is not. Wherefore, justice doth not loose her fetters and let anything come into being or pass away, but holds it fast. Our judgment thereon depends on this: "*Is it or is it not?*" Surely it is adjudged, as it needs must be, that we are to set aside the one way as unthinkable and nameless (for it is no true way), and that the other path is real and true. How, then, can what *is* be going to be in the future? Or how could it come into being? If it came into being, it is not; nor is it if it is going to be in the future. Thus is becoming extinguished and passing away not to be heard of.

Nor is it divisible, since it is all alike, and there is no more of it in one place than in another, to hinder it from holding together, nor less of it, but everything is full of what is. Wherefore it is wholly continuous; for what is, is in contact with what is.

Moreover, it is immovable in the bonds of mighty chains, without beginning and without end; since coming into being and passing away have been driven afar, and true belief has cast them away. It is the same, and it rests in the self-same place, abiding in itself. And thus it remaineth constant in its place; for hard necessity keeps it in the bonds of the limit that holds it fast on every side. Wherefore it is not permitted to what is to be infinite; for it is in need of nothing; while, if it were infinite, it would stand in need of everything.

The thing that can be thought and that for the sake of which the thought exists is the same; for you cannot find thought without something that is, as to which it is uttered. And there is not, and never shall be, anything besides what is, since fate has chained it so as to be whole and immovable. Wherefore all these things are but names which mortals have given, believing them to be true—coming into being and passing away, being and not being, change of place and alteration of bright colour.

Since, then, it has a furthest limit, it is complete on every side, like the mass of a rounded sphere, equally poised from the centre in every direction; for it cannot be greater or smaller in one place than in another. For there is no nothing that could keep it from reaching out equally, nor can aught that is be more here and less there than what is, since it is all inviolable. For the point from which it is equal in every direction tends equally to the limits.

II. The Way of Belief

Here shall I close my trustworthy speech and thought about the truth. Henceforward learn the beliefs of mortals, giving ear to the deceptive ordering of my words.

Mortals have made up their minds to name two forms, one of which they should not name, and that is where they go astray from the truth. They have distinguished them as opposite in form, and have assigned to them marks distinct from one another. To the one they allot the fire of heaven, gentle, very light, in every direction the same as itself, but not the same as the other. The other is just the opposite to it, dark night, a compact and heavy body. Of these I tell thee the whole arrangement as it seems likely; for so no thought of mortals will ever outstrip thee.

(9)

Now that all things have been named light and night, and the names which belong to the power of each have been assigned to these things and to those, everything is full at once of light and dark night, both equal, since neither has aught to do with the other.

(10, 11)

And thou shalt know the substance of the sky, and all the signs in the sky, and the resplendent works of the glowing sun's pure torch, and whence they arose. And thou shalt learn likewise of the wandering deeds of the round-faced moon, and of her substance. Thou shalt know, too, the heavens that surround us, whence they arose, and how Necessity took them and bound them to keep the limits of the stars . . . how the earth, and the sun, and the moon, and the sky that is common to all, and the Milky Way, and the outermost Olympos, and the burning might of the stars arose.

(12)

The narrower bands were filled with unmixed fire, and those next them with night, and in the midst of these rushes their portion of fire. In the midst of these is the divinity that directs the course of all things; for she is the beginner of all painful birth and all begetting, driving the female to the embrace of the male, and the male to that of the female.

(13)

First of all the gods she contrived Eros.

(14)

Shining by night with borrowed light, wandering round the earth.

(15)

Always looking to the beams of the sun.

(16)

For just as thought stands at any time to the mixture of its erring organs, so does it come to men; for that which thinks is the same, namely, the substance of the limbs, in each and every man; for their thought is that of which there is more in them.

(17)

On the right boys; on the left girls.

(18)

Thus, according to men's opinions, did things come into being, and thus they are now. In time they will grow up and pass away. To each of these things men have assigned a fixed name.[5]

Plato and the Theory of Forms

The essential themes of Plato's philosophy are well known. His dialogical understanding of philosophical thinking presented through his characterization of his teacher, Socrates, in the early dialogues is shaped by the representation of the discursive Socrates as an open-minded thinker pursuing, but never grasping, the wholeness of truth. In the dialogues of Plato's mature and later years, this dialogical method seems to take on a more rigorous cast, and Plato has been interpreted as moving incrementally in the direction of a complete philosophic system.

The interpretation of the received Plato as positing a doctrine of eternal ideas or forms that exist as both the ground and the goal of rational explanation makes the dialectic a viable method in the quest for certainty. And it is the aim of both dialogue and the dialectic to arrive at these ideas

---

5. Excerpted from John Burnet, *Early Greek Philosophy* (London: Adam and Charles Black, 1920).

and their systematic relationships. The idealism of the received Plato is an objective idealism in which the real is *ideal* in the sense of being independently existing patterns, structures, or forms that have an originative and sustaining function for order in the world. In his attempt to construct a coherent vision of the unity of things, the received Plato bequeathed to subsequent generations of thinkers a number of persistent problems that have helped to define the character of philosophical speculation ever since. The distinctions between Being and Becoming, permanence and flux, reality and appearance, knowledge and opinion, and so forth, remain intransigent within our philosophic narrative.

This way of reading Plato then, is that he is an abstract formist who provides his Theory of Forms as an objective and universal answer, and thus a closure to all of our most pressing philosophical problems. He is a metaphysical realist who understands the life of the philosopher as a theoretical and spiritual ascent from a world of appearance and mere opinion to that of Reality and the true intellectual knowledge of the unchanging Forms. The escape from the cave in the *Republic*, Diotima's introduction of Beauty-in-Itself to a young Socrates in the *Symposium*, the escape of the soul from the body in the *Phaedo*, are all ways of conveying this intellectual journey and its certain end.

But perhaps a more interesting reading of Plato might be that he is an erotic ironist who advocates philosophy as an open-ended and continuing way of life and growth. For such a Plato, philosophy is a process rather than an end. Plato on this reading is a poet and playwright, a purveyor of metaphor and a subversive artist, and has only been reduced to a metaphysical absolutist because of the melding of Greek philosophy with Christian dogma and twentieth-century scientism. Having acknowledged this more compelling Plato, we must still allow that it is the first interpretation of Plato that has been the received Plato, and that has had such a profound impact on the evolution of Western culture.

Plato's much celebrated "Theory of Forms" is for the most part an evolving hypothesis with only gestures in the direction of any direct proof. Even though its mature statement as a transcendental "two-world" theory does not occur until his middle and later dialogues, we can trace its substance to his earliest dialogues and, in so doing, associate it with his teacher, Socrates. The causal Theory of Forms as an ontological way of explaining the human experience in all of its parts—metaphysics, epistemology, ethics, religion, and so on—has had an enormous influence on the course of Western civilization, especially as it was later appropriated by the Church Fathers as the language and structure for interpreting the Abrahamic religions.

Plato uses many different overlapping terms in constructing his Theory of Forms. This vocabulary includes *idea, morphe, eidos,* and *paradeigma* but also *genos, physis,* and *ousia.*[6] Plato's ontology centers on this notion of Form or Idea, singular and plural, whereby expanding upon this postulate and stipulating new meanings for it, it comes to serve him as a key technical vocabulary to give expression to his highly abstract concept. If we take the term *eidos* as an example, the original Homeric meaning as "what one sees," "appearances," "shape" has a strong emphasis on the visual apprehension of something physical. In the historian Herodotus it becomes an abstract term to mean a "characteristic property" or "type" of something, and in Thucydides he speaks of "the *eidos* of a disease," imparting to it a notion of some constituent and determinative nature.

Plato develops his Theory of Forms in response to the problem of change as his deliberate antidote to the relativization of both epistemology and moral philosophy being advocated by his nemesis, the Sophists. John Dewey describes the impulse behind the thinking of these early Greek philosophers remembered best in the person of Plato, insisting that "the Greeks in initiating the intellectual life of Europe were impressed by characteristic traits of plants and animals, so impressed indeed that they made these traits key to defining nature and explaining mind and society."[7] Dewey singles out two prominent terms in the Greek vocabulary that give expression to this understanding of the underlying design of both things and world, observing that "the conception of *eidos,* species, a fixed form and final cause, was the central principle of knowledge as well as of nature. Upon it rested the logic of science. Change as change is mere flux and lapse; it insults intelligence. Genuinely to know is to grasp a permanent end that realizes itself through changes, holding them thereby within the metes and bounds of fixed truth."[8] And for Dewey, the second term that lends explanation to the actualization of living things is captured in the Greek term *telos,* where "in living things, changes do not seem to occur as they happen elsewhere, any which way;

---

6. Throughout my exploration of the terms through which Greek ontological thinking is expressed I have benefited much from the narrative of the original Greek terms in F. E. Peters, *Greek Philosophical Terms: A Historical Lexicon* (New York: New York University Press, 1967).

7. John Dewey, *The Essential Dewey,* vol. 1, ed. Larry Hickman and Thomas Alexander (Bloomington: Indiana University Press, 1998), 40.

8. Dewey, *The Essential Dewey,* vol. 1, 40–41.

the earlier changes are regulated in view of later results. This progressive organization does not cease till there is achieved a true final term, a *telos*, a completed, perfected end."[9]

We can associate the earliest use of the terms *eidos* and *idea* in Plato's dialogues with Socrates himself when Socrates looks to the religious figure Euthyphro for assistance in defining the single *eidos* of all holy actions. The Greek word that is usually translated interchangeably as "holiness" or "piety" is *hosia*, which carries with it a strong sense of fealty, fidelity, and allegiance. In describing persons, *hosia* means piety or devotion; with respect to things, it means hallowed or sacred; and with actions it means sanctioned by divine law.

The occasion recounted in the *Euthyphro* is one in which Socrates is facing public prosecution on the charge of irreligiousness and impiety, and during the trial on this charge remembered in the *Apology*, he will have to answer his accusers. He meets up with Euthyphro who is also involved in preliminary hearings at the court of the chief magistrate, where he has brought a suit against his own father for murder. It is because Euthyphro is reputed in Athens to have a deep interest in religious matters that Socrates takes this opportunity to seek his counsel.

The dramatic function of Euthyphro's prosecution of his own father is important in clarifying the status of holiness as a universal principle. If we are to apply a single, objective standard, Euthyphro is surely right when he asserts that in "prosecuting a criminal either for murder or sacrilegious theft or some other such thing," divine law would have it that "one must not let off the perpetrator of impiety whoever he should happen to be."[10] Principled justice must be blind. Again, the case brought by Euthyphro against his father is that he had apprehended an employee who in a drunken rage had killed a slave. Binding the culprit and detaining him in a ditch, the father sent to the authorities in Athens for instructions on how to dispose of him. In the interim, the murderer, exposed to the elements, dies from the cold. The dramatic function of Euthyphro's accusation against his father lies in the fact that such a patently tenuous case can hardly be squared with the universal standard being advocated by Socrates.

---

9. Dewey, *The Essential Dewey*, vol. 1, 40.

10. Plato, *The Last Days of Socrates*, trans. Hugh Tredennick and Harold Tarrant (London: Penguin, 2003), 14, 5d–e.

First Anticipation

This anecdote about Euthyphro prosecuting his father is sometimes asso-ciated with a resonant passage in the *Analects of Confucius*: "The Governor of She in conversation with Confucius said, 'In our village there is this young man, "True Goody." When his father stole a sheep, he reported him to the authorities.' Confucius replied, 'Those who are "true" in my village conduct themselves differently. A father would cover for his son, and a son for his father, and being "true" lies in doing so.' "[11] There is a backstory here. While on tour late in his life, Confucius travels south from the state of Cai to visit the region of She in the state of Chu. The duke as governor of the local county is aware of Confucius's reputation as a well-known teacher and moral exemplar, and he wants to impress this man of reputation with the high ethical standards of the people under his jurisdiction and moral sway. The governor relates an incident that involves one particularly "upright" young man in his district known revealingly as "True Goody." The name of this young man, Zhigong 直躬, speaks volumes. *Zhi* 直 means "true" in the sense of being "true, upright, honest." And *gong* 躬 is a term for the body that references specifically a deliberate public display of one's personal merits. In this particular context, the character *gong* conveys a sense of self-righteousness—a sanctimonious person making a conscious display of his virtues for all to see. When Confucius contrasts his sense of what it means to be "true" with "true" as it is baked into the name "True Goody," it recalls Confucius's deeply felt antipathy to anything and anyone that is duplicitous.

By way of interpretation, the position that Confucius is advocat-ing here begins from the Confucian conception of the political as an isomorphism among family, state, and world (*jiaguotianxiatonggou* 家國天下同構) in which state and world are simulacra and thus conceived of on the basis of family relations.[12] For Confucius, a true and trusting relationship among members of a family is the fabric from which the norms of community, polity, and ultimately cosmos draw their tensile

---

11. *Analects* 13.18: 葉公語孔子曰: "吾黨有直躬者, 其父攘羊, 而子證之." 孔子曰: "吾黨之直者異於是. 父為子隱, 子為父隱, 直在其中矣."

12. This assumed isomorphism is pervasive in the philosophical literature and is made explicit in *Mencius* 4A5: 人有恆言, 皆曰 "天下國家." 天下之本在國, 國之本在家, 家之本在身. "There is a popular adage heard among the people who all say: 'The world, the state, the family.' The world is rooted in the state, the state in the family, and the family in one's own person."

strength. As such, Confucius underscores the pressing need to continue to cultivate virtuosity in family relations close to home as the ultimate ground of all familial, communal, and political morality. This assumption that social and political order is the radial extension of what is closest at hand is the same issue when we meet this same governor of She in another passage in the *Analects*. During the twenty-sixth year of King Zhao of Chu (490 BCE) there is an occasion on which the governor asks the itinerant Confucius about governing properly. Confucius replies: "If those near at hand are pleased, those at a distance will repair to you."[13]

This anecdote about True Goody is a much-cited passage from the *Analects* that has produced a veritable avalanche of scholarly literature in recent years, especially in China where there has been a continuing debate about the relationship between Confucian values and a persistent culture of corruption.[14] In the *Analects*, Confucius insists that "family reverence" (*xiao* 孝), when properly understood, far from being a source of nepotistic corruption that would compromise social and political order, is itself respectful of proper authority: "It is a rare thing for someone who has a sense of family reverence and fraternal responsibility (*xiaoti* 孝弟) to have a taste for defying authority. And it is unheard of for those who have no taste for defying authority to be keen on initiating rebellion."[15] What sheds light on this "True Goody" case while at the same time making the situation somewhat more complex is the internal demand in Confucian role ethics to make things right by achieving optimal appropriateness in any particular situation (*yi* 義). To this end, "remonstrance" (*jian* 諫)—that is, the stern obligation that the younger generation has to remonstrate with and try to rectify the conduct of its elders—has a prominent and crucial role in the Confucian literature on family reverence (*xiao* 孝).

---

13. *Analects* 13.16: 近者悅, 遠者來.

14. Articles by Liu Qingping and Guo Qiyong were published in *Dao* 6, no. 1 (2007): "Confucianism and Corruption: An Analysis of Shun's Two Actions Described by Mencius" and "Is Confucian Ethics a 'Consanguinism'?" respectively. Additional articles by them and others can be found in English translation in a special issue of *Contemporary Chinese Thought* (39, no. 1 [2007, Fall]) on "Filial Piety: The Root of Morality or the Source of Corruption?" with an introduction by guest editor Huang Yong 黃勇. Guo Qiyong has edited a collection of articles in 儒家倫理爭鳴集: 以親親互隱為中心 [Debates on Confucian ethics: The mutual concealment among family members] (Wuhan: Jiaoyuchubanshe, 2004). There is also a collection of the articles in this continuing debate at www.confucius2000.com.

15. *Analects* 1.2: 其為人也孝弟, 而好犯上者,鮮矣: 不好犯上, 而好作亂者, 未之有也.

A first impression of many commentators on reading this passage is that it sets up a contrast between an objective principle of justice and a perhaps understandable but illegitimate impulse to protect family members from prosecution. The contrast lies between impartial principles and partial relations, a tension between loyalty to state or to family, that is, a choice between justice and corruption. But this is not the issue here. We must begin again from the Confucian conception of the political as an isomorphism among family, state, and world in which state and world are simulacra for family. At the end of the day, the notion of justice in this Confucian tradition is holistic rather than simply principled and requires a consideration of both higher level norms and particular historical circumstances. The question at issue is not a choice between justice and corruption but how to best achieve justice as an inclusive balance between partiality and impartiality.

There has been much in ethical theorizing late and soon that either ignores or excludes the consideration of the partiality evidenced in family roles as being relevant to moral conduct.[16] By way of contrast, Confucian role ethics begins explicitly from family feeling. Confucian role ethics is not an abstract theory that provides principled moral judgments for hard cases we might encounter along the way, nor does it give primacy to developing a deliberate, rational means to achieve some moral end. Rather than appealing to some set of objective principles then, Confucian ethics offers a way of trying to live consummately in family and community roles through achieving a relational virtuosity (*ren* 仁) in one's conduct that is preemptive of moral transgressions. Such a holistic vision of life within roles and relationships requires the ongoing cultivation of an aesthetic, moral, and religious imagination that will enable one to pursue an optimal and inclusive appropriateness in all that one does

16. A good account of this problem is found in Susan Moller Okin's influential work *Justice, Gender, and the Family*. Okin offers a compelling argument that the contemporary institution of family, with its hierarchical structure of roles saturated by a pervasive gender bias, is fundamentally unjust. And as she properly claims, given the crucial importance of family as the veritable "school of justice" in the moral development and education of our children, the assumption that we can construct a just society on such a tenuous foundation is untenable. This being the case, Okin argues that it is undeniably true and yet at the same time, wholly deplorable that most scholars who would offer us a theory of justice think they can get away with either ignoring family or idealizing it to the extent that its partial concerns locate it beyond the scope of ethics. See Susan Moller Okin, *Justice, Gender, and the Family* (New York: Basic Books, 1989).

(*yi* 義). It is an attempt to use moral artistry in one's roles and relations to live life most significantly.

In the modern Chinese language, the binomial *zhengyi* 正義 is the standard translation of "justice." Equity for each unique person can only be respected and diversity among them achieved by giving full affordance to both particularity and impartiality rather than choosing between them. This being the case, rather than positing a conception of justice that is rendered properly blind in its appeal to an abstract principle applied to equal and thus abstract individuals, a clear-eyed conception of justice with its pursuit of relational equity must do the work of accommodating both particular instances and the generalizations that can be made from them. That is, rather than invoking some transcendental standard or some faculty of impersonal reason as the single warrant for claiming impartiality—a strategy that is necessarily hobbled by the contingencies of always specific circumstances—Confucian philosophy true to its commitment to holism proffers an alternative understanding of impartiality itself that arises as a generalization from particular instances of justice. With the commitment to the postulate of "the inseparability of one and many" (*yiduobufen* 一多不分) in Confucian process cosmology, *zhengyi* must include broad concern for partial relations as well as for any abstract and yet always provisional standard of impartiality.

Such an inclusive holism would mean that Confucian justice is to be sought as fairness within "forms of life" as they are defined by specific patterns of ritual propriety (*li* 禮) achieved within always specific circumstances. Any simple appeal to an abstract, principled understanding of positive law, while on occasion necessary, would at the same time be a signal of communal failure. Again, rather than invoking a rational calibration on the scales of evidence that will enable it to achieve the binary closure of "right or wrong," "guilty or not guilty," the pursuit of *zhengyi* would be a continuing, emergent, and always imperfect process inclusive of multiple perspectives that relies heavily on moral imagination for its compass. With an optimizing symbiosis (*gongsheng* 共生) being both its "objective" and its highest value, such a conception of justice can only be provisional and a matter of degree. Confucian justice, rather than being elevated and reified or institutionalized as an abstract, complete theory, has its origins for the most part in a response to perceived instances of injustice at home. Again, in resisting any persistent formal definition as a concept or principle or ideal, *zhengyi* would reference a quality of agreement achieved through an emergent consensus among a local population: literally (L. *con* + *sentire*), their "shared feelings" in real time.

We might ask whether this speculative reconstruction of *zhengyi* within the Confucian interpretive context is consistent with the real-life experience of the Chinese people. The contemporary Taiwan legal scholar Chang Wejen (Zhang Weiren) 張偉仁 has spent a lifetime reflecting on the subject of law and justice in traditional China. In asking the question of how Chinese people have understood and valorized justice, he concludes that

> the Chinese believe that for a social problem, facts could be seen in different perspectives, especially if one observed their historical developments; when many other factors, including human relations and feelings, were taken into consideration, it was nearly impossible to get a clear, black and white picture. Therefore in many instances, the parties to a dispute did not seek absolute justice, believing that it was not achievable or even desirable; they preferred peaceful coexistence to formal justice that separates them into winners and losers.[17]

***

In the early pages of the *Euthyphro*, Socrates reproaches his "teacher" Euthyphro for giving him only one specific instance of holiness or piety—that is, Euthyphro's own prosecution of his father—when in fact Socrates is asking "for that special feature (*eidos*) through which all holy things are holy. For you were in agreement, surely, that it was by virtue of a single standard that all unholy things are unholy and holy things holy."[18] To begin with, it seems that Socrates is asking for a "real" definition of piety or holiness: not defining the word but what piety really *is*, the universalizable, causal object itself rather than a conception of it.[19] Indeed, there is much in *Euthyphro* as

---

17. Chang Wejen, "Classical Chinese Jurisprudence and the Development of the Chinese Legal System," *Tsinghua China Law Review* 2, no. 2 (Spring 2010): 270.

18. Plato, *The Last Days of Socrates*, trans. Hugh Tredennick and Harold Tarrant (London: Penguin, 2003), 15, 6e.

19. Aristotle observes that Socrates himself "did not separate the universal definition" as having some transcendent and subsistent existence, but Aristotle might in fact be co-opting Socrates for his own rejection of the abstract and transcendental status of

an early dialogue that anticipates Plato's mature statement of the Theory of Forms. We find that, as we work through the several definitions proffered for piety in the dialogue, we are systematically introduced seriatim to the essential vocabulary of Plato's logic of knowing where the objects of true knowledge are these formal "real" definitions.

In Euthyphro's first definition he offers an example of piety, where what is at issue is the need to respect the universal character of *eidos*. We are alerted to the fundamental difference between a "formal" definition that is seeking the selfsame identical and reduplicated characteristic or "form" true of all instances of piety or holiness and mere instances of it. The basis for Plato's principle of individuation and the categorical thinking that follows from it is established by insisting that piety is one thing that supervenes upon all instances of piety.

Euthyphro then proposes as his second definition "what is agreeable to the gods is holy, and what is not agreeable is unholy." Socrates counters this claim by saying that since "the same things are considered just by some and unjust by others" they "would be both holy and unholy by this account."[20] Socrates's response to this second definition provides us with a notion of strict identity and the principle of noncontradiction that follows from exclusive, categorical thinking: that is, the logic that something cannot be both A and not-A at the same time.

Euthyphro then emends this definition by asserting that "what's holy is whatever all the gods approve of, and that its opposite, what all the gods disapprove of, is unholy."[21] Socrates responds to this universalizing definition of holiness by asking, "Is the holy approved by the gods because it is holy, or is it holy because it's approved by the gods?"[22] By manipulating Euthyphro through a rather convoluted grammatical argument, Socrates gets him to agree that "it *gets approved* because it's holy: it's not holy by reason of *getting approved*."[23] Simply put, the "it" and thus the "is" or essence of holiness must precede its approval, elevating the *eidos* of holiness to causal status. Holiness must be singular and independent in the sense that "it is what it is" by virtue of itself. Anything that is loved as holy must itself be

---

Plato's Theory of Forms. See *Metaphysics* 1078b.

20. Plato, *Last Days of Socrates*, 17, 8a.

21. Plato, *Last Days of Socrates*, 20, 9e.

22. Plato, *Last Days of Socrates*, 20, 10a.

23. Plato, *Last Days of Socrates*, 21, 10d.

both logically and temporally prior to its being loved. That is, it must have some essential characteristic that then induces the attribute of its being loved. With this argument, Socrates provides us not only with the ontological essence and attribute distinction but also with the ontological priority of an essential subject to whatever is to be predicated of it as its attributes. He gives us the difference between substances as property-bearers and those properties that are borne by subjects respectively. It is precisely this substance vocabulary that Socrates appeals to when he criticizes Euthyphro for not giving him what he has been asking for, saying, "When asked what the holy is, you don't want to point out the essence for me, but to tell me of some attribute that attaches to it, saying that has the attribute of being approved by all the gods; what it *is* you've not yet said."[24] Importantly, what Socrates is demanding of Euthyphro is not the definition of a mere concept but a theory of meaning grounded in a metaphysics of essences. It is the essence that tells us what *is* what. And by extension, given the ontological priority of this *eidos*, the relationship between "holiness' and the particular instances of it is originative: in Plato's own language, the *eidos* with respect to the particular instances is "in, present to, copied in, participating in, added to, of," and so on. And the consequent relationship of the particulars to the singular *eidos* is they "have, copy, partake in, accept, and get" it. For Plato, these particular instances in their obvious imperfection as mere copies of the original *eidos* stand as clear proof that in order for them to exist, the perfect *eidos* must exist prior to them.

Expressing some frustration with Euthyphro's seeming inability to understand what is being asked of him to identify the universal essence of all instances of holiness, Socrates offers his own definition by proposing "that everything holy is just." On reflection and seeming himself to be thinking aloud, Socrates then qualifies this first statement "that everything holy is just" by asking if it might be "the case that all that's holy is just, whereas not all that's just is holy—part of it's holy and part of it's different."[25] We are given Plato's own answer to this question in the later dialogue *Protagoras*, where he insists that everything that is holy is *by that very fact* just, and everything that is just is *by that very fact* holy. In the debate between Protagoras and Socrates, when someone hypothetically asks about the relationship between justice and holiness, Socrates in making his argument for the unity

---

24. Plato, *Last Days of Socrates*, 22, 11a.

25. Plato, *Last Days of Socrates*, 23, 11e.

of virtue replies, "I should certainly answer him on my own behalf that justice is holy, and that holiness is just."[26] Given that the term "holiness" itself actually means sanctioned by divine law, the divine status of justice would seem to preclude any important distinction between divine justice itself and divinely sanctioned human justice. As such, Socrates initial claim "that everything holy is just" should properly bring closure to their efforts to define holiness. But Socrates's insistence on this further qualification is calculated, allowing him to introduce the genus, species, and differentia distinctions necessary for the refinement of any formal definition: that is, all whales are mammals but not all mammals are whales.

Mary Tiles offers us a summary of what is carried over from Plato as the Aristotelian genera and species mode of taxonomic classification, observing that

> the kind of rational structure which is given prominence in Aristotle's works is the structure of a classificatory system—a hierarchy of kinds of things organised successively by kinds (or genera) and forms of those kinds (or species). (In turn species become in effect genera to be divided into [sub]species and genera grouped into more comprehensive genera.) Definitions were not in the first instance thought to be accounts of words but of the "what-it-is-to-be" a thing of that kind, in other words accounts of essence. To define an object—to give its name a precise or correct use—was to locate it in a classificatory system.[27]

Tiles provides a further account of how the application of Aristotle's classificatory system, grounded as it is in this substance ontology, is thought to lead to what is the discovery of meaning about a given reality rather than the production of additional knowledge. She avers that "this is a hierarchical order based on qualitative similarities and differences. A key assumption underlying such an order is that a thing cannot both have and lack a given quality—the requirement of non-contradiction. Non-contradiction is therefore

---

26. *Protagoras* 331a–b, B. Jowett translation.

27. Mary Tiles, "Idols of the Market Place: Knowledge and Language," unpublished manuscript (n.d.), 5–6. A revised version is available in Mary Tiles, "Images of Reason in Western Culture," in *Alternative Rationalities*, ed. Eliot Deutsch (Honolulu: Society for Asian and Comparative Philosophy Monograph, 1992).

fundamental to this kind of rational order. . . . Knowledge of definitions (or essences) coupled with the principle of non-contradiction can serve as the foundation for further, rationally demonstrable, knowledge."[28]

As we have seen, Plato would define things by appeal to the reduplicated eternal ideals of what he takes to be natural kinds, thus allowing Socrates to make the Pythagorean argument that human beings have an immortal soul. Aristotelian scholar Yu Jiyuan 余纪元 would distinguish Plato's abstract understanding of reality from Aristotle by insisting that, for Aristotle, each "being in itself" has its own unique definition. Yu says that

> according to Aristotle, the essence of a thing is revealed by a definition and is the ontological correlate of definition: "For definition (*horismos*) seems to be of what a thing is" (*Analytica Posteriora* ii.3, 90b3–4). There can never be two definitions of the same thing. Each type of essential predication, therefore, reveals one definite essence. This entails that each *per se* being has its distinct essence. In short, to say that X is a *per se* being means that it is a being with an essence, revealed by a definition of genus + differentia.[29]

Aristotle's hylomorphic understanding of things includes both form and matter, and thus it is that, unlike Plato, he gives ontological privilege to Socrates as the particular thing rather than the ideal. At the same time, in considering his principle of individuation, we have to allow that the material aspect explains the uniqueness of any particular thing while the reduplicated and indivisible formal aspects—its *eidos* and *telos*—define it as one of an inviolate species or kind.

Second Anticipation

As a graduate student at the University of London, I had the happy opportunity to study with and learn from the inimitable Angus Graham. One problem that Graham focused on and pondered throughout his long career was how to understand the Chinese concept *xing* 性 that is

---

28. Tiles, "Images of Reason in Western Culture," 7–8.

29. Jiyuan Yu, *The Structure of Being in Aristotle's* Metaphysics (Dordrecht: Kluwer Academic, 2003), 7–8.

conventionally (and for Graham problematically) translated as "human nature" as it emerged in the mid–Warring States period to become a persistent theme of philosophical debate. Early in his reflection on this concept, Graham opined that

> Chinese thinkers who discuss *hsing* [*xing* 性] seldom seem to be thinking of fixed qualities going back to a thing's origin. . . . Mencius in particular seems never to be looking back toward birth, always forward to the maturation of a continuing growth. This accords with one's general impression when groping towards an understanding of early Chinese concepts, that often they tend to be more dynamic than their nearest Western equivalents, and that English translation freezes them into immobility.[30]

The contemporary philosopher Zheng Kai 鄭開, in his argument against using the Greek term "ontology" to discuss Chinese philosophy as rehearsed in the final chapter of this monograph, makes the compelling case that we have to appeal to *xinxing* theory (*xinxinglun* 心性論) as Chinese philosophy's first philosophy (*benti* 本體) if we are to take this tradition on its own terms. It would seem that Graham in his resistance to an ontological reading of *xing* was on to something fundamental in distinguishing two very different understandings of what it means to be human. And further, Graham's throwaway reflection that early Chinese concepts tend to be "more dynamic" than the English equivalencies we assign to them (such as when we translate *xing* as "human nature") is a fair measure of his penetrating insight into the uncommon assumptions that distinguish Confucian process cosmology that focuses on life (*sheng* 生) from a Greek causal ontology with its pursuit of formal definitions.

In Aristotle, Socrates is described as that person who "fixed thought for the first time on definition."[31] For Socrates, the activity of "real" and

---

30. A. C. Graham, *Studies in Chinese Philosophy and Philosophical Literature* (Albany: State University of New York Press, 1990), 8. The early essay from which this quote is taken was published in 1967. I have tried to chronicle Graham's changing understanding of *xing* in my own essay, "Reconstructing A. C. Graham's Reading of *Mencius* on *Xing* 性: A Coda to 'The Background of the Mencian Theory of Human Nature' (1967)" that was published in *Having a Word with Angus Graham: At Twenty-Five Years into his Immortality*, ed. Carine Defoort and Roger T. Ames (Albany: State University of New York Press, 2018).

31. Aristotle, *Metaphysics*, *The Complete Works*, 987b2.

thus formal definition is the search for what the world is by discovering the objective essences that are defining of natural kinds. Such a rational understanding of reality declines any example of something in favor of its ideal, declines the subjective in favor of the objective, declines the contingent in favor of the necessary, and declines what is changing in favor of what is fixed and certain. The term "definition" itself in setting boundaries on things means literally "to finish, to conclude, to come to an end, to determine with precision."

Classical Chinese thinkers by contrast with their Greek counterparts were not inclined to seek out objective definitions by appeal to "essences" or "natural kinds." There seems to be no hard and fast dichotomy between the subjective and objective, and again there is a keen awareness of the processual nature of experience that would in itself preclude fixed and final boundaries. Indeed, we find that as a method for understanding the meaning of particular terms, instead of seeking to set limits on them, there is a habit among Chinese thinkers of correlating a term with other terms that come to mind through some combination of semantic and phonetic association. "Paronomasia" is the technical term for this practice of correlating terms that sound alike or that have a similar meaning to conjure forth a meaning-producing image. I do not use the word "definition" for paronomasia because as a rhetorical device it is directed at the open-ended adding and disclosing of supplementary meaning through association rather than seeking closure in the sense of setting a boundary on such meaning. Significantly, in this paronomastic process, the expectation is that we are not just "discovering" knowledge about an existing world but actively delineating an evolving world and bringing it into being.

This paronomastic imaging is to be found everywhere in classical Chinese literature.[32] When we consult traditional dictionaries that themselves chronicle the cultural associations being made in this world—the second-century *Shuowenjiezi* 說文解字, for example—we discover that terms are not as much defined analytically and etymologically by appeal to some essential, literal, putatively "root" meanings as they are generally explained metaphorically or paronomastically by their semantic and phonetic associations. The term "exemplary person/s" (*jun* 君), for example, is correlated with its cognate and phonetically similar term, "gathering"

---

32. For discussion and an extended example of this phenomenon, see O'Neill, *Ideography and Chinese Language Theory*, 167–170.

(*qun* 群), an association that arises between the two terms because of the expressed image of people gathering round and deferring to exemplary persons. After all, the *Analects* insists that "virtuosic persons do not dwell alone; they are sure to have neighbors."[33] "Mirror" (*jing* 鏡 or *jian* 鑒) is correlated with "shining radiantly" (*jing* 景) or "looking into, overseeing" (*jian* 監), generating the image of a mirror not simply as the passive source of reflection but also as a source of insight, illumination, and increased information as it casts its light from one particular perspective or another. "Battle formation" (*zhen* 陣) is correlated with "displaying" (*chen* 陳), conjuring up the image of a battle formation's most important function in making a display of strength that will discourage if not deter an enemy.[34] A "ghost or spirit" (*gui* 鬼) is correlated with "returning" (*gui* 歸), suggesting the image of the dispersed *qi* 氣 of the deceased finding its way back to some more primordial home. "Way-making" (*dao* 道) is tellingly correlated with "treading" (*dao* 蹈), invoking the image that the *Zhuangzi* expresses so eloquently, "The way is made in the walking."[35] "King" (*wang* 王) is associated with "going to" (*wang* 往), remembering the image pervasive in Confucian political philosophy of the people repairing to the true king. Such paronomastic examples are legion.

Another example of paronomasia lies behind a family of characters that are associated through a shared phonetic indicator to express a common meaning. For example, there is the character *can* 戔 as the root classifier and phonetic that means "small and thin," followed by a cluster of terms with similar pronunciation that have related meanings: *can* 殘 "incomplete, deficient, remnant," *jian* 帴 "narrow," *qian* 錢 "small coins, money," *qian* 淺 "shallow, superficial," *zhan* 棧 "an animal pen,"

---

33. *Analects* 4.25: 德不孤, 必有鄰.

34. The character "battle formation" (*zhen* 陣) written as "displaying" (*chen* 陳) occurs only three times in the core thirteen chapters of *Sunzi: Art of Warfare* 孫子兵法 and yet occurs over a hundred times in the later, recently recovered *Sun Bin: The Art of Warfare* 孫臏兵法, with it being the main theme in six of the chapters. This fact is an indication of the evolution of military engagement over the centuries of the Warring States period from loose militia to the much more efficient fixed battle formations. See *Sun Bin: The Art of Warfare: A Translation of the Classic Chinese Work of Philosophy and Strategy*, trans. D. C. Lau and Roger T. Ames (Albany: State University of New York Press, 2003), 34–40 and 67–71.

35. *Zhuangzi* 莊子, Harvard-Yenching Institute Sinological Index Series, Supp. 20 (Peking: Harvard Yenching Institute, 1947), 4/2/33: 道行之而成. Importantly, we must translate this passage as "made in the walking" rather than "made in the walking *of it*."

zhan 盏 "a small cup," zhan 醆 "a small wine cup," zhan 虥 "the fine hair of a tiger," zhan 琖 "a small jade wine cup," jian 賤 "low priced, cheap," jian 箋 "small note paper," jian 餞 "a farewell party, a send-off," jian 牋 "a brief memo," jian 俴 "shallow, thin," jian 濺 "splash, splatter," jian 諓 "flattery," and other terms as well.

Another example of a cluster of terms around a phonetic indicator would be shen 申 as root classifier that, in different contexts, means "stretching, extending, prolonging, explaining, expressing, repeating, exhibiting, taking it easy." Its family of characters includes shen 伸 "stretching, extending, straightening, emerging, taking it easy," shen 神 "spirit, divine, god, miraculous, mysteries," shen 呻 "chanting, droning, groaning," shen 紳 "sash, the girdle worn by officials," shen 珅 "a kind of jade," shen 胂 "meat encasing the spine," chen 抻 "pulling out, drawing out, stretching," shen 眒 "wide-eyed," shen 柛 "dead and withered wood of a fallen tree," yin 柬 "a small drum, drawing out," dian 電 "lightning" (understood as a gerund).

What is remarkable about this Chinese paronomastic way of generating meaning is that a term is further elucidated nonreferentially by mining for us who lack the competence that comes with an interpretive context seemingly random associations implicated phonetically or semantically in the term itself. The success of the association and the quantum of meaning derived from it then is dictated by the degree of relevance, with some protean associations being more thought-provoking and productive than others.

Another discernible pattern in this mode of correlating terms is that erstwhile "nouns" default to "verbal nouns" or "gerunds," underscoring the primacy of process over form as a grounding presupposition in this "eventful" cosmology and reminding us of Graham's earlier claim that Chinese concepts tend to be "more dynamic" than the Western equivalencies we assign to them. That is, "things" are defined as "doings"; for example, dao 道 in being defined as "treading" (dao 蹈) gives primacy to "way-making" over the way that is made. Indeed, the imaginative correlation of "events" in the flux and flow of a processual cosmology stands as the classical Chinese counterpart to the Platonic and Aristotelian method of knowing the world through essential definitions rehearsed earlier.

In this zoetological world in which things are constituted by their conditioning relations, meaning is always situational and generative as something done rather than being derived causally from some "essence" as a single, originative source. Meaning arises in situ through the cultivation of a deepening in relations that we have called "the art of contextualization" (*ars contextualis*). "Things" are what they mean for themselves, for their contextualizing others, and for the unsummed totality. Such thick and robust relations are the result of growth in the world, enriching the family, the community, and the cosmos. It is thus that the vocabulary of personal realization in Confucian philosophy is described in the language of growth and extension: "personal virtuosity" (*de* 德), for example, is correlated paronomastically with "getting" (*de* 得) in the sense of those gains in meaning made from the coalescence of relations through a regimen of personal cultivation, "spirituality" (*shen* 神) is "stretching and extending" (*shen* 伸) in the sense of going beyond what is presently known, "becoming human" (*ren* 人) is a "becoming consummately human" (*ren* 仁) in the sense of achieving sustained virtuosity in one's relations with others, and so on.

Given the centrality of formal definition in ontological thinking, clarity, precision, and rigor come to have a high value. In Platonic idealism and its ideographic thinking, existing behind an "idea" is an abstract, eternal pattern or archetype of something. Thus, for Plato and Aristotle, too, "to know" is to define something through grasping its cause and thus calling it by its correct name. This definitional process is true not only of "things" but of abstractions such as "equality," "largeness," and "squareness." By way of contrast, it is a productive vagueness and a consequent efficacy in the generative process of correlating things for added significance that is a dominant value in zoetological thinking. "Knowing" is an amplificatory and incremental process in the sense of an increasing awareness of the associations something has with other things, thus being able to call them by another name. With respect to particular persons, for example, it is to get to know them better in all of the roles and relations that in sum make up their personal narrative as they strive to realize the world in a particular way: as a daughter, a teacher, a spouse, a neighbor, an artist, and so on.

Timothy Michael O'Neill contrasts two distinct ways of thinking about the nature of language and how it functions differently within the ontological assumptions of classical Greece and the early Chinese alternative respectively. He argues that

> the Chinese, unlike Europeans, were not obsessed with transcendental—not of this world, eternal, unchanging, absolutely true in all cases—distinctions when analyzing language (i.e., the

Forms, God, the Active Intellect, universals, nouns, etc.); the philological discussions of the nature of language and its role in society that began in the Warring States period in China always took for granted that language is arbitrary and artificial—that words are units of articulated sound with socio-politically agreed upon meaning, that words change in pronunciation, meaning, and written form through space and time, and that words have no ontologically fixed reference outside of their historical usage by specific human beings.[36]

O'Neill in his reflections on the canonical text, the *Erya*, contrasts the classical Greek understanding of words that are literally "informed" by transcendent forms with the assumption that Chinese "words" (*ming* 名) are arbitrary and contingent. He insists that "the *Erya* is not a book concerned with strong and soft Forms and how they relate to words, but rather entirely as *ming* 名, that is, as artificial (i.e., arbitrary) socially, historically determined signifiers for arbitrary, social, historically deter-mined signifieds."[37]

In translating the title of the *Erya* 爾雅 as "Nearing the Refined Standard," O'Neill offers us a "making words correct" (*zhengming* 正名) interpretation of how this canonical lexical text functions within the early culture. Herein, like the Greeks, importance is invested in the clarity and precision needed from language to stabilize the human experience. The text seeks to overcome the arbitrariness of the language by providing standard meanings that can be relied upon as being crucial to the project of effecting and sustaining the social and political hierarchies of its times. The need for this standard emerges out of the very nature of the human language. O'Neill observes that "visceral emotions, which are directly expressed in otherwise undifferentiated sounds by both humans and animals, become human speech when they are 'patterned,' when they take on the pronunciations of human language. . . . The meaning-bearing aspect of spoken human language, then, is a combination of visceral emotion from the heart and socially agreed-upon and politically-enforced

---

36. O'Neill, *Ideography and Chinese Language Theory*, 165. For a fuller account of this language theory, O'Neill directs his reader to Hu Qiguang 胡奇光, *Zhongguoxiaoxueshi* 中國小學史 [A history of Chinese philology] (Shanghai: Shanghai People's Press, 2005).

37. O'Neill, *Ideography and Chinese Language Theory*, 162.

linguistic norms ('sound patterns')."[38] O'Neill focuses on the task embraced by the sages to establish a refined standard for consistency and efficacy in the way in which terms are deployed in order to maintain social and political order. This form of "making-meaning," in the absence of a metaphysical foundation, requires various strategies for disciplining the language to overcome its contingent nature. For the sages, "the activity of *zhengming*, 'making words correct,' is the quintessential Chinese method of lexical statecraft, a method specifically crafted for producing the social hierarchy fundamental to human coexistence."[39] Here again O'Neill contrasts such a living and changing zoetological world with very different ontological assumptions: "All knowledge of the cosmos in the early Chinese tradition, therefore, is considered concrete historical interventions by humans, literally what the sages had to say about it (rather than 'what it is' by cosmic fixation of its ontological nature, content, and structure at the moment of creation)."[40] O'Neill understands the *Erya* as a semantic and syntactic gloss that would serve the important lexical function of delivering the clarity needed in the effective use of terms but also as a text compiled at a certain time and in a certain place by a certain cohort of scholars as their contribution to the way-making of their world. Allowing for both persistence and change in the way in which language functions, O'Neill explains how texts like the *Erya* stabilize and provide structure for social and political institutions while at the same time giving birth to "offspring" lexical texts such as Yang Xiong's *Fangyan* and Xu Shen's *Shuowen*. He says of the *Erya*: "As early as the Eastern Han, it has, as it were, spawned its lexicographic offspring, who in turn breed their own progeny, and so on and so forth, while *Erya* remains only on the side-lines of the later families of dictionaries, a respected elder statesman, a cherished relic of presumed antiquity."[41] It is no surprise that in O'Neill's explanation of this continuing process, he appeals to family and genealogical metaphors. That is, the disciplining of the arbitrariness in the language is certainly retrospective in "making words correct," but it also has an important prospective aspect in the way in which language-games are woven into and integral to ritual and propriety.

---

38. O'Neill, *Ideography and Chinese Language Theory*, 175.

39. O'Neill, *Ideography and Chinese Language Theory*, 181.

40. O'Neill, *Ideography and Chinese Language Theory*, 163.

41. O'Neill, *Ideography and Chinese Language Theory*, 231.

Language shapes the evolving human experience and contributes to the emerging textual tradition as it comes to constitute a cultural identity.[42]

O'Neill is keen to distinguish the way in which this linguistic tradition functions from the ideological and semantic theories that are underwritten by Greek metaphysics. It is not about ideas and abstract meanings but rather about how lives are lived. With respect to these classificatory schemes, O'Neill insists that

> the content is far less important than the authors; the content is a completely artificial historical artifact of value only because it is filled with the intentions of these sages (and we should be hard-pressed to describe it in any other terms without recourse to ideographic theory). The *zhengming* episteme . . . assumes that such classification is always the work of specific people in specific places at specific historical junctures, in this case Chinese sages in the ancient past. . . . It is the practical use of words by humans according to social order that matters, not what the words "mean" in some kind of abstract ideographic sense.[43]

The zoetological world is uniquely an unbounded "worlding," and the scholar is always an existential and thus intentional perspective embedded within it. Absent a standpoint or basis for persons asserting objective truths about their experience, the line between subject and world, between description and prescription is blurred because subjects are always reflexively implicated in the way in which they organize the world. To say something about the world is to say something about oneself, one's disposition, one's values, and one's purposes. Another consequence of having no fixed objective perspective is that saying, even thinking, something about the world is doing something to the world. Any severe distinction between theory and practice, between word and world, functions to separate speaking from doing and thus trivializes notions such as "freedom of speech" in the sense that speech is merely a saying rather

---

42. I have cited Nathan Sivin's argument for the importance of *zhengming* as "pragmatics" as opposed to classical Greek dialectics previously. See also the entry for *zhengming* in Roger T. Ames, *A Conceptual Lexicon for Classical Confucian Philosophy* (Albany: State University of New York Press, 2022).

43. O'Neill, *Ideography and Chinese Language Theory*, 234–235.

than a doing. What is merely theoretical cannot change the world. In zoetological world-making, thinking and speaking are actions that have real consequences in shaping our environments in one way or another.

We can speak of the "fertility" of language in many different ways. How is it, for example, that the graphs that reference written Chinese characters themselves came to be *wen* 文 and *zi* 字? O'Neill cites the second section of the postface to the *Shuowen* lexicon:

> 說文: 昔者倉頡造書, 以類象形, 故謂之文. 其後, 形聲相益, 即謂之字. 字, 生也. 孳乳浸多也.

> The *Shuowen* says: in antiquity, Cangjie created writing, first relying on the classification *xiangxing* "resemble the shape" and therefore called written words "patterns" [文] (i.e., rebus writing). After this, such written words were combined together according to the *xingsheng* "classifier and phonetic" classification, which are therefore called "offspring" written words [字] (in being the "children" of two or more earlier graphs combined together to write new words—generally, one grapheme used for sound only, one grapheme to help identify which spoken word that sound represents). The word "offspring" in and of itself originally meant "something that is born" [生]. These "offspring" characters grew and multiplied, gradually increasing in number (and hence the term "offspring").[44]

The fertility of language, like the fecundity of *dao*, which means not only "doing" as "way-making" but also "speaking" as "speaking a world into being," lies in activating the indeterminacies that are always available for *ars contextualis*: that is, the omnipresent opportunity for artful recontextualizing. As we have seen, this correlative process can be understood as "paronomasia"—a prospective reconstruing of the contextualizing conditions of any situation that would allow something to be called by "another name" and, in so doing, to produce additional meaning. The liquid we call "water," for example, is certainly a resource that waters plants and produces life, and hence we have come to call it an irrigation

---

44. O'Neill, *Ideography and Chinese Language Theory*, 246. On the bronzes, the character 字 written as ▮ is then glossed as "birthing" (*sheng* 生) and is further explained as "a woman giving birth to a child." See Kwan, "Database," 字父己觶 (商代) CHANT 6270.

system. Water has also been a traditional source of energy and hence in this context we call it hydropower. But with further ingenuity, we might one day be able to transform it through controlled fusion into a novel resource that will drive our cars and fly our planes, and thus we call it by yet another name. This amplificatory process certainly begins from a careful mapping out of names as they have been used—that is, a retrospective "rectification of names"—but it also requires the imagination to use language in an expansive way and to make correlations that will produce novel meaning as a "making" and a "doing" in an ever-changing world.

***

In this early Platonic dialogue, the *Euthyphro*, we are introduced to Socratic irony. The term "irony" itself comes from a dramatic character in Greek comic theater called Airon, who through his superior wit inevitably triumphs over the ever arrogant and bombastic Alazon, thereby reversing the status of their positions. Irony thus comes to mean self-referential inconsistency. In the *Apology* Socrates is the wisest person in Athens because he knows that he isn't wise. In the *Euthyphro*, the self-declared religious expert Euthyphro is a casualty of Socratic irony in Socrates's demonstration that the expert knows nothing. And Socrates, who knows nothing in guiding the dialogue, reveals a true depth of understanding about what holiness must mean. Interestingly and perhaps ironically, the given name "Euthyphro" itself means "sincere," and as the conversation unfolds, Euthyphro's "sincerity" is perhaps the only thing we can claim for his contribution to our understanding of holiness. And ironically again, in an aporetic dialogue that offers no conclusion, we still garner real insight into not only the meaning of holiness but into the Platonic logic of knowing itself.

In spite of the *Euthyphro*'s lack of finality, we do come away from the dialogue with significant understanding of what Socrates takes to be the *eidos* of holiness. From *Euthyphro* we gain the clear impression that holiness for Socrates is a single, originative, unchanging, and universal principle that can serve as an independent, objective standard against which all instances of holiness can be measured and adjudicated. And there are important implications. The *eidos* of holiness that according to Socrates himself is closely aligned with the principle of justice provides divine sanction for a universalistic morality. This assumption taken one step further not only gives us confidence that such a norm exists but that, with effort, this universal standard as the proper object of knowledge can through formal definition be known to us.

At the same time, Socrates exhibits an impatience with the popular anthropomorphic sentimentalization of the gods. He rejects the familiar instrumental understanding of religion as the opportunity to be "practically religious": that is, engaging in the art of commerce between humankind and the gods that pays out dividends. The desired dramatic effect of this dialogue is that whether Euthyphro is in fact expert in religious affairs or just a common Athenian, the general public as it is represented by Euthyphro has no idea of what holiness really means. Following this logic, the only conclusion that can be reached is that the Athenian court composed of Socrates's peers who, in finding him guilty of irreligion and then executing him, has in its gross incompetence made an egregious error.

Although there is no evidence in Plato's own writings themselves, sometime later in Diogenes Laertius we are told that because of this encounter with Socrates, Euthyphro abandoned the prosecution of his father.[45] If this were in fact the case, it might be either because Socrates had undermined Euthyphro's confidence in his own grasp of what holiness actually means, or that Euthyphro had been persuaded by Socrates that if holiness as a universal standard were to be applied to the problematic indictment Euthyphro was bringing against his father, the case would fall far short of satisfying its normative demands.

R. E. Allen, in his monograph *Plato's Euthyphro and the Earlier Theory of Forms*, provides a compelling argument for the incremental development of Plato's Theory of Forms from the earlier to the later dialogues. He insists that it is not until the middle dialogues (such as the *Meno* and *Phaedo*) that "the relation between Forms and their instances is construed as radical dependence and radical separation."[46] In offering further clarification, Allen concludes that "forms are as separate from their instances in the early dialogues as they are later on. For they are not identical with their instances, and are ontologically prior to their instances. That is, they exist 'apart.' The difference between the Theory of Forms in the early dialogues and those which followed does not consist in the fact of separation, but the way in which separation is conceived."[47]

---

45. Https://penelope.uchicago.edu/Thayer/E/Roman/Texts/Diogenes_Laertius/Lives_of_the_Eminent_Philosophers/3/Plato*.html, vol. 2, 29.

46. R. E. Allen, *Plato's* Euthyphro *and the Earlier Theory of Forms* (London: Routledge, 1970), 129.

47. Allen, *Plato's* Euthyphro, 147.

While the relationship between particulars and *eidos* is certainly "explained" in the very tentative causal language of some kind of "participation," the singular and unchanging nature of *eidos* already guarantees the radical dependence of particulars on *eidos* and their separation from it.[48] For Allen then, it is the doctrine of *anamnesis* or recollection in the *Meno* and *Phaedo* in which, in the search for knowledge, sensation is made inferior to reflection as the actual nature of the separation. That is, it is this distinction between the intelligible and the sensible worlds, and between *episteme* and *doxa* that arises from access to these universal principles, that then becomes the two-world doctrine underlying Plato's Theory of Forms.

Third Anticipation

Socrates famously asks Euthyphro whether something is holy because it is loved by the gods or it is loved by gods because it is holy. And Socrates then answers his own question by insisting on the latter. Continuing in this same dialogue, Socrates makes a further point in support of his answer through a grammatical argument that concludes by claiming anything that is loved as holy must itself be holy both logically and temporally prior to its being loved. That is, it must have some essential characteristic itself that then induces the state or accident or attribute of its being loved. For Socrates, you have to have an "it" before "it" can be loved.

Of course, the success of such an argument is wholly dependent upon a logic grounded in a substance ontology that allows for a clear distinction between essences and their attributes, between some discrete thing and its contextualizing relations. But this same argument falters in an event-zoetology where the essence and attribute dualism has no purchase. Given the Confucian commitment to zoetological thinking and its radical empiricism, it would have to contest the causal assumptions both natural and normative that lay behind Plato's Theory of Forms and that derive from the ontological disparity between essence and attribute.

---

48. Even though Aristotle is critical of Plato's abstracted interpretation of the Forms, his own hylomorphic move to make them "immanent" in things as the formal and final causes of an immutable species does not alter the fact that they remain separate and independent, being unchanged as they are by their material conditions. Such immanence is thus transcendent in the sense of a unilateral and independent source that itself remains unchanged in the relationship.

Confucian philosophy would abjure the "Euthyphro problem" that would insist that principles of adjudication must be prior to and separate from the objects of our judgment, where such standards must be determined to be intrinsically good—that is, good in themselves—rather than being deemed good as a summary judgment on what is occurring within an always relational narrative. In its zoetological thinking, what is putatively "essential" is simply a generalization made off of a pattern of evolving relationships within a narrative in which the context and transitivity of all things cannot be denied. That is, something being holy, far from being a quality intrinsic to that standard itself, is a function of what it means for those persons within its always changing context.

An old church in Wales, for example, made quite holy in its own time by a pious congregation, might become someone's house when its parishioners have dispersed and faded away. As such, it is only a provisional convenience if not a grammatical nicety for us to describe the church as "being holy" rather than as "holy-ing" under a specific set of conditions. The holiness of something is situational and transitory. In its own time the church became valorized as holy because of the interest both the gods and the churchgoers have come to invest in it. In this eventful logic, the actual content of something that is "holy-ing" or continually "becoming" holy changes with time rather than being some essential and unchanging property that defines it. All this is but to say that what something is, what it does, and what it means for other things are no more than aspects within the continuing narrative that provides it with its identity.

This same distinction between an essential and a narrative identity applies to persons as well. We will see that Aristotle's ontological and thus isolating "What?" question answers what can be said "of" the man in the market-place, with this question about the reduplicated essence of human "beings" standing in contrast to the subsequent ancillary questions that identify what can be attributed to, and thus be "in," the subject once it is substantially understood. By way of contrast, Sor-hoon Tan invokes John Dewey's "retrospective fallacy" as a challenge to the isolating reduplication of personal identity that occurs when we abstract persons from the connectivity of their narratives. Because all human conduct for Dewey is irreducibly social and organic, Tan observes that

> those still preoccupied with identity often complain that Dewey's view is that of a "self-in-action without a self." They miss

> the point of Dewey's protest against traditional conceptions of the self. For Dewey, there could be no self outside of experience, outside of human doing and undergoing. The distinction between "self" and action is "after the fact." Unity precedes distinctions in experience; to think otherwise is to commit the "retrospective fallacy"—to mistake a distinction introduced into experience by later reflections as fully present in the original experience. . . . Selfhood is an eventual function that emerges with complexly organized interactions, organic and social.[49]

Dewey's retrospective fallacy resonates immediately with Whitehead's fallacies of "simple location" and "misplaced concreteness" that would similarly entail the isolating and abstracting things from their vital relations and, in so doing, make the abstract "thing" more real than its context and its transitivity.

***

Chronologically, the next dialogue we need to consider in the evolution of Plato's ontology is the *Symposium*. In this dialogue from the middle period, Socrates gives an account of an eschatological adventure he had as a young man when, under the spell of Diotima of Mantinea, he is taken on an intellectual and spiritual journey. Given the exalted status of Socrates himself, the description of this steep spiritual ascent that challenges even his formidable stamina is one of the most powerful pieces of rhetoric in the entire history of our philosophical literature. At every advancing step in the ascent, as Socrates encounters beauty in its many different manifestations, he comes upon the source of the stage that came before. At the very end of this climb, a breathless Socrates comes into the presence of the ultimate source of all that is beautiful in the world, and we are made witness to his wide-eyed encounter with the Form of Beauty itself. Although the ascent toward the Form of Beauty is incremental, and is inspired by the apprehension of an always higher level of beauty, in the end the vision of Beauty that "exists as itself in accordance with itself, eternal and uniform," echoes the account of the unity of Being in Parmenides. As with Parmenides, in

---

49. Sor-hoon Tan, *Confucian Democracy: A Deweyan Reconstruction* (Albany: State University of New York Press, 2003), 27.

giving an account of this experience all discriminations and predications must be discounted as being merely metaphorical. At the same time, as in the allegory of the cave in the *Republic*, Plato seems to be arguing that this kind of encounter with Reality itself by philosophers still in the world will yield social dividends in enabling them in their return to the human community to give birth to and to nourish true virtue in all that they do. Perhaps the explanation here is that, even though human *theoria* as momentary access to a kind of divine ecstasy is only itself a fleeting experience, its intensity in making enlightened philosophers "friends to the gods" still has a transformative effect on how they continue to live their lives while still in the world.

***

"These are the activities of love, Socrates, into which you could probably be initiated. I [Diotima] don't know whether you are the sort of person for the final rites and mysteries, for which these former things are the preparation, if one can let go in the right way. So, I'll speak," she said, "and I'll not curtail my enthusiasm. Try to follow as well as you can.

"The person who is going to approach this matter correctly," she declared, "must begin while young to turn toward beautiful bodies, and at first, if he is correctly led by his guide, to love a single body and to bring forth beautiful conversations in that situation. He must then realize that the beauty of any particular body is akin to the beauty of every other body, and that if it is necessary to pursue beauty of form, it is quite mindless not to believe that the beauty of all bodies is one and the same. When he comprehends this, he must become a lover of all beautiful bodies, and he will despise that vehement love of a single body, thinking it a trivial matter.

"After that he must believe that the beauty of souls is more valuable than that of the body, so that if someone who has a decent soul is not very attractive, he will be content to love him, to take care of him, and with him to search out and give birth to the sort of conversations that make young men better. As a result, he will be compelled to study the beauty in practical endeavors and in laws and traditions and to see that all beauty is related so that he will believe that the beauty connected with the body is of little importance.

"After practical endeavors he must be led to examples of knowledge in order that he may see in turn the beauty of knowledge and no longer look upon what is limited to an individual case as being very beautiful, like a house-slave who is enthralled by what is paltry and of little account, lusting after the beauty of a young boy or of some particular person, or of a single practical endeavor. On the contrary, after turning toward the great sea of beauty, he studies it and gives birth to many splendidly beautiful conversations and thoughts in a magnanimous philosophy, until, as he becomes more capable and flourishes in this situation, he comes to see a knowledge of a singular sort that is of this kind of beauty.

"You must try," she continued, "to pay attention to me as closely as you can. The person who has been instructed thus far about the activities of Love, who studies beautiful things correctly and in their proper order, and who then comes to the final stage of the activities of love, will suddenly see something astonishing that is beautiful in its nature. This, Socrates, is the purpose of all the earlier effort.

"In the first place, it is eternal; it neither comes into being nor passes away, neither increases nor diminishes. Therefore, it is not beautiful in one respect while ugly in another, nor beautiful at one time while ugly at another, nor beautiful with reference to one thing while ugly with reference to something else, nor beautiful here while ugly there, as though it were beautiful to some while ugly to others. Moreover, the beautiful will not appear to this person to be something like a face or a pair of hands or any other part of the body, nor will it appear as a particular statement or a particular bit of knowledge, nor will it appear to exist somewhere in something other than itself, such as in an animal, in the earth, in the sky, or in anything else. On the contrary, it exists as itself in accordance with itself, eternal and uniform. All other beautiful things partake of it in such a way that although they come into being and pass away, it does not, nor does it become any greater or any less, nor is it affected in any way. When someone moves through these various stages from the correct love of young boys and begins to see this beauty, he has nearly reached the end.

"In the activities of Love, this is what it is to proceed correctly, or be led by another: Beginning from beautiful things to move ever onwards for the sake of that beauty, as though using ascending steps, from one body to two and from two to all beautiful bodies, from beautiful bodies to beautiful practical endeavors, from practical endeavors to beautiful examples of understanding, and from examples of understanding to come finally to that understanding which is none other than the understanding of that beauty itself, so that in the end he knows what beauty itself is.

"Here is the life, Socrates, my friend," said the Mantinean visitor, "that a human being should live studying the beautiful itself. Should you ever see it, it will not seem to you to be on the level of gold, clothing, and beautiful boys and youths, who so astound you now when you look at them that you and many others are eager to gaze upon your darlings and be together with them all the time. You would cease eating and drinking, if that were possible, and instead just look at them and be with them. What do we think it would be like," she said, "if someone should happen to see the beautiful itself, pure, clear, unmixed, and not contaminated with human flesh and color and a lot of other mortal silliness, but rather if he were able to look upon the divine, uniform beautiful itself? Do you think," she continued, "it would be a worthless life for a human being to look at that, to study it in the required way, and to be together with it? Aren't you aware," she said, "that only there with it, when a person sees the beautiful in the only way it can be seen, will he ever he able to give birth, not to imitations of virtue, since he would not be reaching out toward an imitation, but to true virtue, because he would be taking hold of what is true? By giving birth to true virtue and nourishing it, he would be able to become a friend of the gods, and if any human being could become immortal, he would."[50]

---

50. Plato, The Symposium *and* The Phaedrus: *Plato's Erotic Dialogues*, trans. William S. Cobb (Albany: State University of New York Press, 1993), 47–49, 209e–212a.

Fourth Anticipation

On the oracle bones, the character *mei* 美 written as 羙 depicts a human being with head ornamentation, sometimes interpreted as a feathers-and-hair headdress and sometimes as jewelry made from animal horns.[51] This graph *mei* 美, often translated into English as "beauty," is in fact more appropriately rendered "beautiful." The semantic difference lies in our culturally specific tendency to understand "beauty" either as "beauty-in-itself" or as some given and essential quality that something "has." "Beautiful," on the other hand, is the description of a given thing or event that is being referred to at a particular time within its specific context. As Joseph Needham has observed with respect to early Chinese cosmology: "Things behaved in particular ways . . . because their position in the ever-moving cyclical universe was such. . . . If they did not behave in those particular ways they would lose their relational position in the whole (which made them what they were), and turn into something other than themselves. They were thus parts in existential dependence upon the whole world-organism."[52] Needham here is stating in his own way Tang Junyi's cosmological postulate "one is many, many one" (*yiduobufen* 一多不分)—that is, the insistence that the identity of all things is a function of their particular context at any particular time.[53] Things are what they are because of where they are within a specific manifold of relations and are thus inseparable from their narrative contexts. The difference between a piece of wood and a roof rafter is where it is and its function at that particular time and place. Thus, an account of what something is has to be qualified by the cosmological postulate of "the inseparability of forming and functioning" (*tiyongyiyuan* 體用一源). We might say that the "where" and the "when" is the "what" of things. Again, abandoning the usual synchronic and diachronic binary, we must see time and space as the "taking place" of a particular event, where its temporality is the quantum of its change, and its place is the focus of its activities. Spring as a season is the accelerating pace of the life in the forest, and the forest is the taking place of this life and growth.

---

51. Kwan, "Database," 甲骨文合集 CHANT 0210.

52. See Needham, *Science and Civilisation in China*, vol. 2, 280–281.

53. Tang Junyi, *Complete Works*, vol. 11, 16–17.

As it is observed in the *Zhuangzi*, different contexts produce different conditions for different "beautifuls": "A gorilla will take a female ape as his mate, an elk will mount his doe, and fish will frolic about with other fish. Mao Qiang and Lady Li were eyed as great beauties by the gentlemen, but when fish see these ladies, they dive into the deep, when birds see them, they soar into the skies, and when deer see them, they bolt for their lives. Who among these four animals knows what is the right source of arousal?"[54] There is a general point to be made here with respect to the fundamental nature of the Chinese language itself. In spite of what is suggested by "the Master said" (*ziyue* 子曰) formula ubiquitous at the beginning of so many passages in the *Analects*, neither the *Analects* nor any of the other classical canons are transcriptions of what was actually said. The classical Chinese language is a terse, economical way of preserving ideas that we might associate more with the economy of poetry than the pedestrian nature of expository language, and with rhetorical thrift rather than prosaic bounty. This minimalist Chinese written language was accompanied by a robust and redundant spoken language, where the written text would only become integral to the spoken language through rote memory or through tropes such as the pithy four- and eight-character set phrases called *chengyu* 成語 that often allude to classical texts. It is only as late as the first decades of the twentieth century that the transcription of the vernacular language as a written form became a common practice.

A familiar feature of the spoken and of the modern Chinese written language is that most terms are comprised of two characters and thus function as binomials. Indeed, one of the most important sources of the richness of the Chinese language and its power of description is the binomial structure of terms in which two ideas are correlated not only to generate new meaning but to reflect a focal specificity by setting the conditions of where and when such a description would apply. This particular kind of "beautiful" as meritorious contribution (*gongmei* 功美), for example, occurs only when these specific conditions are satisfied. And it is because this same term *mei* 美 as "beautiful" can be associated with so many different things and situations that it can be parsed to mean a seemingly boundless range of "beautifuls": "fine" (*meihao*

---

54. *Zhuangzi*: 2/6/68–70: 猨，猵狙以為雌，麋與鹿交，鰌與魚游. 毛嬙、麗姬，人之所美也，魚見之深入，鳥見之高飛，麋鹿見之決驟. 四者孰知天下之正色哉?

美好), "handsome" (*jianmei* 健美), "exquisite" (*youmei* 優美), "elegant" (*jingmei* 精美), "dainty" (*jiaomei* 嬌美), "pretty" (*junmei* 俊美, *meimao* 美貌), "pleasing" (*meiguan* 美觀), "improving" (*meirong* 美容), "happy" (*meiman* 美滿), "aesthetic" (*meigan* 美感, *shenmei* 審美), "majestic" (*huamei* 華美), "magnificent" (*zhuangmei* 壯美), "morally excellent" (*meide* 美德), "splendid" (*meimiao* 美妙), "gorgeous" (*xiumei* 秀美), "charming" (*meise* 美色), "perfect" (*wanmei* 完美, *chunmei* 純美), "scenic" (*meijing* 美景), "mellow" (*chunmei* 醇美), "of high repute" (*meiyu* 美譽, *meiming* 美名), "poignant" (*qimei* 淒美), "fertile" (*feimei* 肥美), "delicious" (*meishi* 美食), "tasty" (*xianmei* 鮮美), "voluptuous" (*meiyan* 美艷), "scrumptious" (*bianmei* 便美), "delicate" (*roumei* 柔美), "luscious" (*meiwei* 美味), "sweet" (*tianmei* 甜美), "praiseworthy" (*zanmei* 讚美), "kindly" (*meiyi* 美意), "laudatory" (*meicheng* 美稱), "quiet and happy" (*tianmei* 恬美), "embellishing" (*meihua* 美化), "smug" (*choumei* 臭美). Again *mei* can be further stretched poetically to describe "springtime beautiful" (*chunmei* 春美), "the timely rains" (*meiyu* 美雨), and importantly "the finest of wines and most savory of dishes" (*meijiuzhenzhuan* 美酒珍饌). In the composition of the binomials themselves the primary correlation is between two images; for example, *meiwei* 美味 is the correlation between "beautiful" and "taste" = "delicious." And then there is a second stage of correlation that occasions the term being brought to mind, for example, the "where and when" of grandmother's dinner table calling forth this exclamation.

In other natural languages such as in the kenning of the Anglo-Saxons and in the German language as well, we see this same practice of correlating words to create additional meaning or "knowledge" (*ken* or *Kenntnis*). For example, in the Anglo-Saxon language, a "word-pantry" or "word-hoard" is a dictionary and a "bone-house" is the body. The epic poem *Beowulf* is replete with such examples wherein "battle-sweat" is blood, "sleep of the sword" is death, "whale-road" is the sea, "raven-harvest" is corpses, "sky-candle" is the sun, "ring-giver" is the king, "earth-hall" is a burial mound, "helmet-bearers" are warriors, and so on.

In the evolution of the spoken and now written Chinese language, the artful correlation of two terms produces additional meaning. A snapshot of this continuing process is much in evidence in the second half of the nineteenth century when a new language was self-consciously created out of Chinese characters to synchronize the East Asian languages—Japanese, Chinese, Korean, Vietnamese—with the vocabulary of Western modernity. "Society" (*shehui* 社會) for example is the combination of "the traditional ridgepole that stands in the middle of a community" (*she* 社) and "gathering around = organization, society" (*hui* 會). "Capital" (*ziben* 資本) is "money" (*zi* 資) and "root" (*ben* 本). "Labor" (*laodong* 勞動) is "toil" (*lao* 勞) and "activity" (*dong* 動). And this correlative process continues today with "computer" as "electric brain" (*diannao* 電腦), ATM as "machine for fetching money" (*qukuanji* 取款機), and "video" as "seeing in serial repetition" (*shipin* 視頻).

There are several additional points to be made, beginning with the primacy of situation over agency. A dramatic turn in the *Symposium* occurs when Socrates and then Diotima challenge Agathon, who would attribute all things beautiful to the erotic lover. Socrates argues that since erotic lovers are desirous of beauty, they cannot already be in possession of it. Indeed, since all "good" things are beautiful, such erotic lovers not only lack beauty but virtue and goodness as well. Hence, the locus of all things beautiful is not the erotic lover who is in pursuit but the beloved person who is being pursued. We can thus see in Plato the primacy of agency over situation. This stands in contrast to zoetological thinking in which agency is often a second-order abstraction out of the transactional nature of all concrete situations. In the well-known story of the "happy fish"(*leyu* 樂魚) in the *Zhuangzi*, for example, we are being persuaded that enjoyment does not reference some internal mental state of the fish, of Zhuangzi, or of anything else but is first and foremost a characterization of a happy event taking place on the bridge over the river Hao, where the ambient enjoyment includes the two dueling philosophers, the fish, the bridge, and the river as well.

To underscore the point that *mei* 美 as "beautiful" is a function of an aesthetic that is achieved in particular contexts and specific activities we might appeal to the symbiotic relationship between the making of "music" (*yue* 樂) and the production of "enjoyment" (*le* 樂), a fact reflected in their being represented by the same graph. The character *yue* on the oracle bones is a depiction of a stringed musical instrument made of wood ¥, with the *bai* 白 element added to the graph in the early Zhou bronzes indicating the plucking of the strings 樂.[55] Hence the character does not mean simply "music" but "the making of music," and again it is the making of music for the enjoyment of oneself and others who are present. Intransitive *le* or transitive *yao* is "en-joyment," that is, a rejoicing in the musicality of the human experience that can be shared by all. There

---

55. Kwan, "Database," 甲骨文合集 CHANT 3166 and 春秋晚期 CHANT 233 respectively.

is a suggestive resonance between *le/yao* and the etymology of the word "enjoy" itself. With en- as "making" and Latin *gaudere* "rejoicing in," there is the strong causative sense of producing those conditions for a shared rejoicing and the production of both moral and religious meaning within the fiduciary relationships of family, community, and cosmos.

Much has been made of the fact that the same character 樂 pronounced differently is used to mean "enjoyment" (*le, yao* 樂) and "music" (*yue* 樂), but the fact that this graph references the same basic idea parsed differently should not be overlooked. The playing of music is an obvious source of shared enjoyment that is in competition only with food as being the most essential prerequisite where and whenever human beings gather together. Hence, there is a persistent truth that, in the shared events punctuating the most important moments within the human experience, music, food, and enjoyment usually come together. But it works the other way around as well. That is, shared enjoyment within "harmonious" relationships also confers on human practices their cadence and musicality. Again, *le* is cognate with "medicinal remedies" (*yao* 藥), suggesting that both the enjoyment of music and the musicality of enjoyment have therapeutic and restorative qualities.

Correlating the relationship between making music and generating enjoyment is mutually informative, suggesting as it does that, just as music has breadth and depth and is the source of a broad range of feelings, so too "enjoyment" in its substance and intensity is anything but a simple euphoria. There is much to ponder. What does music as education and refinement mean when we carry it over to think of enjoyment? What does an achieved virtuosity through assiduous practice in music tell us about the meaning of enjoyment? What does the collaborative and performative nature of music suggest for the nature of enjoyment? What does the intensely intimate nature of music reveal for a deeper understanding of enjoyment? What does the profound relationship between music as the sound from the ground and a sense of place contribute to how we would parse enjoyment? At the end of the day, perhaps music and enjoyment overlap most closely at the intersection of a complex human flourishing that in its compass is more a bittersweet poignancy and profound depth of feeling over time than any specific event or emotion.

Enjoyment so conceived is a communal flourishing achieved through the deepening of robust personal bonds, where the meaning that is created becomes the very character of the community itself, its ethos, its song. Again, such enjoyment becomes a profound sense of felt worth and belonging within that community that has truly religious proportions and that is resilient, regardless of the inevitable vicissitudes of a human life. Even in the most unfortunate of circumstances, *le* is an underlying feeling of depth, stability, and contentment. The religious implications of *le* arise from the kind of spirituality that emerges as members of a flourishing community are able to cultivate their unique individuality through participation in its shared practices and to make their personal contribution to the whole. Remembering the resonances between the Confucian of personal cultivation and Emerson's "Divinity School Address," religion thus understood is anything but an institutionally imposed uniformity and is instead the attainment of personal distinctiveness as it is activated to produce a shared well-being for all. As such, Confucian religiousness is the flowering of a communicating family and community composed of unique persons, wherein an aspiring and thus inspired people becomes a spiritual people.

Again there is the pervasive correlation between ritual propriety (*li* 禮) and music (*yue* 樂) in the classical corpus where these two terms appear as a dyadic pair (*liyue* 禮樂). They are perceived to have a collateral function as these practices are embodied and reauthorized in each generation. Ritual propriety and music collaborate as synergistic activities emulated and embodied by succeeding generations to inform and elevate the human experience. Given the perceived coincidence between the human and the cosmic moral order, together ritual propriety and music are understood as providing the very structure and rhythm of the cosmic order itself. In the "Record of Music" (*Yueji* 樂記) chapter of the *Record of Rites* (*Liji* 禮記), it states: "Music is the optimizing harmony of the heavens and the earth; ritual propriety is the cosmic ordering of all things in the world."[56]

***

It is perhaps in the *Phaedo* that Plato with his doctrine of recollection (*anamnesis*) comes the closest to offering what might be interpreted as a proof for the existence of the Forms. The way in which he describes these Forms as in the *Symposium* implies their close association with divine causal

---

56. *Liji* 禮記 (*Record of Rites*), in D. C. Lau and Chen Fong Ching, *A Concordance to the* Liji (Hong Kong: Commercial Press, 1992), 19.4/99/23: 樂者，天地之和也；禮者，天地之序也.

principles embedded in the workings of the cosmos. The independence and perfection of these principles make them singular, uniform, and invariable, establishing the strictly transcendent relationship they have with the world of appearance. To be clear, strict philosophical or theological transcendence asserts that an independent and superordinate Principle A originates, determines, and sustains Principle B, where the reverse is not the case. In the asymmetry of strict transcendence, Principle A has a free hand in determining and sustaining the world; conversely, the world has no effect on what is the perfection and aseity (or self-sufficiency) of Principle A. Hence, such transcendent Principles and the world that is a mere shadow of them stand in a dualistic, "reality and appearance" relationship. Taking this ontological dualism wherein the first term nullifies the second a step further, we have to acknowledge that these Principles standing independent of the world actually negate the world in the sense that the world of appearance is wholly derivative of and has no independent existence or value outside of the perfection of these Principles.

Since the Forms are transcendent, how can they be grasped by the erotic philosopher who belongs to the sensible world? Plato's answer to this question is to ascribe this same kind of reality and appearance distinction to human beings. That is, Plato attributes a divine aspect to humankind by describing the immortal soul as being akin to the Forms in its permanent and unchanging status, and by interpreting death as the liberation of this soul from a sensuous body. Plato argues that genuine philosophers are "training to die" in the sense that they live the life of the intellect where through a process of recollection they come to know their real selves while at the same time they are distancing themselves as much as possible from the distractions of the body.

This deprecation of the body is given dramatic effect by Plato when he makes Socrates's disciple, Phaedo, the narrator of the dialogue. In Diogenes Laertius 2.105, we are offered an account of how Phaedo as a person of high birth was taken prisoner in his youth and came into the hands of an Athenian slave dealer. We know that Phaedo was only a youth from the fact that his hair is described as still long when it was the custom at the time to cut a young man's hair at eighteen years old. Phaedo was sold into service and, as a youth of considerable beauty, was pressed into prostitution. After becoming acquainted over a period of time with Socrates, Phaedo ran away from his master and attached himself to his philosophical mentor. Socrates then arranged for one of his wealthy friends to pay off Phaedo's owner and to free him from this physical bondage and exploitation. Thus it was that

Phaedo himself through the person of Socrates was liberated from the trials of the body and was introduced to the life of the philosopher.

Plato denigrates the human body and at the same time, through his doctrine of recollection, elevates the human soul to divine status. He argues that for ensouled human beings, instead of the Forms belonging to a transcendent and thus independent world out of their reach, they are available to the human intellect through its process of recovering what the soul has always known. We will find that for Aristotle as well it is the active intellect or *nous* and its *theoria* that is the intersection at which human beings overlap with the divine.

***

"If no pure knowledge is possible in the company of the body, then either it is totally impossible to acquire knowledge, or it is only possible after death, because it is only then that the soul will be isolated and independent of the body. It seems that so long as we are alive, we shall keep as close as possible to knowledge if we avoid as much as we can all contact and association with the body, except when they are absolutely necessary; and instead of allowing ourselves to be infected with its nature, purify ourselves from it until God himself gives us deliverance. In this way, by keeping ourselves uncontaminated by the follies of the body, we shall probably reach the company of others like ourselves and gain direct knowledge of all that is pure and uncontaminated—that is, presumably, of Truth. For one who is not pure himself to attain to the realm of purity would no doubt be a breach of the divine order. Something to this effect, Simmias, is what I imagine all real lovers of learning must say to one another and believe themselves; don't you agree with me?"

"Most emphatically, Socrates."

"Very well, then," said Socrates, "if this is true there is good reason for anyone who reaches the end of this journey which lies before me to hope that there, if anywhere, he will attain the object to which all our efforts have been directed in life gone by. So this journey which is now ordained for me carries a happy prospect for any other man also who believes that his mind has been made ready—and pure, so to speak."

"It does indeed," said Simmias.

"And doesn't this 'purification,' as we saw some time ago in our discussion, consist in separating the soul as much as possible from the body, and accustoming it to withdraw from its dispersal throughout the body and concentrate itself in isolation? And to have its dwelling, so far as it can, both now and in the future, alone by itself, freed from the chains of the body. Does not that follow?"

"Yes, it does," said Simmias.

"Is not what we call death a freeing and separation of soul from body?"

"Certainly," he said.

"And the desire to free the soul is found chiefly, or rather only, in the true philosopher; in fact the philosopher's occupation consists precisely in the freeing and separation of soul from body. Isn't that so?"

"Apparently."

"Well then, as I said at the beginning, if a man has trained himself throughout his life to live in a state as close as possible to death, would it not be ridiculous for him to be distressed when death comes to him?"

"It would, of course."

"Then it is a fact, Simmias, that true philosophers make dying their profession, and that to them of all men death is least alarming. . . . If this is so, will a true lover of wisdom who has firmly grasped this same conviction—that he will never attain to wisdom worthy of the name elsewhere than in the next world—will he be grieved at dying? Will he not be glad to make that journey? We must suppose so, my comrade; that is, if he is a genuine 'philosopher,' because then he will be of the firm belief that he will never find wisdom in all its purity in another place."[57]

Fifth Anticipation

The traditional Chinese character for "body" (*ti* 體) in its simplified form that is now standard in China and Japan combines the radical for person

---

57. Plato, *Phaedo*, *Last Days of Socrates*, 128–129, 66e–68b.

(*ren* 人) with the character "root or trunk" (*ben* 本) to form the graph *ti* 体. We can only speculate on the origins of this construction, with the most likely story being that it became a cursive way to write what is otherwise the complicated traditional character. But perhaps thinking of the body zoetologically as "rootedness" is much more than simply a heuristic. What might have prompted the selection of the "root" radical to express the idea of body takes us back to the very earliest usage of this character *ti* 體. Deborah Sommer has observed that "the significance of plant life for the meaning of *ti* merits further consideration, particularly as the term was first used in reference to plant (and also animal) bodies."[58] Whereas the metaphor we associate with "body" in European languages is the main part or "structure" of something, the meaning in the earliest classical Chinese sources is the organic (rather than geometric) form of animal and plant bodies, where in certain contexts it has a horticultural reference as plant vegetation in general (roots, stalks, foliage) and, more specifically, as a rhizome or tuber.[59] In the *Book of Songs* 35, for example, a spurned wife draws a correlation between the harvesting of vegetables, root and greens, and the full acceptance of a married relationship in all of its parts. Addressing her husband she insists that "husband and wife should encourage each other and it is not right for you to give way to angry feelings. In picking turnips and daikon radishes, do we not take them roots and all?"[60]

Sommer on further consideration of this poem's reference to *ti* as a rhizome observes that the *ti* body is "a polysemous corpus of indeterminate extent that can be partitioned into subtler units, each of which is often analogous to the whole and shares a fundamental consubstantiality and common identity with the whole."[61] Sommer's research

---

58. Deborah Sommer, "Boundaries of the *Ti Body*," in *Star Gazing, Fire Phasing, and Healing in China: Essays in Honor of Nathan Sivin*, ed. Michael Nylan, Henry Rosemont Jr., and Li Waiyee, special issue of *Asia Major*, 3rd series, 21, part 1 (2008): 295–296.

59. For this claim about the organic basis of the term *ti*, see Roger T. Ames, "The Meaning of Body in Classical Chinese Philosophy," in *The Self as Body in Asian Theory and Practice*, ed. Roger T. Ames, Wimal Dissanayake, and Thomas P. Kasulis (Albany: State University of New York Press, 1993).

60. 黽勉同心、不宜有怒. 采葑采菲、無以下體. Cf. Sommer, "Boundaries of the *Ti Body*," 297. This story does not have a happy ending. As Sommers reports, the spurned wife like the unused parts of the vegetables is not brought to the banquet table, and in the verse that follows the husband has replaced the wife with another woman.

61. Sommer, "Boundaries of the *Ti* Body," 294.

provides us with real insight into the horticultural origins of the *ti* body, and we learn much from the early sources from which she is drawing her examples. But perhaps there is one point on which we might want further reflection. Sommer sees a fundamental distinction between the human *ti* and that of rhizomes, where the latter "lend themselves to unusual kinds of division and multiplication—processes that rarely occur with other kinds of bodies without killing them . . ."[62] She compares these plants to human and animal bodies, observing that "when living human bodies are divided, they die: halving, quartering, or fragmenting human or animal bodies inevitably results in dismemberment or death."[63]

The suppressed assumption Sommer is beginning from here is the discrete individuality of plants and persons as the basic unit of comparison, then offering a life or death distinction between the division of the rhizome and the human body respectively. But in fact, if a rhizome is simply cut up without further attention to the proper planting that will allow for its own specific method of reproduction, it too will most likely die. In the early writings, there are several different ways of referencing "body." The body depicted in the prestylized graph meaning "vital or lived body" is *shen* 身, which in its earliest form is the body of a pregnant woman ⬛.[64] Sommer in fact uses the language of "parent" and "mother body" in describing the proliferation of the rhizome in a kind of genealogical lineage, remarking that "each new plant produced in vegetative propagation becomes a new plant exactly like its 'parent.' Moreover, each new plant in some sense is still the parent plant, and there exists a material continuity of identity from one life form to the next. . . . Mother and daughter plants are at once autonomous and yet consubstantial."[65] This reference to "mother and daughter plants" being the case, we might ask is the reproduction of the rhizome so different from the way in which the Confucian tradition has conceived of the human experience in which mothers live on in daughters, and ancestors live on in the lives of their progeny? I would suggest that if one thinks genealogically rather than analytically, this alternative method of bodily division and reproduction for human beings within a family lineage is

---

62. Sommer, "Boundaries of the *Ti* Body," 296.

63. Sommer, "Boundaries of the *Ti* Body," 296.

64. Kwan, "Database," 逆鐘 (西周晚期) CHANT 63.

65. Sommer, "Boundaries of the *Ti* Body," 296.

not so much at variance with the rhizome. At the genealogical level, our bodies and the process of human procreativity provide the birthing of distinctive and unique persons from those who have come before, where the language of their "embodied knowing" and their "living on" in their progeny is not meant merely rhetorically. The profound sense of genealogical continuity implied by the expression "living on" is difficult to grasp if the body is taken as "belonging" only to an individual.

The opening chapter of the *Classic of Family Reverence* (*Xiaojing* 孝經) makes it clear that for Confucius, the body is consubstantial as an inheritance that is on loan from one's family lineage and that must be returned to it. According to this text, the first obligation one has to this lineage is to maintain the body's integrity by avoiding any kind of desecration or disgrace. The consubstantiality of the body is most obvious in the transmission of physical likenesses within the family lineage, but perhaps even more important are the embodied continuities of the cultural tradition itself—its language, its institutions, and its values.

The collaterality and consubstantiality between parent and child is captured in the character "familial reverence" (*xiao* 孝) itself as the culture's prime moral imperative, constituted as it is by the combination of the graph for "elders" (*lao* 老) and that for "offspring, son, daughter, child, youth" (*zi* 子). In clarifying the meaning of family reverence as deference between generations, it is important to note that one's immediate family is only the beginning of such deference. *Xiao* must become a pattern of conduct that, with unrelenting attention, is extended out from family to include all members of the community, and polity, and ultimately, to the cosmos itself. Within the human experience, *xiao* is nothing less than the highest value as the motive force behind the intergenerational transmission of the living cultural tradition.

In the first chapter of the *Classic of Family Reverence*, it declares that extending radially outward from a focal center "family reverence begins in service to your parents, continues in service to your lord, and culminates in distinguishing yourself in the world."[66] Then in chapter 7 of this same text entitled the "Three Powers," *xiao* takes on cosmic status as a value that informs the relationship that obtains among the heavens, the earth, and the human world. It is because these three powers (*sancai* 三才) are mutually implicated in each other that such cosmic relations provide a context for the human experience. Importantly, this isomorphism between

---

66. 夫孝始於事親, 中於事君, 終於立身.

family, state, and cosmos begins with the proper accord aspired to in our human institutions and is then extended outward. In recalling the conversation between Confucius and Master Zeng, the text reads: "'Incredible—the profundity of family reverence!' declared Master Zeng. 'Indeed,' said the Master. 'Family reverence is the constancy of the heavenly cycles, the appropriate responsiveness (*yi*) of the earth, and the proper conduct of the people. It is the constant workings of the heavens and the earth that the people model themselves upon. Taking the illumination (*ming*) of the heavens as their model and making the most of the earth's resources, they bring the empire into accord (*shun*).'"[67] Given the central role of family reverence (*xiao*) as the axis for the intergenerational transmission of the living culture, it is significant that in the pre-Qin documents, the graph for the "embodying" (*ti* 體) of the tradition that family reverence enables appears with three alternative semantic classifiers. The *shen* 身 classifier alludes to the lived, vital, and irreducibly social body; the *rou* 肉 semantic indicator suggests the flesh-and-hair, carnal body; and the *gu* 骨 marker references the "bones" and the formal, skeletal structure they provide. We can appeal to these different ways of writing the graph for "body" as a heuristic that will allow us to give fuller value to how each succeeding generation has the responsibility for coming to "know" and to thus embody the cultural corpus that has come before.[68]

Ti with the "lived body" classifier (*shen* 身) 軆 that is found on the early Warring States bronzes (ca. 400 BCE) is the earliest form we have of this character. It references the vital and existentially aware dimension of the embodied experience in its dynamic social relations with others, both lived from the inside and engaged from the outside.[69] As previously mentioned, the body depicted in the prestylized *shen* graph is the profile of a pregnant woman 身,[70] an image of perhaps the most intimate and visceral of all human relations. The "duplicity" or "two-ness" of the pregnant body carries over with *shen* indicating the subjective and existential as well as the more objective dimension of experience with the internalizing of the outside in the process of achieving a personal

67. 曾子曰: 甚哉! 孝之大也. 子曰: "夫孝、天之經也, 地之義也, 民之行也. 天地之經而民是則之, 則天之明, 因地之利, 以順天下.

68. For a fuller discussion of this sense of embodiment, see Ames, *Confucian Role Ethics*, 102–113.

69. Kwan, "Database," 戰國早期 CHANT 9735.3b.

70. Kwan, "Database," 逆鐘 (西周晚期) CHANT 63.

identity. We come to know and express what it means to become consummately human intuitively, where we first "have" feelings in our various lived-body family and social relations and then struggle to organize and make sense of them.

Arguing that structure and function are two aspects of the same thing, medical anthropologist Judith Farquhar searches for an appropriate language that will provide the necessary contrast between the processual understanding of the body in traditional Chinese medicine (TCM), and the very different formal, anatomical assumptions of biomedicine. Farquhar observes that "Chinese medicine most classically envisions embodiment as a dynamic complex of interwoven processes, as a physiology that must be understood in the living through analysis of signs, symptoms, and a subjective sensorium."[71] This functional understanding of formal structures within the correlative cosmology is radically situational and contextual, locating "things" such as the "lived body" or "the body as experienced" within its ever-changing circumstances as a collaboration between an existential and an external landscape.

Farquhar cautions that if we are to overcome "our commonsense commitment to a materialism which must reduce phenomena to synchronically observable collections of objects," we must understand "things" as both existing in time and as entailing a subjective, existential dimension. For TCM, ontological thinking must give way to zoetology. That is, the temporality and reflexivity of "things" must be considered in any and all attempts at understanding them. "Body" must be understood diachronically or "through time" where "it is signs and symptoms, experiences and perceptions, which are the material foundation of medical perception. They are not less concrete than anatomical organs, but they are not conceivable outside of lived time."[72] Thus, any tendency to treat "body" as simply a physical object would violate the existential, contextual, and processional sensibilities of the correlative cosmology in which traditional Chinese medicine is grounded. Unsurprisingly, the personal narrative as the reflexive aspect of corporality is of enormous importance in traditional Chinese medical practices, in which "the evidence here suggests . . . that Chinese medicine accords a certain importance to quotidian self-perception; while never denying the object-nature of

---

71. Judith Farquhar, *Knowing Practice: The Clinical Encounter of Chinese Medicine* (Boulder: Westview Press, 1994), 162.

72. Farquhar, *Knowing Practice*, 386.

bodies, it privileges processes of change that take place in personal time, which can only be entered into medical consideration via the patient's own narrative."[73] The inseparability of the subjective "lived body" and the more objective "body for others" in traditional Chinese medicine provides one way of making sense of ourselves as organisms. Again, body with its body consciousness and body language is discursive, and with the patient's narrative as a necessary factor, it is aural as well as visual. The body—at once the self-conscious "I" as my existential experience and the embedded "me" as "my living body for other subjects"—is an indissoluble continuity between self and world.

Turning to "body" (*ti*) with the "flesh" classifier (*rou* 肉) 軆 , it is found pervasively on the Guodian bamboo strips (ca. 300 BCE) and alludes to the carnal body—that is, the body as flesh, hair, and bone.[74] The modalities of our experience are rooted in and are always mediated through a unique localizing physicality, and are temporally and spatially constrained by this fact. All of our thoughts and feelings are grounded in a complex psychophysical sensorium of seeing, hearing, touching, smelling, and tasting, a sensorium that makes specific demands on our conduct and that registers our pleasures and pain. Philosopher Richard Shusterman has made much of what he has called a "somaesthetic"—that is, the opportunity the "flesh and bone" carnal body provides us for educating its various senses, and how this leads to the civilizing and aestheticizing of the human experience. The body provides us the occasion for developing a keen eye for art, an acute ear for music, a fine sense of touch for the piano keys, an awakened nose for good wine, a discriminating palate for haute cuisine, and much, much more.[75]

The now familiar, traditional form of the character *ti* 軆 with the "bones" classifier (*gu* 骨) as *ti* 體 still in use today in places where simplified characters have been resisted does not occur in our current records until the Mawangdui bamboo strips (168 BCE). This graphic form references our persons as "discursive bodies" that engage in "structuring,"

---

73. Farquhar, *Knowing Practice*, 386.

74. Kwan, "Database," 郭店簡,窮達以時 10.

75. See as a representative example Richard Shusterman, *Body Consciousness: A Philosophy of Mindfulness and Somaesthetics* (Cambridge: Cambridge University Press, 2008). Given the centrality of body in Confucian philosophy, perhaps unsurprisingly there is keen interest Shusterman's work in China where many if not most of his books are now available in good translations.

"configuring," and "embodying" our experience not only cognitively and affectively but also viscerally.[76] We might reflect on the difference implied by "seeing" the world versus "knowing" it as a distinction between experience as immediately "had" and a more reflective and deliberate experience that has been mediated through human epistemic structures. Each of us inherits a worldview and a common sense through our cultural ambiance and collaborates with the world to discriminate, conceptualize, and theorize our experience of it. We embody and give Apollonian form to the contents of our culture, our language, and our habitat, and in this continuing process of shaping and being shaped, our various "languages" speak us as much as we speak them.

Medical anthropologist Zhang Yanhua analyzes the two characters that in modern Chinese as a binomial are usually used to denote "body" (shenti 身體) with their irreducibly subjective and gerundive implications, insisting that "if we have to make a distinction between shen and ti as bodies, we may say that shen implies a socially informed body-person or body-self, while ti, frequently used in or as a verb, emphasizes 'embodying' as a process of knowing and acting. Both concepts resist dualistically positioned mind and body, subject and object."[77] In Confucian role ethics, we can correlate the character for "lived body" (ti 體) and its cognate character (li 禮)—"aspiring to propriety in one's roles and relations"—by arguing that they express two ways of shaping, embodying, and thus "realizing" our personal identities. That is, these two characters point to "a living body" and "embodied living" respectively. Internalizing and embodying our experience is a form of carnal "knowing" that is carried over into the modern Chinese language in which "knowing bodily" (tihui 體會 and tiyan 體驗) means to know something through experiencing it viscerally, but such knowing does not end there. That is, in the process of internalizing our experience of the world, we participate in knowing in the sense of "realizing" it.

In this process cosmology, there is a correlative rather than dualistic relationship between "heartmind" and "body" (xinshen 心身). It should thus not be surprising that Sommer in summarizing her analysis of the ti body as it occurs in the classical literature uses language immediately reminiscent of the body-mind holography that is made explicit in the

---

76. Kwan, "Database," 馬王堆・五十二病方 376.

77. Zhang Yanhua, *Transforming Emotions with Chinese Medicine: An Ethnographic Account from Contemporary China* (Albany: State University of New York Press, 2007), 36.

Book of Changes cosmology. Sommer observes that "when a *ti* body is fragmented into parts (literally or conceptually), each part retains in certain aspects, a kind of wholeness or becomes a simulacra of the larger entity of which it is a constituent."[78] We might take as an example of this holography a passage in which Mencius insists specifically that "the myriad things of the world are all implicated here in me."[79] Mencius is herein averring that the unbounded cosmic totality is implicated in each vital impulse of the embodied lives as they are lived by always unique persons.

The notion of *li* 禮 denotes a continuing, complex, and always novel pattern of invested institutions and significant behaviors that come to be embodied, authored, and reauthorized by succeeding generations as the persistent authority of the culture itself. In so doing, the culture serves to bring together the family lineages (*shizu* 氏族) and clans (*jiazu* 家族) into a specific yet extended body of people (*minzu* 民族) or body politic (*renmin* 人民). For this holistic Confucian philosophy, our unique and embodied persons in their entirety penetrate so deeply into the human experience in all of its complexity that it would be a nonsense to try to separate out some reality that stands independent of them. Said another way, for Confucianism, our reality is our lived, embodied experience and nothing else.

It should be clear that what we are referencing here by "lived body" is not simply the transmission of a physical lineage, although it is that too. The living body and our embodied living is the conveyance of the cultural corpus of knowledge through which a living civilization itself is preserved and extended: that is, its linguistic facility and proficiency, its religious doctrines and mythologies, the aesthetics of refined living, the modeling of mores and values, the instruction and apprenticeship in cognitive technologies, and so on. Our bodies are certainly our physicality, but they are also living conduits through which the entire body of culture is inherited, interpreted, elaborated upon, and reauthorized across the ages.

At the most primordial level, the body via these three mutually entailing modalities—the vital, carnal, and discursive bodies—serves as the bond that coordinates our subjectivity with the internalizing of our various environments and that mediates our processes of thinking and feeling as

---

78. Sommer, "Boundaries of the *Ti* Body," 294.

79. *Mencius* 孟子 7A4: 萬物皆備於我矣.

they are expressed through overt behaviors. If we use the vocabulary of contemporary medical anthropology to capture the nonanalytical relationship between living and embodying, our animated life activities, far from being distinct from our embodiment, are in fact integral to and expressive of it. As Zhang Yanhua in reflecting on the relationship between our life force and our bodies concludes rather succinctly, "*jingshen* 精神 is not perceived as opposite to *shenti* 身體 but constitutive of it."[80]

***

"Does that actual nature of things—their true being which we try to describe in our discussions—remain always constant and invariable, or not? Does equality itself or beauty itself or any other thing as it is in itself ever admit change of any kind? Or does each one of these entities, being uniform and self-contained, remain always constant and invariable, never admitting any alteration in any respect or in any sense?"

"They must be constant and invariable, Socrates," said Cebes.

"Well, what about the many instances of beauty—such as men, horses, clothes, and so on—or of equality or any other things that have the same name as those others? Are they constant, or on the contrary, scarcely ever in the same relation in any sense to themselves or to one another?"

"You're right again about them, Socrates; they are never free from variation."

"And these latter things you can touch or see or perceive by your other senses, but those constant entities you cannot possibly apprehend except by the workings of the mind; such things are invisible to our sight."

"That is perfectly true," said Cebes.

"So you think we should assume two classes of things that may be such-and-such, one visible and the other invisible?"

"Yes, we should."

"The invisible being invariable, and the visible never being the same?"

"Yes, let's assume that too."[81]

---

80. Zhang Yanhua, *Transforming Emotions*, 38.

81. Plato, *Phaedo, Last Days of Socrates*, 146–147, 78d–79a.

***

"Now Cebes," he said, "see whether this is our conclusion from all we have said. The soul is most like that which is divine, immortal, intelligible, uniform, indissoluble, and ever self-consistent and invariable, whereas body is most like that which is human, mortal, multiform, unintelligible, dissoluble, and never self-consistent."[82]

***

"Well," said Socrates . . . "I am assuming the existence of Beauty in itself and Goodness and Largeness and all the rest of them. If you grant my assumption and grant they exist, I hope with their help to explain causation to you . . . It seems to me that whatever else is beautiful apart from Beauty in itself is beautiful because it partakes of that Beauty, and for no other reason. Do you accept this reason?"

"Yes, I do."

"Well, now," he said, "I cannot understand these other ingenious theories of causation. If someone tells me that they reason why a given object is beautiful is that it has a gorgeous colour or shape or any other such attribute, I disregard all of these other explanations—I find them confusing—and I cling simply and straightforwardly, naively perhaps, to the explanation that the one thing that makes that object beautiful is the presence in it or the association with it (in whatever way the relationship comes about) of that other Beauty. I do not go so far as to insist on the precise detail; only upon the fact that it is by Beauty that beautiful things are beautiful."[83]

Sixth Anticipation

In order to clarify the nature of causality assumed in Plato's ontological thinking, David Hall introduces a distinction between the notions of

---

82. Plato, *Phaedo, Last Days of Socrates*, 148–149, 80b.

83. Plato, *Phaedo, Last Days of Socrates*, 175–176, 100b–d.

"power" and "creativity." Beauty-in-Itself as an originative principle having ontological priority is the source of all beautiful things and reflects a mode of causality that, in the melding of Greek philosophy and the Abrahamic religions, predominates in the erstwhile "Creator and creature" relationship between God and world. In distinguishing creativity from power in the relations that obtain among things, Hall observes that " 'creativity' is a notion that can be characterized only in terms of self-actualization. Unlike power relationships that require that tensions among component elements be resolved in favor of one of the components, in relations defined by creativity there is no otherness, no separation or distancing, nothing to be overcome."[84]

Such a collateral definition of creativity that occurs in the relations between persons and their natural, social, and cultural environments—or perhaps better, of co-creativity—cannot be reconciled with notions of external causation that appeal to determination by some independent principle or agency. In fact, there has been a persistent confusion regarding "creativity" within the creatio ex nihilo doctrines familiar in the Abrahamic religious culture that has attended all but the most recent thinking about the necessary conditions for creativity to occur. Hall further avers that "creatio ex nihilo, as it is normally understood, is in fact the paradigm of all power relationships since the 'creative' element of the relation is completely in control of its 'other,' which is in itself literally nothing."[85] The aseity or self-sufficiency of God ascribes "perfection" itself to Godhead, and hence nothing can be added to Him or taken away. We can say that God, as Omnipotent Other Who commands the world into being, is Maker of the world, but because nothing novel emerges in the process, He is not in any interesting sense its "Creator." Any subsequent human acts of "creativity" that by definition ought to entail the spontaneous emergence of novelty can in fact only be secondary and derivative exercises of power. Creativity understood in terms of the spontaneous emergence of novelty can only make sense in a world that would insist upon ontological parity among things. Either everything shares in a process of mutual creativity, or the world is sharply divided into makers and their mere shadows, into Being and its mere appearances. In the latter world, the elements of novelty and spontaneity are fatally

---

84. See David L. Hall, *Eros and Irony: A Prelude to Philosophical Anarchism* (Albany: State University of New York Press, 1982), 249.

85. Hall, *Eros and Irony*, 249.

threatened. Such concerns are precisely what have been at issue in A. N. Whitehead's process understanding of creativity in which things and their contextualizing relations are coterminous and mutually entailing.

Power is to be construed as the production of intended effects determined by external causation. Creativity, on the other hand, is the spontaneous production of additional meaning in the correlative relations that obtain among things and thus, unlike power, is not reducible to an exhaustive causal analysis. While power is exercised with respect to and over others, creativity is always reflexive and is exercised over and with respect to interdependent things that in their relations are inclusive of themselves and their environing others. Taking "persons" as an example, since persons in a processive world are irreducibly social, such co-creativity is a transactional and multidimensional undertaking in which persons are literally "making" each other. We make both our friends and our enemies.

Stated the other way around, it is the transactional, co-creative character of all creative processes in which persons both shape and are shaped by their world that renders personal cultivation irreducibly social. In "creating" oneself as a committed and effective teacher, one is intent on producing extraordinary students. And the standard of teaching demanded by exceptional students produces a committed and effective teacher. Both teacher and student are cause and effect in their transactional relationship. Since all persons are constituted by their relationships, self-creation means being true in one's associations with others. It requires a commitment to the effective cultivation of oneself within one's social, natural, and cultural contexts as the ground from which one's person as simultaneously self and other arise together to maximum benefit. The resolve that animates self-creation determines what persons are becoming and is a function of how well and how productively they are able to fare in their synergistic alliances with their others.

Canonized by Zhu Xi 朱熹 in the Southern Song dynasty as one of the Four Books, *Focusing the Familiar* (*Zhongyong* 中庸) provides us with a dramatic account of precisely this contextualized understanding of creative resolve in personal and cosmic cultivation that enables persons to achieve a quality of consummation:

> Resolve (*cheng* 誠) is self-consummating and its way-making is self-directing. Resolve is the beginning and the end of things, and without this resolve, there would be nothing. It is thus that,

for exemplary persons, it is resolve that is prized. But resolve is not simply the self-consummating of one's own person; it is what consummates everything. Completing oneself is achieving virtuosity in one's roles and relations (*ren* 仁); completing all things is advancing wisdom in the world (*zhi* 知). Such is the virtuosity achieved in one's natural propensities and the way-making that integrates what is more internal and what is more external. Thus, when and wherever one applies this virtuosity, it is fitting.[86]

The character *cheng* 誠 translated here as "resolve" is conventionally rendered "sincerity" or "integrity." In this chapter of the *Zhongyong*, it is not being deployed simply as a human feeling but rather as a technical cosmological term. The Song dynasty scholar Xu Zhongche 徐中車 emphasizes the dynamic aspect of *cheng* by alluding to the phrase in *Zhongyong* 26 that states "the utmost creative resolve is ceaseless" (*zhichengwuxi* 至誠無息), thus defining *cheng* as "a ceaseless process" (*buxi* 不息). Such an interpretation is consistent with Zhu Xi's own generative understanding of *cheng* when he glosses it as 真實不妄: "the genuine and undeflected process of coming to fruition." Similarly, Tang Junyi understands the *Zhongyong*'s use of *cheng* as "continuity itself" (*jixubenshen* 繼續本身), while Wing-tsit Chan 陳榮捷 in translating the *Zhongyong* for a Western audience insists that *cheng* in this text "is not just a state of mind, but an active force that is always transforming things and completing things, and drawing man and Heaven together in the same current."[87] Tu Wei-ming 杜維明 takes this reflection on *cheng* in the *Zhongyong* further in observing that since "the last thirteen chapters deal mainly with the metaphysical concept of *ch'eng* [*cheng*] (sincerity, reality, and truth)," *cheng* "has been somewhat unjustifiably translated as 'sincerity.' "[88] In his monograph-length study of this text, Tu collates earlier commentarial exegesis and argues that *cheng* must be under-

---

86. *Focusing the Familiar* 中庸 25: 誠者自成也，而道自道也. 誠者物之終始，不誠無物. 是故君子誠之為貴. 誠者非自成己而已也，所以成物也. 成己，仁也; 成物，知也. 性之德也，合外內之道也，故時措之宜也.

87. Wing-tsit Chan, *A Source Book in Chinese Philosophy* (Princeton: Princeton University Press, 1963), 96.

88. Tu Wei-ming, *Centrality and Commonality: An Essay on Confucian Religiousness* (Albany: State University of New York Press, 1989), 16–17.

stood as "creativity." In his own words, *cheng* "can be conceived as a form of creativity. . . . It is that which brings about the transforming and nourishing processes of heaven and earth. As creativity, *ch'eng* [*cheng*] is "ceaseless" (*pu-hsi* [*buxi* 不息]). Because of its ceaselessness it does not create in a single act beyond the spatiotemporal sequence. Rather, it creates in a continuous and unending process in time and space. . . . It is simultaneously a self-subsistent and self-fulfilling process of creation that produces life unceasingly."[89]

Cheng as it appears in the *Zhongyong* unquestionably references a generative cosmic process, but remembering David Hall's concern about eliding the distinction between power and creativity, we might want to further note that the only kind of "creativity" relevant in this zoetological, one-world process cosmology is creatio in situ: that is, the co-creativity that takes place in the relationship between particulars and their contextualizing others. Indeed, it is the fact that all real creativity is necessarily co-creativity that would give us a warrant for dropping the redundant "co-" in co-creativity and translating *cheng* simply as "creativity." Of course, the caveat here would be that if we are translating *cheng* on behalf of an English-language readership for whom, under the sway of Abrahamic theology, the predominant understanding of "creativity" would be creatio ex nihilo, we must take just such a prejudice into account. To avoid the default understanding of "creativity" by most Western readers as entailing creatio ex nihilo, I have translated *cheng* as "resolve": that is, the animating spirit behind a situated and always collaborative creativity. Creative resolve is situated and site-specific, and in bringing embedded relationships into clearer focus and resolution, it makes them increasingly meaningful. It is only through such resolve that the highest order of human beings are able to participate fully as co-creators together with the heavens and the earth in their "extending *dao*" (*hongdao* 弘道) and in their commitment to a collaborative "world-making."

***

Chronologically, the next Platonic dialogue to make its contribution to Plato's Theory of Forms is the *Republic*. As we have seen in this chapter, one function of this theory is to provide an answer to the question of the relationship between the one and the many, where the single perfect Form

---

89. Tu Wei-ming, *Centrality and Commonality*, 81–82.

available in the intelligible realm has a causal function in determining and explaining the many imperfect replications of it in the sensual world of appearances. At the same time, this single principle "informs" the language that would give this world its definition. For Plato, in order for this system of objective ideals to achieve a sense of completeness and coherence, it must include a principle of unity that establishes the normative relationship that obtains among the various Forms. Plato's Principle of the Good serves this purpose. This ultimate principle is at the basis of Plato's intuition of the unity of all things, and it is an expression of his sense that order and value are related in such a manner that the richest and most complex order manifests the greatest value.

The dynamic aspect of Plato's philosophy is captured in the desire of philosophers for the completeness of understanding—their *eros*. Predicated upon a lack of knowledge of what is real and what is not, this quest for apodictic knowledge carries with it the need for self-completion and to acquire what is necessary to make oneself whole. We remember in the *Symposium* in the monologue of Aristophanes the amusing myth in which, early on, round human beings were twice what we are today, like two persons grafted into one and with the use of eight limbs rather than the now-standard four. As a consequence of their strength and the hubris that attended it, these superhumans became a threat to the gods who, rather than simply exterminating them, decided to cut them into two. Thereafter, in order to become whole again, these deflated and much diminished agitators were driven to roam the world searching for their other half. Without this erotic pursuit after completeness, the normative aspect of Plato's philosophy that comes to have such significance in neo-Platonism and Christianity would be much less pronounced. The practitioner of dialectic must be prepared to make the final ascent to the unifying principle of knowledge that provides the foundation for the cosmological order. This Principle of the Good encompasses both fact and value, undergirds the unity of knowledge, and is the explanation for the unity of the world as well.

In the *Republic*, Plato uses metaphors, similes, and allegories to lend some persuasive clarity if not actual proof to his hypothesis about the unifying Good. One familiar simile is his distinction between dreaming and waking, where the former he associates with those people who mistake the apparent many for the real one. That is, the dreamer sees beauty in the world as it is manifested in multiple things but fails to seek out the source of that beauty in the Form or Idea of Beauty-in-Itself. The dreamer thus confuses what is only a matter of opinion or belief with the true object of knowledge.

Another related image Plato conjures up for the Good is the analogy of the sun, again underscoring the problem of mistaking a lower level of understanding and its shadowy object for the true knowledge that would provide access to the causal source of what is real. Given the central role that metaphor and analogy play in the correlative thinking of zoetology, we might well ask what then is the role of these same tropes in Plato's ontology? Indeed, in order to distinguish clearly Plato's metaphorical turn from what might seem to be an overlap with zoetology, we must ask after his reasons for moving from dialectic and reasoned explanation to invoking the linguistic devices of simile, metaphor, and analogy.

I would suggest that Plato is using this alternative imagistic mode of explanation as a necessary complement to his ontology in the same way that, in ontological thinking, aesthetic sensibilities lead to the rationalizing of the beautiful as the principle of beauty, that is, Beauty-in-Itself. First, for Plato access of the intellect to the Forms must be the direct experience of philosophers themselves and cannot be made available by any second party. It is thus that the role of the teacher can be no more than that of a guide on the side. As we saw in the *Symposium*, preliminary to the final ascent the erotic philosopher might make in order to encounter the principle of Beauty Itself, exposure to particular instances of beauty can serve as motivation to strive for a higher, more abstract grasp of their ultimate cause. Each step along the way is an explanation for the step that has come before: for example, the one perfect body explains the many imperfect bodies that have been encountered earlier. These suggestive images can function as an indirect method for enabling a process of increasing intellectual clarity in the discovery of what is necessarily a given reality. An encounter with a beautiful body points one in the direction of Beauty Itself. It is important to observe that Plato's analogies are not, as in zoetological thinking, taken to be productive of novel meaning. Rather, they only serve the seekers of knowledge as signposts on their journey to discover what is a transcendent, an independent, and a causal source of meaning. And as we read on in the *Republic*, the analogy of the sun is restated and further elaborated upon with the image of the divided line and the allegory of the cave, where it is the function of all of such tropes to point toward a principled reality.

In Plato's Theory of Forms as it is expressed through these images, we are given his metaphysical realism and its ensuant rational epistemology. First, both the sun and the Good provide intelligibility. The sun connects the human being with the sensible world through sight; the Good makes the connection between the light of reason and reality. Just as we know the world as it is illuminated by the sun, we know the reality of the Forms in light of the Good. The difference between metaphor and reality lies in the fact that everything under the sun is known through the senses only as a matter of opinion, while the Good is the source of the true intellectual knowledge of what is real. And just as the sun presides over the visible world and provides stable access to its terrain, so the Good governs reality itself and reveals not only its internal structure but the relationship between this structure and the sensible world. That is to say, the Good grasped by the intellect not only gives us reality but also makes sense for us of the sensible world as it reflects that reality. Again, both the sun and the Good are "causal" although in very different ways. While the sun has a creative function in giving birth to, growing, and nourishing all things, the Good is the single causal source for the existence and intelligibility of the Forms and further provides the ideal and the teleological account of everything that is informed by these Forms.

The analogy between the sun and the Good also works to shed light on the intellectual ascent of the philosopher. In the allegory of the cave, when philosophers escape from the shadowy cave they are first blinded by the rays of the sun. Gradually their eyes not only become accustomed to the light, but this illumination enables them to see clearly and take full advantage of the sensible world. In the same way, as the philosopher's journey turns from the sensual to the intelligible world, the mind through the illumination provided by the Good is able to overcome its ignorance and to grasp a true knowledge of reality. Philosophers are able to contemplate and fully appreciate the structure of reality itself with all of its moral value and beauty. Having made this ascent, philosophers while they are still in the world of change are then able to use this "insight" into the nature of reality in a way that optimizes the quantum of real human virtue in all of the things that they do.

As remarked upon earlier in the discussion of Parmenides's two-world theory, there are important issues that stand out as unresolved in Plato's use of the sun as a metaphor for the Good. Plato is not unaware of the limits of this metaphor when he himself says of the Good that it is only sun-*like*, and that the knowledge and truth that follow from it are only Good-*like*. First, in the space between the Good and the sun there is the distinction we have made between power and creativity. The "causal" *power* of the Good as the source of being, knowledge, and truth and its capacity to manifest the world is entirely at odds with the *creative*, generative, and life-giving operations of the sun. Here the distinction between their alternative modes of creatio ex nihilo and creatio in situ are important. Again, given that the Good is a unifying principle, the various dualistic dichotomies of ontology's sensible world such as subject and object, mind and world, idea and reality, knower and known can have no purchase. Indeed, in trying to make sense of the philosopher's "relationship" to the Good (if this is even appropriate language), we are thus tasked with formulating an interpretation of the Platonic and Aristotelian notions of *theoria* robust enough to reconcile all of the ontological dualisms.

In the *Republic* then, we begin from Plato's distinction between mere opinion and true knowledge as it is captured in his dreaming and waking simile that would release the philosopher from the apparitions of dreaming to the waking grasp of what is real. Such an awakening to the ideal One behind the apparent many then takes the philosopher out of the shadowy darkness and into the light of the sun.

***

Well, I imagine that audiences and spectators can take pleasure in beautiful sounds and colours and shapes, and everything which is created from the elements, but that their minds are incapable of seeing, and taking pleasure in, the nature of beauty itself.

True.

Whereas those who are capable of approaching beauty itself, and seeing it just by itself, would be few in number, wouldn't they?

Very few.

Take the man who believes in beautiful objects, then, but does not believe in beauty itself, and cannot follow if you direct him to the knowledge of it. Is his life a dream, do you think, or is he awake? Think about it. Isn't dreaming like this? Suppose one thing, A, resembles another thing B. Isn't dreaming the state, whether in sleep or waking, of thinking not that A resembles B, but that A is B?

Well, I would certainly say that someone who made a mistake like that was dreaming.

What about the person who is just the opposite, who believes in beauty itself, who can look both at it and at the things which share in it without mistaking them for it or it for them? Does his life, in its turn, strike you as waking or dreaming?

Waking, he said. Very much so.

In that case, would we be justified in claiming that this man's state of mind, because he knows, is knowledge, and the other man's state of mind, because he merely believes, is opinion or belief?

Yes, we would . . .

Having established these definitions, I have a question to put to that fine fellow who thinks there is no beauty in itself, no form or character of beauty which remains always the same and unchanging, who thinks that beauty is plural—that born spectator who cannot tolerate anyone saying that beauty is one, or justice is one, or anything like that. Well, my friend, we shall ask him, is there any of these numerous beautiful things which cannot on occasion appear ugly? Anything just which cannot appear unjust? Anything holy which cannot appear unholy?

No, he said. They must necessarily appear to be both beautiful and ugly. And the same with all the other examples you ask about.[90]

***

In the world of thought the good stands in just the same relation to thinking and the things which are thought as the sun, in the world of sight, stands to seeing and the things that can be seen. . . . You can say that this thing which gives the things which are known their truth, and from which the knower draws his ability to know, is the form or character of the good. Because it is the cause of knowledge and truth, think of it by all means as something known. But you will be right to regard it as different from, and still more beautiful than, knowledge and truth, beautiful though both of these are. Just as in our example it is correct to think of light and vision as sun-*like*, but incorrect to think that they *are* the sun, in the same way here it is correct to think of knowledge and truth as good-*like*, but incorrect to think that either of them as the good. The good is something to

---

90. Plato, *The Republic*, ed. G. R. F. Ferrari and trans. Tom Griffith (Cambridge: Cambridge University Press, 2000), 179, 476b–d, 183–184, 479a–b). Reproduced with permission of the Licensor through PLSclear.

be prized even more highly. . . . The sun gives to what is seen, I think you would say, not only its ability to be seen, but also birth, growth and sustenance—though it is not itself birth or generation. . . . For the things which are known, say not only that their being known comes from the good, but also that they get their existence and their being from it as well—though the good is not being, but something far surpassing being in rank and power.[91]

Seventh Anticipation

The concept of the Good is introduced to provide unity to Plato's Theory of Forms. In Plato's idealism, the unity is the One behind the many that causes, sustains, and explains the many; it is the single Reality behind a world of mere appearances. Plato uses the metaphor of the sun as the Good to represent not only knowledge in the sense of intelligibility but also as the cause of knowledge and its truth. Yet at the same time, the Good is higher and more beautiful than knowledge and truth. In observing that the Good endows things with their existence and their Being, Plato appeals to the analogy of the sun that is similarly the single source of "birth, growth, and sustenance" of things. But given that Plato's ontology ascribes self-sufficiency to Being and denies the reality of change, the analogy between the Good and the sun fails to the extent that the Good's causal "endowment" bringing all things into existence and making them what they are is an expression of power rather than creativity. The erstwhile "growth" engendered by this self-sufficient transcendent principle can only be understood as causal in the sense of its role as a single, unilateral ex nihilo source. As in the case of power that wholly negates the originality and novelty we would associate with real creativity, Plato's notion of the causal Good contradicts the idea of growth as birth and life in any meaningful sense.

In contrast to this ontological causality that problematizes the notion of life itself, one theme that is pervasive in zoetology is what we have described as a holistic *ziran* 自然 or "self-so-ing" understanding of causality, wherein anything is both the cause and the effect of everything else. One familiar image in zoetology that reflects this situated notion of

---

91. Plato, *The Republic*, 215–216, 508c–509b.

causality is the energy of growth radiating outward from a focal center into to an unbounded field, while at the same time turning back to reflexively deepen and extend the center itself. The center is animated by both a centrifugal and a centripetal energy, outwardly extending and increasing its influence and reflexively focusing and increasing its resolution. Such a reflexive dynamic is captured in the gerundive binomial *jingshen* 精神 that expresses a symbiotic relationship between increasing focal intensity and its extended reach. The binomial *jingshen* as it is used in the modern Chinese language is usually translated as "spirit, vigor, vitality, drive, full of life." If the two characters are taken separately, *jing* 精, conventionally translated as "essence," is not some ontological essence to be contrasted with accidents or attributes. Rather, it is the concentrated, quintessential source of personal vitality, both physical and intellectual, that has been inherited from one's parents and further supplemented from various forms of nourishment. *Jing* is the sap of life, the potency of semen (*jingye* 精液), a tangible, life-giving energy as it is self-consciously felt within and expressed through one's actions in the world.

And the second character *shen* 神, conventionally translated as "spirit," is not the spiritual as opposed to the corporeal. Rather it is this same *jing* vitality that, once activated, then spreads through, expands into, and pervades the functional life activities of mind and body as a whole. *Shen* as it appears on the bronze inscriptions is 𥘞 and is interpreted as a bolt of "lightning" from above.[92] The character consists of the radical *shi* 示, meaning "sacrificial offering, displaying" and *shen* 申, meaning "extending, stretching." Such an etymology suggests the capacity of *shen* we would associate with a kind of "large-souled" spirituality that extends meaning in the world. *Shen* in the context of popular religion is thus often translated as "spirits" or "gods," and it has a range of meaning in Confucian cosmology the scope of which reveals the perceived continuity between three realms: (1) the numinous or divine, (2) human ancestors, and (3) the inspired human experience. The *Shuowen* lexicon states that "the heavenly gods call forth the myriad things" (*tianshenyinchuwanwuzheye* 天神引出萬物者也), with one of the commentaries suggesting that in this fundamentally monsoon agrarian world, there is a correlation between the events of thunder and rain and the fertility, life, and growth on the land that follows in their wake. One meaning of *shen* then is the numinous associated with natural phenomena such as the sky, sun, moon, stars, rivers, mountains, forests,

---

92. Kwan, "Database," 西周中期 CHANT 4174.

valleys, and so on. But importantly, *shen* does not simply reference the numinous; it also extends to human beings and their experience. It refers specifically to human ancestors on the bronze inscriptions and also comes to mean "life" and "spirit." When *qi* 氣 assumes a particular phenomenal form, *shen* as the life and spirit of this phenomenon is also born.

An important point to note is that these various terms are inter-penetrating rather than being categorical, referencing those different nonanalytical aspects necessary to explain the phenomenon of life itself. Zhang Yanhua insists that the vocabulary used for both the formal and the vital aspects of life (*tiyong* 體用) must be understood as resolutely situated, transactional, and imagistic, observing that

> although *jingshen* 精神 is translated in English as "mind" or "spirit," it is very much part of *shenti* [body]. . . . Primary *jing* provides the basis for the process of transforming the energy dis-tilled from food and is enriched and strengthened by "acquired *jing*." Chinese medical theories view *jing* and *qi* 氣 (air, breath, vital energy) as the same life-giving energy. When it is concen-trated, it is *jing*; when it is dispersed it turns into *qi*. If *jing* is the nurturing aspect of this energy, *qi* is the active configurational aspect of the same energy. . . . If *jing* and *qi* are the basis of life, then *shen* 神 is the manifestation of that life. . . . In other words, *shen* is the phenomenon of life activity itself.[93]

The flow of life energy requires coordination and direction by the heartmind (*xin* 心). *Xin* is the projective, intentional process ("bodyheart-minding") that provides the directive force negotiated within and guided by the possibilities inherent in any particular situation. In the human experience, avers Zhang Yanhua, "*xin* is a system of functioning that forms a continuous process of being or becoming a person, involving the physiological, psychological, and sociological. . . . What is particular about this process-centered heart-mind physiology is . . . the commitment to an unobstructed process of transformation in accordance with a given social context and natural environment."[94]

Given the Confucian focus-field conception of persons, we can through a historical example use this language of *jingshen* 精神 to illus-

---

93. Zhang Yanhua, *Transforming Emotions*, 37–38.

94. Zhang Yanhua, *Transforming Emotions*, 41.

trate the perceived symbiotic relationship between the intensity and resolution of a person's focal identity, on the one hand, and the enhanced extension of this person's field of influence on the other. To this end, we might take Confucius as the focal identity of one unique flesh-and-blood person who lived his life some twenty-five hundred years ago. Confucius's reach and influence in the world has extended outward diachronically across the centuries and has spread synchronically from his home state of Lu to encompass China, the Confucian cultures of East Asia, the vast Chinese diaspora, and in our time, is making incursions on world culture broadly construed. Simultaneously, Confucius's focal identity has, with the reflexive and symbiotic internalization of these environing cultures, taken on incrementally increased resolution and meaning, elevating Confucius as a cultural hero from local to global status, from a person of social and political influence to a civilizational force.

***

In the *Timaeus*, we find Plato applying his Theory of Forms in formulating "a likely account" of the construction of a cosmogony that brings with it a strong sense of teleological order. What is causally true of particular things in the world is true of the world as a whole. In this respect, a major distinction between Plato and Aristotle is that Plato posits the demiurge who as a god acts purposefully to impose order on the cosmos and, in so doing, introduces a design or *telos* for the cosmos that not only lifts it out of chaos but also establishes a template for rational and moral order as the highest standard to which human beings can aspire. Both Plato and Aristotle are thinking causally, but by way of contrast, for Aristotle order is inherent in the nature of the cosmos itself and thus has no initial beginning. His Prime Mover has a significant explanatory role in Aristotle's system as the necessary source of motion for an otherwise static reality. In the *Physics* (VIII 4–6), Aristotle, following the logic of Parmenides that nothing comes from nothing, finds "surprising difficulties" explaining even commonplace change and requires "a fair bit of technical machinery." His causal thinking takes on a more complex form. This "machinery" includes the four causes, potentiality and actuality, hylomorphism, and his theory of categories. Further and perhaps most fundamentally, Aristotle insists that "the bare existence of change requires the postulation of a first cause, an unmoved mover whose necessary existence underpins the ceaseless activity of the world of motion."[95]

---

95. Christopher Shields, *Aristotle* (New York: Routledge, 2007), 196, 226.

Although this Prime Mover does not have a direct creative function, it too is a source of order in the sense that with its eternality, it is the inspiration for the constant reproduction and continuity of all of the natural and moral orders. With all things aspiring to the Prime Mover's immortality, the Prime Mover becomes a teleological cause of the coalescence and organic unity in what would otherwise be a fragmented cosmic order.

The demiurge in Plato is a craftsman, and working with the materials at hand, he must function with reason and intelligence on the one hand while deferring to the necessity of what is given on the other. He works to shape the cosmos from an unchanging original model and, in his best efforts to capture its perfection, makes a replica of it for the world of change. In some ways we might extrapolate from the demiurge to the philosopher, where just as the god must craft as stable and complete a copy of the original as he can, so too philosophers must make their account of the original template as reliable as they can. This single god is perfectly rational and good, standing in stark contrast to the conception of capricious gods that in Greece dominated popular religion at this time. It is the fact that Plato's demiurge behaves in a consistent and invariable way that guarantees the underlying order of the natural and moral cosmos.

***

Timaeus:[96] Our starting-point lies, I think, in the following distinction: what is it that always is, but never comes to be, and what is it that comes to be but never is? The former, since it is always consistent, can be grasped by the intellect with the support of a reasoned account, while the latter is the object of belief, supported by unreasoning sensation, since it is generated and passes away, but never really is. Now, anything created is necessarily created by some cause, because nothing can possibly come to be without there being something that is responsible for its coming to be. Also, whenever a craftsman takes something consistent as his model, and reproduces its form and proper-ties, the result is bound in every case to be a thing of beauty, but if he takes as his model something that has been created,

---

96. The following quotations from the *Timaeus* are from Plato, *Timaeus*, in *Timaeus and Critias*, © Oxford University Press, 2008. Reproduced with permission of the Licensor through PLSclear.

the product is bound to be imperfect. The whole universe or world . . . has come to be. After all, it is visible, tangible, and corporeal, and everything with these properties is perceptible, and we have already demonstrated that everything perceptible—which is to say, everything that is grasped by belief with the support of sensation—is subject to creation and belongs to the class of things that have come to be.

Now, we've already said that anything created is necessarily created by some cause. But it would be a hard task to discover the maker and father of this universe of ours, and even if we did find him, it would be impossible to speak of him to everyone. So what we have to ask is, again, which of those two kinds of model the creator was using as he constructed the universe. Was he looking at what is consistent and permanent or at what has been created? Well, if this universe of ours is beautiful and if its craftsman was good, it evidently follows that he was looking at an eternal model, while he was looking at a created model if the opposite is the case—though it's blasphemous even to think it. It's perfectly clear, then, that he used an eternal model, because nothing in creation is more beautiful than the world and no cause is better than its maker. The craftsman of this universe, then, took as his model that which is grasped by reason and intelligence and is consistent, and it necessarily follows from these premises that this world of ours is an image of something.[97]

***

But we need to apply rational thought to achieve more clarity about these matters, by asking the following questions. Is there such a thing as fire which is just itself? And what about all the other things we constantly describe in the same way, as each being just itself? Or is this kind of reality found only in things that are visible or otherwise perceptible by the bodily senses, and is the perceptible world, then, all that exists? . . .

Speaking for myself, this is how I cast my vote: if knowledge and true belief are two distinct kinds of thing, then these

---

97. Plato, *Timaeus*, in *Timaeus and Critias*, trans. Robin Waterfield and intro. Andrew Gregory (Oxford: Oxford University Press, 2008), 16–17, 27d–29b.

entities absolutely do exist in themselves, even though they are accessible only to our minds, not to our senses; but if, as some people think, true belief is no different from knowledge, then we must count all the things we perceive with our bodily senses as the most reliable things in existence.

But we're bound to claim that knowledge and true belief are different, because they occur under different circumstances and are dissimilar. In the first place, the former is a result of instruction, the latter of persuasion; in the second place, the former is always accompanied by a true account, while the latter cannot explain itself at all; in the third place, the former is unmoved by persuasion, while the latter can be persuaded to change; and finally, we have to claim that the former is the property of the gods, but of scarcely any human beings, while the latter is something every man has.

This being so, we have to admit that there exists, first, the class of things which are unchanging, uncreated, and undying, which neither admit anything else into themselves from elsewhere nor enter anything else themselves, and which are imperceptible by sight or any of the other senses. This class is the proper object of intellect. Then, second, there is the class of things that have the same names as the members of the first class and resemble them, but are perceptible, created, and in perpetual motion, since they come into existence in a particular place and subsequently pass away from there. This class is grasped by belief with the support of sensation.[98]

Eighth Anticipation

In the *Timaeus*, Plato's teleology establishes a necessary link between the intelligent design of the cosmos and human values, where mankind does well to live and think in a way that is modeled on and consistent with the rational perfection inherent in the natural and moral order. The lives of humankind with all of their imperfections are lived in a cosmos of divine origin and purpose, and it behooves human beings in all they do to conform to this bequest of an independent and unchanging standard of what is good. As Timaeus speculates:

98. Plato, *Timaeus*, 44–45, 51b–52a.

Let's simply state that the reason and purpose of this gift is as follows: the gods invented and supplied us with vision to enable us to observe the rational revolutions of the heavens and to let them affect the revolutions of thought within ourselves (which are naturally akin to those in the heavens, though ours are turbulent while they are calm). That is, the gods wanted us to make a close study of the circular motions of the heavens, gain the ability to calculate them correctly in accordance with their nature, assimilate ours to the perfect evenness of the god's, and so stabilize the wandering revolutions within us.[99]

What is divine in the human being has been endowed in us by an independent, divine source, and the best way to nurture this aspect is by living the life of the philosopher. In so doing, we are able to restore our endowment to its original condition:

But there is only one way that anyone can take care of anything, and that is by giving it food and exercise that is congenial to it. So, since the movements that are naturally akin to our divine part are the thoughts and revolutions of the universe, these are what each of us should be guided by as we attempt to reverse the corruption of the circuits in our heads, that happened around the time of our birth, by studying the harmonies and revolutions of the universe. In this way, we will restore our nature to its original condition by assimilating our intellect to what it is studying and, with such assimilation, we will achieve our goal: to live, now and in the future, the best life that the gods have placed within human reach.[100]

Human conformity to a transcendent and thus independent divine source as its model of self-realization stands in stark contrast to the collateral relationship between *tian* 天 and human beings in Chinese cosmology. The inseparability of *tian* and the human world in this cosmology is often expressed with the mantra "the continuity between and inseparability of *tian* and human beings" (*tianrenheyi* 天人合一). This statement is consistent with Tang Junyi's cosmological postulate "the

99. Plato, *Timaeus*, 38, 47b–c.

100. Plato, *Timaeus*, 96, 90c–d.

inseparability of one and many" (*yiduobufenguan* 一多不分觀) where the mutual shaping and being shaped of one and many again provides a clear contrast with the causal "One-behind-the-many" model implicit in the theology of the *Timaeus*. The relationship between the one and many becomes a vitally important religious question because it is in this respect that Confucian religiousness stands in greatest divergence to the asymmetry between human beings and their God as it is commonly understood in the Abrahamic religions, informed as these religions have been historically by the causal language of Greek philosophy. In this mainstream Abrahamic theology, the aseity or self-sufficiency of a perfect and thus unchanging God, means that human morality at the end of the day is entirely derivative of God, and that human beings do not make a difference in themselves. God is everything; human beings are nothing. And the role of the human being is simply to worship and to obey.

In the language of the theologian Friedrich Schleiermacher, who describes such religiousness as a doctrine of "absolute dependence," one can hear the echoes of Greek ontology, the unity of being, and the causal language through which this unity of being is expressed. For Schleier-macher, "the feeling of absolute dependence . . . is not to be explained as an awareness of the world's existence, but only as an awareness of the existence of God, as the absolute undivided unity."[101] Schleiermacher uses this language of "absolute dependence"—a self-abnegating defer-ence to a self-sufficient, independent Deity—as a positive expression of religious humility. But contrary to Schleiermacher who finds great solace in this claim, others within the Abrahamic tradition itself might regard such a doctrine in relieving human beings of any responsibility save faith and obedience to be morally questionable if not indeed repugnant. At issue here is what William James as a term of abject criticism calls "a block universe"—a world devoid of individuality and particularity. John Dewey, in explaining the expression "a block universe" as it is used by his visionary mentor James states that

> mechanism and idealism were abhorrent to him [William James] because they both hold to a closed universe in which there is no room for novelty and adventure. Both sacrifice individuality and all the values, moral and aesthetic, which hang upon indi-

---

101. Friedrich D. E. Schleiermacher, *The Christian Faith*, ed. H. R. Mackintosh and J. S. Stewart (London: T & T Clark, 1999), 132.

viduality, for according to absolute idealism, as to mechanistic materialism, the individual is simply a part determined by the whole of which he is a part. Only a philosophy of pluralism, of genuine indetermination, and of change that is real and intrinsic gives significance to individuality. It alone justifies struggle in creative activity and gives opportunity for the emergence of the genuinely new.[102]

One understanding of the liberating humanism of the European renaissance is that by insisting upon the intrinsic worth of human beings in themselves without reference to a transcendent and thus independent God, such humanistic values were a direct challenge to just such a hegemonic and oppressive religiousness. Historically, what follows from renaissance humanism is a basic distinction between the "strict transcendence" that grounds Greek ontology and the dualistic worldview that follows from it, on the one hand, and the pantheistic "transcendentalism" that we associate with the British Romantics such as Coleridge and Wordsworth, and importantly, with Ralph Waldo Emerson, on the other. These two terms—transcendence and transcendentalism—are obviously similar, and as consequence, the important distinction that separates them is often elided. If we take Emerson as an example, he famously says "trust thyself: every heart vibrates to that iron string"[103] and seems to celebrate the kind of "individuality" that Dewey defines as "the realization of what we specifically are as distinct from others."[104] Indeed, it is particularly in the example of the singular person of Emerson himself that we have the strongest sense of the inimitable worth of each person. Emerson exhorts us:

> Be yourself; no base imitator of another, but your best self. There is something which you can do better than another. Listen to the inward voice and bravely obey that. Do the things at which you are great, not what you were never made for. . . . The energetic action of the times develops individualism, and the religious

---

102. John Dewey, *The Moral Writings of John Dewey*, ed. James Gouinlock (New York: Prometheus Books, 2002), 35.

103. Emerson, "Self-Reliance."

104. John Dewey, *Early Works, 1892–98*, 5 vols., ed. Jo Ann Boydston (Carbondale: Southern Illinois University Press, 1971), vol. 3, 304.

appear isolated. I esteem this a step in the right direction. Heaven deals with us on no representative system. Souls are not saved in bundles.[105]

Quite early in his career, Dewey like Emerson before him rejects conventional "religion" as institutionalized dogmatism competing with equally misguided modern science in its claims about "Truth." Yet Dewey in his writings still insists on retaining not only the term "religious" but even the term "God" to connote "the sense of the connection of man, in the way of both dependence and support, with the enveloping world that the imagination feels is a universe."[106] Dewey not only rejects supernaturalism but sees the organized religion built around it as a very real obstacle to the possibility of realizing a religiousness that, far from being a separate kind of experience, is a quality that can be achieved in all aspects of the human experience. The institutions and rituals of conventional religions promote a kind of assimilation of and uniformity among their practitioners, and they not only fail to produce the religious quality of experience for these adherents but in fact are anathema to the distinctive individuality that Dewey believes to be the substance of such inspired living. In Dewey's own words, "It is conceivable that the present depression in religion is closely connected with the fact that religions now prevent, because of their weight of historic encumbrances, the religious quality of experience from coming to consciousness and finding the expression that is appropriate to present conditions, intellectual and moral."[107] It is for this reason that Dewey is unwilling to surrender religiousness to those who, in either affirming or denying it, assume that by definition religiousness requires supplication to some transcendent and supernatural object of worship. In his own historical context, Dewey is radically iconoclastic in his "firm belief that the claim on the part of religions to possess a monopoly of ideals and of the supernatural means by which alone, it is alleged, they can be furthered, stands in the way of the realization of distinctively religious values inherent in natural experience."[108] Indeed, Dewey is uncompromising and even harsh in calling for

---

105. Emerson, "Self-Reliance."

106. Dewey, *Later Works*, vol. 9, 36.

107. Dewey, *Later Works*, vol. 9, 31.

108. Dewey, *Later Works*, vol. 9, 33.

"the emancipation of the religious from religion."[109] Within the Western narrative itself, we can find a clear distinction between Schleiermacher's mainstream God-centered religiousness that uses the language of "absolute dependence" and the liberating countercurrent of an alternative, human-centered religiousness we find among the transcendentalists and the classical pragmatists as well.

When we turn to Confucian human-centered religiousness, what is important and fundamentally different from the mainstream Judeo-Christian theology as it was informed by Greek philosophy is that *tian* and human beings have a collateral although hierarchical relationship in which they are defining of each other, with *tian* occupying the higher position in the hierarchy. *Tianrenheyi* 天人合一 as the mantra invoked to describe Confucian religiousness describes the inseparability between the numinous and the human experience, and between the cultural and natural context and the human thinking and living that takes place within it. Importantly, given the resolutely inseparable *heyi* relation that obtains between humans and their context, this expression is not describing the putting together of what were originally two separate things. Indeed, since it is the relation between humankind and *tian* that is first order with *tian* and humanity being second-order abstractions from the relationship, the project then is not to integrate two aspects of our experience that are originally independent of each other but rather to optimize the correlative and interdependent possibilities of what is a shared experience.

The *heyi* relation is a *yinyang* contrastive yet mutually entailing relationship of two inseparable, "aspectual" features of experience that have to be understood in terms of each other. Like the heavens and the earth (*tiandi* 天地), the numinous and the human (*tianren* 天人) are also one and two at the same time. It is thus that such correlative expressions are not simply descriptive but are also prescriptive. The normative concern is with the "depth of coalescence" (*du* 度) that can be cultivated and achieved in their first-order relationality. The relationship itself is fecund and generative, with *tian* and *ren* working together collaboratively to build the connector for their own time and place and to extend the cosmic order in doing so, what is expressed as the world-making of *hongdao* 弘道 and *dadao* 达道. And *tian* and *ren* in their dyadic yet resolutely constitutive relationship are to be understood as mutually doing and undergoing, shaping and being shaped.

---

109. Dewey, *The Essential Dewey*, vol. 1, 410.

It is clear that human beings in this *tianren* relationship derive much benefit from the ancestral/numinous/cultural/natural resources denoted by *tian*. *Tian* certainly provides human beings with the context for flourishing and serves us as a model of order to emulate and revere. But since the relationship between *tian* and human beings is irreducibly collateral, we have to ask: What does *tian* get in this relationship from human beings? Even with *tian*'s higher status, far from *tian* being independent of human beings, it is often anthropomorphized to take on a human visage. That is, one way in which the Confucian canons invest the opaque notion of *tian* with meaning and make it in degree determinate for their readers is by putting a human face on what would otherwise remain a remote and recondite concept. Just as persons of stature and accomplishment in traditional Chinese paintings are depicted as proportionately much larger than their retinue, so too in the canonical description of consummate persons there is a tendency to present them hyperbolically in celestial terms.

In the literature, culturally significant human beings—persons such as the Duke of Zhou and Confucius—are analogized as the sun and moon and thus ascend to become the countenance of *tian*, where *tian* itself is made determinate in their narratives as persons. Not only does *tian* entail anthropomorphism, thereby making "gods" human-like, but *tian* is also a euhemeristic "theomorphism" wherein truly worthy persons as exemplars and sages become god-like. Worthiness in the human world expands and contributes to the meaning of *tian*. As a narrative infused by the contributions of a long lineage of ancestors and cultural heroes, we have a warrant for asserting that *tian* itself is thus genealogical and biographical.

What it means to become human is constantly being reshaped by *tian* that serves as the natural and cultural context for personal cultivation, where the richer the context, the more resources are available for this Confucian project. At the same time, the sages as the highest order of human beings are generative of additional cosmic meaning and thus have a role in the increase in the resources available for personal cultivation. Again, *tian* itself is being shaped and extended symbiotically by sagacious conduct as it thus elevates the human experience. That is to say, *tian* is a living, cumulative, and normative regularity, inclusive of nature and nurture, that is not only inseparable from the human experience but is in important degree expressive of it. Persons are born into a world informed by the language and values of a particular cultural legacy, and in this context, they have the opportunity to enculturate themselves and to thus refine and even enchant the human experience. The sages as the most successful among these cultivated human beings in turn contribute a new quantum of meaning to *tian* as the aggregating cultural legacy, with the intimate relationship between humankind and this world-centered sense of the divine continuing to evolve.

Aristotle: Socrates as a Human Being

The civilizations that share the Indo-European group of languages are certainly many and diverse, but by virtue of trade, travel, war, population movements, and the imperceptible dissemination of ideas entailed by their complex narratives, they have over past millennia developed a cultural family resemblance. Friedrich Nietzsche asserts that presuppositions behind a particular worldview have over time been sedimented into the family of Indo-European languages that both shape and constrain the semiotic structures of these disparate yet in some ways continuous cultures. As a consequence of this shared history, the culturally specific Indo-European languages in their various modes of expression encourage certain philosophical possibilities while discouraging others. Nietzsche observes: "The strange family resemblance of all Indian, Greek, and German philosophizing is explained easily enough. Where there is an affinity of languages, it cannot fail, owing to the common philosophy of grammar—I mean owing to the unconscious domination and guidance by similar grammatical functions—that everything is prepared at the outset for a similar development and sequence of philosophical systems; just as the way seems barred against certain other possibilities of world-interpretation."[110] Moving exclusively among these kindred Indo-European languages can over time "naturalize" what are actually culturally specific assumptions and can lull us into a sense of common conceptual commitments that become illusory when we look to traditions that lie beyond this shared history.

To take just one example, in the Western cosmogonic traditions such as the book of Genesis, Hesiod's *Theogony*, and Plato's *Timaeus*, the particular understanding of causal "beginnings," whether they pertain to the cosmos as a whole or to the creatures that populate it, has a determinative influence over the way a culture comes to conceive of the nature and order

---

110. Friedrich Nietzsche, *Beyond Good and Evil*, trans. W. Kaufmann (New York: Vintage, 1966), 20.

of things.[111] In fact, the causal thinking so prominent in Plato, and many but not all of the early Greek philosophers who preceded him, is rooted in a certain kind of cosmogonic speculation. In classical Greek philosophy, the term *kosmos* itself connotes a clustered range of meanings, including *arche* (originative, material, and efficient cause/ultimate indemonstrable principle), *logos* (underlying organizational principle), *theoria* (contemplation/thinking thinking itself), *nomos* (law), *theios* (divinity), *nous* (active and passive intellect). In combination, this cluster of terms conjures forth a notion of a single-ordered Divine universe originated and governed by natural and moral principles ultimately intelligible to the human mind.[112] Simply put, the cosmic structure is derived from and patterned after the causal agency that is responsible for the construal of a *kosmos* out of chaos. In such a *kosmos* that by definition derives from a single principle of order, everything is "in principle" explicable.

In ancient Greece, the preference for permanence and "being" over process and "becoming" requires a causal agency to account for change. In a metaphysical cosmogony, the originative principle (examples being Plato's demiurge, Aristotle's Prime Mover, and the Abrahamic God) stands independent of its creatures in bringing order to chaos. Natural change is then driven by a linear teleology that takes us from creation to the realization of the given design. Such cosmogony is very ambitious: that is, the philosophical move is to trace the "many" back to the ordering "One" and, in so doing, to cancel contingency and render all things intelligible.

Aristotle's cosmology is certainly different from Plato's, but for all of their vaunted differences, this teacher and student do share a significant number of dispositions that render their disputes in large measure family quarrels among proponents of a common culture. Both of them take metaphysics to be the search for ultimate causes and hence believe in a single-ordered world. Both have faith in the efficacy of reason in the search for the laws that define the structure of the world and the relation of the human mind to that structure. And this faith in reason in turn leads each to defend the

---

111. For an extended discussion of alternative conceptions of beginnings taken from a comparative perspective, see François Jullien, *The Book of Beginnings* (New Haven: Yale University Press, 2016).

112. Not all cosmogonies in the classical Greek tradition entail a single-ordered world. Indeed, the notion of *kosmos* as a single-ordered world is relatively late, with early Greek philosophers such as Anaximander and Empedocles, for example, having multiple world cosmogonies.

ideal of a philosophical system that reflects the structure of the world and the human relationship to it. With respect to *eidos* itself, it is the formal cause of things, where with Aristotle's *eidos* being immanent in matter rather than transcendent of it, it still directs the formation of things. Aristotle's *eidos* defines the origins of things and is coupled with their final cause or *telos* that specifies their given purpose and end. For Plato and Aristotle both, *eidos* as the intelligible essence of existents is the proper object of knowledge and thus serves as the foundation for their taxonomical epistemologies. Against the background of such profound ontological agreements, their significantly different attitudes toward the disposition and importance of the phenomenal world in philosophical thinking seems somewhat less dramatic.

Aristotle in his application of this causal thinking, like Hegel as mentioned before, was concerned with the question of where the philosophical investigation begins. And in looking for this beginning, we can say that Aristotle also like Hegel, but much earlier, took the question What is a person? as the starting point of his inquiry. That is, Aristotle's *Categories* is the first text of the *Organon* in the standard *Corpus Aristotelicum*. And Aristotle's initial project in the *Categories* is to identify the full set of questions that must be asked to give a comprehensive account of what can be predicated of a subject, with his own concrete example of this subject being "the man in the market-place." In the several different versions of these categories found throughout his corpus, "What?" is not only his first question but also his primary one. The primacy of the "What?" question lies in the fact that, in Aristotle's answer to it, he introduces an ontological disparity by first identifying and privileging the necessary essence or substance of the subject (Gk. *ousia*, L. *substantia*)—that is: What "is" a man? It is only when the subject has been thus identified that we can then follow up with questions that distinguish this person's various secondary and contingent attributes: "What can be said about and is thus 'in' a man?"

Aristotle explains this ontological distinction between substance and attribute in the following terms:

> Of things said without any combination, each signifies either substance or quantity or qualification or a relative or where or when or being-in-a-position or having or doing or being-affected. To give a rough idea, examples of substance are man, horse; of quantity: four-foot, five-foot; of qualification: white, grammatical; of a relative: double, half, larger; of where: in the Lyceum, in the market-place; of when: yesterday, last-year; of

being-in-a-position: is-lying, is-sitting; of having: has-shoes-on, has-armour-on; of doing: cutting, burning; of being-affected: being-cut, being-burned.[113]

Stated the other way round, what cannot be said about a man and is not "in" a man is the primary substance (*protai ousiai*) that makes him a particular person. We might take Socrates who seems to actually have made his home in the agora as our example of "the man in the market-place." Aristotle states clearly that "every substance seems to signify a certain 'this.'" As regards the primary substances, it is indisputably true that each of them signifies a certain 'this'; for the thing revealed is individual and numerically one."[114] Aristotle then further clarifies the primary subject as a distinctive and phenomenal "this" by observing that

> a *substance*—that which is called a substance most strictly, primarily, and most of all—is that which is neither said of a subject nor in a subject, e.g., the individual man or the individual horse. The species in which the thing's primarily called substances are, are called *secondary substances*, as also are the genera of these species. For example, the individual man belongs in a species, man, and animal is a genus of the species; so these—both man and animal—are called secondary substances.[115]

The person of Socrates is thus hylomorphic, adding to his primary and individuating material substance (*hyle*) what are his formal aspects (*eidos* and *telos*) as the secondary substances. Substance (*ousia*) as subject is "that which underlies." The primary substance itself "is neither said of a subject nor in a subject," and what can be said "of" Socrates but are not present "in" him are secondary substances. Secondary substances are a hierarchy of universals that begin with what is closest to him, the species (*eidos*) "man" and then the increasingly abstract genera more distant from him: hominoid, mammal, animal, animate creature, and so on, and are essential to Socrates in the sense that without them he could not be Socrates. And again, the

113. Aristotle, *Categories*, *The Complete Works*, 4, 1b25–2a4.

114. Aristotle, *Categories*, *The Complete Works*, 6, 3b10–12.

115. Aristotle, *Categories*, *The Complete Works*, 4, 2a14–19.

species and genera are the only things that can be said about the subject to be called secondary substances "for only they, of things predicated, reveal the primary substance."[116]

In this hierarchical taxonomy, the relationship of the primary substance to the secondary substances is repeated in the relationship between what is more specific and more general in the relationship between species as *eidos* and genera. Aristotle argues that "as the primary substances stand to the other things, so the species stands to the genus: the species is a subject for the genus (for the genera are predicated of the species but the species are not predicated reciprocally of the genera). Hence for this reason too the species is more a substance than the genus."[117] For Aristotle, the "What?" question has primacy because it provides us with the hylomorphic, essential subject. The "What?" identifies the underlying primary and secondary substances that are defining of who Socrates *is*. The various other questions that are prompted by the remaining nonsubstance conditions—quantity, quality, relation, place, time, position, state, action, and affection—seek to provide us with the full complement of attributes that are "in" Socrates as a subject or can be said "of" him as a subject. These attributes or accidents describe Socrates as contingent and conditional predicates, none of which can exist without supervening on this particular subject. Aristotle, in giving ontological primacy to the phenomenal subject, insists that "all the other things are either said of the primary substances as subjects or in them as subjects. . . . So if the primary substances did not exist it would be impossible for any of the other things to exist."[118] It is interesting and important to note that the set of questions Aristotle asks in search of a complete predication do not include "How?" or "Why?" This omission is because in his substance ontology, the inherent causal entailments—that is, his *eidos* and his *telos* as his formal and final cause respectively—already answer the "How?" and "Why?" questions. Socrates, given his formal definition, has the potential that when actualized makes him fully a man. Hence, the presence of the formal essence and the final *telos* as a man makes the explanatory questions of How? and Why? moot. Aristotle assumes that a complete propositional description of the subject does not require such further causal

116. Aristotle, *Categories*, *The Complete Works*, 5, 2b30.

117. Aristotle, *Categories*, *The Complete Works*, 5, 2b18–20.

118. Aristotle, *Categories*, *The Complete Works*, 5, 2b3–6.

explanation, an assumption that we will see is untenable in Chinese process cosmology.

Angus Graham in reflecting upon Aristotle's strategy for providing a complete description of something, and on what this strategy reveals about Aristotle's categories, observes that "Aristotle's procedure is to isolate one thing from others, treating even transitive verbs ('cuts,' 'burns') as objectless, and even the relative ('half,' 'bigger') as not relating two things but said of one with reference to the other."[119] We can say of the man in the market-place that "he-burns" or "he-cuts" as a predicate without the need of stipulating the object of these actions, and we can say "he-is-bigger" as a characteristic "of" him in reference to a second person rather than describing the relationship between the two.

Aristotle's substance or essentialist ontology introduces a notion of discrete individuality that, with the further implications of self-sufficiency and simple location, favors grammatically the noun form. His first example of a subject, the "man in the market-place," is the bearer of the attributes that can then be ascribed to him. David Weissman, in his work on social ontology, describes Aristotle as asserting a kind of discrete identity that makes human "beings" into first-order individuals, who then, on the basis of second-order, external relations, come into association with other persons. In Weissman's reading of Aristotle, "things that have matter and form—primary substance—are freestanding. Each is self-sufficient. . . . Aristotle would have us believe that a thing's relations to other things—including spatial, temporal, and causal relations—are incidental to its identity. He reasoned that identity is established by form, so that relations to other things may only support, somewhat disguise, or threaten the thing."[120]

One of the corollaries of an Aristotelian substance ontology that would give privilege to Socrates as a discrete, individual subject is that our experience of this world is one populated by isolatable things or objects that, like Socrates, "object" to us in standing off as being independent of us. And a second corollary of this ontology is the doctrine of external relations entailed by the independence of things. That is, substance ontology construes these various independent objects each with its own essential integrity as first-order, discrete things—what they really *are*. Then any relations that might bring them into association and conjoin them with other things are

---

119. Graham, *Studies in Chinese Philosophy and Philosophical Literature*, 380.

120. David Weissman, *A Social Ontology* (New Haven: Yale University Press, 2000), 95.

only second-order, contingent relations that they subsequently contract. Socrates as the man in the market-place is first and foremost a discrete, self-sufficient, and independent individual. Any and all of his relationships with his various protégés including Plato himself that are remembered in the dialogues, as important as they are, can only be second-order and thus contingent rather than constitutive relations.

In formulating his substance ontology, Aristotle seems to be responding directly to what we too might find most unsatisfying in Plato's objective idealism: that is, Plato's failure to give us a clearer account of the relationship between the universal Form and the particular instances of it.[121] In Plato, the Forms are given ontological priority and have transcendent status as what is really real. Individual things being causally dependent upon these Forms are in some sense a copy of them and are thus less real. Plato states explicitly that the Forms are "the real nature (*ousia*) of any given thing—what it actually is."[122] Aristotle is impatient with Plato's transcendentalism, and in his hylomorphic understanding of concrete things as being a composite of form and matter, he reverses Plato's ontological priority by making the individual things themselves primary and basic. In making this argument, Aristotle avers that "another characteristic of substances is that there is nothing contrary to them. For what could be contrary to a primary substance? For example, there is nothing contrary to an individual man, nor yet is there anything contrary to man or animal."[123]

For Aristotle, ontology begins with the vital Socrates for whom there is no opposite either as a unique person or as a species called humans or animals. Socrates is real rather than being a mere appearance of some higher order reality and, in this respect, is one of a kind. And if we confine ourselves to the *Categories*, Aristotle is asserting that even though the formal and final causes (*eidos* and *telos*) persist unchanged through change, he says explicitly that these secondary substances could *not* exist independent of individuals such as Socrates. Again, although these unique hylomorphic substances themselves "have" no contraries, they are able to "receive" contraries. He again observes explicitly that what is most distinctive of substance is "that what is numerically one and the same is able to receive contraries. . . . For

---

121. Plato himself is also keenly aware of what he calls "the dilemma of participation" and tries to give an account of it in *Parmenides* 131a–c.

122. Plato, *Phaedo, The Last Days of Socrates*, 126, 65e.

123. Aristotle, *Categories, The Complete Works*, 7, 3b24–27.

example, an individual man—one and the same—becomes pale at one time and dark at another, and hot and cold, and bad and good."[124]

Even though there is no contrary to Socrates as a person, he is disposed to the contingent contraries of being young or old, of being wise or foolish, of being handsome or otherwise. Aristotle is here asserting the uniqueness of Socrates and thus affirming the reality of the phenomenal world in which we and Socrates both live. At the same time, in claiming immanental status for the secondary formal substances, Aristotle is attempting to escape Plato's transcendental idealism. But does he? With Aristotle's insistence that species (*eidos*) and final causes (*telos*) only exist in particular things, these formal aspects are still immutable universals and, as such, continue only in an immanental form Plato's objectivism and foundationalism. At the end of the day, Aristotle's *eidos* and *telos* are still "transcendent" in the sense that as the causal explanation of things, they remain separate, independent, indivisible, and unaffected by the material and efficient causes. As Aristotle himself insists, Socrates cannot be any more or less a "man" than any other, "for substance, it seems, does not admit of a more and a less. . . . For example, if this substance is a man, it will not be more a man or less a man either than itself or than another man. For one man is not more a man than another . . . [and] is not called more a man now than before. . . . Thus substance does not admit of a more and a less."[125]

Ninth Anticipation

The identities of Plato and Aristotle's discrete human "beings" are first explained in a causal, substance language and are then conjoined by second-order, external, and contingent relations. Confucian human "becomings," by way of contrast, are holographic, interpenetrating, focal centers of constitutive relations in what we have called a focus-field conception of persons. To be clear, focal "things" and the vital relations that constitute them are both first order as two ways of perceiving the same phenomenon. In the process cosmology that sets the interpretive context for the Confucian understanding of persons, this alternative, holistic, focus-field model begins from the primacy of vital relationality. In clarifying the nature of "relations" that is relevant to this Chinese cos-

---

124. Aristotle, *Categories, The Complete Works*, 7, 4a10–21.

125. Aristotle, *Categories, The Complete Works*, 7, 3b35–39.

mology, Angus Graham uses his own his language of first-order, "concrete patterns" versus second-order, abstract "relations between things" and is thus introducing a distinction between internal, constitutive relations versus external, contingent relations. He avers that "as for 'relationships,' relation is no doubt an indispensable concept in exposition of Chinese thought, which generally impresses a Westerner as more concerned with the relations between things than with their qualities; but the concern is with concrete patterns rather than relations abstracted from them."[126] Graham is thus invoking a distinction between a doctrine of internal relations that are actually constitutive of erstwhile "things" and those second-order external relations that would merely conjoin things that are themselves discrete and independent of other things. In the former model, given that things are constituted by their relations, the familiar distinction between what something "is" and its relations has no purchase. Further, if everything is constituted by its relations, and if these relations have no boundary either synchronically or diachronically, then every particular thing is, more or less, relevant to any other particular thing. The primary consideration in identity formation then is proximity. That is, identity is a function of the relative importance and the priority to be given to the environing others within an always unique matrix of relations.

To invoke a concrete focus-field example, one explanation for the primacy of family as a model of order within classical Confucian philosophy is that each person is conceived of as a unique focus within their own specific field of family relations. The meaning of the family is implicated in and dependent upon the productive cultivation of each of its members, and the genealogy of both family lineage and the culture it embodies is transmitted through these human conduits. By extension, the meaning of the entire cosmos is in turn implicated in and dependent upon the productive cultivation of each person within family and community, and it expands accordingly to become a more meaningful cosmos. Personal cultivation thus produces not only familial and communal but also cosmic dividends. Importantly, while existential narratives themselves are certainly the lived lives of particular persons, they are also unbounded and interpenetrating stories within their natural, social, and cultural ecologies. Each person is nonfungible as a unique perspective on family, community, polity, and cosmos. And through a

126. Graham, "Replies," 288–289.

dedicated regimen of deliberate growth and articulation, everyone has the possibility of bringing focal resolution and thus a clearer and more meaningful intensity to their field of relationships.

I have previously given an account of the familial source of the ecological focus-field language and have tried to develop a more nuanced understanding of what the extended and unbounded "field" might mean in a "focus-field" notion of human agency. We might now turn to a closer reflection on what the process of particular persons "focusing" their field would entail and how such language might be useful in expressing a more complex and, at the same time, perhaps a more empirically coherent conception of personal identity and of its agency. We might begin by responding to a concern voiced by philosopher David B. Wong. Wong finds it unproblematic to allow that "fields take on definition through individuals and their relationships and in that sense are constituted by them." At the same time, Wong worries that "it is more difficult to say how a field constitutes individuals."[127] We might restate his concern here with a few specific examples. Wong is saying that it is easier to see how a family takes on its definition by virtue of the members who constitute it than it is to see how the family lineage comes to constitute each of its members. Or it is easier to see how history is constituted by a sequence of particular events than it is to see how each event has implicated within it the entire course of history. Or it is easier to see how a particular person speaks a language than it is to see how the language speaks the person. What I want to do here in explaining this notion of focus-field agency is to try to address the perceived asymmetry Wong feels between the unproblematic fields being constituted by their foci, on the one hand, and the less clear sense of foci being constituted by their fields on the other.

To begin with, just as we would want to distinguish between a leg and walking, we have to avoid our tendency to equivocate on the distinction between a body and a person, especially given the habituated individuating language we use such as "somebody," "everybody," "nobody" and "someone," "everyone," "no one." Indeed, we must acknowledge that walking unlike a leg is a focal, psycho- and sociosomatic event performed in and together with an unbounded world. In just this same way, we would do best within this relational cosmology to register a

---

127. David B. Wong, "Cultivating the Self in Concert with Others," in *Dao Companion to the Analects*, ed. Amy Olberding (Dordrecht: Springer, 2014), 191.

distinction between complex persons and their bodies and to think of persons as focal, narrative events who achieve their transactional and interdependent identities in and with the world around them.

Still, even as we can fairly claim that the unbounded totality is present within each moment of each eventful person's always unique experience, what prevents such an observation from being overwhelming is the meaningful resolution established through graduated degrees of relevance. In the focal identities of family members, for example, immediate, intimate relations are certainly closer to the focal center than distant relatives and those distant relatives closer than remote strangers. What is of key significance for particular persons in shaping the characteristic conduct that constitutes their unique identities is what nexus of relations within their field actually becomes focal, resolute, and habituated. We might want to think of our focal identities as the clines or gradients of what becomes most immediately significant for each of us as we try to bring our unique manifold of relationships into its most meaningful resolution. And again for most of us, what is focal and thus has such individuating privilege is our "embodied living" (*li* 禮) or perhaps "forms of life" within the continuing narrative of our roles and relations as they are lived in families and communities. At the same time, our many roles are performed through the always transactional activities we identify with the "living, existential body" (*ti* 體) inherited genealogically through our family lineages.

Indeed, this "narrative" understanding of persons that would allow the parsing of them as discrete and isolated individuals only as a convenient, functional abstraction provides us with the beginning of an answer to Wong's question about the kind of focal agency I have ascribed to Confucian role ethics. Although Wong in his reflections on Confucian ethics moves decisively in the direction of relational persons, he does not seem to take the primacy of relationality as far as we would want to go with it. Indeed, beyond "How does the field constitute the focus?" he asks a second question: "Who is 'in' the relationship?" Wong frames his second question thusly: "If I am the sum of my relationships, then who or what is the entity standing in each of these particular relationships?"[128] In asking this question, it would seem that Wong wants to maintain the primacy of first-order, discrete entities over their second-order relations with others and thus maintain a doctrine of external relations that are

---

128. Wong, "Cultivating the Self," 192.

formed only subsequently to conjoin such entities. And it would seem that Wong's answer to his own question, developed in his earlier work and retained in his most recent publications, is: "We begin life embodied as biological organisms and become persons by entering into relationship with others of our kind."[129] For Wong, simply put, there must be, both logically and temporally, two "entities" before there can be a relationship between them. He retains this position in spite of his specific reference to "biological organisms" that would seem by definition to embed such entities within the social and physical ecology of their environing others. In order to be clear in formulating our own answer to Wong's question about this focus-field agency, we will need to return to the distinction between the doctrines of external and internal relations.

In my answer to "Who is 'in' the relationship?" I would refrain from introducing post hoc divisions into the original experience that would then retrospectively abstract persons out of their family and social ecologies. Said another way, in a doctrine of internal and constitutive relations, the ostensive distinction between "things" and "their relations" has no purchase. Simply repeating my answer to Wong's first question, I would claim that focal persons who are constituted by fields of relations are not only "in" but quite literally *are* these first-order relations. I have never been a critically, self-conscious, and purposeful "me" without this "me" being this son, this brother, this husband, this teacher, this dad, this Canadian and then American immigrant, and so on. Quite simply, we are our narratives and all of the relational events that are pertinent to the story. And there is no need to reduplicate this intense and habitual focus or center of constitutive relationships by positing an antecedent and discrete "subject" within which this field of relationships must inhere.

William James warns us against such "substance" thinking and our "inveterate trick" of turning eventful referents into "things" when he observes that

> the low thermometer to-day, for instance, is supposed to come
> from something called the "climate." Climate is really only the

---

129. Wong, "Cultivating the Self," 192. See also his "Relational and Autonomous Selves," *Journal of Chinese Philosophy* 34, no. 4 (December 2004), and "If We Are Not by Ourselves, If We Are Not Strangers," in *Polishing the Chinese Mirror: Essays in Honor of Henry Rosemont, Jr.*, ed. Marthe Chandler and Ronnie Littlejohn (New York: Global Scholarly, 2008).

name for a certain group of days, but it is treated as if it lay behind the day, and in general we place the name, as if it were a being, behind the facts it is the name of. But the phenomenal properties of things . . . do not inhere in anything. They adhere, or cohere, rather, with each other, and the notion of a substance inaccessible to us, which we think accounts for such cohesion by supporting it, as cement might support pieces of a mosaic, must be abandoned. The fact of the bare cohesion itself is all the notion of the substance signifies. Behind that fact is nothing.[130]

In spite of our growing awareness of the resolutely ecological nature of the human experience, the tradition of substance ontology sedimented into our language, along with the doctrine of external relations that it entails, still continues to be our shared and default common sense. Such an ontology guarantees the primacy and the integrity of the discrete and independent entities Wong is positing when he allows that we as separate organisms "become persons by entering into relationship with others of our kind." But the movement away from assumptions about such a foundational individualism is becoming increasingly marked even within the mainstream Western discourse. For example, research scientist John Henry Clippinger in his monograph *A Crowd of One*, locates erstwhile individuals within this kind of relational nexus—albeit the "crowd" rather than the "family"—by appealing to biological metaphors. Clippinger challenges the ostensive boundaries that separate and delineate persons specifically as individual existents. For Clippinger, "there is no such thing as the 'individual' independent of the group. We are a crowd of one. There are no sharp dichotomies between species and environment, between one species and another, and between one race or religion and another."[131] Such a recent turn away from foundational individualism echoes the relationally constituted conception of persons posited by the classical pragmatists. Almost a century ago, in his *Individualism Old and New*, John Dewey worried over the growth in his time of an aberrant form of individualism that had broken with Emerson's promise to conjure forth for us a nonconformist and self-reliant American soul. Dewey rued

---

130. James, *The Works of William James*, vol. 1, *Pragmatism*, 46.

131. John Henry Clippinger, *A Crowd of One: The Future of Individual Identity* (New York: Public Affairs, 2007), 179.

the fact that real "individuality" as "the most characteristic activity of a self"[132]—that is, the Emersonian project of each of us aspiring after the highest quality of our own personal uniqueness—had degenerated into the then prevailing mercantile creed of a self-interested and contentious "individualism."

Dewey, in setting up a distinction between his own neologism "individuality" and what had become a then-decadent "individualism," goes on to exhort philosophers in their search for the Great Community to step up to the challenge of formulating a new conception of persons within the social organism that embodies the very "idea" of democracy as a personal, social, political, and ultimately religious ideal. Indeed, for Dewey, "the problem of constructing a new individuality consonant with the objective conditions under which we live is the deepest problem of our time."[133] Dewey challenges us to aspire after a relationally constituted "individuality" in which full personal realization and the communal flourishing that emerges from these achieved individualities are coterminous and mutually entailing.

Dewey in his advocacy for this intersubjective "individuality" can be read as a precursor to prominent contemporary philosophers such as Charles Taylor and Michael Sandel and their more recent reflections on how we become persons.[134] Charles Taylor in his *Sources of the Self* and continuing in his more recent monograph, *The Language Animal*, marries a doctrine of socially embedded persons who exemplify irreducibly "embodied agency" emerging within their "webs of interlocution," with a historically and culturally self-conscious form of a communicating communitarianism.[135] In Taylor's view, it is not only that we discover things about who we are through communicating with others, but much more radically, we can only become persons by narrating shared worlds of embodied experience.

---

132. Dewey, *Later Works*, vol. 7, 286.

133. Dewey, *Later Works*, vol. 5, 56.

134. A. T. Nuyen, "Confucian Role Ethics," *Comparative and Continental Philosophy* 4, no. 1 (2012): 141–150, offers some examples of recent Western ethical theorists who offer a relational and role-based conception of persons: Taylor, *Sources of the Self*; Dorothy Emmett, *Rules, Roles and Relations* (London: Macmillan, 1967); Marion Smiley, *Moral Responsibility and the Boundaries of Community* (Chicago: University of Chicago Press, 1992); and Larry May, *Sharing Responsibility* (Chicago: University of Chicago Press, 1992).

135. Taylor, *Sources of the Self* and *The Language Animal*.

As early as his *Liberalism and the Limits of Justice*, Michael Sandel too has been strongly critical of the deracinated self that serves as a starting point for the Kantian-cum-Rawlsian deontological conception of the individual.[136] Sandel in searching for a different and more interesting place to start, looks to an alternative "intersubjective" or, what he terms perhaps more accurately, an "intrasubjective" conception of self that the Rawlsian position by implication has clearly ruled out. Sandel in invoking the organic "intra-" as a preferred prefix to the atomistic "inter-," is making an important distinction here. Indeed, it is the distinction between a doctrine of internal versus external relations.

Aristotle's Causal Thinking

For Aristotle, with metaphysics being the search for ultimate causes (*aitia*), a responsible account of any item of experience must have recourse to a complete "causal" analysis. He defines four types of causes: the efficient (*kinoun*), material (*hyle*), formal (*eidos*), and final (*telos*) causes. We might summarize his own description of these causes in the *Metaphysics* in the following terms:

> We call a cause (1) that from which (as immanent material) a thing comes into being, e.g., the bronze of the statue and the silver of the saucer, and the classes which include these (2) the form or pattern, i.e., the formula of the essence, and the classes which include this, (e.g., the ratio 2:1 and number in general are causes of the octave) and the parts of the formula. (3) That from which the change or the freedom from change first begins, e.g., the man who has deliberated is a cause, and the father a cause of the child, and in general the maker a cause of the thing made and the change-producing of the changing. (4) The end, i.e., that for the sake of which a thing is, e.g., health is the cause of walking. For why does one walk? We say "in order that one be healthy," and in speaking thus we think we have given the cause.[137]

136. Michael Sandel, *Liberalism and the Limits of Justice* (Cambridge: Cambridge University Press, 1982).

137. Aristotle, *Metaphysics*, *The Complete Works*, 1600, 1013a24–36.

The material cause names the stuff of which this object is comprised. The formal cause designates its structure or pattern. The efficient cause is the agent or process that brings the object into being and maintains its existence. And the final cause names the end for which it exists or was made—its function and purpose. Previously, in rehearsing Aristotle's account of a full predication of "the man in the market-place" taking Socrates as our example, with the exception of Socrates's father as the efficient cause that transmits the formal and final causes, we saw that Aristotle was indeed employing a full causal analysis.

Such causal thinking was not new with Plato and Aristotle. Both of them referred to the earliest Greek philosophers, such as the Milesian thinkers Thales, Anaximander, and Anaximenes, as *physikoi*: those who sought the *logos* or explanation of things in their originating cause or *physis*. And the three Milesians gave as their answers to this explanatory cause: water, *apeiron* (infinite vortex), and air respectively.[138] For these early Milesians, we can speculate that they generally understood *physis* as: (1) the process of growth or *genesis* of things, (2) the physical stuff of which things are made, (3) the internal, organizational principle or structure of things, and (4) as something living, having a divine reference. David Skrbina in his work on panpsychism within the Western philosophical narrative argues that hylozoism was implicit in early Greek philosophy, insisting that "for the Milesians, matter (*hyle*) possessed life (*zoe*) as an essential quality. Something like hylozoism was simply accepted as a brute condition of reality."[139] Indeed, the complex understanding of *physis* with its assumed and uncritical doctrine of vitalism implicit in most of these early Greek thinkers was made explicit in the fragments of Heraclitus in which he uses the language of both *zoe* (life in the eternal and unbounded sense) and *bios* (life in the finite and individuated sense).

Aristotle, in the *Metaphysics* and following fast upon his discussion of the four causes enumerated earlier, provides his own summary account of *physis*, translated here as "nature," that echoes the understanding of the erstwhile "Presocratics":

> We call nature [*physis*] (1) The genesis of growing things. . . .
> (2) The primary immanent element in a thing, from which
> its growth proceeds. (3) The source from which the primary

---

138. Plato, *Phaedo* 96a; Aristotle, *Metaphysics*, *The Complete Works*, 1005a.

139. David Skrbina, *Panpsychism in the West* (Cambridge, MA: MIT Press, 2005), 24.

movement in each natural object is present in it in virtue of its own essence. . . . (4) Nature is the primary matter of which any non-natural object consists or out of which it is made, which cannot be modified or changed from its own potency, . . . where the first matter is preserved throughout. In this way people call the elements of *natural* objects also their nature, some naming fire, others earth, others air, others water, others something else of the sort, and some naming more than one of these, and others all of them. (5) Nature is the substance of natural objects. . . . And from this sense of "nature" every substance in general is in fact, by an extension of meaning, called a "nature," because the nature of a thing is one kind of substance.[140]

This hylozoistic reading of *physis* covers much of the ground of Aristotle's four causes, but his own interpretation of *physis* is not how the Milesian *physikoi* were characterized by those who came later. Indeed, the problem of misinterpreting these early Greek thinkers only begins with the anachronistic "Presocratic" label that has been applied to them since the late eighteenth century.[141] This label is inappropriate in suggesting that the Milesians are somehow preliminary to and less than Socrates, that there was some unifying theme that would bring them together under one term, and that they were concerned solely with cosmological issues rather than the ethics and politics that interested Socrates. At the same time and perhaps most importantly, such a description invites a systematic reading of the fragments of these early Greek thinkers through a lens that is not of their own making.

Aristotle himself characterizes the Milesians whom he himself calls *physikoi* to be the first "materialists," suggesting that their philosophies are incomplete because they evidence only one or at best two of his four causes while neglecting the others. In this description of the Milesians, Aristotle uses the term *hyle* or matter that he himself stipulates as being inert and formless. Even though *hyle* as a material "cause" does have its own a kind of potency, Aristotle's materialist designation of the Milesians largely ignores their more robust understanding of *physis* that includes vital and even theo-

---

140. Aristotle, *The Complete Works*, 1602, 1014b16–1015a13.

141. The term "Presocratic" was first coined and used by the German philosopher J. A. Eberhard as *vorsokratische Philosophie* in the late eighteenth century. See André Laks and Glenn Most, *The Concept of Presocratic Philosophy: Its Origin, Development and Significance* (Princeton: Princeton University Press, 2018), 1.

logical connotations such as growth, a principle of internal organization, and originative power.

Tenth Anticipation

Those modes of causal analysis couched in terms of the rational dominant are based on the notion of logical order and the rationalization of the human experience. The source of order and its design are antecedent to the process, where particulars are only relevant to the extent that they satisfy a given rationalized order. We might take a Platonic understanding of a triangle as an absolute, unchanging truth as an example, where the abstract, formal aspect of the triangle negates any material considerations. By way of contrast, aesthetic, first problematic assumptions we would associate with a work of art would lead us to characterize the pattern evidenced by things in a distinctly different manner. Causal language is the discourse of substances; correlative language is the discourse of processes. While logical order is disclosed by patterned regularity indifferent to the actual content of the particulars constituting the order, aesthetic order discloses an emergent ad hoc unity formed by irreplaceable details. The insistent particularity of these details stands in tension with the provisional harmony of the ad hoc unity, since the harmony cannot be appreciated except as a harmony of just those specific particulars. Logical order reveals a closed patterned unity; aesthetic order discloses its unique particulars.

Greek idealism with its causal thinking gives us the reductionist logic of one design behind the many. In this discourse of substances, to the extent that we as human beings have the same *eidos* and *telos*, we constitute one univocal order. Confucian process cosmology is fundamentally a holistic, aesthetic order. The language of consummate persons/conduct (*ren* 仁) and virtuosity (*de* 德) begins from the insistent focal particularity of each human becoming and stands in tension with the provisional harmony of the ad hoc unity we call *dao* 道. *Dao* is the unsummed totality of just those particulars that constitute it: the "myriad of things" characterized in the language of *wanwu* 萬物 or *wanyou* 萬有.

Later, in responding to and trying to explain Joseph Needham's claim that early Chinese cosmology has "its own causality and its own logic," I will describe an alternative, correlative sense of "causality" that I call *ziran* 自然 causality. This aesthetic understanding of "causality" contrasts with the Greek rationalized version in precisely these same holistic terms, beginning as it does from the insistent particular as the ultimate ordering factor. Instead of positing an antecedent source of order that then replicates its predetermined design, in this aesthetic *ziran* causality any particular thing is both the cause and the effect of everything else. With the Mona Lisa as an example, every concrete detail interpenetrates with every other detail as both cause and effect in producing the totality of the effect. And the totality of the effect, like *dao* as described earlier, is the unsummed totality of just those particulars that constitute it.[142] The tension between these specific particular details and the ad hoc unity we find in the totality of the effect arises because the work of art is always being interpreted and appreciated from one particular perspective or another.

In the place of causally oriented science, those who think correlatively investigate the concrete items of immediate feeling, perception, and imagination related in aesthetic or mythopoetic terms. While causal thinking is "vertical" in tracing events back to antecedent origins, correlative thinking is primarily "horizontal" in the sense that it involves the association of concrete experienceable items and events, usually without recourse to any supramundane realm. From the perspective of correlative thinking, to explain an item or event is first to place it within a scheme organized in terms of analogical relations among items selected for the scheme, and then to reflect and act in terms of the suggestiveness of these relations. Correlative thinking involves the association of image clusters related by meaningful disposition rather than by physical causation. Such thinking is a species of imagination grounded in necessarily informal and hence ad hoc analogical procedures presupposing both association and differentiation.

A simple illustration might clarify this point. In the most superficial understandings of totemic classifications, for example, the associating of a clan, a family, or a group with a particular animal or natural object is not based upon claims of a shared essence or upon an observed or inferred causal connection but on the assignment of a meaningful correlation. The meaning is a "created meaning" in the sense that selected characteristics of the totemic object elicit feelings or behaviors in the

---

142. For a substantial discussion of the important differences between classical Greek causality and this notion of *ziran*, see Zheng Kai, *The Metaphysics of Philosophical Daoism*, trans. Hanliang Ruan (New York: Routledge, 2021), 58–71.

human beings associated with it that help to establish the character and import of their own self-understanding as individuals, as well as their patterns of communal association. Totemic classification establishes a field of meaning among those individuals represented by various images.

Those who are suspicious of the explanatory force of such totemic correlations are so precisely because such schemes resist causal analysis. Correlative schemes would seem altogether arbitrary to a mind shaped by causal thinking. A rational individual is accustomed to assuming an objective ground that can underwrite standards of evidence, allowing for claims to at least plausibility if not certitude. But from the correlative perspective, the quest for certainty is overridden by a search for significance and efficacy. We need only to reflect on the immediate tension that often arises between advocates of biomedicine and traditional Chinese medicine to find a clear instance of causal versus correlative thinking.

When we look for some counterpart to early Greek cosmological theology, perhaps this distinction between causal and correlative thinking might provide some clarification. We find that just as with our prevailing systematic interpretations of Plato and Aristotle, there is a parallel attempt among sinologists to formulate and impose what is perhaps an overdetermined and unwarranted coherence on the evolution of early Chinese cosmology. It was in fact Nathan Sivin in his seminal essay "The Myth of the Naturalists" who brought some light to our still inadequate understanding of early *qi* 氣 cosmology. In tracing out what he takes to be three transitions in the evolution of the *yinyang* and five phases vocabulary, Sivin recounts how

> at the end of the Chou [Zhou] dynasty, in certain contexts, *wu hsing* [*wuxing* 五行] was a set of moral categories that could plausibly be linked to Mencius . . . [that] put individual self-cultivation at the center of the philosophic quest, and focused its disciplines increasingly on nurturing the "all-encompassing *ch'i* [*qi* 氣]" of the cosmos within oneself. . . . The second change, equally gradual, adapted this new emphasis to the urgent task of inventing a new political order as the old one collapsed once and for all. . . . By the end of the first century, *yin* and *yang* . . . and *wu hsing* . . . were . . . sets of qualifiers used to describe either two or five aspects of *ch'i*. They shared certain important characteristics: they were dynamic (accounting for change), relational (an attribute is defined by its relation to

others within the system of two or five), and aspectual (the choice between *yin-yang* and Five-phases analysis depends on what aspect of the phenomena one wants to discuss).[143]

Sivin's main point here is that relations among the notions of *yinyang*, *wuxing*, and *qi* certainly underwent a process of development. But far from these terms constituting a systematic and technical cosmological terminology used to describe physical phenomena, from the very outset they were fundamentally a morally and politically invested vocabulary constituting a loose, often disjointed framework for understanding, explaining, and prescribing the human experience in its broadest terms. Sivin and other scholars have cautioned us against an unjustifiable confidence in what we know about the development of this early cosmology. Instead, their more modest, correlative explanations of *wuxing* allow for a nuanced approach to the important and pervasive notion of *qi* that becomes explicit among philosophers in the late fourth and early third centuries BCE.

In much the same vein as Sivin, Michael Nylan surveys the early philosophical literature through the Eastern Han to attempt to dispel exaggerated assurance in how we understand what sinologists have been loosely calling a Chinese "correlative cosmology." In her account, Nylan resists uncritical assumptions about some essential unity suggested by this rubric, challenging the notion that the initially separate concepts *yinyang*, five phases (*wuxing*), and *qi* had fused early in this development. Her point is to underscore the paucity of evidence available for making unjustified claims regarding an erstwhile consistent, shared cosmology in these early texts.[144] In many ways, the Sivin and Nylan critique of the systematizing of Chinese cosmology parallels a concern we ought to have about the confidence that has emerged in our overdetermining the interpretation of the early Greek philosophers that, like the Chinese case, is based upon only the most fragmentary of evidence understood primarily through an Aristotelian lens.

---

143. Sivin, *Medicine, Philosophy and Religion in Ancient China*, vol. 4, 5–6.

144. See Michael Nylan's essay "*Yin-yang*, Five Phases, and *Qi*," in *China's Early Empires: A Re-appraisal*, ed. Michael Nylan and Michael Loewe (Cambridge: Cambridge University Press, 2010).

Plato and Aristotle on *Theoria*: The Life of Thinking

I have tried to tell the story of ontology by selecting out salient passages from Parmenides, Plato, and Aristotle in order to allow these philosophers to speak on their own terms. Although I have noted ways in which Aristotle sees his own variation on ontological thinking to be a corrective on his teacher's transcendentalism, perhaps the clearest statement of the continuity between Plato and Aristotle is their commitment to the Parmenidean logic of the changeless. If "only Being is" then the philosophical life they have called *theoria* is one of dialectical ascent toward what is divine in the human being, with the ultimate occupation of the philosopher, even if only in rare moments, being the reflexive and self-sufficient life of thinking thinking itself. Going all the way back to Parmenides, this mode of thinking is the point of convergence at which the distinction between thought and being has no purchase.

The Greek term *theoria* has conventionally been translated as "contemplation" and is thus often understood as and problematically associated with a spectator conception of knowing and a correspondence theory of truth. A first step in understanding the role of *theoria* in early Greek philosophy is to disassociate it from the theory and practice binary as it is popularly understood. Further, the translation as "contemplation" is perhaps too passive to capture what in fact seems itself to be an activity, both as a continuing way of life and as the experience of *theoria* itself. In reflecting on Parmenides, Plato, and Aristotle, in all three cases the experience of *theoria* only becomes possible as an intellectual achievement at the end of an assiduous journey that must itself be understood as integral to the goal itself. It is not simply beholding reality but a pleasurable and morally transformative intuition: that is, a kind of knowing accessible only to those who have lived the intellectual life to its fullest such that thinking, thought, and being have in the end become one.

Classicist Pierre Hadot disambiguates *theoria* from theory by providing us with a clear distinction between the "theoretic" that we would associate with the "theory and practice" binary and what he calls the "theoretical":

> In modern parlance, "the theoretic" is opposed to "the practical" the way the abstract and the speculative is opposed to the concrete. From this perspective, then, we may oppose a purely theoretic philosophical discourse to a practical, lived philosophical life. Aristotle himself, however, uses only the word "theoretical"

[*theoretikos*], and he uses it to designate, on the one hand, the mode of knowledge whose goal is knowledge for knowledge's sake, and not some goal outside itself; and on the other, the way of life which consists in devoting one's life to this mode of knowledge.[145]

Hadot observes in summary that the " 'theoretical' can be applied to a philosophy which is practiced, lived, and active, and which brings happiness."[146]

For Aristotle, *theoria* as *bios theoretikos* or "the philosophical life of the individual" is an end in itself, where its ultimate goal is associated immediately with the active as opposed to the passive intellect or *nous*, as the self-initiating and unmoved source of thinking. *Theoria* is used in his *Metaphysics* interchangeably with expressions such as "unmoved moving," "life living eternally," "thought thinking itself," "God," "pure actuality," and "light." Such a mode of thinking is not a "doing" that would locate it in the changing world of potential and actualization, but it is the highest quality of self-sufficient, self-animating, reflexive thinking dependent upon nothing other than itself. As pure actuality, its cyclical motion as "motion without change" that inspires all natural cycles does not itself fall within the bounds of temporality. Importantly, in *theoria*'s guise as Aristotle's Prime Mover, it is at once a teleological cause and the highest good. The Prime Mover's eternal, unmoved moving is the inspiration that animates all motion and that unifies all of the specific, lesser goods inherent in the individuated formal causes.

David Hall and I have argued that the important difference between *theoria* and what Hadot calls "the theoretic" as the opposite of practice, is that *theoria* both as a way of life and as life's ultimate goal must be understood not as second-order theoretical thinking that informs and enhances practice but indeed as the intuitive wonder of first problematic thinking. As Hall insists in his monograph *Eros and Irony*, "The realm of *theoria* patterned by the realization of the end of *eros* is fundamentally a realm of mystical insight. . . . *Theoria* names the intuitive mode in accordance with which one receives the welter of experience unconditioned by the desire for consistent, coherent, systematic engagement with the world."[147] In our *Anticipating China*, Hall and I revisit this same issue in arguing that after

---

145. Pierre Hadot, *What Is Ancient Philosophy?*, trans. Michael Chase (Cambridge, MA: Belknap Press of Harvard University Press, 2002), 80–81.

146. Hadot, *What Is Ancient Philosophy?*, 81.

147. Hall, *Eros and Irony*, 240.

Plato and Aristotle, the philosophical life itself was being redefined to the extent that "the movement of Greek thought was away from the wonder associated with the original attitude of *theoria*, which involved the desire to celebrate the splendors of the world, and toward what we shall later associate with formal, theoretical understandings motivated by the desire for internal coherence, rigor, and consistency."[148] I have selected passages from Plato and Aristotle themselves to make an argument on behalf of an understanding of *theoria* as the life of thinking itself. It is this mode of thinking that is an inspiration that makes the intellectual and spiritual ascent desirable and, again, *theoria* being what is divine in the human experience, awaits philosophers although only intermittently, at the end of their quest.

In the *Theaetetus*, Plato portrays the philosophical life for "those at the top" in a humorous way. The consuming and solitary preoccupation with seeing the Good raises such persons out of the ordinary business of their lives and, for others around them, makes such persons seem to be living in a world of their own. The persistent theme of their dialectical ascent is captured in the "star gazing" metaphor ascribed to the dysfunctional philosophers who seem wholly distracted. Sustained philosophical reflection removes them quite literally from the most basic tasks needed to function as normal human beings. It draws their thoughts up into the heavens, leaving their defenseless bodies behind, and thus makes their very survival in the world rather precarious.

***

SOCRATES: Let's speak then . . . about those at the top—for why should one speak of those who spend their time in philosophy so poorly?—it's surely these who since their youth, first of all, don't know the way to the marketplace, or where's a court, council house, or anything else that's a common assembly of the city. And laws and decrees, spoken or written, they neither see nor hear, and the serious business of clubs for gaining office, and meetings, banquets, and revelries with flute girls—it doesn't even occur to them to do them in their dreams. And whether someone has been well-born or base-born in the city, or whether someone has incurred some evil from his ancestors, on the men's or women's side—he's less aware of it than of the proverbial

---

148. Hall and Ames, *Anticipating China*, 54.

pitchers of the sea. And he doesn't even know that he does not know all these things, for he's not abstaining from them for the sake of good repute, but in truth his body alone is situated in the city and resides there, but his thought, convinced that all these things are small and nothing, dishonors them in every way and flies, as Pindar puts it, "deep down under the earth" and geometricizes the planes, "and above heaven," star gazing, and in exploring everywhere every nature of each whole of the things which are and letting itself down to not one of the things nearby.

THEODORUS: How do you mean this, Socrates?

SOCRATES: Just like Thales, Theodorus, while star gazing and looking up he fell in a well, and some gracefully witty Thracian servant girl is said to have made a jest at his expense—that in his eagerness to know the things in heaven he was unaware of the things in front of him and at his feet. The same jest suffices for all those who engage in philosophy. For someone of this sort has truly become unaware of his neighbor next-door, not only as to what he's doing but almost to the point of not knowing whether he is a human being or some different nursling. But what a human being is and in what respect it's suitable for a nature of that sort to act or be acted on that's different from all the rest—he seeks that, and all his trouble (*pragmata*) is in exploring it. Surely you understand, Theodorus, or don't you?[149]

***

In the *Symposium*, this idea of *theoria* is expanded upon in describing Socrates's unmediated encounter with the object of his enlightened vision, where Beauty "as itself in accordance with itself, eternal and uniform," is not portrayed as one object among many but as everything all at once. For Plato, who claims that knowledge is virtue, there is a coincidence between beauty, justice, and the good, and seemingly between thought and being, with this concurrence being that which is most desirable. I repeat this wholly repeatable passage here.

---

149. Plato, *The Being of the Beautiful: Plato's Theaetetus, Sophist, and Statesman*, trans. Seth Bernardete (Chicago: University of Chicago Press, 1984). *Theaetetus* 173c–174b.

"In the first place, it is eternal; it neither comes into being nor passes away, neither increases nor diminishes. Therefore, it is not beautiful in one respect while ugly in another, nor beautiful at one time while ugly at another, nor beautiful with reference to one thing while ugly with reference to something else, nor beautiful here while ugly there, as though it were beautiful to some while ugly to others. Moreover, the beautiful will not appear to this person to be something like a face or a pair of hands or any other part of the body, nor will it appear as a particular statement or a particular bit of knowledge, nor will it appear to exist somewhere in something other than itself, such as in an animal, in the earth, in the sky, or in anything else. On the contrary, it exists as itself in accordance with itself, eternal and uniform. All other beautiful things partake of it in such a way that although they come into being and pass away, it does not, nor does it become any greater or any less, nor is it affected in any way. When someone moves through these various stages from the correct love of young boys and begins to see this beauty, he has nearly reached the end.

"In the activities of Love, this is what it is to proceed correctly, or be led by another: Beginning from beautiful things to move ever onwards for the sake of that beauty, as though using ascending steps, from one body to two and from two to all beautiful bodies, from beautiful bodies to beautiful practical endeavors, from practical endeavors to beautiful examples of understanding, and from examples of understanding to come finally to that understanding which is none other than the understanding of that beauty itself, so that in the end he knows what beauty itself is.[150]

***

Again, toward the end of the *Republic*, Plato explains that the education necessary for those philosophers who would govern the state is the dialectical ascent to the experience of the Good itself that stands as the cause of all that is good, just, and beautiful. While most of their lives happily

---

150. Plato, The Symposium *and* The Phaedrus, 48, 211a–211c.

occupied with philosophy will be shaped by the vision of this Reality, they are compelled by necessity in their proper turn to administer the governance of the state and its people.

***

"Isn't 'dialectic' the name you give to this journey? . . . The upward path from the underground cave to the daylight, and there the ability to look, not in the first instance at animals and plants and the light of the sun, but at their divine reflections in water and the shadows of real things, rather than in shadows of models cast by a light that is itself a shadow in comparison with the sun? All of this practice of the sciences we have just outlined has precisely this power to direct the best element in the soul upwards towards the contemplation of what is best among the things that are—. . .

Do we insist also that the power of dialectic is the only power that can reveal this? . . . The dialectical method is the only one which in its determination to make itself secure proceeds by this route—doing away with its assumptions until it reaches the first principle itself."[151]

***

Then when they are fifty years old, and those who have survived and been completely successful in every sphere, both in practical affairs and in their studies, should now be conducted to the final goal, and required to direct the radiant light of the soul towards the contemplation of that which itself gives light to everything. And when they have seen the Good itself, they must make that their model and spend the rest of their lives, each group in turn, in governing the city, the individuals in it, and themselves. They can spend most of their time in philosophy, but when their turn comes, each group must endure the trials of politics and be rulers. They will regard it as a necessity rather than a privilege. In this way, after educating a continuous

---

151. *Republic* 241–242, 532b–533a.

succession of others like themselves, and leaving them behind to take their place as guardians of the city, they will finally depart, and live in the islands of the blest.[152]

***

We turn next to Aristotle on *theoria*, where he like Plato associates it with what is divine in mankind, but beyond Plato he tries to provide a fuller if not equally enigmatic account. In trying to understand what Aristotle means by *theoria*, we perhaps do best to begin from how Aristotle takes it to be the sole occupation of the Prime Mover who reflexively thinks thought itself. In Aristotle's formulation of this idea of the Prime Mover whom he sometimes calls God, he is perhaps inspired by Plato, who earlier in defining the human soul states that "every soul is immortal. That is because whatever is always in motion is immortal, while what moves, and is moved by, something else stops living when it stops moving. So it is only what moves itself that never desists from motion, since it does not leave off being itself. In fact, this self-mover is also the source and spring of motion in everything else that moves, and as a source has no beginning."[153]

For Aristotle, his notion of the Prime Mover seems to be Plato's conception of the human soul scaled up to world-soul as God: that is, to be a self-sufficient, unmoved and unmoving, yet still self-moving actuality. Since motion in the world as understood by Aristotle has no beginning and no end, the idea of the Prime Mover is a necessary condition in the explanation of what sustains this motion. The Prime Mover existing outside of the temporal process of potential being actualized is the inspiration for the eternal cyclical processes of motion that animate the world. All of the cycles we experience—day and night, the seasons, the turning of the heavens, the life cycles of plants and animals, the flourishing and decline in the human experience—are aroused and explained by this eternal, self-moving substance.

Since such cycles entail motion, we needs must ask whether they are not in fact temporal and historical examples of change. Indeed, can there be motion without change? As one line of response we might recall John Dewey's essay on the influence Darwin has had on philosophy. Alluding

---

152. *Republic* 250, 540a–c.

153. *Phaedrus* 245c5–9, cited in Jiyuan Yu, *The Structure of Being in Aristotle's* Metaphysics, 186–187n7. I am much indebted to Yu Jiyuan in my discussion of Aristotle's Prime Mover.

to Aristotle's understanding of *eidos* as "species," Dewey asserts that "few words in our language foreshorten intellectual history as much as does the word species. . . . In living beings, changes do not happen as they seem to happen elsewhere, any which way; the earlier changes are regulated in view of the later results. This progressive organization does not cease till there is achieved a true final term, a τέλος, a completed and perfected end."[154] Because the "process" in these self-fulfilling cycles that eventuates in the completion of the object itself is in fact built into the formal definition of the object from the outset, Dewey would argue that what seems to be an erstwhile process does not in fact entail change in the sense of history or temporality. Dewey insists that as a consequence of this atemporality, science in seeking to know and to explain such cycles "is compelled to aim at realities lying behind and beyond the processes of nature, and to carry on its search for these realities by means of rational forms transcending ordinary modes of perception and inference."[155] In Aristotle, it is some kind of cyclical and yet unchanging motion that is ascribed to the Prime Mover. The "Unmoved Mover" is moving, but being a self-sufficient pure actuality, it neither moves other things nor is moved by them. It is in this sense then that *theoria* as "thinking thinking itself" still belongs to Parmenides's logic of the changeless.

Thus, the Prime Mover is not an efficient cause in the sense of being a Creator God or initiating motion in the world. For Aristotle, to assert that the Prime Mover originates motion would violate the Parmenidean logic of precluding any "before and after"; that is, it would introduce some state antecedent to the Prime Mover's introduction of motion and, hence, open a space for the claim that something can come from nothing. Again, to be consistent with this same logic, there must be a self-sufficiency of the Prime Mover as the reflexive "thought thinking itself" or as "life living eternally." Hence, for Aristotle, the eternal Unmoved Mover can only be causal in the teleological sense of being some kind of final cause. But how does this work? How can this Unmoved Mover be an explanation for the movement in other things?

Each particular thing in the plant and animal world as a member of a species has a formal cause that defines what it will become as its own specific good. As a composite, hylomorphic thing comprised of form and matter, however, it is mortal in the sense of living and then dying. This

---

154. Dewey, *The Essential Dewey*, vol. 1, 40.

155. Dewey, *The Essential Dewey*, vol. 1, 41.

being the case, the process of its reproduction in which it passes on its formal cause to its progeny is motivated by its desire for immortality. This desire for eternal life of each member of its species is inspired by the Prime Mover who is pure actualized life itself.

Although the Prime Mover is described as "unmoved," its substance is further defined as "actuality." Yu Jiyuan explains how this divine thinking sustains motion in the world, observing that "a potential member of a species is generated by one actual member of the same species, and the form is transmitted. This desire for eternity explains not only why it is a general law of nature that like produces like, but also accounts for why this form comes into being in the first place. It is through the individual members' desire for eternity that a species lasts."[156] Hence, while the formal cause in each thing is its specific good, the Prime Mover as eternal living itself is properly described as the higher good to which all living things aspire. Indeed, Aristotle describes this God and the actuality of its thinking precisely as life without beginning or end: "And life also belongs to God; for the actuality of thought is life, and God is that actuality; and God's essential actuality is life most good and eternal. We say therefore that God is a living being, eternal, most good, so that life and duration continuous and eternal belong to God; for this *is* God."[157]

We can perhaps clarify the role of the Prime Mover by comparing Aristotle's cosmological theology with that of his teacher, Plato. In the *Timaeus*, we saw that the demiurge is causal as a craftsman who works from the template of a perfect *kosmos* and does his best to replicate its natural, rational, and moral order within the world of change. In Plato's model, perhaps inspired by Anaxagoras who has appealed to "intellect" (*nous*) as the source of cosmic order, Plato has gone beyond the earlier Greek philosophers whom he interprets as having offered only naturalistic explanations such as water and air as the ordering cause. With Plato's demiurge we are given a rational, intelligent agent of design working from the necessity of a given, unchanging reality to produce a natural and moral universe.

For Aristotle, the relationship between the Prime Mover and cosmic order is also causal but in an importantly different way. The formal cause (*eidos*) that determines what any living thing will become can only exist within the particularity of things themselves and is then passed on in their process of reproduction. The Prime Mover does not have a role in creating

---

156. Yu Jiyuan, *The Structure of Being in Aristotle's* Metaphysics, 194.

157. Aristotle, *Metaphysics, The Complete Works*, 1072b1.

the cosmic structure that is immanent in all things individually and serves as their specific goods but does produce motion by being loved. That is, it is only by virtue of the desire that all living things have for immortality inspired by the higher good of this Prime Mover that the given cosmic order finds its coalescence and is perpetuated. Aristotle states plainly that the cosmic order as a whole is brought together into organic unity by virtue of this higher good and by the inspiration that the Prime Mover provides, "for the good is found both in the order and in the leader, and more in the latter; for he does not depend on the order but it depends on him. And all things are ordered together somehow, but not all alike."[158]

Yu Jiyuan again provides us with a summary statement of this teleological role that the Prime Mover has in the ordering of things, serving as both the unifying force that brings the cosmic order together as an organic whole and again as the teleological cause of that order. Yu observes that

> since all things are ordered to one end, and each operates as its nature allows, the result is that all the things in the universe form an orderly whole in which each thing's position is determined by its own nature. It is in this sense that we can see why the Prime Mover is the order as well as the cause of the order. . . . The entirety of nature becomes a hierarchically ordered body. In this organic whole, each can actualize and re-actualize its own form, and by doing this unceasingly, it contributes to the common good. . . . The order of the universe emerges when each thing desires the eternity that the Prime Mover represents.[159]

What is interesting in Aristotle's account of the Prime Mover is that in spite of the fact that this God does not itself act upon the world, the idea itself still falls clearly within the bounds of Aristotle's causal thinking. Aristotle insists that "the seed comes from other individuals which are prior and complete, and the first thing is not seed but the complete being, e.g., we must say that before the seed there is a man,—not the man produced from the seed, but another from whom the seed comes."[160] Indeed, Aristotle in this passage from the *Metaphysics* when he insists that the Prime Mover as pure actuality must have logical and temporal priority over potentiality, and that

158. Aristotle, *Metaphysics*, *The Complete Works*, 1075a.

159. Yu, *The Structure of Being in Aristotle's* Metaphysics, 199.

160. Aristotle, *Metaphysics*, *The Complete Works*, 1072d–1073a.

such actuality must be complete in itself, is in fact making the *Euthyphro* argument that holiness itself must be antecedent to its being loved and is thus loved by the gods because it is holy.

Another important claim that Aristotle carries over from Parmenides and that informs Plato as well is the insistence that thinking and the object of thought are one and the same substance. It is in this sense that the Prime Mover and *theoria* are described repeatedly as the substance of thought thinking itself. For Plato, the dialectic is an ascent from the many to the one, where finally any binary distinctions such as those between subject and object, and between thought and the object of thought, collapses, and both seeing and being seen are integral to this ultimate "one." This substance is without magnitude and, being without parts, is indivisible. Like Parmenides, too, Aristotle attempts to overcome the ambiguity of "one" by introducing a distinction between "one" as a measure and "one" in the sense of a self-sufficient simple, where it is the second that describes *theoria*.

***

There is therefore also something which moves them. And since that which is moved and moves is intermediate, there is a mover which moves without being moved, being eternal, substance, and actuality. And the object of desire and the object of thought move in this way: they move without being moved. The primary objects of desire and of thought are the same. For the apparent good is the object of appetite, and the real good is the primary object of wish. But desire is consequent on opinion rather than opinion on desire; for the thinking is the starting point. And thought is moved by the object of thought, and one side of the list of opposites is in itself the object of thought; and in this, substance is first, and in substance, that which is simple and exists actually. (The one and the simple are not the same; for "one" means a measure, but "simple" means that the thing itself has a certain nature.) But the good, also, and that which is in itself desirable are on the same side of the list; and the first in any class is always best, or analogous to the best.

That that for the sake of which is found among the unmovables is shown by making a distinction; for that for the sake of which is both that *for* which and that *towards* which, and of these the one is unmovable and the other is not. Thus it produces motion by being loved, and it moves the other moving things. Now if something is moved it is capable of being otherwise than as it is. Therefore if the actuality of the heavens is primary motion, then in so far as they are in motion, in *this* respect they are capable of being otherwise,—in place, even if not in substance. But since there is something which moves while itself unmoved, existing actually, this can in no way be otherwise than as it is. For motion in space is the first of the kinds of change, and motion in a circle the first kind of spatial motion; and this the first mover *produces*. The first mover, then, of necessity exists; and in so far as it is necessary, it is good, and in this sense a first principle. For the necessary has all these senses—that which is necessary perforce because it is contrary to impulse, that without which the good is impossible, and that which cannot be otherwise but is *absolutely* necessary.

On such a principle, then, depend the heavens and the world of nature. And its life is such as the best which we enjoy, and enjoy for but a short time. For it is ever in this state (which we cannot be), since its actuality is also pleasure. (And therefore waking, perception, and thinking are most pleasant, and hopes and memories are so because of their reference to these.) And thought in itself deals with that which is best in itself, and that which is thought in the fullest sense with that which is best in the fullest sense. And thought thinks itself because it shares the nature of the object of thought; for it becomes an object of thought in coming into contact with and thinking its objects, so that thought and object of thought are the same. For that which is *capable* of receiving the object of thought, i.e., the substance, is thought. And it is *active* when it *possesses* this object. Therefore the latter rather than the former is the divine element which thought seems to contain, and the act of contemplation is what is most pleasant and best. If, then, God is always in that good state in which we sometimes are, this compels our wonder; and if in a better this compels it yet more. And God *is* in a better state. And life also belongs to God; for the actuality of thought is life, and God is that actuality; and God's essential actuality is life most good and eternal. We say therefore that God is a living being, eternal, most good, so that life and duration continuous and eternal belong to God; for this *is* God.

Those who suppose, as the Pythagoreans and Speusippus do, that supreme beauty and goodness are not present in the beginning, because the beginnings both of plants and of animals are *causes*, but beauty and completeness are in the *effects* of these, are wrong in their opinion. For the seed comes from other individuals which are prior and complete, and the first thing is not seed but the complete being, e.g., we must say that before the seed there is a man,—not the man produced from the seed, but another from whom the seed comes.

It is clear then from what has been said that there is a substance which is eternal and unmovable and separate from sensible things. It has been shown also that this substance cannot have any magnitude, but is without parts and indivisible. For it produces movement through infinite time, but nothing finite has infinite power. And, while every magnitude is either infinite or finite, it cannot, for the above reason, have finite magnitude, and it cannot have infinite magnitude because there is no infinite magnitude at all. But it is also clear that it is impassive and unalterable; for all the other changes are posterior to change of place. It is clear, then, why the first mover has these attributes.[161]

***

We must consider also in which of two ways the nature of the universe contains the good or the highest good, whether as something separate and by itself, or as the order of the parts. Probably in both ways, as an army does. For the good is found both in the order and in the leader, and more in the latter; for he does not depend on the order but it depends on him. And all things are ordered together somehow, but not all alike,—both fishes and fowls and plants; and the world is not such that one thing has nothing to do with another, but they are connected. For all are ordered together to one end. (But it is as in a house, where the freemen are least at liberty to act as they will, but all things or most things are already ordained for them, while the slaves and the beasts do little for the common good, and for the most part live at random; for this is the sort of principle

---

161. Aristotle, *Metaphysics, The Complete Works*, 1072a–1073a.

that constitutes the nature of each.) I mean, for instance, that all must at least come to be dissolved into their elements, and there are other functions similarly in which all share for the good of the whole.[162]

Eleventh Anticipation

An important point that Aristotle wants to make in his discussion of *theoria* is that in its relationship to practical wisdom (*phronesis*), it is "a thing apart." Practical wisdom is associated with the composite, hylomorphic nature of human beings, their various activities, and their moral excellence. But *theoria* is self-contained and has "no aim beyond itself." In this sense, it can be associated with the singular and unmixed spiritual life of the gods as the source of the highest pleasure for them and, by extension, for us as well. The scholar of classical Greek and Hellenistic philosophy Pierre Hadot is making this same distinction between practical wisdom and *theoria* among the ancient thinkers when he insists that, for them, "philosophy is not wisdom, but a way of life and discourse determined by the idea of wisdom."[163]

Aristotle's distinction between practical wisdom and *theoria* might have important relevance for how we are to parse the historical transition in the occupation of the philosopher in the Western narrative, from the early days of philosophy as an ethical and spiritual way of life to the theoretical and logical pretensions of professional philosophy today. Within its own context, Hadot's work is certainly a timely corrective on the sins of the discipline of professional philosophy as it exists within the contemporary Western academy. Philosophy has become a predominantly theoretical and polemical activity that is perhaps something less than a way of life and as an academic subject seems to show little if any interest in the pursuit of either practical wisdom or *theoria*. Further, as a discipline it is anachronistic in that it construes its own historical narrative largely in these same terms. Hadot himself in answering the question as to where and how philosophy became primarily an abstract and theoretical exercise seemingly divorced from the project of *askēsis* or "self-transformation" sees academic pedantry emerging as early as

---

162. Aristotle, *Metaphysics*, *The Complete Works*, 1075a.

163. Hadot, *What Is Ancient Philosophy?*, 46.

Roman philosophy and reports on a clear theoretical ascent occurring in the Middle Ages with the growing dominance of philosophical commentary on Aristotle as integral to a university culture.

Allowing Hadot to speak for himself, he describes the life lived in Plato's academy as an example of philosophy as a way life and says that,

> in Plato's time, dialectics was a debating technique subject to precise rules. . . . By dint of sincere effort, the interlocutors discover by themselves, and within themselves, a truth which is independent of them, insofar as they submit to the superior authority of the *logos*. Here, as in all ancient philosophy, philosophy consists in the movement by which the individual transcends himself toward something which lies beyond him. For Plato, this something was the *logos*; discourse which implies the demands of rationality and universality. . . . Plato affirms that we must exercise the superior part of the soul—which is none other than the intellect—in such a way that it achieves harmony with the universe and is assimilated to the deity. . . . It is an exercise of death because death is the separation of the soul and the body, and the philosopher spends his time trying to detach his soul from his body. . . . This exercise was, indissolubly, an *askēsis* of the body and of thought—a divestment of the passions in order to accede to the purity of intelligence.[164]

Hadot in this description seems to give a fair account of Plato and Aristotle's understanding of *theoria* as being both the way of life and the ultimate goal of the spiritual ascent that can only be achieved through dialectic. And in its purest form, it is only through *theoria* that human beings can experience an intermittent intersection of the active human intellect with the eternal actuality of divinity thinking itself.

In reflecting upon the actual substance of the "spiritual exercises" and "self-transformation" that Hadot takes to be proper to the philosopher's "way of life," he sees an engagement with practical life not as an end in itself but only as an expedient means of ultimately according with the standards and norms of reason. In so doing, philosophers ascend to, apprehend, and ultimately conform to the demands of the abstract and theoretical as an end in itself. Hadot's philosophers so described in

---

164. Hadot, *What Is Ancient Philosophy?*, 62, 66, 67.

different ways and at different times privilege the reductive rationalization of the human experience through "the lived practice of the virtues of logic, physics, and ethics" that make them better persons than the unprincipled sophists and elevates them above the rest of humankind.[165] Hadot appeals to the *Phaedo* as an example of the spiritual exercises that constitute a distinctively philosophical way of life where this later Platonic dialogue not only explicitly denigrates the role of somaticity and the emotions in the project of personal cultivation but further offers us a moral vision for externally related, self-sufficient individuals—individuals without the intrinsic and constitutive relations that would make them responsive to the needs of others.

Hadot's compelling argument is that classical Greek philosophers epitomized by Plato and Aristotle within the Academy and the Lyceum respectively, created the curriculum and the community as a way of life with its goal being personal cultivation and transformation. Such language would seem to resonate immediately with the Confucian philosophical tradition that would use similar terms in describing their own project of personal cultivation. But while Hadot does seem to be giving a fair account of a kind of Greek philosophical eschatology, the question is whether from a Confucian perspective we can endorse this same regimen of spiritual exercises as "a way of life." Although superficially resonant with Confucian philosophy perhaps, this putatively "philosophical" way of life is markedly different from an embodied, aesthetic, holistic, and inclusive vision of the art of living we have come to associate with the transformative education advocated in the Confucian canons. In these Confucian texts we do not find the ostensive authority of predetermined norms and principles or a curriculum dominated by rational practices. Perhaps what marks the greatest difference is with the Greek positing of a salvific *theoria* in which philosophers have momentary experience of what is divine as the ultimate goal of their philosophical lives. In reflecting on thinking independent of practice, Confucius famously remarks, "Once, lost in my thoughts, I went a whole day without eating and a whole night without sleeping, and I got nothing out of it. I would have been much better off devoting my time to learning."[166] Rather than either theoretical and spiritual ascent or intermittent access to the life of the gods, the reversal of gravity we find in Confucian philosophy takes us in quite the

---

165. Hadot, *What Is Ancient Philosophy?*, 172.

166. *Analects* 15.31: 吾嘗終日不食，終夜不寢，以思，無益，不如學也.

opposite direction. Confucian practices seek a deepening measure (*du* 度) in optimizing the creative possibilities of the human experience, looking to enchant the everyday and to elevate the most ordinary in human life, thereby making it extraordinary. In this family-centered culture, the love of a grandmother for her grandson is at once the most common and the most precious of things we can know.

I find welcome corroboration for this decidedly Confucian alternative to *theoria* as the goal of the philosophical life when Stephen Angle compares the Confucian with the Greek understanding of sagehood. Angle observes that

> ideas of sagehood in Greece are often bound up with a conception of divinity, which is a realm of perfection separate from humanity. Only gods are truly wise, though humans can and should aspire after wisdom (*sophia*); those who do so are lovers of *sophia*, or "philosophers." Since these individuals love and aspire to something that is fundamentally different from our limited human knowledge, though, Greek theorists generally recognize that its pursuit requires a rupture with everyday life. They argue that people should seek to shape their lives by spiritual exercises that bring divine wisdom tantalizingly closer. For many thinkers, the best life (that is, the life of happiness or "eudaimonía") is the life of contemplation ("theōria").[167]

Angle then brings Aristotle's *phronimōs*—the practically wise person—into the discussion as a distinctly different Greek achievement that cannot easily be reconciled with the alternative Greek ideal of *theoria* as "a thing apart." The Confucian project is a journey along the pathway from achieving the status and function of consummate persons (*renzhe* 仁者) to apprenticing as scholar-officials (*shi* 士), to graduating in becoming exemplary persons (*junzi* 君子), and finally to becoming sages (*shengren* 聖人) as the highest order of humanity. The way is long and arduous, but each stage is continuous with the one before, with the goal of living a consummate life to simply live the consummate life, and the goal of becoming exemplary as a person to simply be exemplary in one's relations with others. Angle also cites Yu Jiyuan, who insists that "in Aristotle,

---

167. Stephen C. Angle, *Sagehood: The Contemporary Significance of Neo-Confucian Philosophy* (New York: Oxford University Press, 2009), 22.

the fulfillment of the practical self does not lead to the fulfillment of the theoretical self, and vice-versa. These are two models of human flourishing that cannot be fulfilled within a single career, and Aristotle ranks the actualization of the theoretical self higher than the actualization of the practical self. In contrast, in Confucius, there is only one continuous process of the development of the relational self, in which one's virtuous character keeps deepening and perfecting."[168]

***

Perhaps the most complete statement we have on *theoria* as the specifically philosophical life of reflexive thinking available to human beings is found in book 10 of the *Nicomachean Ethics*. When we turn from other life forms to humankind, we must begin from the first sentence in the *Metaphysics*: "All men by nature desire to know." Integral to the formal cause of human beings is the intellect (*nous*) where the passive aspect of the intellect receives the intelligible forms of things *sans* matter and, in so doing, enables us to know the world around us. The mysterious active intellect on the other hand is analogized as light in the sense of the intellectual activity that makes things intelligible. This active mind is described as "separable, impassible, unmixed, since it is in its essential nature activity."[169] It is separable in the sense that it is not dependent upon any element within the body and itself has no magnitude; it is impassible in the sense that it is purely active and not passive or acted upon; it is unmixed in the sense that it does not have a nature other than its own activity. And in contradistinction to the perception of the passive intellect that has the external world impressed upon it, active mind is self-sufficient and reflexive. This active intellect as *theoria* is the highest good in human beings and is their link to both divinity and immortality. As the highest good for both humans and the gods, *theoria* is the ultimate source of happiness for them both.

Theoria for this active mind is reflexive thinking in which the distinctions between subject, object, and the life process have no purchase. Such thinking is divinely infused in the sense that humankind's love of this active intellectual life as their highest good, and their desire to achieve and then sustain it, is inspired by the Prime Mover. It is the coincidence between the

---

168. Yu Jiyuan, *The Ethics of Confucius and Aristotle: Mirrors of Virtue* (New York: Routledge, 2007), 204.

169. Aristotle, *De Anima*, *The Complete Works*, 430a15–18.

inspiration of the Prime Mover as pure thinking thinking itself and human beings having the occasional experience of their own active intellect giving them access to what is divine that animates their desire for eternal life as the highest good.

We know that Plato and then Aristotle in their fellowship with other philosophical travelers followed a rigorous theoretical regimen that lay at the heart of their curriculum. They must have found something in the life of their own intellection that led them to an association between this reflexive mode of thinking they identify as *theoria* and the cluster of terms used to define their cosmological theologies: the highest Good, reality, eternal life, God, light, pleasure, human flourishing, and so on. They take this self-sufficient mode of thinking called *theoria* to be the divine aspect of the human being, and then by externalizing and hypostasizing it, it becomes their causal explanation for a divinely sanctioned cosmic order.

In positing *theoria* as the highest Good, the equation that Plato and Aristotle draw between reality and what is most abstract has persisted in philosophy. The Western philosophical narrative with metaphysics and episte-mology at its core became the quest for knowledge of the first causes—that is, a search for origins that promises the philosopher a firm grasp on both reality and truth. On such a reading, it would seem then that what Richard Rorty has called the "mirror of nature" works in both directions. On the one hand, we have the familiar correspondence theory of truth wherein our passively derived ideas correspond to facts about the real world. On the other hand, there is perhaps a less familiar notion of correspondence between how the active intellect of human beings works and the projection of this sublime activity of pure thinking or *theoria* being writ large as a theological explanation for the ultimate cause of cosmic order.

***

If happiness is activity in accordance with excellence, it is reasonable that it should be in accordance with the highest excellence; and this will be that of the best thing in us. Whether it be intellect or something else that is this element which is thought to be our natural ruler and guide and to take thought of things noble and divine, whether it be itself also divine or only the most divine element in us, the activity of this in accordance with its proper excellence will be complete happiness. That this activity is contemplative we have already said.

Now this would seem to be in agreement both with what we said before and with the truth. For this activity is the best (since not only is intellect the best thing in us, but the objects of intellect are the best of knowable objects); and, secondly, it is the most continuous, since we can contemplate truth more continuously than we can *do* anything. And we think happiness has pleasure mingled with it, but the activity of wisdom is admittedly the pleasantest of excellent activities; at all events philosophy is thought to offer pleasures marvellous for their purity and their enduringness, and it is to be expected that those who know will pass their time more pleasantly than those who inquire. And the self-sufficiency that is spoken of must belong most to the contemplative activity. For while a wise man, as well as a just man and the rest, needs the necessaries of life, when they are sufficiently equipped with things of that sort the just man needs people towards whom and with whom he shall act justly, and the temperate man, the brave man, and each of the others is in the same case, but the wise man, even when by himself, can contemplate truth, and the better the wiser he is; he can perhaps do so better if he has fellow-workers, but still he is the most self-sufficient.

And this activity alone would seem to be loved for its own sake; for nothing arises from it apart from the contemplating, while from practical activities we gain more or less apart from the action. And happiness is thought to depend on leisure; for we are busy that we may have leisure, and make war that we may live in peace. Now the activity of the practical excellences is exhibited in political or military affairs, but the actions concerned with these seem to be unleisurely. Warlike actions are completely so (for no one chooses to be at war, or provokes war, for the sake of being at war; any one would seem absolutely murderous if he were to make enemies of his friends in order to bring about battle and slaughter); but the action of the statesman is also unleisurely, and—apart from the political action itself—aims at despotic power and honours, or at all events happiness, for him and his fellow citizens—a happiness different from political action, and evidently sought as being different. So if among excellent actions political and military actions are distinguished by nobility and greatness, and these are unleisurely and aim at an end and are not desirable for their own sake, but the activity of intellect, which is contemplative, seems both to be superior in worth and to aim at no end beyond itself, and to have its pleasure proper to itself (and this augments the activity), and the self-sufficiency, leisureliness, unweariedness (so far as this is possible for man), and all the other attributes ascribed to the blessed man are evidently those connected with this activity, it follows that this will be the complete happiness of man, if it be allowed a complete term of life (for none of the attributes of happiness is incomplete).

But such a life would be too high for man; for it is not in so far as he is man that he will live so, but in so far as something divine is present in him; and by so much as this is superior to our composite nature is its activity superior to that which is the exercise of the other kind of excellence. If intellect is divine, then, in comparison with man, the life according to it is divine in comparison with human life. But we must not follow those who advise us, being men, to think of human things, and, being mortal, of mortal things, but must, so far as we can, make ourselves immortal, and strain every nerve to live in accordance with the best thing in us; for small in bulk, much more does it in power and worth surpass everything. This would seem, too, to be each man himself, since it is the authoritative and better part of him. It would be strange, then, if he were to choose not the life of himself but that of something else. And what we said before will apply now; that which is proper to each thing is by nature best and most pleasant for each thing; for man, therefore, the life according to intellect is best and pleasantest, since intellect more than anything else is man. This life therefore is also the happiest.

But in a secondary degree the life in accordance with the other kind of excellence is happy; for the activities in accordance with this befit our human estate. Just and brave acts, and other excellent acts, we do in relation to each other, observing what is proper to each with regard to contracts and services and all manner of actions and with regard to passions; and all of these seem to be human. Some of them seem even to arise from the body, and excellence of character to be in many ways bound up with the passions. Practical wisdom, too, is linked to excellence of character, and this to practical wisdom, since the principles of practical wisdom are in accordance with the moral excellences and rightness in the moral excellences is in accordance with practical wisdom. Being connected with the passions also, the moral excellences must belong to our composite nature; and the excellences of our composite nature are human; so, therefore, are the life and the happiness which correspond to these.

The excellence of the intellect is a thing apart; we must be content to say this much about it, for to describe it precisely is a task even if it be greater than our purpose requires. It would seem, however, also to need external equipment but little, or less than moral excellence does. Grant that both need the necessaries, and do so equally, even if the statesman's work is the more concerned with the body and things of that sort; for there will be little difference there; but in what they need for the exercise of their activities there will be much difference. The liberal man will need money for the doing of his liberal deeds, and the just man too will need it for the returning of services (for wishes are hard to discern, and even people who are not just pretend to wish to act justly); and the brave man will need power if he is to accomplish any of the acts that correspond to his excellence, and the temperate man will need opportunity; for how else is either he or any of the others to be recognized? It is debated, too, whether the choice or the deed is more essential to excellence, which is assumed to involve both; it is surely clear that its completion involves both; but for deeds many things are needed, and more, the greater and nobler the deeds are. But the man who is contemplating the truth needs no such thing, at least with a view to the exercise of his activity; indeed they are, one may say, even hindrances, at all events to his contemplation; but in so far as he is a man and lives with a number of people, he chooses to do excellent acts; he will therefore need such aids to living a human life.

But that complete happiness is a contemplative activity will appear from the following consideration as well. We assume the gods to be above all other beings blessed and happy; but what sort of actions must we assign to them? Acts of justice? Will not the gods seem absurd if they make contracts and return deposits, and so on? Acts of a brave man, then, confronting dangers and running risks because it is noble to do so? Or liberal acts? To whom will they give? It will be strange if they are really to have money or anything of the kind. And what would their temperate acts be? Is not such praise tasteless, since they have no bad appetites? If we were to run through them all, the circumstances of action would be found trivial and unworthy of gods. Still, every one supposes that they *live* and therefore that they are active; we cannot suppose them to sleep like Endymion. Now if you take away from a living being action, and still more production, what is left but contemplation?

Therefore the activity of God, which surpasses all others in blessedness, must be contemplative; and of human activities, therefore, that which is most akin to this must be most of the nature of happiness. This is indicated, too, by the fact that the other animals have no share in happiness, being completely deprived of such activity. For while the whole life of the gods is blessed, and that of men too in so far as some likeness of such activity belongs to them, none of the other animals is happy, since they in no way share in contemplation. Happiness extends, then, just so far as contemplation does, and those to whom contemplation more fully belongs are more truly happy, not accidentally, but in virtue of the contemplation; for this is in itself precious. Happiness, therefore, must be some form of contemplation.

But, being a man, one will also need external prosperity; for our nature is not self-sufficient for the purpose of contemplation, but our body also must be healthy and must have food and other attention. Still, we must not think that the man who is to be happy will need many things or great things, merely because he cannot be blessed without external goods; for self-sufficiency and action do not depend on excess, and we can do noble acts without ruling earth and sea; for even with moderate advantages one can act excellently (this is manifest enough; for private persons are thought to do worthy acts no less than despots—indeed even more); and it is enough that we should have so much as that; for the life of the man who is active in accordance with excellence will be happy.

Solon, too, was perhaps sketching well the happy man when he described him as moderately furnished with externals but as having done (as Solon thought) the noblest acts, and lived temperately; for one can with but moderate possessions do what one ought. Anaxagoras also seems to have supposed the happy man not to be rich nor a despot, when he said that he would not be surprised if the happy man were to seem to most people a strange person; for they judge by externals, since these are all they perceive. The opinions of the wise seem, then, to harmonize with our arguments. But while even such things carry some conviction, the truth in practical matters is discerned from the facts of life; for these are the decisive factor. We must therefore survey what we have already said, bringing it to the test of the facts of life, and if it harmonizes with the facts we must accept it, but if it clashes with them we must suppose it to be mere theory.

Now he who exercises his intellect and cultivates it seems to be both in the best state and most dear to the gods. For if the gods have any care for human affairs, as they are thought to have, it would be reasonable both that they should delight in that which was best and most akin to them (i.e., intellect) and that they should reward those who love and honour this most, as caring for the things that are dear to them and acting both rightly and nobly. And that all these attributes belong most of all to the wise man is manifest. He, therefore, is the dearest to the gods. And he who is that will presumably be also the happiest; so that in this way too the wise man will more than any other be happy.[170]

Twelfth Anticipation

Herodotus had high praise for the eloquent Pythagoras, who on the basis of his own holistic, practical, and intelligent way of life was the first to call himself a philosopher—"a lover of wisdom."[171] While certainly celebrating the formulation of abstract, theoretical science, Pythagoras as a person was committed to periodical ascetic observances, to a complex

---

170. Aristotle, *Nicomachean Ethics*, *The Complete Works*, 1177a12–1179a32.

171. Cicero, *Tusculan Disputations* 5.3.8–9, and Diogenes Laertius, *Lives of the Eminent Philosophers* 1.12, 8.8.

program of social and political reform, to sustained ethical reflection, to oratory and the making of music, to a physical regimen, to religious practices based upon assumptions about the immortality of the human soul, and even to rigorous dietary prescriptions and prohibitions. In book 15 of Ovid's *The Metamorphoses*, Pythagoras is described specifically as a passionate vegetarian who is sickened by the slaughter of living things, as holding a doctrine of transmigration and the immortality of the soul, and who also teaches a doctrine of metamorphosis in which "the heavens and all things beneath the heavens change their forms—the earth and all that is upon the earth; and since we are parts of the world, we, too, are changeable."[172]

But Pythagoras's holistic vision of the good life as the highest aspiration of *philosophia* faded in time, and what had been a truly "philosophical" journey—that is, a quest for both practical wisdom in living a moral life as well as theoretical knowledge—gave way to quite a different pilgrimage. As we have seen, in Plato and Aristotle the life of philosophical ascent in important degree became the rational search for abstract, apodictic knowledge and its promise of certain truth. It became a lifelong discipline rewarded by intermittent moments of a kind of divine, intellectual pleasure they called *theoria*. With the melding of the Greek and the Christian traditions, medieval scholastic philosophy was placed in the service of theology, and reverence for the theoretically and spiritually abstract meant that in the fullness of time, practical wisdom, rhetoric, and the aesthetic were relegated to the downside of a prevailing dualism. In this evolving philosophical narrative, we witness that a growing preoccupation with ontological and metaphysical questions led to a more rarified and pointed search for an abstract, unconditional knowledge and its promise of epistemic certainty. *Lógos* that had originally encompassed both *ratio* and *oratio*—both rational explanation and rhetoric—became heavily weighted on the side of the former. *Philosophia*, "the love of wisdom," had for all intents and purposes become *philoepisteme*, "the love of apodictic knowledge." "Knowledge" and "truth" became the defining vocabulary of systematic philosophy, and "wisdom" became and remains today a largely obsolete term in the corridors of the Western philosophical academy.

---

172. Ovid, *The Metamorphoses*, trans. Allen Mandelbaum (New York: Everyman's Library, 2013), 510.

Richard Rorty is not atypical of contemporary Western philosophers in being persuaded that philosophy's turn away from personal cultivation and the pursuit of wisdom has been a desirable advance in its narrative. He observes that "philosophy in the West started off its career as an answer to the question 'What is the good life for the human being?' To gain wisdom was to have learned the answer to that question. . . . Most Western philosophers no longer try to be sages, and they are quite rightly suspicious of Eastern philosophers who suggest that wisdom is still the goal of philosophical study."[173]

But we might speculate that there are still some philosophers for whom wisdom is not altogether expendable. Whitehead, for example, diagnoses what he calls the "fallacy of misplaced concreteness" as that error in reasoning committed when the formally abstracted and decontextualized is taken to be what is most real and concrete.[174] He then rehearses the history and the consequences of this "fatal virus" that has come to inhibit our understanding of the intrinsic, constitutive, and productive nature of relatedness. Indeed, he accuses Epicurus, Plato, and Aristotle of being "unaware of the perils of abstraction" that render knowledge closed and complete and that, in so doing, precludes the possibility of attaining wisdom. According to Whitehead, "the history of thought" that he associates with these great men "is a tragic mixture of vibrant disclosure and of deadening closure. The sense of penetration is lost in the certainty of completed knowledge. This dogmatism is the antichrist of learning. In the full concrete connection of things, the characters of the things connected enter into the character of the connectivity which joins them."[175] What Whitehead means here by "the sense of penetration" that is vitiated by the assumption that certain knowledge can be attained is the creative advance made possible by achieving productive relations among unique persons. Indeed, Whitehead uses "friendship" as his example of such relationality that he calls "the character of the connectivity." It is this cultivated, creative application of insight into how persons can best relate to each other to optimize the

173. Richard Rorty, "Philosophy and the Hybridization of Culture," in *Educations and Their Purposes: A Conversation among Cultures*, ed. Roger T. Ames and Peter D. Hershock (Honolulu: University of Hawai'i Press, 2007), 48.

174. Whitehead, *Process and Reality*, 10.

175. Whitehead, *Modes of Thought*, 58.

possibilities of their relations that is the real meaning of wisdom. For Whitehead, friendship is a relationship that is constituted by the unique character of the two persons involved, where the quality of a real meaningful friendship is a matter of vibrant disclosure in which two persons "appreciate" each other in the most "concrete" sense of this term: that is, they enlarge and increase the weight and measure of each other. Importantly, the realization of this vital relationship is not at the expense of their personal uniqueness or integrity but indeed a consequence of it. Integrity means both the persistent particularity of each friend and the "becoming one together" that is the substance of a truly significant relationship and a source of added cosmic meaning. In the growth of this achieved friendship, it is ultimately the persons as individuals that become the second-order abstraction, and it is the first-order, shared friendship that is what is most concrete.[176]

This understanding of vital relationality as intrinsic, constitutive, and productive is what Whitehead means by a holistic "aesthetic" as opposed to a reductionistic "rational" order in the sense that any aesthetic achievement aspires to the fullest disclosure of those specific particular details in the totality of the achieved effect—in this case, the "connectivity" of the friendship itself.[177] If "knowledge" is putatively to be found in the rational comprehension of some abstract and universal truth, then "wisdom" is to be found in the pragmatic, aesthetic project of correlating and harmonizing concrete relationships in service to an optimizing of their possibilities. There is for Whitehead real wisdom to be found in his example of "true" friendship.

Whitehead criticizes the classical Greek aesthetic sensibility harshly for losing sight of the balance that needs to be struck and sustained between the particular details and the achieved harmony. He insists that "the enjoyment of Greek art is always haunted by a longing for the details to exhibit some rugged independence apart from the oppressive harmony. In the greatest examples of any form of art, a miraculous balance is achieved. The whole displays its component parts, each with its own value enhanced; and the parts lead up to a whole, which is beyond themselves, yet not destructive of themselves."[178] When applied to the

---

176. Whitehead, *Modes of Thought*, 58–59.

177. Whitehead, *Modes of Thought*, 60–63.

178. Whitehead, *Modes of Thought*, 62.

human experience, disclosure in our relationships is what makes this family and community meaningful or, said perhaps more dynamically, is what makes these social relationships a situated case of "meaning-making." Any understanding of harmony that emphasizes an abstract conformity at the expense of disclosing its particular details in doing so sets limits on the possibility of attaining wisdom and is thus, quite literally, life-threatening. Whitehead observes that "our lives are passed in the experience of disclosure. As we lose this sense of disclosure, we are shedding that mode of functioning which is the soul. We are descending to mere conformity with the average of the past. Complete conformity means the loss of life. There remains the barren existence of inorganic nature."[179] The point that Whitehead is making here is that the productive harmony achieved by optimizing relationships can only emerge out of the real, shared experience of always unique persons. As such, this emergent harmony—indeed, another name for wisdom—will always be multilateral rather than unilateral, correlative rather than univocal, and a case of disclosure rather than closure. Wisdom is intelligent practice that reveals the appropriate balance between the concrete and local, on the one side, and a more abstract, sustained harmony on the other.

An important point to be made here before we "assay adventure" into the very different Chinese philosophical narrative is that Whitehead is not advocating a replacement of the abstract by the concrete but rather an appropriate, complementary balance between the two of them. After all, philosopher Pythagoras beyond his search for practical wisdom had an important contribution to make to theoretical mathematics as well, and it has served humankind well. What we are going to find is that, to the degree that the narrative of Western philosophy has stressed the abstract and impartial as the foundation of ethics, and to the degree that the narrative of Confucian philosophy has emphasized partiality and family feeling as the entry point for cultivating a moral life, they are in important degree complementary and thus have much to say to each other in a conversation that will enrich them both.

---

179. Whitehead, *Modes of Thought*, 62.

Chapter 5

Classical Chinese Zoetological Thinking

Zoetology and Its Far-Reaching Implications

Just as with Greek "ontology" and its profound influence on the evolution of the Western philosophical narrative, I have identified what I take to be an alternative, equally engrained "prejudice" in classical Chinese cosmology that has persisted over the centuries. By way of summary, I am borrowing the Greek term *zoe* for "life" and am appealing to the organic and ecological thinking made explicit in the "Great Commentary" to the *Book of Changes* (*Yijingdazhuan* 易經大傳) to create the neologism "zoetology," which I would translate into modern Chinese as *shengshenglun* 生生論 or "the art of living." In trying to clarify what has come to be called ontology as a Greek understanding of its own first philosophy, I have cited the classical Greek philosophers at some length to allow them to speak on their own terms. In this chapter then, reference to the *Book of Changes* as the first among the Chinese classics can serve a comparable function for speaking on behalf of zoetology and shedding light on a Chinese formulation of its alternative first philosophy.

As a text, the *Book of Changes* can itself be taken to be an object lesson in the ecological worldview it attempts to present. That is, within this processual understanding of cosmic order with primacy being given to vital relationality, it requires of us that we reflect on the nature of interpenetrating "events" rather than discrete "things." We quickly discover that the relationship of these particular foci to their fields lends itself to an organic and holographic understanding of world systems. In such a cosmology, the unsummed totality or unbounded field is both adumbrated in and construed from the unique perspective of each particular focus—in this case, the *Book of Changes* itself. Indeed, the "Great Commentary" to the *Changes* makes just such a holographic, focus-field claim in announcing its importance as a canonical text, asserting that "as a document, the *Changes* is vast and far-ranging, and has everything complete within it. It contains the way of the heavens, the way of human beings, and the way of the earth."[1]

Edward Shaughnessy in his translation of the "Great Commentary" (or *Xici*) on the *Changes* observes that "the worldview of its *Xici* or *Appended Statements* Commentary—integrating man and nature through the medium of the *Yijing*—is arguably the most sophisticated (it is certainly the most subtle) statement of the correlative thought that has been so fundamental to all of China's philosophical systems."[2] Shaughnessy is not exaggerating when he says that, "indeed, so central has the *Yijing* been to Chinese thought over these two millennia that a history of its exegetical traditions would require almost a history of Chinese thought."[3] Indeed, it is this open-ended classic with its millennia of accruing commentaries that has set the terms of art for the persistent yet evolving cosmology and for a deeply engrained cultural common sense. As such, it provides a shared interpretive context for the unfolding of the Confucian, Daoist, and Buddhist traditions over the centuries and, most recently, for an increasing engagement of these same philosophies with the Western philosophical narrative.

In the Chinese language as in English, the profoundly ambiguous term "change" covers a broad range of meanings: "transforming" *hua* 化, "being in flux" *bian* 變, "removing" *qian* 遷, "replacing" *geng* 更, "taking the place of, substituting for" *ti* 替, "transferring, altering" *yi* 移, "reforming" *gai* 改, "exchanging" *huan* 換, "peeling away" *ge* 革, "increasing, adding, profiting" *yi* 益, and many more. The early commentaries correlate the *yi* 易 modality of change we find in the title of the *Yijing* 易經 or *Book of Changes* paronomastically with its homophone *yi* 益 that means "increasing, adding, profiting," a *kind* of change that is consistent with the self-consciously declared claim of the text that it provides its sagely counsel as catalytic to making the most out of the human experience. The contemporary commentator Guo Moruo 郭沫若 argues that the term *yi* 易 in fact should be read as an early abbreviated form of the graph *ci* 賜, meaning "gifting," "transacting,"

1. Ames, *Sourcebook*, 91: 《易》之為書也, 廣大悉備. 有天道焉, 有人道焉, 有地道焉.

2. Edward L. Shaughnessy, trans., *I Ching: The Classic of Changes* (New York: Ballantine, 1997), 1.

3. Shaughnessy, *I Ching*, 1.

"exchanging." In a cosmology that gives primacy to vital relationality and in which nothing does anything by itself, the transactional "ex-changing" modality of "change" that produces growth is foundational as the ultimate source of value and increased meaning. From this perspective then, Guo's suggestion is compelling.[4] On the other hand, it is perhaps the inclusive ambiguity of the term "change" itself rather than referencing any specific form of change, that allows the process to be understood in a holistic and inclusive way, recommending to us the "Book of Changes" as a translation rather than a more exclusive "Book of Exchanges."

The *Book of Changes*, thus taking the generic and productively vague notion of "change" (*yi* 易) as its title, explains the motive force within the unfolding of cosmic order specifically and denotatively as the "ceaseless procreating of life" itself. *Sheng* 生 as change—the life, the growth, and the specific kind of genealogical birthing that occurs within this vital process—is real and will not be denied. This *Book of Changes* cosmology gives privilege to events as irreducibly relational "becomings," and it provides the correlative *yinyang* categories needed to "speak" process and its eventful content. A popular mantra often invoked to capture the spirit of the *Changes* is "procreative living is without end, and its creativity never ceases."[5]

One term the *Changes* appeals to in expressing its generative worldview is *dao* or "world-making"—metaphorically, the existential journey each one of us takes and that we take together through life. In setting out its terms of art, the text states:

> It is because of the sheer opulence of way-making (*dao*) we call it "the grand workings"; it is because of its daily renewal we call it "copious virtuosity"; it is because of its ceaseless procreating we call it "the changes" (*yi*). The prospective forming of images we call *qian*; the bringing about of their specific contours we call *kun*. Providing foreknowledge of what has yet to come through exhaustive calculations we call prognostication. The continuity in flux we call events. And what cannot be fathomed by appeal to *yinyang* correlative thinking is what we call the truly mysterious (*shen*).[6]

---

4. See the entry for 易 in Kwan, "Database."

5. 生生不已, 創造不息.

6. Ames, *Sourcebook*, 103–104: 富有之謂大業, 日新之謂盛德. 生生之謂易, 成象之謂乾, 效法之謂坤, 極數知來之謂占, 通變之謂事, 陰陽不測之謂神.

Each phrase in this passage isolates one specific generative way of looking at *dao* from within our continuing life experience and then gives this particular aspect a denotative name: its opulence, its fecundity, its productivity, its giving shape to things, its presaging, its eventfulness, and its inexorable mystery.[7] Each name references one dimension of *dao* or "world-making" as the cosmic order is unfolding within the human experience. The last phrase in this passage then takes us back to where we began, reminding us of the open-endedness of the processes of change as they are describable in the language of *yinyang* 陰陽 correlations and of the limits of our own capacity to fully understand these changes. Whatever "things" in this cosmos might be, their ever-changing and phasal identities within the forming and functioning (*tiyong* 體用) of their contexts must be understood as uniquely centered and transforming foci constituted by a manifold of vital relations within a boundless ecological field. This passage recalls a related description in this same text where it says specifically of the sages as the highest order of humanity that "in their mysterious progresses they remain undefined, and in their changes they have no set structure."[8]

In this processual cosmology, the growth that attends such generative living is not only ceaseless and boundless but is further elevated to be celebrated as the most vigorous potency of the cosmos itself:

> The greatest capacity (*dade* 大德) of the cosmos is life itself. The greatest treasure of the sages is their attainment of standing (*wei* 位). The means for maintaining their standing is aspiring to become consummate in their conduct (*ren* 仁). The way of attracting and mobilizing others is to put all available resources to good use. Regulating these resources effectively, insuring that language is used properly, and preventing the common people from doing what is undesirable is what is said to be optimally appropriate and most meaningful (*yi* 義).[9]

---

7. There is an important grammatical distinction we find throughout the *Changes*. At times the text uses the denotative formula "is what is meant by" (*zhiwei* 之謂) and, at other times, the conative formula "is called or termed" (*weizhi* 謂之) formula. The former expression defines its antecedent explicitly, while the latter connotes or references what is only one "aspect" of some greater whole.

8. Ames, *Sourcebook*, 101: 神无方而易无體.

9. Ames, *Sourcebook*, 112: 天地之大德曰生, 聖人之大寶曰位. 何以守位曰仁, 何以聚人曰財, 理財正辭、禁民為非曰義.

Life as growth in relations is the magic behind what is fundamentally a moral cosmos. It is the nature of life to seek out those conditions for its optimal and most meaningful growth. Thus, the full complement of Confucian values is expressed as the assiduous cultivation of growth in all of the various dimensions of the human experience, from the sages achieving moral stature to best practices in the use of resources, and in the effecting of robust social and political order as well. Meaning is not available to us from putative metaphysical foundations—what David Keightley has described as "a Platonic metaphysics of certainties, ideal forms, and right answers."[10] Instead, in this Confucian world, such deliberate, meaningful growth is the substance of moral education and of lives that flourish as they are cultivated through human ingenuity. A fundamental value that is expressed here is the symbiotic relationship between the welfare of the people and the moral standing of those who take responsibility for effecting the social and political order.

To underscore the claim of the *Changes* that it is "living, growing, birthing" (*sheng* 生) that is most basic in this classical Confucian cosmology, we might take a passage from the text that rehearses a key cluster of philosophical terms that are invoked to give this cosmology expression and explanation. As we can see, the meaning of each one of these terms is rooted in the vital process of life and growth:

> It is because the *Book of Changes* is modeled on the heavens and the earth that it is able to cover the full complement of their operations (*dao* 道). Looking upward, the sages observed the constellations in the heavens (*tianwen* 天文), and looking downward, they discerned the topography of the earth (*dili* 地理). It is thus that they came to understand the source of both what is apparent and what is obscure. In tracing things back to their origins and then following them to their end, they came to understand what can be said about life and death. The condensing of *qi* constitutes all things (*jingqiweiwu* 精氣為物), and the wanderings of the life-forces animates all change. It is thus that the sages came to understand the actual circumstances of the gods and spirits. Because the sages are comparable to the heavens and the earth, they do not run contrary to them. Because

10. David N. Keightley, "Shang Divination and Metaphysics," *Philosophy East and West* 38, no. 4 (October 1988): 376.

they have a comprehensive understanding of all that is, and a way that gives the world what it needs, they do not overstep its boundaries. Because they act circumspectly without getting carried away, they find pleasure in *tian* (*letian* 樂天); because they are fully cognizant of the propensity of circumstances (*zhiming* 知命), they are free of all anxieties. Because they are at ease in their place and genuine in their consummatory conduct (*dunhuren* 敦乎仁), they are able to be loving (*ai* 愛). Because they embrace the transformations of the heavens and the earth without going beyond them, because everywhere they bring all things to fruition without leaving anything behind, and because they have a penetrating understanding of the pathway from day to night, in their mysterious progresses they remain undefined, and in their changes they have no set structure.[11]

This cluster of philosophical terms around which the "Great Commentary" is constructed reveals the world as it is immediately experienced, providing us with a steady proliferation of correlated yet oppositional dyadic terms such as upward and downward, the heavens and the earth, the origins and the ends, the apparent and the obscure, life and death, gods and spirits, things and their changes, night and day, and so on. By way of contrast with causal, ontological thinking that in explaining change must appeal to some Prime Mover or some other external source, it is the correlative, bipolar, and dynamic tensions inherent in this zoetological lifeworld that produces its own internal energy of transformation. Given that the locus of life is always the relationship between the organism and its environment, and given that it is the nature of life itself to seek to optimize its conditions for growth, pressures and strains are generated among the many life-forms as the vital cosmos itself negotiates an optimizing symbiosis for its constituents. And it is the site of these same dynamic tensions between what is determinate and what is still indeterminate that is the locus and source of new growth.

Important in this passage from the *Changes* is a description of how things and events, from the most ordinary and everyday to the noncorporeal world of gods and spirits, are formed and eventually dissipate. They are animated by

11. 《易》與天地準, 故能彌綸天地之道. 仰以觀於天文, 俯以察於地理, 是故知幽明之故. 原始反終, 故知死生之說. 精氣為物, 遊魂為變, 是故知鬼神之情狀.與天地相似, 故不違. 知周乎萬物, 而道濟天下, 故不過. 旁行而不流, 樂天知命, 故不憂. 安土敦乎仁, 故能愛. 範圍天地之化而不過, 曲成萬物而不遺, 通乎晝夜之道而知, 故神无方而易无體.

both oppositional and collaborative tensions in their relations and take shape as continuing perturbations in the hylozoistic *qi*. Importantly, the correlative relationship of the dyadic pairs such as "living and dying" (*sisheng* 死生) and "gods and spirits" (*guishen* 鬼神), in which each is implicated in the other, reflects the porousness of such classifications and the absence of the categorical thinking that would set any final and exclusive limits on them. To take one example, in a genealogically driven, living cultural tradition rooted in ancestral sacrifices, those who have gone before are very much present in the lives of the living. And to take another example, where gods and the human spirit in ontological thinking are usually construed as exclusive categories, in this zoetological world cultural heroes and high ancestors such as Confucius and the Yellow Emperor, respectively, are what it means to be gods.

What is of important note in this passage is the collaborative relationship between humankind, on the one hand, and the heavens and the earth on the other. This triad is often referenced as the "three forces" (*sancai* 三才): "because the sages are comparable to the heavens and the earth, they do not run contrary to them." Throughout the *Changes*, the language cluster usually used to express the various modalities of what is specifically human virtuosity—"consummatory conduct in roles and relations" (*ren* 仁), "love" (*ai* 愛), "awareness, wisdom, understanding" (*zhi* 知), and so on—is naturalized to be integral to the workings of the cosmos. Such a shared, human-in-the-world vocabulary reflects the perceived isomorphism we find between the human and the natural worlds. Love, for example, is not to be isolated as a powerful, internal human feeling that draws people together. Rather, love is situational as a collaborative and unbounded force as it is fostered within the stabilizing conditions necessary for and integral to the positive growth of such feelings. Love is in the world, and it belongs to the human experience in all of its parts. And it is because the vital and transformative relationship between the sages and their world is collateral in mutually shaping and being shaped that the sages in their activities remain resistant to any set definition or fixed structure.

A good example of this isomorphism between humankind and its world is the relationship between the two seemingly distinct human and natural versions of the "five phases" (*wuxing* 五行) doctrines: a regimen of moral habituation we associate with Zisizi and Mencius, on the one hand, and on the other the later cosmological postulate of the five phases ascribed to Zou Yan 鄒衍 (305–240 BCE) that occur within the natural factors of "water" (*shui* 水), "fire" (*huo* 火), "metal" (*jin* 金), "wood" (*mu* 木), and "earth" (*tu* 土).

In the recently recovered document *Five Modes of Virtuosic Conduct* (*Wuxingpian* 五行篇) and again echoed in the *Mencius*, there is the phasal doctrine of the "five modes of virtuosic conduct" (*wuxing* 五行) as they are defined in the human world—"consummatory conduct in roles and relations" (*ren* 仁), "aspiring to an optimal appropriateness" (*yi* 義), "propriety in roles and relations" (*li* 禮), "living wisely" (*zhi* 知), and "sagacity" (*sheng* 聖). The interlinear commentary included in the Mawangdui version of the *Five Modes of Virtuosic Conduct* is explicit in referencing *xin* 心 or "bodyheartminding" as the personal identity that is consolidated when these five phases are set as the root of a growing habitude of virtuosic conduct. The commentary on the Mawangdui version of this text states that, "having thus set these five modes of conduct, they become one. This 'one' then refers to the five modes of virtuosic conduct that, once consolidated as the [one] bodyheartminding (*xin*), is then taken as one's personal identity."[12] In this continuing, phasal process of growing and consolidating a personal identity we find the familiar cosmological postulate "one is many, many one." At the end of the first chapter of *Five Modes of Virtuosic Conduct*, it states explicitly that "efficacy is human way-making, while moral virtuosity is the way-making of *tian*."[13] And yet consolidated moral virtuosity (*de* 德), far from being the exclusive way-making of *tian*, stands and is expressed as a collaboration between *tian* and the way-making of the highest order of humanity, the sages, that achieves proper measure (*du* 度). To appreciate what is meant here by the distinction between "human way-making" and "the way-making of *tian*" we need first to suspend our uncritical yet default Abrahamic theological assumptions and thus resist any temptation to think that this distinction is referencing two exclusive domains. The human-*tian* collaboration in way-making captured in the mantra "the continuity between and inseparability of the human and the cosmic orders" (*tianrenheyi* 天人合一) is an emergent, increasingly inspired way of being in the world that always has both a human and a cosmic aspect. The text states that a harmonious integration of the first four modes of virtuosic conduct as moral virtuosity (*de* 德) produces human efficacy (*shan* 善). But when the fifth mode of virtuosic conduct is added to this harmony—that is, the sagacity

---

12. 獨然後一，一也者，夫五為□(一)心也，然後得之. See a fuller account of this process in Roger T. Ames, *Human Becomings: Theorizing Persons for Confucian Role Ethics* (Albany: State University of New York Press, 2021), 310–312.

13. 善，人道也; 德，天道也. See Ames, *Sourcebook*, 621–622.

of human beings (*sheng* 聖)—it produces a moral virtuosity (*de*) to be associated with *tian*.

Importantly, the human-*tian* relationship itself is first order, while *tian* and humankind are a second-order abstraction from this relationship that is one and two at the same time. Given that the sages are the paramount exemplars of what is humanly possible, this moral virtuosity is manifested in the world as the consummate expression of the operations of both sagacious human beings and the contextualizing *tian* as, in their collaborative activities, they find a real depth of coalescence and meaning. Not only is such sagacity to be understood as the human being achieving the reach and influence of *tian*, but moreover *tian* itself is deepened and extended by this accumulating human sagacity. Just as human sagacity is naturalized to become integral to the cosmic order, *tian* and the natural order are socialized to become integral to the human experience. The ruler is described as the offspring of *tian* (*tianzi* 天子), and the "constancy (*jing* 經) of the heavenly cycles" and "the appropriate responsiveness (*yi* 義) of the earth" are described in terms of family reverence (*xiao* 孝).[14] This shared virtuosic conduct not only underscores the primacy of the *tianren* relationship over the secondary distinction between *tian* and *ren*, but it also makes the important point that human beings in their role as sages can continue and extend the work of *tian*.

Somewhat later than the *Five Modes of Virtuosic Conduct*, a cosmological doctrine designated by the same term, *wuxing* 五行, appears with the modal "five cosmic phases"—that is, "water" (*shui* 水), "fire" (*huo* 火), "metal" (*jin* 金), "wood" (*mu* 木), and "earth" (*tu* 土). Both the human and the natural versions of *wuxing* are "phasal" in the sense that each of the five phases is an aspect of a continuing process. Again, in traditional Chinese medicine (TCM), the natural five cosmological phases are dynamic and interdependent aspects of the *qi* 氣 life force that, when they sustain a proper balance and are able to function without obstruction, promise a healthy life-form. As referenced earlier, in this Confucian process cosmology, the energy of transformation arises from the negotiated strains and tensions as well as the mutual collaborations between organisms and their environing others. The well-being of lived human bodies in all of their aspects from family and communal roles to exercise, diet, feelings, sexual practices, morality, and so on, is to be understood and explained in terms

---

14. The *Classic of Family Reverence* 7: 夫孝, 天之經也, 地之義也.

of achieving proper measure in the coordination of these five cosmological phases. And disease in the human body, both physical and emotional, is explained as blockage, stagnation, and deficiency in this life process. From the ecological perspective of "one is many, many one," these two moral and natural, human and cosmological *wuxing* phasal doctrines, rather than being understood as exclusively human or cosmic, share much by way of resonance and interpenetration between them.

The *Changes* is a normative text that reports on a common moral cosmos shared symbiotically by human beings and the natural environment. The mysterious penumbra that honeycombs the unfolding of the cosmic order extends this process beyond what is determinate and intelligible. As the sages embody the cosmic transformations in everything they do, the insights they glean from such operations and the influence they themselves come to exert on the life process is unbounded and beyond rationalization. The story of how this canonical text has been compiled by the sages as a primer for the human life and how it appeals to imagistic thinking in the production of meaning is described specifically in terms of change and transformation:

> The sages set out the hexagrams and observed the images. Attaching their commentaries to them, they made clear what is auspicious and inauspicious. The firm and the yielding lines displacing each other produce the changes and transformations. It is thus that auspiciousness and inauspiciousness are the images of gaining and losing, that regret and care are the images of anxiety and concern, that change and transformation are the images of advancing and withdrawing, that firm and yielding are the images of day and night. The movement of the six lines is the unfolding of the world-making (*dao*) engendered by the three ultimates: that is, the heavens, the earth, and humankind.[15]

The sages have created a dynamic, imagistic discourse drawn from their understanding of the generative procreativity of the cosmos to communicate their insights into how to usher the human experience forward deliberately and productively, enabling it to unfold within the context of the heavens and the earth in the most auspicious way. Philosophers such as Mark Johnson

---

15. Ames, *Sourcebook*, 97–98: 聖人設卦觀象, 繫辭焉而明吉凶. 剛柔相推而生變化. 是故吉凶者、失得之象也, 悔吝者、憂虞之象也, 變化者、進退之象也, 剛柔者、晝夜之象也. 六爻之動、三極之道也.

and John Dewey before him in their own reflections on the holistic nature of the human experience are making an argument for image-schemata as a continuing source of meaning that resonates with the pattern of images we find here in the *Changes*. The imagistic discourse of the sages is certainly descriptive of the physical operations of the cosmos. But through the promotion of benign growth, this discourse becomes a generative resource for the human being to elevate the language and create the higher-order concepts and values that make the human experience increasingly moral, aesthetic, and intelligent.

The subtitle of Johnson's monograph *The Body in the Mind* explicitly insists upon *The Bodily Basis of Meaning, Imagination, and Reason*.[16] In this work, Johnson has done much to argue for the bodily ground of human meaning-formation and also for what is ultimately the aesthetic ground for human flourishing. He maps out the way in which through the metaphorical projections and elaborations of our imagination, the barest of physical image-schemata are extended to generate complex cognitive and affective patterns of meaning, insisting that "our world radiates out from our bodies as perceptual centers from which we see, hear, touch, taste, and smell our world."[17]

For Johnson, the formal, logical structures of human understanding are a direct extension of the activities of our lived bodies, with such higher-order intelligence emerging through the exercise of our seemingly boundless imagination. Such is the human capacity to produce culture in all of its complexity. Johnson identifies his own basic image-schemata as "containment," "force," "balance," "cycles," "scales," "links," and "center-periphery." In his reflection on "learning to become human," Johnson has urged the view "that understanding is never merely a matter of holding beliefs, either consciously or unconsciously. More basically, one's understanding is one's way of being in, or having, a world. This is very much a matter of one's embodiment, that is, of perceptual mechanisms, patterns of discrimination, motor programs, and various bodily skills. And it is equally a matter of our embeddedness within culture, language, institutions, and historical traditions."[18] In appreciating this evolving formation of the structures of human

---

16. In many ways Johnson is following John Dewey's pioneering work, *Experience and Nature* (Mineola, NY: Dover, 2000).

17. Mark Johnson, *The Body in the Mind: The Bodily Basis of Meaning, Imagination, and Reason* (Chicago: University of Chicago Press, 1987), 124.

18. Johnson, *The Body in the Mind*, 137.

understanding, we have to be wary of a simple epiphenomenal interpretation that would separate root from tree as cause and effect. Indeed, root and tree are a holistic, symbiotic process where they grow together or not at all. Intellection is always an expression of our embodied living, and body itself with its visceral memory is both conscious and discursive. In this sense, lived bodies (*ti* 體) and our embodied living (*li* 禮) are two aspectual ways of looking at the same symbiotic process of growth, with bodies themselves becoming increasingly aware, complex, and intelligent.

The image-schemata we find here in the *Changes* are captured in the correlative images as the early sages have described them and are reflective of the primacy given to vital relationality in the classical Chinese zoetological cosmology. That is, these always situated images are understood in fundamentally and irreducibly relational terms with agency usually being a second-order consideration. Such an imagistic discourse in surrendering conceptual boundaries and formal definitions in favor of always shifting horizons does not and cannot generate the putative precision and clarity promised by more systematic, theoretical thinking. On the other hand, these images describe the vital, transactional, and thus generative relationships that locate and amplify meaning in the activities of organisms within their human and natural ecologies.

To give just one example of how higher-order thinking might be the extension of bodily actions, it is not difficult to conceive of how reflection on recurrent, habituated physical patterns such as giving and getting, rising and falling, balance and imbalance, and agitation and equilibrium could be elevated and metaphorically extended and transformed to produce higher-order economic and political concepts defining of a mature culture such as "relational equity" and "social justice." Again, such higher-order and still generative imagistic constructs are reflexively internalized to become integral to our complex body consciousness.

The *Changes* has been formulated and passed on within the historical narrative by the most sagacious of our progenitors as they have strived to coordinate the human experience most effectively within the ambient, changing cosmic processes. For Confucian philosophy, morality itself is understood as a cosmic phenomenon emerging out of the symbiotic and synergistic transactions that take place between the operations of nature and the concerted efforts of the higher orders of humanity to refine and aestheticize what it means, both individually and as a species, to become consummately human.

Yi 易 as *Shengsheng* 生生:
Construing Change as Procreative Living

On the oracle bones, the character *sheng* 生 as "living, growing, birthing" appears as 㞢 and is explained by traditional commentators as the sprouting of plant growth as it breaks through the earth.[19] Hence, there is an immediate correlation between the human experience and environmental concerns, and what it means for humankind to optimize the growth made possible by a fertile and generous earth. At the same time, on further reflection we can see an obvious and interesting contrast between the horticultural implications for the term "birth" suggested by this image of a plant breaking ground and our more immediate association of birthing with mother and child. In our commonsense thinking, human procreating is "derivative" in the sense that the mother bears the child and gives birth to an independent existent; mother in this process is one becoming two. Indeed, in the English language to refer to the sprouting of plant growth breaking ground as an image of "birthing" is a stretch and sounds at best figurative and metaphorical, if not misplaced.

To find contrast with this derivative sense of human birthing, we might describe horticultural growth as transmutative, where some inchoate form of plant life internalizes the resources provided by its environment as its nourishment for growth to become a collaboration between organism and environment. When as prompted by our common sense we think about plant growth ontologically, with the suppressed premises of formal and final causes, we assume that corn seed in its growth will naturally become stalks of corn and nothing else. But when we think zoetologically, given the radical contextuality of procreativity, we must acknowledge the fact that only one in a million kernels of corn actually grows into a stalk of corn, while most corn seed in fact transmutes to become something else, such as a cow, a slice of cornbread, or perhaps a pig.

Sheng is conventionally translated in its noun form as "birth, life, and growth" and verbally as "giving birth to, bearing, living, growing, producing." Adjectivally *sheng* means "raw, unworked, fresh, strange" with the implication being that the bearer of this property is a new and thus unfamiliar quantum of life available for further refinement. Thinking gerundively and thus eventfully,

---

19. Kwan, "Database," 甲骨文合集 CHANT 1381.

the scope of *sheng* as "living" takes us generatively and qualitatively through the process from birth and growth to a life lived well. *Sheng* as a "doing" guides us from the beginnings of an activity to its consummate fruition, and as a "making" it leads us from raw, unworked ore to the refined product of an exquisite ceremonial *gu* 觚, a bronze libation vessel. The early *Shuowen* lexicon defines *sheng* as "plant growth breaking through the earth," but it also references the evolving life that follows from this erstwhile beginning as "advancing, extending, and spreading out" (*jin* 進).

Although the complex and ambiguous concept of "change" (*yi* 易) is defined in the *Book of Changes* as a generic "ceaseless generating and pro-creating" (*shengsheng* 生生), the traditional commentaries as we have seen do provide some specificity in characterizing this process. When the early sources correlate the term *yi* 易 paronomastically with the homophonous *yi* 益 as "increasing, gaining, profiting, adding to," we can infer that in the ecological economy of the *Book of Changes*, such autopoietic, transactional change is expansive and advantageous growth in the vital, situated relations that enrich experience. *Sheng* occurs synchronically in situ and diachronically in medias res as mutual interest is expressed in the first-order and consti-tutive relations that obtain among things, where such growth "appreciates" things in the sense of adding value to both themselves and their worlds.

The primacy of vital relationality has real implications for the way in which we parse the meaning of "birth" within an ecology of life and growth, and it requires that we qualify any uncritical, default assumptions we might have in our image of the birthing of discrete existents. As Tang Junyi in reflecting on the meaning of "natural propensities" (*xing* 性) observes, the answer to the question "Whither?" would seem to give us more important information than to the "What?" question: "Take the fact that a concrete existent has life. In speaking of its natural propensities (*xing*), what is import-ant is not remarking on *what* the *xing* of this entity is, but in assaying *the direction of its existence*."[20] It is only in having life and living its own story that something has *xing*. Everything as a "becoming" that is transforming in real time, is at once what it is for itself, for its specific context, and for the unsummed totality. Important in an understanding of this *sheng* vocabulary is the gestalt shift from the Greek noun-dominated, substance thinking with its world of human "beings" living their lives within a world of essential "things," to the Confucian gerundive assumptions about the always eventful

---

20. Tang Junyi, *Complete Works*, vol. 13, 28: 然就一具體存在之有生，而即言其有性，則重要者不在說此存在之性質性相之爲何，而是其生命存在之所向之爲何.

nature of "human becomings" living their interpenetrating and entwined lives within their natural, social, and cultural ecologies.

Just as human flourishing arises from positive growth in the relations of family and community, the isomorphic cosmic flourishing is an extension of this same kind of transactional growth but simply on a more expansive scale. Indeed, human values and the moral cosmic order are both grounded in life and its productive growth, and they are thus continuous with each other as interpenetrating complementarities. In canonical texts such as *Focusing the Familiar* (*Zhongyong* 中庸) and the *Classic of Family Reverence* (*Xiaojing* 孝經), what are specifically human moral imperatives such as "sincerity, resolution, co-creativity" (*cheng* 誠) and "family reverence" (*xiao* 孝) respectively, are also norms discerned in the natural order of things and are thus elevated as cosmic values beyond and yet inclusive of the human experience. At the same time, generic terms that describe erstwhile cosmic forces such as "way-making" (*dao* 道), "imaging" (*xiang* 象), and "patterning" (*li* 理) are also used to express the human capacity as meaning-makers to forge their way in the world, to transform images into institutions, and to structure the human experience with an achieved intelligence.

"Things" as constituted by their relations are continually being redefined by the growth they experience in their intercourse with other things. We might appeal to the metaphor of language usage and its compositing of words. Like words in a sentence, relational meaning begins from the conventional grammar that provides the basic ordering of these words required for them to be intelligible. Then in the deliberate process of "com + position," words are rearranged in their relations and are thus reinvested with significance, where the productive association they come to have with each other expands upon their meanings. The rhetorical effectiveness of a sentence is pursued as the relations among the words are cultivated and are thus grown in their meanings to become increasingly eloquent in their expression. And the sentence then rises to the level of poesy through optimizing the contribution that each inimitable word, drawing upon its own history of associations, is able to afford its specific others. Just as the grammatical and rhetorical relations among words can be cultivated to elevate language to the level of song, so too when relations among things are properly attended to, all things can aspire to a cosmic musicality.

The living world as it is constituted by the interpenetration of interdependent "things" (or better, "events") requires a doctrine of intrinsic, constitutive relations to describe them. Erstwhile "things" do not occupy a discrete place in the sense of simple location; rather, as living, focal "events" they are "taking place" with time and space being aspectual descriptors rather than separate dimensions. Time is a quantum of growth; space is the "taking place" of such growth. Given its broadest compass, the cosmological postulate we might translate as "persisting in change" (*biantong* 變通) and its later echo in Wang Bi's 王弼 expression "forming within functioning" (*tiyong* 體用) provides us with a summary language for how the activity of the always situated procreating process (*shengsheng* 生生) is understood and explained in the *Book of Changes*. Such an aspectual, processual vocabulary provides insight into both the determinate and the vital nature of these happenings:

> Thus, the closing of the swinging gate is called receptivity (*kun* 坤); the opening of it is called penetration (*qian* 乾). The ongoing alternation of openings and closings is called flux (*bian* 變), and the inexhaustibility of the comings and goings is called persistence (*tong* 通). When something is manifest, it is called an image (*xiang* 象), and taking on physical form it is called a phenomenon (*qi* 器). To get a grasp of these things and employ them is called emulation (*fa* 法). Putting them to good use so that all of the people can take advantage of them is called insight into the mysteries of the world (*shen* 神).[21]

This passage describes step by step the presencing of events within a vital landscape characterized by both determinacy and an ever-present, indeterminate penumbra, the symbiotic relationship between their forming and functioning, the manifesting of a patterned yet changing imagistic configuration among them (*xiang* 象), their acquiring and then shedding phenomenal forms (*qi* 器), and the unfathomable "more" that honeycombs things and goes beyond our capacities of perception (*shen* 神). This language speaks metaphorically to the different modalities of interaction and intercourse such events have within the flux and persistence of experience (*biantong*). The unsummed totality of the cosmic ecology termed *dao* is the confluence of the always unique narratives of these interpenetrating events. There is a transactional coalescing of each focal event (*de* 德) through nurturing and being nurtured in its relations with its environing others (*de* 得), and it is from the perspective of each of these events that its own specific journey or way-making (*dao*) is being construed.

---

21. Ames, *Sourcebook*, 110: 是故闔戶謂之坤, 闢戶謂之乾, 一闔一闢謂之變, 往來不窮謂之通, 見乃謂之象, 形乃謂之器, 制而用之謂之法, 利用出入, 民咸用之謂之神.

Appealing to the concrete example of human identity formation, a person's own potentialities, far from being causally frontloaded by locating their latent qualities as some inherent nature that is then available for actualization, arises pari passu in their collaboration over time with their environments: that is, a person's identity is continually forming as they participate in the various operations taking place in the world around them (*tiyong* 體用). It is thus that persons, rather than being self-standing human "beings," can best be characterized in the language of human "becomings" who are constantly internalizing their environing conditions to grow their personal identities, and who, in this process, are intentionally shaping the identities of their environing others. Such human "becomings" are vital, interpenetrating, and irreducibly social "events" that create meaning through the continuing cultivation of their relations with others, thus providing them with the opportunity to transform what is ordinary experience into something extraordinary.

We begin from the fact that the phenomenon of life itself, always a collaboration between organism and environment, seeks naturally to optimize its conditions for its growth. The purpose of life and the form it takes is thus explained by the inclination of the natural world toward a shared synergy and an optimizing symbiosis in the relations among the things that constitute it. This perceived proclivity of ecologies to make the most of their resources is captured in the Confucian prescriptive language in *Focusing the Familiar* (*Zhongyong*) of achieving "balance and equilibrium" (*zhong* 中) and sustaining a "superlative harmony" (*he* 和). And human "becomings" have the capacity as co-creators in this natural world to participate fully in this living process, coordinating the human life experience with all things to further enhance the flourishing of the cosmic order. To human beings as cosmic meaning-makers falls the responsibility for cultivating and aestheticizing the human experience and for lifting it out of its animality through a contrapuntal, expansive relationship with the heavens and the earth. The civilizing of the human experience that brings with it elegance and refinement is genealogical and naturalistic—it is "turtles all the way down" in the sense of making no appeal to the intervention of some external, metaphysical or supernatural source. The phenomenal world in classical China of which humankind is one aspect is an endless stream, evidencing its determinate character only within the generative process of "trans-*form*-ation." The formal aspect of experience, always attended by temporality, is the rhythmic cadence of life that, when properly cultivated, becomes its musicality.

Zoetology's Relational Equity as an Alternative to a Foundational Individualism

We might recall the argument for why, in ontological thinking, the entrenched notions of autonomous individuality and simple equality of persons continue to trump the alternative conception of what Zhang Yanhua has described earlier as irreducibly "physiological, psychological, and sociological" persons embedded in a living ecology. Political theorists dating back to the classical Greeks have certainly acknowledged that we are all social creatures strongly influenced by the others with whom we interact and, further, are fully cognizant of the fact that we are deeply influenced by the different cultures within which we live our lives. As Aristotle has remarked, a person who could live apart from society might be a beast or a god but is not a human being.[22] At the same time, however, this social and cultural dimension of individual persons has rarely been regarded as defining of our humanity at its moral, political, biological, and metaphysical levels.

The reasoning is that within our personal narratives, our socially defined selves cannot be regarded as being of compelling worth because we have had little control over the contingencies out of which the concrete circumstances of our lives have emerged. That is, we do not ourselves determine our time and place, our ethnicity, our family lineage, our gender, and so on. Consequently, on this individualistic view, what must establish the primary worth of human beings—their dignity, their integrity, and their ultimate value—is the capacity of individuals to act purposively and to be self-determining, that is, their autonomy. It is individual autonomy that must command the respect of us all. Of course, in order for these individual human beings to be truly autonomous, they must be free and rational in the choices that they make rather than being coerced or governed by instinct or passion. And since all human beings are valorized in terms of their autonomy, even though they may in many ways be significantly different from each other, the value invested in their shared individual autonomy makes them essentially equal in their humanity and trumps what are in comparison only incidental differences.

John Stuart Mill is a fair example of a philosopher who begins from just such an assumption about the discreteness of individuals, insisting as he does that all social activity can be traced back to a fixed and individuated human nature. Mill insists that "the laws of the phenomena of society are,

---

22. Aristotle, *Politics, The Complete Works*, 1253a.

and can be, nothing but the laws of the actions and passions of human beings united together in the social state. Men, however, in a state of society are still men; their actions and passions are obedient to the laws of individual human nature."[23] The renowned sociologist Fei Xiaotong 費孝通 in positing an alternative to the kind of foundational individualism we find in Mill introduces distinctions that he would argue establish an important contrast between Western and Chinese models of social organization. Reflecting on the deep-rooted history of Western individualism, Fei describes this "organizational mode of association" (*tuantigeju* 團體格局) as groups of discrete individuals constructing rule-governed social organizations that function within clearly defined boundaries. The image Fei uses for this organizational mode is of individual straws collected and bound together to form a haystack—that is, a bundle of discrete, individual entities brought together under a common principle.

For Fei, the contemporary configuration of a very different Chinese kinship-based sociopolitical model of governance can be attested to as early as the bronze inscriptions and the canons of the early Zhou dynasty.[24] Fei contrasts the Western organizational mode of association with a Chinese kinship model he calls "the differential mode of association" (*chaxugeju* 差序格局)[25] and provides us with what has now become a familiar idea in our thinking about a Chinese alternative to the ontology of self-sufficient individuals. The image Fei uses for the focal identity of persons within the Chinese kinship model of personal and social organization is "concentric circles formed when a stone is thrown into a lake."[26] Fei insists that Confucian ethics must be conceived of within the context of always unique "centers fanning out into a web-like network"[27] that are "composed of webs woven

23. J. S. Mill, *A System of Logic, Ratiocinative and Inductive; Being a Connected View of the Principles of Evidence and the Methods of Scientific Investigation*, 8th ed. (London: Longmans, Green, 1930), book 6, chap. 7, sec. 1.

24. Yiqun Zhou, *Festival, Feasts, and Gender Relations in Ancient China and Greece* (New York: Cambridge University Press, 2010), 147, also argues that "the home, where one engaged in daily practices of kinship-centered moral precepts and religious ceremonies, was the site for the most fundamental education in Zhou society."

25. Fei Xiaotong, *From the Soil: The Foundations of Chinese Society*, a translation of *Xiangtu Zhongguo* 鄉土中國 by Gary G. Hamilton and Wang Zheng (Berkeley: University of California Press, 1992), 63.

26. Fei Xiaotong, *From the Soil*, 63.

27. Fei Xiaotong, *From the Soil*, 68.

out of countless personal relationships."[28] This dynamic image of a stone thrown into a lake is reinforced by the fact that the character for "ripples" or "rippling" (*lun* 淪) is cognate and homophonous with the graph for "human relations" (*lun* 倫): that is, the first-order "bonds" (*guanxi* 關係) that are formed through the transactions and associations taking place within our roles and relations as they at once come to constitute and to conjoin us.

Fei would further claim that this predominant pattern of Chinese kinship relations with its hierarchically defined roles and relations produces its own distinctive kind of morality within which "no ethical concepts . . . transcend specific types of human relationships."[29] That is, kinship as the root of all human relations is defined by the cluster of values that surround "family reverence" (*xiao* 孝) and "fraternal deference" (*ti* 悌) as they conduce to growth in human relations within the family and the community more broadly.

Returning to Mill, in one chapter of *On Liberty* entitled "On Individuality, as One of the Elements of Well-Being," he reflects further on his understanding of the discrete nature of the individual. Using the metaphor of a tree for the individual person, he observes that "human nature is not a machine to be built after a model, and set to do exactly the work prescribed for it, but a tree, which requires to grow and develop itself on all sides, according to the tendency of the inward forces which make it a living thing."[30]

Mill would seem to offer us a decontextualized understanding of a tree that would make it analogous to "individual human nature" governed by the tendency of its inward forces.[31] By way of contrast with this notion of a self-sufficient tree, Zhao Tingyang argues that the arboreous metaphors of "setting the root" (*zhagen* 扎根) and "growing therefrom" (*shengzhang* 生長)—that is, rootedness and collaborative growth—are the two images most expressive of an alternative Chinese "ontology" of "doing" and "making" rather than "being." Mill's teleological reading of the growth of a tree as a solitary, internal affair is an example of causal thinking that ignores the fact that trees as stands, as groves, and as forests are naturally located within the synergy of an unbounded, living ecology. As an alternative to

---

28. Fei Xiaotong, *From the Soil*, 78.

29. Fei Xiaotong, *From the Soil*, 74.

30. J. S. Mill, *On Liberty in Focus*, ed. John Gray and G. W. Smith (London: Routledge, 1991), 75.

31. Mill, *On Liberty*, 75.

Mill's perception of trees as individuated and self-contained entities, there is much to be appreciated in Fei Xiaotong's contextualizing metaphor for growth wherein persons are construed as focal radial centers that, with a stone being thrown into a lake, ripple outward. Fei describes these focal centers as being hierarchically interrelated, where "one touches different circles at different times and places."[32]

All good, but from a zoetological perspective, Fei's suggestive image does have its limitations. For example, one association that would distance Fei's metaphor from zoetological thinking is the independent agency for the stone to be thrown into the lake. An alternative image more appropriate than the notion of an external causal agency would bring with it a *ziran* 自然 relational understanding of causality wherein anything is the cause and effect of everything else. Yet another way in which Fei's rippling water metaphor might be supplemented is to underscore the sense of vitality that comes with rootedness and collaborative growth. Again, remembering the interpenetration of organism and environment and thus the "shaping and being shaped" activity of all growth, it would seem that in order to respect the always collateral nature of relationality and to acknowledge the mutual imbrication and interdependence of the focal centers, Fei's centrifugal image could also be complemented by a reflexive, centripetal metaphor. The growth of persons is always collateral: both a doing and an undergoing.

As a corrective on Mill's image of the individual and self-sufficient tree and as a complement to Fei's rippling water metaphor then, we might appeal to how trees actually grow and explore the internalizing and embodying dynamics that are at work in the formation of their annual rings (*nianlun* 年輪). Over time through radial expansion this vital, centripetal process comes to form the pith and heartwood of the tree and tells the detailed story of its rooted growth. Such a reflexive image in turning the always collateral growth process back upon itself, supplements Fei's analogy of a center's centrifugal ripples (*lun* 淪) spreading outward. That is, persons themselves both shape and are shaped by their vital network of relations. Being located within this contextualizing pattern of vital relations, while drawing upon and internalizing these external resources in achieving their own personal identities, at the same time they in analogous degree act upon others.

With the passage of the seasons, the rings of a tree are formed from the reflexive and synergistic process of internalizing the external environment in its pattern of growth. For example, in the annual cycle the seasons are

---

32. Fei Xiaotong, *From the Soil*, 63.

taken in, with the lighter colored portion of the rings being formed as the spring and summer growth while the darker section comes along with the late summer and autumn growth. The size of the rings corresponds to the availability of and fluctuations among the resources needed for healthy growth, where years of abundance and distress are clearly marked in the configuration of the rings. Negative conditions such as drought, excessive rain, fire, insect plagues, disease epidemics, injuries, thinning, air pollution, all leave their mark within a tree's annual growth rings, as do those positive environmental circumstances that conduce to its thriving.

Within the trunk there is a fundamental distinction between the heartwood and the sapwood. The outer bark protects the tree from invasive threats, while the inner bark is the conduit through which the food-bearing sap circulates throughout the tree. The heartwood absent living cells is hard and durable, heavier in weight, and resistant to pathogens. It grows in circumference with age, secures and sustains the tree, and together with a system of roots usually three times the diameter of the branches and canopy gives the tree its structural strength and support. The sapwood is the outer region under the layers of bark where the new growth of the tree is taking place. It is lighter in color, softer and less durable in being vulnerable to pathogens. Proportionally it is relatively constant as the component that conducts water and nutrients, and stores up wood. The sap of the tree is its life force, circulating to repair and rejuvenate the root system, trunk, and branches where and whenever needed and, in so doing, enabling the healthy new growth that in turn produces additional sap. The root system then serves as the organs of the tree that produces and stores up its nutrients.

While the dynamics of the life of a tree certainly has this centripetal aspect, internalizing its environments in service to its own identity, it still has a collateral relationship with its environment. The tree gives back. Trees produce oxygen essential to all life and absorb carbon dioxide that is harmful to life, and in so doing forested areas combat climate change. Their shade cools the planet and their root systems not only filter water of its toxins but also protect against extreme weather events by absorbing water and stabilizing the soil in which they grow. Trees provide the habitat for most living species and offer them their protection from exposure to harsh conditions. And again, trees as a counter to urbanization are an important factor in both human leisure activities and mental health.

How then does this image of a tree complement Fei Xiaotong's "stone in the lake" centrifugal image and correlate with the human experience? The growth of the tree can be interpreted as the emergence of a particular focal identity that is one and many at the same time. Just as with a human life, there is a marked difference in the quantum of growth, where saplings like children grow remarkably quickly, and the size of the rings in older trees become progressively smaller as they age. Each episode in the tree's narrative as told in its rings is unique to its growth and incremental to its focal identity. At the same time in its immediate environment, the tree has its place among at least a stand or sometimes a forest of trees that reflects both the continuity and the diversity within its family and community. Again, each tree is one phase in a genealogical lineage of trees, and it serves as the connector between the prior generation of progenitors and the next generation of its progeny. And in the relations this tree has within its living environment, it experiences much more collaboration than contest among the various species of plant and animal growth.[33]

When we reflect on the story told by each tree, just as with human "becomings" the tree is a unique event rather than a "thing"; a cultured, narrative "tree-becoming." All of the familiar idioms used to express the formation of personal identities such as "forming and functioning" (*tiyong* 體用), "persistence through change" (*biantong* 變通), and "one is many, many one" (*yiduobufen* 一多不分) have application to the career of a tree. At its center providing structural stability and resilience against the elements, the internalized record in the heartwood tells its own unique story. Its continuing growth in the inner bark and sapwood is only possible because of what has come before, and what has been passed on as integral to its identity. And this new continuing growth in due course contributes incrementally to provide the tree with its cultivated strength and endurance. It has a focus-field identity in which its "when" and "where" have become its "what"—its own focal character. In terms of temporality, we can say that trees grow rapidly in the spring, but we can also say that springtime is the rapid growing of trees.

This image of tree and root again stands as a corrective on our dualistic penchant for separating cause from effect, creator from creature, human nature from narrative, and root from tree. Just as leaves and roots draw their energy from the unbounded heavens above and the earth below respectively, in the collaboration of these leaves and roots they conspire together to achieve a shared symbiosis (*tiandigongsheng* 天地共生) that, playing on the mantra "the continuity between the cosmic and human relations"

---

33. John L. Culliney and David Jones, *The Fractal Self: Science, Philosophy, and the Evolution of Human Cooperation* (Honolulu: University of Hawaiʻi Press, 2017).

(*tianrenheyi* 天人合一), we might characterize as "the continuity between and the inseparability of the arboreous and cosmic orders" (*tianmuheyi* 天木合一). The system of roots and the canopy of leaves of any particular tree are synergistic and grow each other within an unbounded ecology. There is a seeming symmetry with its roots as branches stretching down into the ground and its branches as roots reaching up into the sky.

And particular trees are only one aspect of a shared, relational ecology that has no end and that brims with countless different forms of life. Not only trees and humans, but all, always unique life-forms in any ecology internalize their environments as their resource for growth. In zoetological thinking inspired by such growth, and in the nature of life itself, normativity in its broadest sense as morality, creativity, beauty, civilization, flourishing, and so on, lies in always situated and thus unique growth, together with the shared making of meaning that is the product of that growth.

Peter Hershock in his monograph *Valuing Diversity* reflects specifically on two different models used to interpret human flourishing that align with our distinction between ontological and zoetological thinking.[34] Each of these models advocates for specific values that have real consequences for growth within the human ecology in its broadest compass. Individual autonomy and equality are desideratum within the ethical discourse of liberal thinking. They are high values grounded in ontological thinking that bring with them the familiar language of individuality, rationality, freedom, rights, and personal choice. Drawing upon East Asian Buddhist values and practices that for the most part share as their interpretive context the process cosmology of Confucian philosophy, Hershock is able to formulate a clear alternative to autonomy and equality that are prioritized in liberal thinking. The counterpart to these liberal values in the ethics of zoetological thinking would be what Hershock terms an inclusive "relational equity" and the "achieved diversity" that follows from it.

Hershock's reasoning is as follows. Both autonomy and equality are grounded in an ontological doctrine of external relations that subordinates our relationships with other people to our individual selves. A doctrine of external relations prioritizes our personal integrity as human "beings" over our interdependence with each other and, again, the ostensive sameness that obtains among us—our "equality"—over our many differences. Thus, the notions of autonomy and equality as they attach to individuals give us

---

34. Peter D. Hershock, *Valuing Diversity: Buddhist Reflection on Realizing a More Equitable Global Future* (Albany: State University of New York Press, 2012).

a sense of personal differences as mere "variety"—differences that do not make much of a difference. That is, we certainly do have differences among us that we do best to register and tolerate, but such differences are in some important degree mitigated by the assumption that, having the integrity of autonomous individuals, we are still to be treated as equals. And as persons who would assert their individual autonomy, the relations they enter into remain external and contingent rather than intrinsic and constitutive.

The zoetological alternative to ontology's autonomy and equality is a relational equity that respects difference, and a first-order, nonfungible relationality that is grown into an achieved diversity as its outcome. This distinction is captured nicely in the Confucian mantra "harmony not uniformity" (*he'erbutong* 和而不同), where equity and diversity that would make the most of the possibilities of any particular situation are the values behind the pursuit of an optimizing symbiosis. Comparative equality and individual autonomy guarantee that difference can only be variations among basically similar people (variety). By way of contrast, in the zoetological model, the inclusive pursuit of relational equity and an achieved diversity in first-order, constitutive relations allows for the continuing diversification of qualities and propensities that grow our differences into resources for mutual enrichment (diversity).

In the liberal model of autonomous and equal individuals, persons can only count as such when they have reached majority and have the capacities to function as fully rational creatures. If we focus on family and community in the holistic zoetological model, human beings have their differences at the various stages that together constitute a full life, from infants to doting seniors. Including all of the phases of a personal career, human beings are most distinctive in the scale to which one person differs from another in their interests and their circumstances. Valorizing relational equity begins not only from an acknowledgment but also from an appreciation of such differences, and its goal is to achieve fairness in serving the interests of all within their different and always changing circumstances. Being much more complex than simple equality, equity allocates resources and opportunities that respect differences in the pursuit of social justice for all and for their shared well-being. And the outcome in this quest for social justice is an achieved diversity realized in the conserving and coordinating of personal differences that would seek to take full advantage of the creative possibilities of any situation.

Relational equity and an achieved diversity can be scaled up from the cultural differences among persons within a particular community to the differences that obtain among the thick cultures within a world community. An exclusive monochrome culture existing within its own parameters has little to offer its own inhabitants or those of other cultures save stability and continuity. When cultural differences within any level of community are merely tolerated but do not produce growth, the community has variety perhaps, but very little diversity. But when there is relational equity among cultures and all of them in their differences are included and treated fairly, there is a mutual accommodation among their different ways of living and thinking in which the cultural differences interact with each other to generate an achieved diversity. Simple variety among equals stands in rather stark contrast to the complex diversity that can only be achieved by fully activating and appreciating the important differences we have from each other. That is, we need to acknowledge not only that we differ *from* each other (variety) but that this gives us the opportunity to actively differ *for* each other, and in so doing to allow our differences to really make a difference (diversity). This pursuit of an optimizing symbiosis that begins from respecting differences is captured in the Confucian mantra "seeking superlative harmony rather than sameness" (*he'erbutong* 和而不同), and in the *Analects* it is given specific political application as "associating inclusively without being partisan" (*zhou'erbubi* 周而不比) and "gathering together with others without forming cliques" (*qun'erbudang* 群而不黨).[35]

There are two important corollaries to the zoetological valorization of relational equity and achieved diversity that we might note. First, within the human ecology, equity and diversity cannot be engineered by individual agents (who do not exist) but instead must emerge as a function of the coordinated activity among relationally constituted members of a family, community, and environment. And second, these same values of equity and diversity in the absence of individual agents are holistic in their compass and extend beyond our human parameters to guarantee the mutual implication and inseparability of ethical, economic, and importantly, ecological and environmental considerations.

In thinking zoetologically and extending the values of relational equity and achieved diversity to an unbounded cosmic ecology, we might observe that the healthy growth of trees is one vital aspect among many within the abundance of life-forms that are integral to producing a cosmic musicality. Growth as happiness, as beauty, and as morality is located within the achieved diversity of an ecology that emerges through the cooperation and

---

35. See *Analects* 13.23, 2.14, and 15.22.

coordination of its constituents rather than through the interventions of particular agents. When in the fullness of time the mature tree is harvested to become an aesthetically charged resource for the cabinetmaker, the skilled eye and hands of the carpenter and the beauty of the wood itself collaborate to make the most of the possibilities that come out of their shared synergy. And rather than being isolated after the fact by binaries such as subject and object, agent and action, or cause and effect, such collaboration takes on many different forms, all of them to be construed as growth in first-order relations.

Two Modes of Procreative Living:
"Derivation" (*paisheng* 派生) and
"Transmutation" (*huasheng* 化生)

Previously, I remarked on the ontological assumptions that would understand human "birthing" in terms of derivation, that is, mother *with* child becoming mother *and* child, with one human being becoming two. This animal sense of "birthing" stands in contrast to zoetological assumptions that favor a horticultural model where plant life internalizes the resources of its environment in coming to fruition, a transmutation model of growth that entails both continuity and change (*biantong* 變通). I am borrowing this derivation versus transmutation language from contemporary philosopher Pang Pu 龐樸, who by appealing to these two contrastive modalities in his explanation of the process of "procreating" (*sheng* 生) provides us with an illuminating distinction.[36] The first mode is procreating in a "derivative" sense (*paisheng* 派生) with one thing giving birth to another as the source of an independent existent: for example, a mother having a child or a hen laying an egg or an oak tree producing an acorn. Given the suppressed teleological assumptions characteristic of ontological thinking where a selfsame identical form is being reduplicated to produce a proliferation of the same natural kind, this causal and derivative sense of procreating has become a default common sense. Such ontological thinking gives rise to a perception of the world as being populated by discrete and independent things conjoined

---

36. Pang Pu, "Yizhong youji de yuzhou shengcheng tushi: Jieshao Chujian Taiyi sheng-shui" 一種有機的宇宙成圖式: 介紹楚簡《太一生水》 [An organic schematization of the universe: an introduction to the Chu bamboo slips "Taiyishengshui"], *Daojia wenhua yanjiu* 道家文化研究 17 (1999): 303.

by second-order, external relations, a world in which growth is construed teleologically as an inchoate potential internal to something that is then actualized.

The second model of procreating is in a "transmutative" sense (*huasheng* 化生) in which one thing transforms into something else, such as summer becoming autumn, and autumn becoming winter. Although Pang Pu has given us this important distinction, upon reflection we find that empirically these two senses of "procreating" are, at least in the birthing phase, profoundly asymmetrical to the extent that they challenge our default teleological assumptions. That is, in the *paisheng* "derivative" modality of growth, we must allow that it is only one egg in a million that is incubated to become a chicken, and only one acorn in a million that takes root to become an oak tree. For humans too, at least in their reproductive phase, the same is again true with the tournament narrowing down from millions to the marriage of a single sperm and a single ovulated egg. In the dominant *huasheng* "transmuting" modality of change, we must again acknowledge that most chicken eggs in fact become omelets and most acorns, squirrels. And even in the rare cases wherein a hen's egg actually does become another chicken, the erstwhile discreteness of such an "independent existent" must again be qualified by the thick genealogical continuities that obtain between progenitor and its progeny.

This genealogical model of procreation is also an encouragement to think of the human experience in a different way. While ontological thinking with its teleological assumptions does privilege a derivative understanding of procreation as its default common sense, both of these modes of procreation—derivation and transmutation—have immediate relevance to Chinese cosmology as complementaries rather than as alternatives. Importantly, as we have seen with the hen and her egg, the discreteness and independence entailed by *paisheng* is heavily qualified by the processual, genealogical, and contextual assumptions of *huasheng*. As we might note in reflecting upon the changing of the seasons, given the consummatory and episodic nature of life captured in the idea of *paisheng*, the processual continuity of *huasheng* is punctuated with divisions into days, weeks, and months, promising us always unique temporal "events." And when we turn to the complexities of the human experience, the possibilities for an achieved uniqueness of each member within a continuing genealogical lineage are again profound. Neither the uniqueness claimed by derivation nor the continuity promised by transmutation will yield to the other; both derivation and transmutation are significant, and mutually entailing.

The doctrine of internal relations that allows for the uniqueness and distinctiveness of particular things, on the one hand, and for the continuity that obtains among them on the other, disqualifies part-whole analysis and requires instead a gestalt shift to focus-field thinking in which this erstwhile "part" and this "totality" are two nonanalytic foregrounding and backgrounding perspectives on the same phenomenon. Carrying this mode of thinking over into the human experience, each member within a family lineage is a particular focus within a continuing and unbounded genealogical field that has neither beginning nor end.

In pursuing the distinction between "derivation" and "transmutation," Pang Pu is alerting us to a further refinement needed in cosmological thinking as we parse the transition from what comes before and what follows from it. Taking human genealogy as our specific, concrete example, while common sense prompts us to understand the progenitor and progeny as a derivative series in which there is an independence of the latter from the former, genealogy in early Chinese cosmology is clearly a combination of both *paisheng* as "derivative of" and *huasheng* as "transmuting into." While *this* progenitor certainly gives way to *this* unique progeny, at the same time, *this* progenitor as integral to the continuing family lineage also lives on as a defining force within the same progeny. The child has a certain "independence" from the parents, and yet the continuity with those who come before only begins with the obvious physical resemblances between bodies that are perceived in Chinese cosmology as having been inherited from the ancestors. More significant then, is the genealogical transmission of their cultural identity in the broadest and deepest sense, as the parents and their culture live on in their children, and in their children's children too. While such continuity is certainly true, again there is the possibility that any member in a family lineage can achieve the personal distinction that contributes to the prestige of both those ancestors who have come before, and those descendants who will follow behind.

With the emphasis in Confucian philosophy on family, on ancestor reverence, on the intergenerational transmission and embodiment of a living tradition, and on a continuing cultural identity, there has been a powerful sense of genealogical continuity. The progeny is a holographic foregrounding of this particular person within a continuing family lineage, and within an evolving Chinese cultural identity. One's family surname (*xing* 姓) is the first and continuing source of identity, while one's given name (*ming* 名) within the course of one's lifetime is complemented by a proliferation of assumed style names (*zi* 字), sobriquets (*hao* 號), and a web of specific family designations such as "uncle number two" (*ershu* 二叔) and "auntie number three" (*sanzhou* 三妯), with a series of professional titles such as "teacher" (*laoshi* 老師) and "director" (*zhuren* 主任), and then when all is done, with a usually (but not always) celebratory posthumous title (*shi* 諡).[37] Each one of these different names designates the many roles a particular person lives within a complex narrative and is a reflection of this person's unique contribution to the meaning of family and community. Again, with the holographic "continuity within change" (*biantong* 變通), the entire story is present within each ensuing episode of the life as it is lived.

But in this same process of transmutation with identity emerging as integral to a genealogical and cultural lineage, there resides a challenge to naïve assumptions about prospective historicity itself by moving in a retrospective direction as well. The progeny as heirs to the tradition certainly embody what has come before. But at the same time, not only can the distinctive lives of the progeny affect the stature of the continuing lineage, but the histories through which they narrate their own origins are not solely or even primarily aimed at accurately depicting an erstwhile closed past. Instead their story can be intended to disclose a trajectory of change projected into an open and yet more or less anticipated future.

We might also want to recall that the early image for birth, life, and growth in the Chinese commentary is the sprouting of plant growth breaking ground rather than human beings giving birth. Rather than confounding our derivative assumptions about birthing, this horticultural understanding of "birth" carries over to assist us in rethinking the case of human birthing within a continuing genealogical narrative. That is, the genealogical understanding of *sheng* reflects the cosmological assumptions in which *dao* 道 is

---

37. In the *Mencius* 4B2 there is a passage: 暴其民甚\, 則身弒國亡; 不甚, 則身危國削. 名之曰 "幽厲," 雖孝子慈孫, 百世不能改也 (When a ruler inflicts real violence on his people, he will be assassinated and his state will perish. Where such negligence is in a lesser degree, his person will be endangered and the territory of his state will be pared away. Such rulers will become known as "the Benighted" and "the Cruel," and even if they have the most dutiful and affectionate sons and grandsons, their progeny will be unable to change this stigma for a hundred generations). As a historical example of Mencius's warning, there are many stories that remember the last ruler of the Shang dynasty, the tyrant Zhou 紂, in the recounting of his debauchery and cruelty to all of those around him. He was given to punishments that maim and mutilate, and making it even worse, many of his victims were elder members of his own extended family. It is for this reason that he was given the posthumous name Zhou 紂: a horse crupper that, in securing the saddle at the back, is the most likely link in the equestrian accessories to be fouled by the defecating horse.

frequently characterized as the "mother" and thus the "fetal source" (*shi* 始) of the myriad things (*wanwu* 萬物). The *Daodejing*, for example, observes that "indeterminacy names the fetal beginnings of the world, and determinacy names the mother of all things. . . . These two aspects emerge from the same source yet have different names; together we call them dark. Darkest of the dark, they are the swinging gateway of the manifold mysteries."[38] The term *shi* 始 translated here as "fetal" rather than initial "beginnings" is found on the bronzes as  and is defined in the *Shuowen* lexicon as a woman giving birth.[39] This notion of a natal beginning is associated with a series of cognate characters: the fetus (*tai* 胎) that in its maturation comes to inherit a world "bequeathed" to it (*yi* 詒) and "passed on" (*yi* 貽) from progenitors who have come before. The language of birthing is pervasively genealogical and ancestral (*zong* 宗), including within this vocabulary rather vague expressions such as "lord" (*di* 帝) and the often-anthropomorphic *tian* 天 that straddle the human and the numinous realms of ancestors and gods respectively.

The predominant metaphor in this world-making process is the mother and the birthing canal from which everything issues forth, itself being a pathway (*dao* 道) that opens through the swinging doors into the life experience. Images such as the opening gateway and *xuan* 玄 as "dark" with the red-black color that produces a darkening red underscore this amniotic association. Indeed, in understanding *dao* in its relation to the myriad things, we have to resist our default derivative assumptions about procreativity that attends such a birthing. *Dao* and the myriad things, far from fitting the familiar Abrahamic model of some transcendent and thus wholly independent Creator as the causal source of His creatures, are simply two aspectual ways of looking at the same phenomenon and the *ziran* 自然 causality that animates it. It is the vitality as it is expressed in the collaboration between determinacy and the ever-present penumbra of indeterminacy that explains the presencing of a persistent and yet always novel world.

The genealogical "cosmogony" offered here is a natal and historical account that occurs within the unfolding process of "worlding" rather than a description of some metaphysical intervention from outside. It references a birthing from an inchoate, incipient life-form that presupposes genealogy and progenitors rather than originative principles or divine design, and a

38. *Daodejing* 1: 無名天地之始; 有名萬物之母 . . . 此兩者, 同出而異名, 同謂之玄. 玄之又玄, 眾妙之門.

39. Kwan, "Database," 西周晚期 CHANT 4338.

pattern of always situated and cultivated growth in meaning rather than the linear actualization of some predetermined potential. This is what Frederick Mote means when he argues that "the genuine Chinese cosmology is that of organismic process, meaning that all parts of the entire cosmos belong to one organic whole and that they all interact as participants in one spontaneously self-generating life process."[40] We repeatedly encounter this alternative understanding of what "procreativity" means in the *Daodejing* in the way in which it deploys the term *sheng* 生, conventionally translated as "giving birth to." For example, D. C. Lau with "begets" being his rendering of the term *sheng* translates the cosmological if not cosmogonic lines in *Daodejing* 42: "The way [*dao*] begets one; one begets two; two begets three; three begets the myriad creatures . . ."[41] Such an interpretation or some equivalency ("gives birth to," "engenders," "produces") is standard and ubiquitous in the literature, with this conventional rendering locating *dao* as antecedent to its progeny. With the understanding that *dao* is the source of one, two, three, and then all things, it reinforces the sense that *dao* is logically and temporally prior to and again is independent of its creatures. For the English language reader, this uncritical "derivative" reading of *sheng* as simply "birthing" construes *dao* as some ultimate and primal source that produces everything that is and, in so doing, overwrites Chinese cosmology with an ontological model of cosmogony not its own. Indeed, such an equivocation on "birthing" begins with John Chalmers's 1888 translation of the *Daodejing* as *Speculations on Metaphysics, Polity, and Morality of the "Old Philosopher" Lau-tsze* and persists with Arthur Waley's *The Way and Its Power* (1934) and Ursula Le Guin's popular translation as *Tao Te Ching: A Book about the Way and the Power of the Way* (1998).

If, however, we read *sheng* here in the holographic way consistent with early Chinese cosmology, it precludes any exclusive separation between creator and creature, between focus and field, between derivation and transmutation, with each being implicated in the other. This *Daodejing* cosmogonic passage is simply describing the synchronic and diachronic "presencing" of the world around us as it is experienced from one particular perspective or another. We might acknowledge an immediate association between *sheng* as it is used here and the generative notion of the "self-so-ing" (*ziran* 自然) causality that would express the simultaneous presencing of the particular

---

40. Frederick Mote, *Intellectual Foundations of China* (New York: McGraw-Hill, 1989), 15.

41. *Daodejing* 42: 道生一, 一生二, 二生三, 三生萬物. *Lao Tzu: Tao Te Ching*, trans. D. C. Lau (London: Penguin Books, 1963), 49.

and the totality, of this focus and its field. This understanding allows us to interpret and then translate this *Daodejing* 42 passage as "Way-making (*dao*) entails continuity, continuity difference, difference plurality, and plurality the manifold of all that is happening."[42] *Dao* and all that is happening are simply two different aspectual expressions for the same procreative process. Given that *dao* is at once continuity and proliferation, *dao* in its relationship to the myriad things (*wanwu* 萬物) provides a good example of Tang Junyi's cosmological postulate *yiduobufenguan* 一多不分觀 as "many is one, one many." That is, it precludes the individuating assumption that one is one in the sense that it is independent and self-contained, and that many are many in the sense of a variety of discrete entities.

Zoetology and Its "Self-so-ing" (*ziran* 自然) Causality

Joseph Needham describes the early Chinese processual and organic cosmology as producing "a characteristic thought-form of its own." He invites us, like Alice sliding down the rabbit hole and finding the other side of the looking glass, to share his encounter with a wonky, wobbly world that has "its own causality and its own logic."[43] Unlike the Greeks who begin from the unconditioned certainty guaranteed by ontology as "the science of being in-itself," in zoetological thinking it is living and growing that are taken as the point of departure, and primacy is given to the constitutive nature of vital relationality. Reflecting on zoetology's alternative, aesthetic causality, we might describe it as a *ziran* 自然 causality wherein anything is both the cause and the effect of everything else. That is, the narrative of any particular thing emerges genealogically in medias res or "in the middle" and pari passu or "along with everything else" as the presencing of a focal and vital center within an unbounded field of experience: a narrative beginning nested within narratives within narratives.

Aristotle's linear causality gives us the binary of cause and effect. That is, a thing's specific efficient, material, formal, and final causes in sum produce its ultimate effect, the actualization of its potential, and its purpose.

---

42. For an extended discussion, see Brook Ziporyn, "Vast Continuity versus the One: Thoughts on *Daodejing* 42, *Taiyishengshui*, and the Legacy of Roger T. Ames," in *Appreciating the China Difference: Engaging Roger T. Ames on Methods, Issues, and Roles*, ed. James Behuniak (Albany: State University of New York Press, 2018).

43. Needham, *Science and Civilisation in China*, vol. 2, 280.

It is a rationalized order in the sense that the causal source of order and the design itself are antecedent to the ultimate realization of the order. In the alternative zoetological *ziran* causality, order begins from the life of the insistent particular, where any particular thing is causally implicated in everything else within the unbounded ecology. Said another way, when something is a matrix constituted by its vital relations, and when these same relations have no boundary, then everything is implicated in any particular impulse. And again everything thus being relevant to the totality of the effect, the ad hoc emergent order is the unsummed totality of just those particular details that constitute it.

Philosophically nuanced interpreters reflecting on the use of this term *ziran* in the canonical texts often choose to render it "self-so-ing." *Ran* 然 means "so-ing-ly" or "such-ing-ly" in the holographic sense of how things are emerging and presencing, with the graph's suggestive image being the roasting of dog meat and, by extension, "the flaring up of the fire." *Ran* has an adverbial function where in binomials such as *huran* 忽然 or *biran* 必然 or *anran* 安然 it adds the "-ly" to "suddenly" or "inevitably" or "peacefully" respectively. In *ziran* as "self-ly" or "self-so-ing-ly," *ran* is complemented by a notion of *zi* 自 or "self-" that has three aspects.

First, this *ziran* causality means that the "self" in the "self-so-ing" process is uniquely what it is, one of a kind; it is a continuing, vital, and specific identity constituted by an unbounded and dynamic manifold of always unique relations. Second, this *zi* identity has both an objective and subjective dimension to it, perceived and engaged from the outside but also lived from the inside. It is this existential self-awareness that prospectively negotiates its *zi* identity from within, and that has some projective influence in the setting and fusing of its horizons with its environing conditions. It is this existential and vital dimension of *zi* that would give *ziran* explanatory force when the *Changes* correlates the processes of change themselves (*yi* 易) with procreativity (*shengsheng* 生生). And it is the verbal *zi* as "living" (*sheng* 生) that is the antecedent to the adverbial *ran* as "livingly" or "presencing" Again, when the *Daodejing* declares that "*dao* emulates self-so-ing" (*daofaziran* 道法自然), *ziran* is the explanation of the specific way to understand *dao* as the genealogical "source" or metaphorically the "mother" of all things, an understanding of causality that stands in stark contrast to the familiar creator/creature causal versions of cosmogony.

And third, since this *zi* identity is constituted by an unbounded field of relations, the *zi* is what it is by virtue of the quality of the coalescence it has been able to achieve within the matrix of vital relations that conspire together to make it insistently so (*ran* 然). Said simply, since everything causes anything, any particular thing is both the cause and the effect of everything else.

Viewed from the perspective of classical Greek metaphysics, we might say that this Confucian cosmology and its alternative *ziran* causality shaves with Ockham's razor not once, but twice. Chinese cosmology, instead of appealing to a notion of some transcendent and independent principle as the cause and architect of the world, begins instead from what is happening within the vital, autogenerative world itself. This "worlding" is an inside without an outside. For Confucianism, the world is an autopoietic, "self-so-ing" process (*ziran'erran* 自然而然) wherein the energy of its ongoing transformation resides within the continuing narrative itself as the strains and tensions as well as the collaborations that emerge among all of its particular aspects. Indeed, in its presencing it has on offer a genealogical religiousness wherein all things can cultivate a sense of contribution and belonging to the totality without reference to a God—an alternative family-centered religious sensibility affirming a spirituality and sacredness that emerges out of inspired human living itself.

The Confucian cosmology shaves a second time by beginning not from an essentialized and causal human nature as an analog to the causal nature of God at the scale of cosmic design but from a phenomenology of what unfolds and compounds as moral habits within the narrative of particular persons themselves. Analogous to the positing of a world that exists without reference to a divine substratum as its source and design, persons too are theorized with no appeal made to some independent, reduplicative, and causal human nature or soul or self as the endowed source of human conduct. The source of a person is their narrative, the collaboration of the vital manifold of relations that together tell their always unique stories.

How then are we to understand the generative notion of *sheng* 生 conventionally translated as "gives birth to, engenders, begets, produces" in a cosmogony in which *dao* 道 and the myriad things (*wanwu* 萬物) do not have the linear creator and creature causal relationship that we find as a commonplace in metaphysical cosmogonies? The source of everything, regardless of how it is parsed, is to be explained as "self-so-ing" (*ziran* 自然) within the "self-so-ing" processes of the cosmos itself. In the *Daodejing* 道德經, the title of which might be translated as "the classic of *this* focus and *its* field," for example, the text observes that just as *dao* as the unsummed totality of world-making "emulates" and is to be explained as self-so-ing," this same model of causality is at the same time true of any aspect or *de* within this world-making process as well. For example, "we the people all say of ourselves that we are self-so-ing."[44] *Dao* is the unsummed totality including "we the people" and everything else. And it unfolds in its continuing transformation as a function of the ceaseless procreation that is occurring at the autopoietic and vital interface between the indeterminate (*wu* 無) and what is becoming determinate (*you* 有). Through the "opening and closing of the gates," an always novel world emerges. The holography in this focus-field cosmology means that the unsummed totality is implicated in each focal particular, and that *dao* is thus present in each moment lived in the lives of ordinary people. Rather than field and focus "begetting" each other in a derivative sense, *dao* and each impulse of life arise together, either backgrounded as this unbounded field construed from this particular focal perspective, or foregrounded as this focus within its particular and yet unbounded field. While *dao* must be understood as an ad hoc and unsummed totality of all orders rather than a rationalizing superordinate and single order, when the *de* orders that constitute *dao* achieve real depth (*du* 度) in their coalescence with each other, they produce a cosmic aesthetic and its musicality.

By way of clarifying this *ziran* causality in perhaps more familiar language, we might appeal to the classical pragmatists who, as themselves zoetological thinkers, also posit a focus-field conception of persons. Dewey provides an organic, ecological image that illustrates how the holographic focus of our habitual behaviors, in having both "everything" and "all the time" as their penumbra, is thus a construal of the synchronic and diachronic totality from one particular perspective. Dewey insists that with the process of habit-formation "an environment both extensive and enduring is immediately implicated in present behavior. Operatively speaking, the remote and the past are 'in' behavior making it what it is. The action called 'organic' is not just that of internal structures; it is an integration of organic-environmental connections."[45] In whatever way we choose to go about explaining the phenomenon we call "thinking," it is clear to Dewey that each moment in this continuing process, far from being isolatable or discrete, has implicated within it an often unclear but always unbounded field of experience. For Dewey, "it may be a mystery that there should be thinking but it is no mystery that if there is thinking it should contain in a 'present' phase, affairs remote in space and in time, even to geologic

---

44. *Daodejing* 25: 道法自然 and 17: 百姓皆謂我自然.

45. Dewey, *Later Works*, vol. 1, 213.

ages, future eclipses and far away stellar systems. It is only a question of how far what is 'in' its actual experience is extricated and becomes focal."[46]

William James in his *Pluralistic Universe* uses a phenomenology of consciousness to reflect on and to give vivid expression to what he calls "the pulse of inner life," a pulsation that, in being both holistic and specific at the same time, requires that we abandon any notion of "inner" and "outer," "subjective" and "objective," "existential" and "phenomenal" as exclusive domains and reconceive their relationship in focus-field, holographic terms. These correlative categories are simply two ways of foregrounding and emphasizing different aspects of the same phenomenon, or stated more concretely, they foreground our focal personal identities within the boundless field of our complex narratives. "Inner" is a self-conscious awareness of the cultivated quality of my relations making a difference within my field of experience; "outer" is the question of how in my deferring to my contextualizing others, my field of experience acquires enhanced extension and resolution from the perspective of those affected by it. James observes that

> in the pulse of inner life immediately present now in each of us is a little past, a little future, a little awareness of our own body, of each other's persons, of these sublimities we are trying to talk about, of the earth's geography and the direction of history, of truth and error, of good and bad, and of who knows how much more? Feeling, however dimly and subconsciously, all these things, your pulse of inner life is continuous with them, belongs to them and they to it.[47]

In this same passage, James goes on to appeal explicitly to a language of focal centers and extended fields as his way of getting past the intellectualist habit of fragmenting our experience into separate "things." He insists that

> the real units of our immediately felt life are unlike the units that intellectualist logic holds to and makes its calculations with. They are not separate from their own others, and you have to take them at widely separated dates to find any two of them that seem unblent. . . . My present field of consciousness

---

46. Dewey, *Later Works*, vol. 1, 213.

47. William James, *A Pluralistic Universe* (New York: Longmans, Green, 1912), 286.

is a centre surrounded by a fringe that shades insensibly into a subconscious more. . . . Which part of it properly is in my consciousness, which out? If I name what is out, it already has come in. The centre works in one way while the margins work in another, and presently overpower the centre and are central themselves. What we conceptually identify ourselves with and say we are thinking of at any time is the centre; but our full self is the whole field, with all those indefinitely radiating subconscious possibilities of increase.[48]

It is clear that in passages such as these, the pragmatists Dewey and James are offering us a focus-field conception of persons that is radically disjunctive within their own philosophical narrative dominated as it has been by a foundational individualism. Indeed, such a challenge to old ways of thinking is perhaps an important reason why decades had to elapse before these early pragmatists have come to be recognized and understood by the mainstream discipline of philosophy as the original and important philosophers they are.

Zoetology and Its Generative Logic

In the world of the classical Greeks, Aristotle's logic grounded in strict identity and the principle of noncontradiction gives us the one method of establishing demonstrable truth. But zoetology's alternative, generative logic requires analogical reasoning that has the capacity to produce new meaning. If, as Needham says, "the sum of wisdom" is a deliberate increase in "the number of intuited analogical correspondences in the repertory of correlations," how then do we follow this path to an increase in wisdom?[49] How do we in our relations achieve that quality of resolution and produce that quantum of meaning needed to live sagaciously?

I have brought John Dewey and William James into the conversation to reiterate the point that zoetological thinking and its *ziran* causality is by no means exclusively Chinese. Again, resisting Needham's language that would give Chinese cosmology its "own" exclusive logic and in so doing further exoticize it, we can find analogy with the logic of another classical

---

48. James, *A Pluralistic Universe*, 286–288.
49. Needham, *Science and Civilisation in China*, vol. 2, 290.

pragmatist, C. S. Peirce.[50] Peirce wanted from reasoning the capacity to produce new ideas—to go beyond what is already stated in the premises and to augment these ideas with additional information and content. To this end, he found it necessary to develop the concept of "abductive" or "explanatory" or "presumptive" reasoning as a necessary supplement to the more familiar notions of deductive and inductive reasoning. Deduction from a given hypothesis is not generative of new meaning, and while enumerative induction is content-increasing by generalizing a particular sample to a population, the extra content is not new but rather an amplificatory generalization made from the content of the premises. Deductive and inductive reasoning are thus used for justificatory purposes to confirm the validity of a given hypothesis and thus serve as an important source for security in our thinking. Abductive reasoning on the other hand is not only ampliative (amplifying the content as induction does) but is also a distinctively generative activity that is productive of new ideas. Abduction is the process of surveying the facts and then coming up with a theory that can best explain them, and it is thus often described as "inference to the best explanation." Further, abduction has the function of not simply justifying hypotheses but of belonging to that phase of inquiry in which a theory is formulated in the first place.

There are several different interpretations of abductive reasoning. A more conservative one would construe it as form of sleuthing or diagnostics that produces an educated guess as to the best explanation that then becomes available for further testing. While such abductive reasoning is short on security in having to rely upon deductive or inductive reasoning to confirm its conclusions, it is nonetheless taken to be strong on uberty: that is, it is fruitful and a source of copiousness.[51] But the perceived strength

---

50. This is not to say that the examples of a generative logic do not abound within the Chinese literature itself. As in the final chapter of this present monograph, we might appeal to Zhang Xianglong's 張祥龍 distinction between imagistic and conceptual thinking or Zhao Tingyang's 趙汀陽 distinctions between a metaphysics of "things" and of *facta* 事, between "creatiology" and ontology. See Zhang Xianglong, 概念化思維與象思維 [Conceptualizing thinking and imagistic thinking], 杭州師範大學學報 [Journal of Hangzhou Normal University] no. 5 (September 2008), and Zhao Tingyang, 赵汀阳: 作为创世论的存在论 [Creatiology as ontology], 哲学研究 [Philosophical research] no. 8 (2012).

51. Igor Douven, "Peirce on Abduction," "Abduction," in *The Stanford Encyclopedia of Philosophy* (Spring 2011 edition), and Stathis Psillos, "Abduction: Between Conceptual Richness and Computational Complexity," in *Abduction and Induction: Essays on Their Relation and Integration*, ed. A. K. Kakas and P. Flach (Dordrecht: Kluwer, 2000).

of abduction so conceived is also its weakness. On this reading, abduction still entails a logic of discovery rather than describing real creative advance and thus precludes reasoning from being a source of new information and ideas. What it makes "newly available" is information about an existing world rather than occasioning the spontaneous emergence of true novelty.

A second, liberal, and more interesting reading of Peircean abduction is that it is the open-ended and unbounded process of making productive correlations, of generating new meaning, and of taking as its boundaries only the limits of our imagination. Steve Coutinho observes that "successful abduction requires accumulated knowledge, extensive experience and a lively imagination. We start with a mystery, a perception, a text; these provide the 'evidence' consisting of a small number of clues, or traces. We then use our imagination, informed and constrained by our extensive experience, and accumulated knowledge to construct an explanation."[52] Such penumbral thinking is an attempt to exploit the always attendant indeterminacy that honeycombs determinate vocabularies as an open and bottomless source of increased meaning.

Elsewhere and early on, David Hall and I coined the term *ars contextualis* as our way of expressing this meaning-productive art of making correlations and recontextualizing different aspects of experience.[53] And the general vision of *ars contextualis* takes us one step beyond this second, more interesting interpretation of Peirce's abductive thinking with any theory and praxis binary it might still suggest to make it clear that zoetology requires of the human being nothing less than full participation in the generative project of world-making itself. It takes us from reasoning about the world to the practical capacity and responsibility of the human being to "extend *dao*" (*hongdao* 弘道) and to thus become a creative collaborator with the heavens and the earth in its "world-making." R. P. Peerenboom, in his argument against a naturalist interpretation of this process cosmology, insists that "*dao*—both normatively, as the sanctioned way, and descriptively, as the order of the universe, the environment, the society, the person—emerges out of our contextual choices rather than as an instantiation of a predetermined blueprint. It is the result of a creative, active, participatory process. The kind of world we live in, in terms of our ethical as well as natural environment,

---

52. Steve Coutinho, *Zhuangzi and Early Chinese Philosophy: Vagueness, Transformation and Paradox* (Aldershot, UK: Ashgate, 2004).

53. See Hall and Ames, *Thinking Through Confucius*, 246–249; *Anticipating China*, 273–275; *Thinking from the Han*, 39–43, 111–112.

depends in part on the choices we humans make."[54] *Ars contextualis* as a practical endeavor is a term that describes the peculiar art of contextualization that allows focal individuals to ally themselves relationally with those contexts that they will come to internalize and that in turn will be shaped to constitute their contextualizing others. There is no One behind the many; there are, rather, many unique ones, many particular focal particulars that construe and organize the fields about them. Absent is any one-many or part-whole model that, like the one-many-ness of a jigsaw puzzle, would serve as an overarching context determining the shape of all other figures within the puzzle. Instead, the world is an open-ended, ecological affair comprised of "thises" and "thats" construable from any number of distinct perspectives. The art of contextualization is an aesthetic project involving the production of more or less harmonious correlations among the myriad of unique details that make up the world.

A corollary to *ars contextualis* that distinguishes zoetology's generative logic from ontology is that "knowing" is not confined to the zero-sum kind of discrimination of what is antecedently real, where knowing is an "either you know it or you don't" affair. And meaning is not limited to a given reality itself that, conditioned by the necessity of "being in-itself," is thus available for rational discovery. Rather, zoetological knowing is the procreative process of "realizing" in the incremental sense of both cognizing what is available and then attracting the resources necessary to make a possible world real. Knowing is to participate in the always local process of world-making. Zoetology as "the art of living" aligns itself with what in the environment can be nurtured and grown, and is thus "realizable" within the human experience. It is the fundamentally aesthetic process of cultivating meaningful relations under the various rubrics that capture this vital growth: education, morality, beauty, creativity, religiousness, technology, culture, and so on.

Linguistically too, zoetology favors an active language that can express the process of growth. Ontology establishes identity through formal causes and thus allows for the formal definition of things. In construing the world as being constituted by discrete "things" and in defining these things as essentially self-sufficient, it favors the noun form that gives generic "names" to specific things. Ontology discriminates what can be said about something

---

54. R. P. Peerenboom, "Beyond Naturalism: A Reconstruction of Daoist Environmental Ethics," in *Environmental Philosophy in Asian Traditions of Thought*, ed. J. Baird Callicott and James McRae (Albany: State University of New York Press, 2014), 163.

from what is contingently in it, with the subject being a necessary condition for the subsequent attributes or "accidents" that are supervened upon it. The noun, thus deployed, separates and sets boundaries on things and, in so doing, establishes a distinction between the essential subject and its contingent attributes, thus giving us a subject-complement grammar. Further, such an ontological disparity between essence and attributes introduces a doctrine of second-order, external relations as they come to conjoin otherwise independent and self-sufficient entities.

Zoetology by contrast construes experience in terms of interpenetrating events, where linguistically an eventful, gerundive language is privileged, and the erstwhile distinction between "things" and "relations" has no purchase. *Dao* 道 as a vital ecology of experience is everything that is happening as it is constituted by the relations obtaining among things: not "*the* Way," but a collective "way-making" or "world-making" as it is being construed from each particular perspective along the way. That is, vital relations are themselves first order and constitutive of the unfolding pattern of events, and the focal events themselves are holographic with their own particular fields implicated within them. This is but to say that human "becomings" as an example of such events are radically situated within and constituted by their unbounded roles and relations.[55]

Zoetology and the Principle of Individuation

Yet another important observation we might make that follows from categorical versus analogical thinking is that ontology and zoetology have alternative understandings of the principle of individuation. Ontological thinking, in defining the world in terms of genera and species, generates categories in which the members of any particular species are defined essentially by some selfsame, reduplicative characteristic (*eidos*). All members of humankind, for example, have a claim on being human "beings," an essential and antecedent

---

55. With respect to this relational understanding of persons, there is momentum in the contemporary Western philosophical literature broadly represented by figures such as John Dewey, George Herbert Mead, and more recently by a range of scholars who might be represented by Charles Taylor. These scholars are taking the discussion of persons away from old assumptions about discrete individuals and in the direction of relationally constituted entities who engage each other through their patterns of relations within their "horizons of relevance" and "webs of interlocution." See Taylor, *Sources of the Self* and *The Language Animal*.

formal definition that cannot be negated while at the same time allowing them to be included as a member of that category. For zoetological thinking that does not assume any concept of strict, reduplicative identity, inclusion in always provisional categories is constituted analogously by perceived similarities and resonances. Such categories, far from being formal, definitive, and thus closed, are processual, emergent, open-ended, and a matter of degree. As open and evolving categories, shifting horizons within the uncontained ecology do the work of ontological boundaries. Hence humankind is constituted by what is most fundamentally a continuing confluence of always particular narratives of this analogically constituted and always evolving "kind." Classifications such as humankind are a matter of continuing, situated disclosure and persistent evolution, a way of interpreting the human experience consistent with our best science. Since "human" is the story of something *done* rather than what persons *are*, zoetology gives us a world not of discrete human beings but of interdependent and thus always plural human "becomings."[56]

Viewed synoptically in terms of cosmic order, ontological thinking is again categorical and causal in positing a rationalized and reductionistic part-whole model with the ideal and individuating "One" standing behind its derivative many. The *kosmoi* are disciplined by the originative laws of a single-ordered *kosmos*, and their plurality is regulated by antecedent first principles to constitute a *uni*-verse. By contrast, zoetological thinking posits a holistic, aesthetic, and genealogical understanding of an unsummed cosmic order in which all the unique details are relevant to the totality of the effect, a world in which there is no ultimate boundary, no final beginning or end, and no privileged single order. Acknowledging Tang Junyi's cosmological postulate of "the inseparability of one and many" (*yiduobufenguan*), the language of a continuous and unbounded *dao* and the myriad happenings (*wanwu* 萬物) that constitute it, is to be understood as two aspectual, nonanalytical ways of referencing the same, unfolding "one is many, many one" process. It is for this reason that zoetological cosmology lends itself to aesthetic analogies in which the quality of world-making or *dao* 道 in its disclosure of precisely those specific details that produce its effect lends itself to a comparison with this sublime piece of music or this exquisite painting.

Tang Junyi's characterization of Confucian cosmology with "one is many, many one" is also important in providing us with a way of conceiving of the dynamic process of identity formation in which persons achieve their

---

56. I have made this argument in detail in Ames, *Human Becomings*.

individuality. Tang would insist that this protean expression *yiduobufen* is a distinctive, generic feature of the Chinese processual cosmology locating our persons as vital and specific focal centers that have implicated within each one of us a boundless field of relations. Importantly, *yiduobufen* is another way of describing the zoetological doctrine of intrinsic, constitutive relationality that has been set in contrast with the ontological doctrine of external relations. It is, simply put, the assumption that in the compositing of any "one," there is implicated within it the contextualizing "many." This *yiduobufen* proposition can be read in many different ways, as it speaks at once to the inseparability of the one and the many, to the continuity between particular identity and its context, to the co-presence of uniqueness and multivalence, to the mutuality of continuity and multiplicity, to the inclusiveness of integrity and integration, to the dynamics of a shared harmony emerging out of relational tensions, to the expression of the specific details in the totality of the effect, and so on.[57] It also restates in a different language the focus-field conception of persons, where each self-conscious person, and each impulse in the life of each person, has implicated within it the boundless "many." This defining feature of Chinese natural cosmology is fundamental to our understanding of the relationally constituted, focus-field conception of persons. As Mencius declares, "The myriad things of the world are all implicated here in me."[58]

Cosmologically, this proposition of the inseparability of one and many is an alternative principle of individuation. All unique events or focal centers—particular persons, as an example—are constituted by an unbounded field of more or less relevant relations that collaborate together to sponsor them. Importantly, rather than beginning as individuals, persons achieve their individuated identities as a function of the quality of coalescence they are able to achieve within these unique fields of relations. That is, moving from description to prescription, a dynamic reading of *yiduobufen* is a summary of the way in which the opportunity is available for each of us to optimize the boundless possibilities that honeycomb the relationships between ourselves as particular persons and our environing conditions. Tang Junyi's postulate asserts not only that persons like any other phenomenon in our field of experience has implicated within them the contextualizing, unbounded many, but further that as a uniquely "one" matrix of relations, persons can find self-conscious resolution and purpose, and become focused in many

---

57. Tang Junyi, *The Complete Works*, vol. 11, 16–17.

58. *Mencius* 7A4: 孟子曰: 萬物皆備於我矣.

different ways according to the multiplicity of roles that are defining of their narratives. Importantly, any claim to their uniqueness and individuality, far from excluding their relations with others, is a function of the quality that this person has been able to achieve within the unique configuration of these same relations. Through an assiduous regimen of personal cultivation, persons become increasingly distinctive and even distinguished within a community of the many others who come to confer this recognition upon them.

The Mohists in explaining the process of individuation give us another version of this same situated and situational dynamic of "one and many individuation" wherein the contextualizing many confer individuality on the one. In the later Mohist canons, there is reference to the "unit" or "one" (*ti* 體), and its "complex" or "many" (*jian* 兼), or stated more concisely perhaps, some "thing" and its "context."[59] Again, on the bronzes, the character *jian* 兼 appears as two sheaves of grain 兼, an ideogram that expresses the idea of "in combination," "together," and "simultaneously connected."[60] But this distinction between unit and complex, far from being simple, is being offered to make the point that any fixed and final sense of individuation—of one elemental unit or "thing"—is in fact problematic. To begin with, according to the *Shuowen* lexicon, *ti* as a "bodily" unit is again a complex divided into the four subcategories of head, trunk, arms, and legs, with each of these units again being divided into three more subcategories for a total of twelve. This fluidity between one and many is consistent with the observations of Deborah Sommer cited earlier, who, reporting on the occurrence of the tuber or rhizome as a "subterranean body" (*xiati* 下體) in the early literature, observes that "when a *ti* body is fragmented into parts (literally or conceptually), each part retains in certain aspects, a kind of wholeness or becomes a simulacra of the larger entity of which it is a constituent."[61] John Dewey in his *The Public and Its Problems* makes this same point about individuation and the tentative nature of any designated "one." What we might refer to as "one unit" or an "individual" cannot be separated from "its connections and ties" nor from "the consequences with respect to which it acts and moves." Dewey observes:

> We are compelled to say that for some purposes, for some results,

---

59. See A. C. Graham, *Later Mohist Logic, Ethics and Science* (Hong Kong: Chinese University Press, 1978), 265.

60. Kwan, "Database," CHANT 戰國 11379.

61. Sommer, "Boundaries of the *Ti* Body," 294.

the tree is the individual, for others the cell, and for a third, the forest or the landscape. Is a book or a leaf or a folio or a paragraph, or a printer's em *the* individual? Is the binding or the contained thought that which gives individual unity to a book? Or are all of these things definers of an individual according to the consequences which are relevant in a particular situation? Unless we betake ourselves to the stock resort of commonsense, dismissing *all* questions as useless quibbles, it seems as if we could not determine an individual without reference to differences made as well as to antecedent and contemporary connections. If so, an individual, whatever else it is or is not, is not just the spatially isolated thing our imagination inclines to take it to be.[62]

In this Chinese cosmology, there are no assumed ultimate elements or simples. Instead, the formal aspect of *ti* or "unit," like a distinguished member of the community, emerges in many different roles and relations according to the functional situation: that is, through the inseparable processes of "forming and functioning" (*tiyong* 體用). In this Mohist terminology, the particular unit—that is, what makes the *ti* a "one"—is always a function of how we choose to locate and foreground it. This thumb is a *ti* unit to this hand that serves as its *jian* complex; the hand is a *ti* to this arm as its *jian*; this arm is a *ti* to this body as its *jian*; and so on. This thumb is only this thumb by virtue of its location within this hand and by the self-conscious process of extending its context to include this arm, this body, this hitchhiking situation, and so on. Something or someone is not "one" in itself but becomes uniquely one by virtue of how it becomes focused in its relations within the dynamic field of others. That is, the most familiar way of looking at this thumb is to foreground it as an individuated unit, but a more important observation is to see it as being "aspectual" and "functional" by situating it within its relational *and eventful* context not only as an integral feature of this hand but as being integral to the experience of *what this hand is doing*.

Corollary to the primacy of relationality and its doctrine of internal, constitutive relations is the fact that the field of any particular thing—the thumb in this case—is necessarily unbounded; its web of relations does not terminate anywhere but keeps on expanding outward. Hence, all correlations we make between thumb and hand are abstractive rather than final,

---

62. Dewey, *Later Works*, vol. 2, 352.

functional rather than absolute, and narrative rather than essential. This being the case, the thumb is "one" as an always fluid center of relationships where, as an aspectual center, it can be focused and reconceptualized in many different ways. This thumb is a necessary collaborator in finger-snaps or shakas, is a main actor in the familiar gesture of being extended upward as an emphatic "yes," or when turned downward, of an equally emphatic "no," and can be seen as the responsible digital member for manipulating the spacebar when it is resting on the computer keyboard. And the individuation of the thumb so described is a simulacrum for that of persons who are conventionally conceived of as individuals, where such individuation is also abstractive, functional, and ultimately narrative. That is, they become distinctive as individuals not exclusive of their relations but because of the quality achieved in them; not because of who they *are* but what they *do*; not because of some ontological claim but by virtue of the meaningful and influential lives that they live.

Chapter 6

In Their Own Words and on Their Own Terms

Contemporary China's Comparative Philosophers

During my years as a graduate student at the University of London, and then for the decades that followed until the time of his passing, it was my good fortune to be able to call myself an eager student of D. C. Lau 劉殿爵, one of the century's most distinguished translators and interpreters of the classical Chinese philosophical canons. One thing I learned almost immediately about Lau was that even if only making a passing comment, when he said something I would do well to listen closely and give it some careful thought. One day over tea Lau remarked that what is unique to a classical Chinese theory of knowledge and its vocabulary that makes it different from Greek thinking about an exclusive "reality" and the "truth" in apprehending it is that "knowing" seems best captured with the eventful metaphor of first "mapping out" and reconnoitering a particular situation in a search for the best way forward, and then walking the walk. What Lau was suggesting is that knowing as a "doing" is an incremental world-making.

When under the sway of the Confucian holistic, process cosmology we reflect on the vocabulary of "knowing" itself, the term *zhi* 知 conventionally translated as "to know," rather than promising any particular cognitive truth, allows for the practical efficacy of a productive "forging ahead" within a particular situation—that is, a constructive way forward that we can rely upon for welcome outcomes. Given the inseparable relationship between *episteme* and *eidos* that we find in early Greek epistemology, there is the danger that the term "epistemology," like "ontology" when carried over into the Confucian context, might obscure what is a very different understanding of what it means to know. In this alternative Confucian theory of knowledge, the sense of mapping is present in the modern Chinese language where the functional equivalent for the expression "I know" is quite literally "I am walking and thus realizing our way forward" (*wozhidao* 我知道). This incremental process of a shared knowing suggests both a specific bearing and how best to get there. If we reflect on the etymology of the character *dao* 道, the image we have for knowing is to understand the signposts as we walk together in the most appropriate or "true" direction.[1] To know is to be cognizant of the prevailing conditions, to have the imagination to see their possibilities, and through virtuosic relationality (*ren* 仁) within one's own community, to have achieved the deference of others necessary to rally support behind, and enthusiasm for, a shared direction and a common future.

Importantly, in the transitive "I know the way" (*wo zhidao* 我知道) or perhaps better "we have the know-how and are making our way," "the way" (*dao*) is not simply the "object" of knowledge as such but has a real subjective and performative dimensions as well. *Dao* defies Aristotle's philosophy of a subject-object grammar and his categorical, "either-or" epistemology, having as much to do with the quality of one's understanding as it does with the conditions of the world as understood. *Dao* is a holistic, qualitative way of conducting one's life in the world inclusive of both subject and object, with specific reference to the attributes of the subject as well as to the modality of the actions being carried out. Knowing tells us as much about the quality of the person who "knows" as it does about something known, and as much about this person's particular disposition to act as it does about the modality of acting itself.

Other Chinese expressions for "knowing" in frequent use today also carry this same sense of "mapping out" a situation: for example, "unraveling and interpreting the changing patterns within this context" (*lijie* 理解), "seeing and understanding with full clarity" (*liaojie* 瞭解), "getting through with insight and alacrity" (*tongda* 通達), "being well acquainted with everything involved" (*baishitong* 百事通), and so on. Even the complimentary description conferred on foreigners by Chinese colleagues in praise of their understanding of China—*Zhongguotong* 中國通—expresses this same sense of penetrating and unobstructed insight into things Chinese. Consistent with this pragmatic method of finding a way forward, any final distinctions

---

1. See the entry in Ames, *A Conceptual Lexicon for Classical Confucian Philosophy*, 19–28.

between subject and object, between fact and value, and between the theoretical and the practical are moot.

We might recall a popular, often repeated saying in modern Chinese: "I cannot see the genuine face of Mount Lu because I am standing within this mountainscape."[2] An ontological reading of this adage would assume the point being made is that it is only the external, objective perspective free of subjective bias that can provide access to the singular certainty of "the true face of Mount Lu." The realist notion of a fixed perspective in the visual arts comes immediately to mind. Such objectivity is the negation of subjectivity and promises the one, necessary truth on what is real rather than a cacophony of competing opinions.[3] In looking for an alternative zoetological reading for this popular saying, we might begin by translating the whole Su Shi 蘇軾 poem from which it is excerpted to provide it with a context. Su Shi's famous verse, "Written on the Wall of the Western Forest Temple" 提西林壁 reads:

> Panoramically I see the ridges, vertically, the peaks;
> Far or near, high or low, each affords a different view.
> I cannot see the genuine face of Mount Lu
> Because I am standing within this mountainscape.[4]

Indeed, the poem begins first by asserting that there are a countless number of competing vistas within the changing landscape of Mount Lu that provide alternative perspectives on it. Further, and most profoundly, that there is never an "outside" of this mountainscape, but only an inside, necessarily seeing it from one vantage point or another. It is in order to avoid prompting the binary "true or false" that, for the English reader, I would translate the term *zhen* 真, conventionally rendered "true," as "genuine" or "authentic." Following the same logic, perhaps the claim being made is that the best way of looking at Mount Lu or anything else in the human

---

2. 不識廬山真面目, 只緣身在此山中.

3. A similar question might arise in reading the *Zhuangzi* passage: 《莊子》寓言篇: 親父不為其子媒. 親父譽之, 不若非其父者也 "A father will not act as matchmaker for his son because whatever the father might say in praise of him is not as persuasive as it would be coming from someone else." While the father is not a proper fit as a matchmaker because of his intimate relationship with his son, in coming to really know who the son is, the father's opinion is probably second to none.

4. 橫看成嶺側成峰, 遠近高低各不同. 不識廬山真面目, 只緣身在此山中.

experience is to have the most comprehensive view that includes as many different perspectives as possible. This then is an argument for a "comprehensiveness" (*quan* 全) theory of knowledge where at the end of the day, the best we are entitled to is not an objective truth or some unconditional certainty but only an open, inclusive, intelligent, and edifying conversation that within real time will make available to us the most panoramic view of things and thus enable us to make our way forward together in the most productive way.

There is another important point to be made in our reflection on this "comprehensiveness" theory of knowledge as it informs a resolutely processual understanding of the human experience. We must allow that the interpretation of the "text" is open-ended, emergent, and never final. We might return to Gadamer and the observations he makes on cultivated hermeneutical sensibilities. He begins by insisting on the full autonomy of the text in the sense that its "language just stands for itself," and in this sense, "it brings itself to stand before us."[5] Gadamer is keen to insist that there are limits on interpretation, and that we must respect the integrity of the text. He concludes: "It is a mistake, I think, to try to make this endless multiplicity a denial of the unshakable identity of the work. . . . The work, the text we read, is not something we dream up."[6] But the integrity of the text is anything but a boundary on its meaning. Gadamer addresses this multivalence in the bottomlessness of aesthetic appreciation when he asserts that "the work of art distinguishes itself in that one never completely understands it. . . . An artwork is never exhausted. It never becomes empty."[7] In this same vein, Gadamer argues that the language of the text, and the commentary as well, is presentation rather than representation, observing that "the 'use' of words is not a 'using' at all. Rather language is a medium, an element: language is the element in which we live, as fishes live in water. . . . In the exchange of words, the thing meant becomes more and more present. A language is truly a 'natural language' when it binds us together in this way."[8]

Such an understanding of how the language of interpretation functions when taken to its logical conclusion means that the text is always being extended and enriched through our commentarial practices. Indeed, one of

5. Dave Ramsey Steele, ed., *Genius in Their Own Words: The Intellectual Journeys of Seven Great 20th-Century Thinkers* (Chicago: Open Court, 2002), 217.

6. Steele, *Genius in Their Own Words*, 217.

7. Steele, *Genius in Their Own Words*, 222.

8. Steele, *Genius in Their Own Words*, 196.

Gadamer's most distinguished students, the Italian philosopher and parliamentarian Gianni Vattimo, reinforces this claim for the intimate relationship between text and commentary by insisting on the generative, dare I say zoetological, role of interpretation. In clarifying this relationship, Vattimo observes: "By the productiveness of interpretation, I mean that interpretation is not only an attempt to grasp the original meaning of the text (for example the authorial intention) and to reproduce it as literally as possible but also to add something essential to the text (to understand it better than its author, the adage resonating in eighteenth-century hermeneutics)."[9] And in further explaining what he means by "adding something essential to the text," Vattimo goes so far as to insist that "the European culture of late modernity 'discovered' the productiveness of interpretation or—which is the same—the nonepiphenomenality, instrumentality, or secondariness of the commentary."[10] That is to say, the evolving commentary becomes integral to and grows the meaning of the text itself. Facility with the text is to literally cultivate its meaning.

In this monograph, I have coined the neologism "zoetology" as my own strategy for setting a clear contrast between what Angus Graham has described as truth-seekers with their epistemology of certainty and way-makers with their "comprehensiveness" theory of knowledge.[11] That is, we can draw a contrast between a commitment to substance ontology that offers a foundational, rationalized way of thinking in search of certainty, on the one hand, and an emergent, aesthetic way of thinking that is rooted in the primacy it gives to the art of living on the other. Although there is perhaps some novelty in my approach that arises from including a philosophical perspective at some real distance from Mount Lu, I would suggest that, consistent with our claim that there is only one world cultural ecology, there is in fact no "outside" of this mountainscape. What the method of comparative cultural hermeneutics does is simply add additional breadth to the attempt to be as inclusive and comprehensive in our conversation as possible by expanding its purview. At the same time, and most importantly, it requires of us that this increasingly expansive conversation continue.

In service to this continuing conversation, I want to highlight the voices of several of contemporary China's most distinguished comparative philosophers. I will argue that they are themselves clearly aware of the perils of

---

9. Gianni Vattimo, *After Christianity* (New York: Columbia University Press, 2002), 62–63.

10. Vattimo, *After Christianity*, 63.

11. Graham, *Disputers of the Tao*, 3.

eliding the distinction between what I am calling Greek ontological assumptions and the Chinese zoetological alternatives, and that they too endorse the imperative that we bring further clarity to the profound differences between what are two alternative first philosophies. In this final chapter I include four of China's most influential thinkers. In my best effort to stay close to their own representative voices, I have provided paraphrased summaries of some of their ideas as they have been presented in recent publications. In spite of the fact that each of these philosophers uses a different vocabulary and has a uniquely distinctive approach to the comparisons being made, I find important corroboration for my ontology and zoetology distinction in what they are saying, and in the edifying contrasts they are able to make. My goal in this chapter, then, is to invite these scholars to join this conversation on first philosophies and to share their perspectives that, in sum, will give us our most panoramic and intelligent view of Mount Lu.

Zheng Kai 鄭開

Figure 6.1. Zheng Kai.

Zheng Kai 鄭開 received his PhD from Peking University in 1999. He is now director of the Chinese Philosophy Section as well as the director of the Center for Daoist Studies at Peking University. He is the author of several acclaimed books on pre-Qin Chinese philosophy and philosophical Daoism, including *Between* De *and Rituals: History of Thought in the*

Pre-Hundred-Schools-of-Thoughy Period (德礼之间: 前诸子时期的思想史; 2009) and *Lectures on the Philosophy of Zhuangzi* (庄子哲学讲记; 2016). His monograph *The Metaphysics of Daoist Philosophy* (道家形而上学研究; 2018) has been translated by Ruan Hanliang (2021) and is now available in an English-language version. The most recent book by Zheng Kai is *A Survey of Daoist Political Philosophy* (道家政治哲学发微; 2019).

Zheng Kai 鄭開:
From Ontology to *Xinxing* Theory (*XINXINGLUN* 心性論)

Our conversation on comparative philosophy in China today begins with a summary of what Zheng Kai 鄭開 takes to be the continuing problem of using ontological language to explicate Chinese philosophy. Consistent with Zheng's exhortation that the tradition must speak on its own terms, he provides us with a detailed account of the direction he would want to take research in Chinese philosophy by anchoring it not in appeals to ontology but in the alternative vocabulary of the indigenous *xinxing* theory (心性論). In formulating the interpretive problem Zheng calls "misplaced ontology" (本體論誤置), he states that,

> in research on Chinese philosophy in recent times, it is a commonplace to see the term "ontology" misapplied, since the notions of "ontology" and "being" that originate in classical Greek philosophy are not appropriate to the notion of "what is most basic" or "first philosophy" (*benti* 本體) within the context of Chinese philosophy. What is both necessary and important in getting clear on this problem is the following. If we are going to really grasp the appropriate method of theorizing Chinese philosophy, we must understand the notion of first philosophy from within the context of Chinese philosophy itself that offers its own paradigm of *xinxing* learning (*xinxingxue* 心性學).[12]

In formulating and advancing this criticism of "misplaced ontology," Zheng cites from the writings of several of contemporary China's most

---

12. 鄭開, 中國哲學語境中的本體論與形而上學, 哲學研究2018年第一期, 77: 近代以來的中國哲學研究, "本體論"概念的誤置屢見不鮮, 因為源自古希 臘哲學的"本體"和"存在," 並不符合中國哲學語境中的"本體." 澄清這一問題的必要 性和重要性在於: 要想準確而內在地理解中國哲學理論範式, 就必須從心性論層面把握中國 哲學語境中的"本體."

prominent and respected philosophical figures such as Tang Yongtong 湯用彤, Fang Dongmei 方東美, Zhang Dainian 張岱年, and Mou Zongsan 牟宗三. Mou Zongsan, for example, interprets the entire vocabulary of neo-Confucian philosophy through an ontological lens, rendering Confucian philosophy itself into what he calls "a system of ontological being" (本體論的存有之系統). Zheng Kai argues that there is certainly much for reflection in Zhang Dainian's 張岱年 attempt to clarify "ontology" from a comparative perspective, and in Tang Yongtong's ascription of "meta-ontology" (*chaoyue-bentilun* 超越本體論) to the "dark learning" (*xuanxue* 玄學) of the Wei-Jin period. And in bringing in other contemporary voices, Zheng allows that there are interesting points being made in Li Zehou's 李澤厚 introduction of terms such as "affect-ology" (*qingtilun* 情體倫) and "historical ontology" (*lishibentilun* 歷史本體論), and again in Chen Lai's 陳來 invention of the neologism "the ontology of 'learning to become consummate'" (*renxueben-tilun* 仁學本體論). But at the end of the day, even while these distinguished scholars insist on important differences from Greek ontology, the lines they would draw between their own novel applications of the term "ontology" and the original Greek notion remain so painfully unclear that such an appeal cannot escape making their alternatives little more than footnotes to Aristotle's ontology as it has been formulated in the *Categories*.

Zheng takes us back to the earliest pre-Qin usages of the language of first philosophy that references what is most basic in the Chinese narrative: that is, the terms "root" (*ben* 本), "body, embodying, root, tuber" (*ti* 體), and the language associated with it such as "root, source, origin" (*bengen* 本根), "root, source" (*benyuan* 本原), "primary, basic, foundational" (*yuan* 元), where the common usage of *ben* 本 and *ti* 體 themselves refer to living things, including both plants and animals. Of course, *ti* 體 also has the meaning of "the whole" (*quanti* 全體), of "observing, experiencing, and understanding" (*ticha* 體察), and of "knowing through experience and practice" (*tiyan* 體驗). At the end of the Han dynasty with the introduction of the binomial "forming and functioning" (*tiyong* 體用), the important relationship between *ti* as "forming" and *yong* as "functioning" emerged to become a ubiquitous way of reflecting on and analyzing philosophical problems.

Zheng Kai avers that classical Greek ontology is closely connected with epistemology and logic, and is the outcome of essentialistic thinking that proceeds from reflection on the separation between a phenomenon and its essence or substance. And as Aristotle makes clear, this notion of essence is associated with the concept of reality. While Greek ontology provides this essence as the object of knowledge for its epistemology, Chinese expressions such as "root and canopy" (*benmo* 本末) and "forming and functioning" (*tiyong* 體用) as they have evolved within the paradigm of *xinxing* theory are located within a complex theoretical matrix that extends over epistemology, ethics, and even logic. And in contrast with Greek ontology that, through the discovery of reality and truth as its ultimate goal would promise us unconditional knowledge, such Chinese terms reference the attainment of different levels of spiritual insight and different approaches to practical wisdom that we would associate with both human and cosmic flourishing.

What is most basic in Chinese philosophy is to avoid isolating, hypostasizing, and reifying its primary ideas such as *dao* 道, *li* 理, and *wu* 無 and instead understand them in terms of their relationality. As examples, we must read the relationship between the phenomenon and what is most basic from the perspective of the inseparability of the subjective and the objective (主客合一), the mutuality of *dao* and phenomena (道器相即), and the aspectual nature of forming and functioning (體用一如). If we were to say that the theoretical framework of Western philosophy from the ancient Greeks on is bound up with epistemology and logic, we can say that from the Warring States period onward, the theoretical framework of Chinese philosophy has been *xinxing* theory, and if the starting point of the former is the separation between the subject and object, the latter is committed to breaking through any erstwhile boundary between the subject and object and attaining a spiritual level wherein there is a coalescing of the two.

Zheng allows that, viewed from the assumptions that ground Western philosophy, Chinese philosophy seems to be rather bizarre. Rather than being analytical in a way that delimits, defines, and clarifies things, Chinese philosophy looks to the continuities that obtain among them: "the continuity between and inseparability of *tian* and the human world" (天人合一), "the inseparability of knowing and doing" (知行合一), "the inseparability of heartmind and the world" (心物合一), "the shared source of forming and functioning" (體用一源), "the mutuality of something and nothing" (有無雙遣), "the interpenetration of *dao* and phenomena" (道器貫通), "the nondual nature of the cosmos and what is most basic in it (*benti*)" (宇宙本體不二), "the spirit and aura of the sages" (聖人氣象), "spiritual levels" (精神境界), and so on. Such ideas, observes Zheng, form a vocabulary that from the perspective of Western philosophy is just "too unphilosophical" (太不哲學). The problem becomes: How in advancing along the narrative shared by Chinese and Western philosophy today can Chinese philosophy taken on its own terms receive greater recognition and understanding?

Zheng sees the first philosophical breakthrough in Chinese philosophy as having occurred at the transition between the Spring and Autumn, and the Warring States periods with Confucius and Laozi formulating their alternative doctrines grounded in the notion of *dao* 道. But Zheng's focus in locating what is most basic (*benti*) lies with a second iteration of this breakthrough that occurs in the middle years of the Warring States period with the doctrines of Mencius and Zhuangzi. He highlights their sustained discussions on the topics of "heartmind" (*xin* 心) and "human propensities" (*xing* 性), with the subsequent emergence of what he calls *xinxing* theory (*xinxinglun*). Since many contemporary scholars express some frustration in trying to understand the meaning and implications of *xinxing* theory, Zheng sets out with a careful analysis of the *Mencius* to try to bring some clarity to this paradigm.[13] In this respect, Zheng takes Mencius to be nothing less than a revolutionary turn in the development of classical Confucianism, and he sees his *xinxing* theory to be a philosophical innovation that not only sets the bearings for historical Confucianism but that also serves as the underlying inspiration for the most prominent of the neo-Confucian thinkers as well.

Until very recent times, the important story of an evolving Confucianism that took place during the span of years separating the lives of Confucius and Mencius has been shrouded in mystery. However, over the past half-century the philosophical discourse has been animated by a significant trove of philosophical documents that have been recovered from a series of exciting archaeological finds. Drawing on these new materials, Zheng appeals to philosopher Chen Lai 陳來, who in seeking to clarify the notion of "human propensities" (*xing* 性) cites two different versions of the recently recovered document "Human Propensities (*xing* 性) Emerge from the Force of Circumstances (*ming* 命)" found at the Guodian site in Hubei and in the Shanghai Museum collection, entitled *Xingzimingchu* 性自命出 and *Xingqinglun* 性情論 respectively. Chen insists that this document reflects the mainstream debate on the concept of human propensities (*xing*) during this period in which, according to Chen Lai,

> the doctrine of human natural propensities (*xing*) as it emerges in the discussion of the nature and the function of human propensities found in these two versions of the document appeals to the logical chain of "Heaven" (*tian*)—"the force of circumstances" (*ming* 命)—"human propensities" (*xing* 性)—"human affect/ actuality" (*qing* 情)—"way-making" (*dao* 道). This document

---

13. 鄭開, 試論孟子心性論哲學的理論結構 [On the theoretical structure of Mencius's philosophy of *xinxing* theory], 國際儒學 2021 2期1卷.

maintains that "the force of circumstances" descends from *tian*, that "human propensities" emerge from the "force of circumstances," that "human affect/actuality" is expressed out of "human propensities," and that "way-making" finds its beginnings in "human affect/actuality." . . . This view that it is the spontaneity of life itself that constitutes human propensities (以生之自然為性) is close indeed to the naturalistic thesis of "spontaneous or 'self-so-ing' human propensities" (自然人性論). . . . Just such a naturalistic understanding of human propensities was in fact the mainstream doctrine in early Confucian philosophy. And by way of contrast, the Mencian notion that "human propensities tend toward efficacious conduct" (人性善) and the Xunzian claim that "human propensities are base" (人性惡) were anomalous exceptions within the development of early Confucianism.[14]

Mencius was heavily influenced by the tradition of the earlier philosopher and grandson of Confucius, Zisizi 子思子 (or Kongji 孔伋), and did much to further develop and elaborate upon his trajectory in Confucian thinking. Although the later followers of Confucius branched out into many different streams, given the distinctively creative and enticing contributions introduced by the arm of Confucianism associated with Zisi and

---

14. Chen Lai 陳,《竹帛 "五行" 與簡帛研究》[Research on the five phases from silk and bamboo manuscripts] (Beijing: Sanlian, 2009), 77:《性自命》等篇的人性說, 從天—命—性—情—道的邏輯結構來討論人性的本質和作用. 它主張命自天降、性自命出、情出於性、道始於情, . . . 這種以生之自然為性的看法, 還是接近於自然人性論. . . . 這種人性說其實是早期儒家人性思想的主流. 而孟子的性善論和荀子的性惡論, 在儒家的前期發展中反而是較為獨特和少有的. There is some real ambiguity with how we are to read the notion of "naturalistic" in a cosmology that eschews any nature-nurture binary and thus would preclude a natural and normative dichotomy. One reading of naturalism we would associate with classical pragmatism is that it is simply a rejection of supernatural or metaphysical causal claims. At the other extreme would be an ontological naturalism in which a reductive physicalism consistent with the argument for causal closure would make all mental activities a direct function of physical causes. In between would be a nonreductive physicalism that tries to make sense of "special causes" for mental states that "realize" certain outcomes without being reducible to physical causation, where such claims seem to move in the direction of a Cartesian dualism. In contrast with ontological naturalism, then, there is a methodological naturalism that would argue science and philosophy are engaged in the same practices, using similar methods to achieve similar aims. See David Papineau, "Naturalism," in *The Stanford Encyclopedia of Philosophy* (Fall 2023 edition), ed. Edward N. Zalta and Uri Nodelman, https://plato. stanford.edu/archives/fall2023/entries/naturalism/.

Mencius called the SiMeng lineage, it became the most important among them. Chen Lai's point here is that this earlier naturalistic understanding of "spontaneous human propensities" was more or less the orthodoxy among the later students of Confucius, and it had a significant influence on Xunzi's theorizing of *xing*. Again, far from being superseded by Mencius's redefinition of *xing*, the notion of spontaneous human propensities continued to be the mainstream doctrine on human propensities until the Song and Ming dynasties when the neo-Confucians elevated Mencius and his doctrines to become the new orthodoxy. For this reason, given Mencius's rejection of the dominant theory on human propensities that prevailed during his time, given his introduction of a novel conception that "human propensities tend toward efficacious conduct" (*xingshan* 性善), and given his positing of an alternative *xinxing* theory, we should refer to his historical contribution as "an unconventional countercurrent." This is but to say that Mencius's *xinxing* theory was the metamorphosis and sublimation of the earlier concept of "human propensities," and his claim that "to say heartmind is but to say human propensities" (即心言性) became one of the core theories of Confucian philosophy.

The prevalent view among linguists is that the event of the two characters "heartmind" (*xin* 心) and "living" (*sheng* 生) being combined to constitute a third character "human propensities" (*xing* 性) probably occurred during the middle years of the Warring States period. This would suggest that a mature conception of "human propensities" was emerging at this time, and that the *xinxing* theory developed by Mencius and Zhuangzi was a turning point that reflected the deepening of this theme in the philosophical discourse.

Zheng Kai then turns to an analysis of Mencius's notion of human propensities (*xing*), making the point that the naturalistic conception of "spontaneous human propensities" (自然人性) prevailing at that time is not valorized as either tending toward efficacious conduct or being base. Hence, when Mencius makes the normative argument that human propensities tend toward efficacious conduct, he is not just saying that humans are "good." Rather than simply appealing to their naturalistic propensities, Mencius is in fact including their prosocial proclivities. In his own words regarding the social nature of persons, Zheng observes that

> Confucians firmly believe that human beings are not isolated and discrete but have a social existence. Or said another way, their basic nature is itself determined by their social relations. What is the difference between the human community and the animal

world? From the Confucian perspective, in the structuring of social relations there is a proper order established between old and young, and proper distinctions are made between noble and base. Mencius's insight is perhaps that it is only with human beings that there are complex and orderly social and political institutions; it is only with human beings that there is the capacity to experience a moral life; it is only with human beings that the real possibility emerges of pursuing moral perfection and self-awareness.[15]

Having gone through the various arguments in the *Mencius* that are meant to clarify Mencius's innovative conception of "human propensities" (*xing*), Zheng then uses characterizations drawn from passages in the *Mencius* itself to summarize how this canonical text would define this term:

> *Xing* is what each person has as their inherent and innate nature: something that "everyone has" (人皆有之) and that "is inherent in me" (我固有之). . . . Of course, what Mencius places the most emphasis upon and gives more importance to is an understanding and explanation of the concept of *xing* from the perspective of "heartmind" (*xin* 心), "reasoning" (*li* 理), and "appropriateness" (*yi* 義), meaning that Mencius seeks to reconstruct the concept of *xing* and to further introduce his own novel theory regarding it. It is only in implanting a moral and rational *xing* in what it means to be human and by making it clear that human beings must have a moral consciousness and pursue an ethical way of life that would distinguish them from animals . . . that Mencius is able to make the most of the dignity and magnificence of what it means to be human.[16]

---

15. 鄭開, 試論孟子心性論哲學的理論結構, 14: 儒家堅信人不是孤立的, 而是具有社會性的存在, 或者說人的本性或本質是由其社會關係決定的. 人類社會和動物世界之間的根本區別是什麼? 在儒家看來就是長幼有序、貴賤有等的社會關係及其秩序. 孟子的洞見也許是, 唯有人類才有複雜而有序的社會政治制度, 唯有人類才可能過倫理生活, 唯有人類才能真正追求道德的完善與自覺.

16. 鄭開, 試論孟子心性論哲學的理論結構, 17: 性是每个人所固有的内在本质, 是"人皆有之""我固有之"的东西. . . . 当然, 孟子更重视也更强调的是从"心""理""义"的角度和方向对性的概念进行理解与阐释, 这就意味着他必须重构一种人性概念, 进而创造一种新的人性理论. 将道德理性植入人性以表明人 (类) 必须拥有道德意识与伦理生活方能有别于"禽兽," . . . 才能真正发扬人性的尊严与光辉.

***

In my own author's aside here, I want to join A. C. Graham in expressing my concern about the entrenched convention of translating *xing* 性 into English as "human nature." We begin from the fact that when Mencius has been interpreted through languages shaped by ontological thinking, he is for the most part read as ascribing a fixed, essential, innate, and universal human nature to human beings. Michael Sandel, underscoring the weight and persistence of early Greek idealism and teleology as it has shaped our own common sense, has observed that "to speak of human nature is often to suggest a classical teleological conception, associated with the notion of a universal human essence, invariant in all times and places."[17]

It is for this reason that, when Angus Graham cautions us to distinguish clearly between Greek substance ontology and Chinese process cosmology, he uses the specific case of translating the Mencian use of the term *xing* 性 as "human nature" to argue that this rendering has led to a profound and persistent misreading of Mencius. Allowing Graham to speak for himself, he says that when we ascribe a theory of "human nature" to Mencius, the very "translation of *xing* 性 by 'nature' predisposes us to mistake it for a transcendent origin, which in Mencian doctrine would also be a transcendent end."[18] That is, as Sandel has anticipated, with such idealism and teleology shaping our own common sense, translating *xing* as "human nature" suggests to us that human "beings" have as their *eidos* or formal cause "a universal human essence, invariant in all times and places" and as their erstwhile final cause a human *telos* or end. It is only by following Zheng Kai in locating the Mencian notion of *xing* with its own *xinxing* theory as its interpretive context that we can avoid such causal thinking with its ontological assumptions, and locate our understanding of *xing* within its own empirical, holistic, nondualistic, processual, and historicist terms.

---

17. Sandel, *Liberalism and the Limits of Justice*, 50. In order to preclude such uncritical assumptions, Sandel suggests that we must be self-conscious about how we parse the notion of self or person even when moving among the various philosophical positions as they are formulated within our own academy. I would only add that of course this is all the more true when we go beyond the borders of our own philosophical narrative and venture into other cultural traditions.

18. Graham, "Replies," 287.

When Graham insists that we must not think of *xing* as having "a transcendent origin" or "a transcendent end," he references specifically the interdependence that the terms *tian* and *dao* have with human beings: "In the Chinese cosmos all things are interdependent, without transcendent principles by which to explain them or a transcendent origin from which they derive. . . . A novelty in this position which greatly impresses me is that it exposes a preconception of Western interpreters that such concepts as Tian 'Heaven' and Dao 'Way' must have the transcendence of our own ultimate principles."[19] Hence, when the opening line of the *Zhongyong* states, "What *tian* commands is what is meant by the human propensities" (天命之謂性), we have to distinguish between the unilateral endowment of a universal human nature by a transcendent God on the one hand, and the endowment of "human propensities" (*xing*) in a cosmology in which *tian* and humankind are interdependent and mutually shaping on the other. Given the interpenetration presupposed in the doctrine of the "three powers" (*sancai* 三才), what it means to be human emerges out of a collaboration between what human beings have made out of themselves and how this ongoing redefinition of humanity is constantly impacting the natural and cultural context into which the human being is born, and within which the continuing human drama is unfolding.

***

Having thus clarified the social and normative entailments of "human propensities" (*xing* 性), Zheng Kai then explores the connection of *xing* with the "heartmind" (*xin* 心) aspect of *xinxing* theory. Given that human propensities themselves are determined by social relations, moral competence emerges when the prosocial "four inclinations" (*siduan* 四端) of the incipient human heartmind are cultivated and grow within the social and political life of the community. Zheng notes that Mencius in observing that human beings "have these four inclinations just as they have their four limbs" is importantly using a "physical" analogy that entails growth rather than invoking a predetermined "metaphysical" condition.[20] Indeed, Mencius goes on to underscore the social nature of these inclinations that locate us in our

---

19. Graham, "Replies," 287.
20. *Mencius* 2A6: 人之有是四端也, 猶其有四體也.

roles and relations, claiming that such inclinations are not only a necessary condition for qualifying as a human person, but further that

> our heartmind in feeling pity at perceived suffering disposes us toward consummate conduct in our roles and relations (*ren* 仁); our heartmind in feeling shame at perceived crudeness disposes us toward appropriate conduct in our roles and relations (*yi* 義); our heartmind in its feelings of modesty and deference disposes us toward propriety in our roles and relations (*li* 禮); our heartmind in feeling a sense of discrimination disposes us toward wisdom in our roles and relations (*zhi* 智).[21]

Further elaborating upon "heartmind" (*xin* 心) as it appears and is developed in the early philosophical literature, Zheng observes that

> if we examine the contents of *Mencius*, the "Great Commentary" of the *Book of Changes*, and *Focusing the Familiar*, we find a faint, always distinctive and yet continuous thread to the extent that we can say that these texts are all incubating and developing the Confucian *xinxing* theory. One point we might emphasize is that the importance Mencius invests in "heartmind" (*xin*) and "thinking" (*si* 思) and his best efforts to promote a theoretical connection between "heartmind" and "human propensities" (*xing* 性) can in its beginnings already be found there in the Zisi lineage.[22]

Citing the words of Confucius on *xin* who says that "in exercising it you preserve it; in giving up on it, it perishes,"[23] Mencius contends that those who care for the heartmind (*cunxin* 存心) and make the most of it (*jinxin* 盡心) can become as worthy as the sages Yao and Shun.

Zheng searches for the most appropriate language to explain *xinxing* theory as a conjunction of "heartmind" (*xin*) that defines what it means to

---

21. *Mencius* 2A6: 惻隱之心，仁之端也；羞惡之心，義之端也；辭讓之心，禮之端也；是非之心，智之端也.

22. 鄭開，試論孟子心性論哲學的理論結構，21: 從內容上考察，《盡心下》與《易傳》《中庸》之間隱約藕斷絲連，甚少可以說它們都醞釀併發展了儒家心性論哲學. 我們特別強調的一點就是，孟子重視"心""思,"並且力求將"心""性"概念聯繫起來的理論意圖其實在子思學派那裡已見端倪.

23. *Mencius* 6A8: 操則存，舍則亡.

be human and "human propensities" as an endowment invested in human beings described in the opening line of *Focusing the Familiar*: "What *tian* commands is what is meant by the human propensities" (天命之謂性). In so doing, Zheng turns away from unilateral metaphysical claims and toward the robust and polysemous notion of *cheng* 誠 as it is developed in both *Mencius* and *Focusing the Familiar*. For Zheng, it is *cheng* that reconciles "the way of becoming human" (*rendao* 人道) and "the way of *tian*" (*tiandao* 天道), bringing them together as one. Zheng cites a passage in *Focusing the Familiar* that would associate *cheng* with the virtuosity of the gods and spirits, and the way in which the numinous virtuosity of these forces imperceptibly nurtures all things in the world: "The virtuosity activated by the gods and spirits is truly profound. . . . Such is the way that the inchoate becomes manifest and that *cheng* becomes irrepressible."[24]

Zheng cites Xu Fuguan 徐復觀, who describes *cheng* as "the emergence of the perfected consummate heartmind" (*renxin* 仁心), allowing that while Xu's observation is certainly an important insight, it is still only one part of the story. In the early literature, *cheng* is understood to be the subjective capacity to combine both consummate conduct (*ren* 仁) and wisdom (*zhi* 智) to the extent that *cheng* references the spiritual level in which this coalescence is fully achieved. Yet at the same time, there are many other passages in this text in which *cheng* seems to be the objective foundation of all things in the cosmos. For example, "*cheng* is the happening of things from beginning to end; without *cheng* there is nothing."[25] Again, "the utmost *cheng* is ceaseless. . . . The way of the cosmos can be captured in one phrase: Since things are never duplicated, their production is unfathomable."[26] How then asks Zheng are we to understand a notion of *cheng* that, in addition to referencing a subjective achievement, is also an essential factor in "the consummating of things" (*chengwu* 成物), in "the covering of things" (*fuwu* 覆物), in "bearing things up" (*zaiwu* 載物), and in "engendering things" (*shengwu* 生物)?

Zheng, in his best effort to reconcile the subjective and objective dimensions of *cheng*, begins from the subjective in arguing that *cheng* brings "consummate conduct" (*ren*) and "wisdom" (*zhi*) together. In this sense, *cheng* has to be understood as a special kind of spiritual awareness defined explicitly in *Focusing the Familiar* as "achieving equilibrium and focus without

---

24. *Zhongyong* 中庸16: 鬼神之為德其盛矣乎! . . . 夫微之顯, 誠之不可揜如此夫!

25. *Zhongyong* 中庸 25: 誠者物之終始, 不誠無物.

26. *Zhongyong* 中庸 26: 故至誠無息 . . . 天地之道可壹言而盡也: 其為物不貳, 則其生物不策.

coercion, succeeding without reflection, and freely and easily traveling the center of the way. It is the sage."[27] With respect to the objective dimension of *cheng*, Zheng again brings in the earlier Zisi tradition and observes that "in the Zisi lineage, *cheng* is not limited to the subjective and the human way alone (*rendao*) but in fact brings together internally oriented 'consummate conduct' (*ren*) and the external world of things. The process of 'consummating oneself' (*chengji* 成己) must extend toward consummating things (*chengwu* 成物) in what is called 'the way of integrating what is more internal with what is more external' (*heneiwaizhidao* 合內外之道)."[28]

For Zheng, *cheng* is a kind of perspicacity, a spiritual awareness that is discriminating and that can penetrate into the operations of the cosmos to discern how all things unfold. It is only with *cheng* consciousness and its spiritual awareness that the "heartmind" (*xin*) and "human propensities" (*xing*) as they are in themselves can be spontaneously revealed. The SiMeng lineage's transformation of *cheng* in their theorizing is an attempt to elevate the way of human beings to the level of the way of *tian*, where the key lies in taking *cheng* that has been characterized primarily as a concept of psychological awareness and transforming it into a conception of what is most basic, that is, the way of *tian*. The understanding of *cheng* in the *Mencius* and *Focusing the Familiar* lies at the intersection of the mutuality of the subjective and objective, and of the interpenetration of the horizons of *tian* and the human. In this way, *cheng* in blurring any exclusionary lines between the subjective and objective is a way of thinking that seeks to overcome any subject/object dichotomy.

Mencius was able to systematize his "making the most of heartmind" (*jinxin* 盡心), "knowing human propensities" (*zhixing* 知性), and "knowing *tian*" (*zhitian* 知天) and, in so doing, to deepen and thus refine his understanding of the concept of "human propensities" (*xing* 性). This theorizing was possible because he could draw upon the legacy of Zisi thinking and, in using the concept of *cheng* 誠 to restructure his understanding of "heartmind" (*xin*), could make *cheng* one of the most profound doctrines in Confucian philosophy. In short, Mencius self-consciously inherited and further developed Zisi thought, reconstructed the concept of "human propensities" (*xing*), and creatively reinterpreted the notion of "heartmind"

---

27. *Zhongyong* 中庸 20: 誠者, 不勉而中, 不思而得, 從容中道, 聖人也.

28. 鄭開, 試論孟子心性論哲學的理論結構, 25: 在子思學派看來, "誠" 不囿于主觀、人道 的方面, 而是兼及了内向的 "仁" 和外在的 "物," 從某種意義上說, "成己" 必須向 "成物" 拓展, 這就是所謂的 "合内外之道."

(*xin*). In deepening his interpretation of the concepts of "heartmind" (*xin*) and "human propensities" (*xing*), Mencius was at the same time establishing a relatively systematic and compelling interpretation of *xinxing* philosophy.

From the ancient Greeks on, the mainstream of Western philosophy has been its tradition of epistemology. Looking at topics such as *cheng* 誠 and "everything is one" (*wanwuyiti* 萬物一體) in Mencian *xinxing* philosophy through the lens of Western epistemology, such themes are not only difficult to grasp but spill over into a kind of mysticism. Zheng sees this mystical dimension of Mencius's *xinxing* philosophy as a foil that brings into relief the complexity and profundity of its orientation toward attaining levels of spirituality and practical wisdom.

While some would interpret Mencius's claim that "the myriad of things are all implicated here in me" as an anomalous, purely rhetorical flourish, for Zheng Kai it in fact points to the necessary and logical outcome of Mencian philosophy.[29] And while some might wonder at the relevance of the statement that follows this first assertion about the myriad things, that is, "looking inward I am *cheng*" (反身而誠), for Zheng such a claim in fact sets the precondition for the myriad things all being here in me. In this SiMeng literature there is a progression from "caring for the heartmind" (*cunxin* 存心), to "making the most of human propensities" (*jinrenzhixing* 盡人之性), to "making the most of the propensities of things" (*jinwuzhixing* 盡物之性), to "knowing *tian*" (*zhitian* 知天), and to "finding contentment in life" (*liming* 立命). The final step then is attaining the spiritual level of "assisting the heavens and the earth in their transforming and nurturing activities" (赞天地之化育) and thus "becoming a triad with the heavens and the earth" (*yutiandican* 与天地参). Zheng cites *Focusing the Familiar* where it makes this same point explicitly: "Only those in the world with the utmost *cheng* are able to separate out and braid together the many threads on the great loom of the world. Only they set the great root of the world and realize the transforming and nourishing processes of the heavens and the earth."[30] Zheng suggests that this same passage might serve as a footnote to Mencius's claim that "the myriad of things are all implicated here in me," noting that the core Confucian ethical vocabulary is focused on relationships among persons and the depth (*du* 度) that can be achieved in these relations through a regimen of personal cultivation.

---

29. *Mencius* 孟子 7A4: 萬物皆备於我矣.

30. *Zhongyong* 中庸 32: 唯天下至誠唯天下至誠, 為能經綸天下之大經, 立天下之大本, 知天地之化育.

Response

Zheng Kai's argument for the central role of *cheng* 誠 in *xinxing* theory 心性論 is compelling. As Zheng has observed, *cheng* resists the separation between subjective and objective, between human feelings and cosmic creativity, between the human way and the way of *tian*, and between what is most basic and life's fullest consummation. In so doing, it vitiates our binary subject-object grammar and presents us with some very real difficulty in understanding the meaning of *cheng*, and then on that basis, finding an adequate English translation for the term itself. Perhaps one way of bringing this recondite term into clearer focus would be to apply our comparative cultural hermeneutics as a method that would take into account the interpretive context within which *cheng* must be located. At the very least, it is an exercise that will enable us to repeat some of Zheng's insights into a Chinese first philosophy, but in a different language.

Beginning from the *Shuowen* as one of the earliest lexicons, we find that in these traditional dictionaries the two terms *cheng* 誠 and "living up to one's word" (*xin* 信) are frequently glossed by appeal to each other. Just as *cheng* turns binaries such as subject and object (*zhuke*), and the human and *tian* (*tianren*) into interdependent *yinyang* aspects of a continuous relationship, the term *xin* 信 also denotes a situation- rather than an agency-centered relationship that combines "credibility" and the concomitant "trust" that such credibility inspires. That is, *xin* describes a fiduciary situation in which its participants as benefactors and beneficiaries conduct themselves sincerely and honestly with mutual regard. From a human perspective, *cheng* is also situational as a necessary condition for the integrative and creative process of growing oneself in one's relations with others to become consummately human. The *Expansive Learning* (*Daxue* 大學) defines the technical expression *shenqidu* 慎其獨, interpreted by commentators as both "internalizing and consolidating virtuosic conduct as one's habituated disposition for action" and "being circumspect when dwelling alone," specifically as "becoming resolute in one's thoughts and feelings" (*chengqiyi* 誠其意). That is, *cheng* like *xin* has a strong sense of generative intentionality that is expressed consistently as that stern resolution in conduct that reflects a commitment to growth in moral virtuosity. It is not "being whole" but the intentional and dynamic project of "becoming whole" within the multilateral relations that constitute a person's natural, social, and cultural environments.

The cluster of four alternative yet overlapping English translations of *cheng*—"sincerity, resolve, integrity, and creativity"—are justified etymologically by the fact that the "creative" sense of the graph *cheng* 誠 is reflected in its cognate term *cheng* 成—"consummating, completing, finishing, bringing to fruition"—that together with the discursive signific "speech" classifier (*yan* 言) makes up the character. This etymology suggests that *cheng* is the cultivation of a fiduciary community achieved through the various modalities of persons communicating effectively with one another. In this process, "sincerity" as "the absence of duplicity" is a necessary condition for cultivating relations, "resolve" is the staunch and steadfast intentionality that animates this regimen of cultivation, "integrity" is the pursuit of a "consummating wholeness" that comes from such cultivation, and a situated "creativity" describes the multilateral processes leading to the achievement of such wholeness. Each of these terms can within different contexts be viable translations. Such a reflection on *cheng* and its range of meaning are further consistent with Zhu Xi's commentary on the *Zhongyong* in which he defines *cheng* as 真實不妄: "the genuine and undeflected process of coming to fruition." As Zheng Kai suggests, such a generative process is certainly expressed through the effects of practical wisdom, but it also requires the attainment of that more exalted spiritual level reached when the highest order of humans as cosmic co-creators are able to assist the heavens and the earth in the production of their bounty.

The cultivation of these fiduciary relationships entails integrity in the sense of acknowledging the insistent particularity of always unique persons, and in the integrative sense of accommodating such persons as they become one together in their concrete, social relationships. Under such circumstances, "integrity" is not simply retaining what you "have" or "being who you are"; it is what you "do" and "become" in coalescing effectively within your relations with family, community, and world. And "sincerity" then connotes the subjective form of feeling that is a necessary condition for this creative process to proceed. That is, it suggests that sincerity is the genuineness that serves as the indispensable ground for growing interpersonal relationships.

This inseparability of integration and creativity is reinforced explicitly in the notion of *ren* 仁, the correlative, consummatory notion of "persons" in which the ongoing realization of oneself and of other persons is mutuality entailing. And the spontaneous emergence of significance in these relationships is the very meaning of this collaborative personal creativity. Indeed, the prefix "co-" in "co-creativity" is made redundant by the fact that it is this kind and only this kind of situated co-creativity—at once cognitive and affective, aesthetic and intensely religious—that can legitimately be called "creativity." Or stated the other way around, given the radical contextuality of this vital, ecological cosmology, there is no such thing as creatio ex nihilo—the erstwhile creativity of some agency that as a self-sufficient "creator" would stand independent of its creatures that in themselves are nothing.

In our translations of the canons, we have certainly respected the familiar "sincerity" and "integrity" renderings for *cheng*. In a cosmology of ever-changing, interpenetrating events, "integrity" further suggests the active process of bringing relationships into focus and securing sufficient resolution in them to achieve their optimum meaningfulness. But when this term *cheng* appears as a central cosmological idea found in the Mencius and is then elaborated upon in some detail in *Focusing the Familiar* (*Zhongyong*), we have also introduced "creativity" and "resolution" as additional dimensions of meaning. The appropriateness of using "creativity" and "resolve" as translations for *cheng* lies in acknowledging the "self-so-ing" (*ziran* 自然) causal assumptions underlying the classical Confucian worldview where it is growth of resolution in focal relations rather than independent causal agency that is the source of enhanced meaning.

The parsing of *cheng* in some contexts principally as "creativity" rather than "sincerity" or "integrity" brings attention to the central role in the Confucian tradition broadly of human participation in the shaping of the cosmic order, and as how this co-creativity is the main theme of *Focusing the Familiar* in particular. When we couple Confucius's introduction of the neologism *zhongyong* 中庸 ("focusing the familiar," "hitting the mark in the everyday") with the Mencian elevation of the human feeling of *cheng* 誠 to the level of a cosmic force, we can then parse *cheng* further as the "resolve and commitment" that animates this creative process. The collateral role of a distinctly human creativity within its larger cosmic context is described in the *Mencius* when it states that "creative resolve is the way-making of *tian* while reflecting on things with resolution is the way-making of human beings."[31] There is a passage in *Focusing the Familiar* seemingly inspired by if not bor-

---

31. 孟子 4A12: 誠者天之道也, 思誠者人之道也.

rowed directly from this Mencian cosmic turn in the meaning of *cheng*, observing that "creative resolve is the way-making of *tian*; applying this creative resolve is the way-making of becoming human. Such resolve is achieving equilibrium and coalescence without coercion; it is succeeding without reflection. Freely and easily traveling at the center of the process of way-making—this is the sage. Resolve is selecting what is efficacious and holding on to it firmly."[32] In interpreting such passages, we must resist our theological tendency to separate the secular from the sacred, the way of humankind from the numinosity of their context. Indeed, we must constantly return to the correlative relationship they have in shaping and being shaped by each other. In the *Mencius* and in these middle passages of *Focusing the Familiar*, *cheng* is a human sentiment that has been elevated and projected onto the cosmos to describe the process of procreation itself, making the resolve of intense human feelings not only integral to its operations but a source of the world's boundless capacity for growth. At the same time, *tian* and humankind, rather than standing independent of and thus external to each other, are aspects of a shared, first-order relationship. This means that what is ascribed to either one of them is always implicated in the other.

This process of cosmic co-creativity is elaborated upon and described perhaps most clearly and powerfully in *Focusing the Familiar* when it states that "resolve (*cheng* 誠) is self-consummating and its way-making is self-directing. Resolve is the beginning and the end of things, and without this resolve, there would be nothing. It is thus that, for exemplary persons, it is resolve that is prized."[33] The meaning of *cheng* here is extended from the familiar personal attitude of sincerity and integrity to describe the cosmic process of world-making in which the sages (*shengren* 聖人) as co-creators play a key role. The discursive element *yan* 言 included in the *cheng* 誠 graph suggests that creativity involves a dynamic, discursive, and transactional partnership between the living human world and its natural, social, and cultural contexts. It is through effective communication that consummation is pursued in family and community, and is the substance of contrapuntal and productive

---

32. *Zhongyong* 中庸 20: 誠者, 天之道也; 誠之者, 人之道也. 誠者不勉而中, 不思而得, 從容中道, 聖人也. 誠之者, 擇善而固執之者也.

33. *Zhongyong* 中庸 25: 誠者自成也, 而道自道也. 誠者物之終始, 不誠無物. 是故君子誠之為貴. 誠者非自成己而已也, 所以成物也. 成己, 仁也; 成物, 知也. 性之德也, 合外內之道也, 故時措之宜也.

transactions between humans and their natural context. *Focusing the Familiar* goes on to identify optimum human creativity with sagacity, where cosmic creativity itself is enhanced dramatically by the virtuosic contributions of this highest level of humanity. The sages (*shengren*) are able to orchestrate the communal discourse and coordinate it with the heavens and the earth to achieve a cosmic flourishing.

In fact, the etymology of the character for "sage" (*sheng* 聖) that appears on the oracle bones 𝕲 and the bronzes ▓ is a combination of "ear" (*er* 耳) and "mouth" (*kou* 口).[34] The early commentaries tell us that this character for sage has the same root as two other characters having the same meaning and being close in pronunciation: "orality, sound, voice" 𝕲 (*sheng* 聲) and "aurality, listening, hearing" 𝕲 (*ting* 聽).[35] Given this close association between sagacity and effective discourse, we might surmise that sages are those virtuosic communicators belonging to a particular epoch who, in all of their listening and speaking, are able to raise their voices to sing the songs of the people. Language becomes music when its composition achieves a coalescence, cadence, and harmony among its speakers in all of their differences. Thus, the musicality that can be ascribed to sagacity is a function of "one is many, many one," where the sages in their depth and measure have emerged as the one voice inclusive of the aspirations of all of their people. Hence *Focusing the Familiar* elevates these cultural avatars to celestial proportions, stating that "only those of utmost sagacity in the world . . . appear and all defer to them, they speak and all have confidence in what they say, they act and all find pleasure in what they do. . . . Thus it is said that they are the complement of *tian* 天."[36] Notions such as "commitment" and "resolve" give rise to the issue of agency, and we have to remember that in this *ziran* causality with primacy given to vital relationality, situation takes precedence over individual agency. Said another way, since in this focus-field holography, anything is both the cause and the effect of everything else, agency is always situated and a matter of degrees of relevance. It is the "one is many, many one" identity of the sages that brings continuity and coherence to the unsummed totality. As Zheng Kai has made clear, *cheng* is what reconciles the subject-object, *tian*-human, and what is

---

34. Kwan, "Database," CHANT 0693 and CHANT 10175.

35. Kwan, "Database," 一期甲骨續一 四五六 三期殷虛書契後編上 七, 一零.

36. *Focusing the Familiar* 31: 唯天下至聖 . . . 見而民莫不敬, 言而民莫不信, 行而民莫不說. . . . 故曰配天.

most basic-cosmic flourishing dichotomies. In all cases, the relationship is first order and the erstwhile dichotomies are themselves two aspects of the same phenomenon, where the quality of its focal resolution is a function of the "depth and proper measure" (*du* 度) achieved in the human-and-world relationship itself.

The main theme of *Focusing the Familiar* is to clarify the relationship between human beings and world captured in the mantra "the continuity of and inseparability between the human and *tian*" (*tianrenheyi* 天人合一). There is ample textual evidence that human sagacity is the measure of the of coalescence achieved in this collaborative, first-order *tianren* relationship. As we witness throughout the canonical Confucian texts, the otherwise vague notion of *tian* takes on the visage of a particular human face as the texts repeatedly correlate these always unique sages with *tian* by characterizing the sages metaphorically in grand, celestial terms such as the turning of the seasons, the sequencing of the sun and the moon, shining like the brightness of the heavens, and so on. Moral virtuosity (*de* 德), far from being described as the exclusive quality of either *tian* or human beings, is expressed as a point of intersection and collaboration between *tian* and the way-making of the sages who stand as the highest order of humanity.

Given that the sages are the paramount exemplars of what is humanly possible, this moral virtuosity is manifested in the world as the consummate expression of the operations of both sagacious human beings and the contextualizing *tian* as this first-order relationship continues to deepen in their collaborative activities. Not only is such sagacity to be understood as human beings such as Yao, Shun, and Confucius themselves achieving the reach and influence of *tian*, but moreover *tian* itself being deepened and extended by this accumulating human sagacity. This shared virtuosic conduct underscores the primacy of the *tianren* relationship over the secondary distinction between *tian* and human beings, and it also makes the important point that human beings in their role as sages can continue and extend the work of *tian*. The highest achievements of human beings constitute nothing less than a co-creative and transformative moral force in the cosmos.

True to the particular and sustained emphasis in the *Mencius* on proper governance, this canonical text establishes an immediate symbiosis between personal cultivation, governing effectively, and a flourishing cosmos. The feeling of resolve (*cheng* 誠) in personal growth is elevated as a natural force that correlates the inner intensity of human feelings with cosmic influence, galvanizes the institutions that enable the civilizing of the human experience, and establishes humankind as a co-creator with the heavens and the earth in a triad described as the "three forces" (*sancai* 三才). Elevating such resolve to an intensity that not only impacts but has a dramatic shaping influence on the emerging natural order locates human life and growth as integral to what is fundamentally a moral cosmos.

Zhang Xianglong 張祥龍

Figure 6.2. Zhang Xianglong.

Zhang Xianglong 張祥龍 was a professor of philosophy at Peking University. He holds a PhD from the State University of New York at Buffalo, an MA from Toledo University, and a BA from Peking University. His research areas include Confucian philosophy, phenomenology, and comparative philosophy, and he has published monographs and many articles in all of these areas. One of his early books, *From Confucius to Phenomenology*, brought the Chinese and Western philosophical narratives into conversation and in its time became a popular bestseller. His most recent focus was on Confucianism and the philosophy of family, with *Family and Filiality: An Intercultural Perspective* now available in English translation by Kevin J. Turner (State University of New York Press). As a senior fellow at the Peking University

Berggruen Research Center, Professor Zhang led projects on science fiction and the philosophy of family.

Zhang Xianglong 張祥龍: "Image" and "Concept" Thinking

The distinguished contemporary philosopher Zhang Xianglong 張祥龍 makes a useful distinction between what he calls "image or imagistic thinking" (*xiangsiwei* 象思維) that we might associate immediately with the *Book of Changes* and the "conceptual or conceptualizing thinking" (*gainiansiwei* 概念思維 or *gainianhuasiwei* 概念化思維) that was characteristic of early Greek ontological thinking.[37] In the *Book of Changes*, both cosmic and human change is described in terms of the strains and tensions within the aspectual and processual images of symbiotic bipolar opposites such as "flux and continuity" (*biantong* 變通), "alternating succession" (*yinyang* 陰陽) and "penetration and receptivity" (*qiankun* 乾坤). Such correlative images complement each other and together provide a generative account of the ongoing process of transformation that continues without respite within an unbounded totality. It is within this flux and flow that the transactional human life unfolds, with the challenge for human beings to fathom these cosmic operations and then to correlate the events of their own lives with the emergent cosmic order to optimum effect.

Let me paraphrase the substance of what Zhang takes to be the important distinction between these two different ways of thinking. With respect to "conceptual thinking," Zhang begins by pointing out the term *gainian* 概念 that translates "concept" is not a traditional Chinese term but is one of many *kanji* loanwords in modern Japanese that were coined to translate European, and especially English terms.[38] During the second half of the nineteenth century beginning in Meiji Japan, the institutions and curricula of Western education were imported wholesale into East Asia. Within this context, a new language constructed with Chinese characters was created to synchronize the East Asian languages with the vocabulary of Western modernity. Within the Western philosophical narrative, "concept"

---

37. Zhang Xianglong, 概念化思維與象思維 [Conceptualizing thinking and imagistic thinking].

38. Zhang's observation that *gainian* 概念 as "concept" is an example of the invention of this new vocabulary is confirmed by Liu, *Translingual Practice*, 286. In this study, Liu lays out this complex process of constructing a new language in detail and reflects upon its political implications.

in contrast to "image" or "intuition" or "feeling" reflects a formal tendency that takes thinking in the direction of the fixed, the determinate, and the abstract definition of things, and tends to arrest the processual nature of experience by privileging the spatial over the temporal and the generic over the particular. In traditional studies in logic, the notion of concept that would distinguish A from not-A provides the principle of noncontradiction as the starting point for the logical method of analysis. In standard Western dictionaries, concept is defined as an abstract and more generic idea as it is generalized from particular instances. Although in its more popular usage today the term "concept" in some degree sheds its theoretical origins ("Do you get the concept of American football?"), still in its stricter usage such as "whiteness" or "beauty" it still remembers this philosophical history. Broadly speaking, "concept" suggests a clear awareness of some stable meaning and, more narrowly, some general idea abstracted out of concrete instances. Philosophically, it can be either the methodological practice of "conceptualizing" or the noun form that is the product of such activity.

Zhang describes five characteristics he would associate with "conceptual thinking." (1) It is a universalizing or generalizing way of thinking (*pubianhua* 普遍化 or *yibanhua* 一般化) that would abstract definitions out the shared features of things rather than dealing with these things concretely and specifically. It is thus abstract rather than particular and purports to grasp what is universal in experience. It tends to ignore the particular and changing lifeworld activities in favor of those theories and truths that can be universalized. Perhaps the clearest example in this respect is Plato's *eidos* as the basis of his Theory of Forms.

(2) In seeking out the erstwhile unchanging essences of things rather than dealing with the changing things themselves, conceptual thinking takes what is most dependable, foundational, static, and logical as its subject matter and thus provides thought with a stabilizing function (*jingtaihua* 靜態化). Particular, concrete phenomena can change, but their essential identities available for conceptualization do not. It is in this way that the essential, rational concepts of the philosopher part ways with the concrete ideas expressive of emotion and imagination that are the currency of literature and poetry.

(3) Conceptual thinking takes abstract, objective principles as the substance of reality and as the subject of its intellectual reflection: beauty-in-itself, courage-in-itself, the principle of justice, and so on. In this sense, it is a form of higher-order objectification (*gaojieduixianghua* 高介對象化). These rationalized, hypostasized objects of knowledge in being intelligible only to the mind are different from the phenomena that belong to a world of time

and space, and thus generate a subject/object dualism. That is, even though the internal, subjective concepts do not have the same reality as their objects, a consciousness of them does effect a kind of subjective universalism as its epistemology. Further, while "horse" or "human being" for example can be conceptualized, there are other ideas that would resist this process, such as *dao* 道 in Lao-Zhuang Daoism, *qi* 氣 in Chinese cosmology broadly, and notions such as a round square or the lowest common denominator.

(4) Concepts do not in their meaning and existence belong to a situation as it is happening because within a process that is changing and taking shape, the experience of the particular and the universal, as well as the objective and the subjective, cannot be separated. We can say that conceptual thinking belongs to a specifically conceptualized understanding of philosophy. There is a philosophical method guided by conceptualized thinking that takes as its subject matter the content of retrospective reflection on things and events (*shihoufansi* 事後反思) rather than of immediate empirical experience. As such, it cannot cover all of philosophy. G. W. F. Hegel in explaining his philosophy of history near the end of his preface to the *Philosophy of Right* writes, "The owl of Minerva spreads its wings only with the falling of dusk." What Hegel means with this metaphor is that the objects of all philosophical understanding are, by necessity, only those things that have already been experienced and that have thus been deduced rationally from principles already known. Such objects can only be known in hindsight. Only the past can be the object of philosophy. Karl Marx, in his famous eleventh thesis on Feuerbach, reflects on this kind of retrospective philosophy and rejects it in insisting that the first duty of philosophy is not just to explain the world but to change it.

(5) Summarizing these first four characteristics of conceptual thinking, it can be characterized as "non-meaning generating" (*bushengchengyiyide* 不生成意義的) in the sense that it is limited to an intellect that would arrange, organize, and systematize meaning but that does not produce it.

Zhang Xianglong rehearses the history of this conceptual thinking as it takes root within the early Greek philosophers and becomes firmly set with Plato and Aristotle. Such conceptual philosophy in giving privilege to the theoretical mode of thinking produces a spectator theory of knowledge—what has been described as the mirror of nature. Importantly, while nascent and sporadic challenges to this entrenched way of thinking certainly emerge much earlier in the Western tradition, it is not until the second half of the nineteenth century that the internal critique within its own philosophical narrative becomes a sustained revolution against such categorical assumptions. Even so, such conceptual thinking as integral to a persistent common sense has in some important measure been recalcitrant and thus difficult to overcome.[39]

Zhang, having thus reflected on the nature and history of conceptual thinking, then turns to describe those very different characteristics he would ascribe to "imagistic thinking" (*xiangsiwei* 象思維):

(1) Such an imagistic way of thinking is a generative source of meaning (*yuanfaxing* 原發性) in the sense of a "doing" that constitutes the doer, what is being done, and what has been initiated within the continuing process itself. It is a way of thinking in which the production of meaning and one's own identity are mutually bound up in one another. Investing oneself utterly in some particular activity, a person in a peripheral way is still able to feel that this same doing allows for one's own identity to be shaped and, again from the new meaning that is being produced, for the doing itself to be afforded its novelty. In more philosophical language, it is allowing persons in following a process of dynamic growth the possibility of participating in the process itself, thereby triggering a way of thinking that brings with it an increase in awareness. Unlike conceptual thinking that would abandon the transitory and conjunctive patterns of growth in phenomena, imagistic thinking invests itself in this same empirical process to make adjustments, repair, and reconstruct the content of experience. Images are the womb of and give birth to both apprehending and participating in what is happening in the world in the fullest sense, and imagistic thinking thus constitutes a level of thought that conceptual thinking does not and cannot reach.

(2) This understanding of image-thinking is nonobjectifying (*feidui-xianghua* 非對象化) in several senses. That is, images cannot be used to capture some object nor are they themselves objects; where image-thinking is happening, the object has yet to take shape. Imagistic thinking does not objectify experience as in the bureaucratic structure of conceptual thinking that would result in definition but instead makes meaning, determines meaning, and makes clear the pathway through which meaning and its structure is manifested. It distinguishes the levels and functions of meaning and permits meaning to methodically and without interruption appear and transform. More than other ways of thinking, the office of imagistic thinking, without itself having any fixed mode of expression, is image-enabling and combining, and at the most crucial moment it is catalytic, with its capacity to induce meaning and to activate the first stages in the growth of meaning.

---

39. As we have seen, Nietzsche would argue that this obstacle to alternative ways of thinking arises from the ontological assumptions sedimented into the grammar and semantics of Indo-European languages themselves, prompting some philosophical questions while precluding others. See Nietzsche, *Beyond Good and Evil*, 20, cited on 157 in this volume.

Imagistic thinking emerges from some hidden, secreted place to occasion the forming of some aspect or class of meaning. It occasions the image but does not predetermine what is conjured forth as the image.

(3) We can see that even though images do not have a fixed form, imagistic thinking has an occasioning structure of arising in the wake of images and of supplementing experience, causing people to ponder deeply and truly in the responses they make to images. Images have a randomness, a gracefulness, a depth, and a clarity that brings about an unforeseen feeling of being pleasantly surprised or unpleasantly disgusted. And it is not clear what it is that is being supplemented. Supplementing in the sense of "repairing" is a response to something broken, strange, uncomfortable, or painful, and it is not clear in advance what that something is. Imagistic thinking functions to bring insights and alternative perspectives with it that will have a complementary "repairing and elaborating" (*bu* 補) function in the growth of meaning (*budui'ershengcheng* 補對而生成), making those adjustments and modifications that will reinstate equilibrium and balance.

(4) Since images will neither resolve to the form and formless distinction nor do they entail some native stuff, we can only think of them in terms of a pure tendency or as a state of emerging and dissipating (*chunshitai* 純勢態), a rising and falling wave, carrying with them the distinction between a living image and one that is dying. An image is something that carries information. And herein lies the difference between a living and a dying image, with the dying image being clearer in its details, while the living image is not.

(5) There is a holographic latency or potentiality (*qianzaiquanxi* 潛在全息) in images that resists definition or boundary. Each image carries with it an ellipsis (. . .) or omission and has implicated in it something disconcerting. With an image, one seems not to know, and yet at the same time, to understand more expansively and more deeply. Each time one encounters an image, there is a beginning for understanding that then sets off a surge of meaning, giving one entry into layered fantasy worlds in which love becomes ever deeper, and hatred ever fiercer. Since it is an image induced by love, at the same time one is able to love the love and to renew it by continually making allowances for any shortcomings. And for hate, too, one is able to find in the image seemingly bottomless reasons for hating. By way of contrast, conceptual thinking is a one-way mirror in which the capturing of the image in the reflection does not move people like poetry or provide them the stimulation occasioned by drama.

For persons who are living in images, it is like living in a dream. Is there the possibility of waking up from the dream? Is there the possibility of a dreamless night? How would one know that yesterday I had a dreamless night? This then is precisely the basic enabling capacity of the image—the great image, the pure image. So that if there is an awakening, it is not the image that does it, nor is it an awakening during a dreamless night.

(6) Images are vital and temporalizing (*shihua* 時化), and they have a life of their own that contrasts with the hardening and reifying of the conceptual. We might say that an image is a living time. This kind of temporality finds one following the image and latching on to its meaning, where following after its meaning is again to participate in the production of its temporality. Each moment inherits the inexhaustible sedimentation of the past and the uncertain withholdings of the future. Images necessarily arise suddenly and yet seem to have been anticipated for ever so long. It is thus that *yinyang* is first a temporal image rather than some primordial structure of the cosmos. Certainly, its meaning comes from a distinction, but the first of its distinctions is that between the past and the future.

(7) One other pathway through which human beings experience images is through language. The fact that children can learn human languages but birds and animals can only learn their own "languages" is because human beings live in a world of images. Their languages are imagistic, riding as they do upon waves of underlying images (*yuanchudiyuyanhua* 原初地語言化): what George Lakoff and Mark Johnson call "metaphors we live by." The fact that persons born deaf and dumb can learn human languages, and yet persons with a complete sensorium cannot learn the languages of birds and animals is because human languages are imagistic. Images are neither universalistic nor particular, and what gives expression to an image is neither a proper name nor a concept. Images change and grow according to the linguistic context, and they activate the growth and formation of new meaning.

Heidegger says that "language is the house of being" because the source of language and the way it works is through the enabling of images. Regardless of whatever kind of human community is referenced, all populations have their languages in the same way that they all take nine months to incubate a fetus. And yet how very different these languages are. While there is no way they can translate each other's languages through conceptual correspondences, all of them can achieve some degree of mutual understanding in the translation process. In translating poetry, humor, and profanity, loss in flavor and intensity is unavoidable, and yet if one's own language has something equivalent, we can usually follow the main drift of what is being said. This is all because of the image. Not only does language give us the capacity to conjure up images, it also allows for both proliferation and depth in this process.

In this world, the Chinese language is something special. In a flesh and blood way, the script still connects us to a world of more than three thousand years ago. Poetry with its rhymes and characters on bamboo strips recovered from more than twenty-three centuries ago can in an instant stir us directly. Moreover, calligraphy produced with these characters has become an art form connected with painting that is purposed to be not only graphic forms or phonetic sounds, but also to be image enablers. Does this say more about the antiquity or the sensitivity of the language? Probably both, but especially the latter. After all, it is only with this need for connectivity and the sensitivity of the language that we can, in the present, use what is ancient to write the future.

RESPONSE

The term that Zhang Xianglong is appealing to in drawing the contrast between the conceptual or categorical thinking we would associate with ontology and the imagistic thinking that resonates with zoetology is *xiang* 象, a character that can be parsed in different contexts as "image, imaging, imagining, figure, figuring, figuring out, configuring." One of Zhang's most powerful insights here is that conceptual thinking that takes a given, unchanging reality as its starting point can certainly promise transparency, clear definition, and analytic rigor. But as the inspiration behind this quest for certainty and universality, its object is fixed and atemporal, and thus not productive of additional meaning. Imagistic thinking, on the other hand, functions within concrete practices, and while it is lacking in the formal boundaries that allow for rigor and objectivity, in its creative vagueness it is alive and generative of novel meaning. In order to get the most out of Zhang's abstract reflection on this important distinction, it might be helpful to return to the canonical texts from which he is drawing his insights, and see how imagistic thinking functions in making these documents not only meaningful but fecund and open-ended in the sense of inspiring generation after generation of evolving commentary.

To begin with, the character *xiang* appears on the oracle bones as 𧰨 and is clearly a pictograph of an elephant. The *Shuowen* lexicon defines *xiang* in precisely such terms: a large animal found in the southern reaches of China and Southeast Asia that has a trunk, tusks, and ears, and that has a three-year gestation period (actually twenty-two months).[40] We have archaeological evidence that elephants once existed in northern China and that ivory carving as a (now banned) contemporary Chinese art form is one of its oldest arts that was already highly developed as far back as the Shang dynasty. An analysis of this evidence suggests that

---

40. See J. Norman and T. Mei, "The Austroasiatics in Ancient South China: Some Lexical Evidence," *Monumenta Serica* 32 (1976): 274–301.

the elephant like the whale and the rhinoceros were rare species imported from outside of China and, if available at all, were because of their novelty used primarily for display. Thus, a creature known but rarely seen came to be used to denote the presentational act of "conjuring" or "imaging."

The early Legalist text *Hanfeizi* is corroborative in providing its explanation for how this term has come to mean "imaging, conjuring, image," stating that "people have rarely seen live elephants but have found the skeleton of the dead animal. On the basis of this experience, they have been able to conjure up its living form. It is for this reason that those things the multitude are able to conjure forth are all called 'images.' "[41] The elephant as an unfamiliar creature requires us actively and with imagination to "imagine" it and "conjure" it up. Thus, *xiang* comes to mean "imaging, imagining, figuring out, configuring" and, by extension and as the outcome of the process, carries us in the direction of "a figure, an image, a presentation" that reveals both the process and the product of our conjuring. At the same time, just as we must resist objectifying the active process of "way-making" (*dao*) into "the way," we must resist hypostasizing the process of *xiang* thinking and thereby reduce it to the production or recovery of images. Imaging and imagining are fundamentally gerundive, and will not surrender themselves to the formal and final. And given their fertility, they provide us with a dynamic role both in retrospectively analogizing and in prospectively configuring the world around us, a world that through our vision of its possibilities reveals itself to us.

The images associated with the hexagrams of the *Book of Changes* are efficacious because they are heuristics and have a communally experienceable character. That is, the image of "fire," for example, might bring to mind particular experiences of the phenomenon of fire through recourse to communal institutions and social memory. An understanding of traditions, institutions, ritual practices, music, literature, and so on, forms a cultural consciousness embodied in the individual consulting the *Changes*. In the classical Confucian cosmology, image is the evoking of a world constantly being reconfigured at the concrete and historical level. Indeed, the living and evolving image can provide more stimulation and thus explanatory force than a logical account that, in arresting the processual nature of things, would distort the experience.

Willard Peterson in fact argues that the term *xiang*, conventionally translated as "image" or "model" as it appears in the *Changes*, ought to

---

41. 《韓非子 解老》："人希見生象也，而得死象之骨，案其圖以想其生也，故諸人之所以意想者皆謂之"象"也.

be rendered "figure" both in the sense of "figuring" and "figuring out": that is, "giving or bringing into shape."[42] This is what is meant by the *Changes* when it reports that "the sages, having the capacity to survey the complexities of the world, found correlations among the vital shapes and the appearances of things, and thus conjured up suitable images for them. It is for this reason they are called 'images.'"[43]

There is a reported conversation in the *Book of Changes* between Confucius and his disciples that is an encouragement to read the didactic function of the *Analects* itself as a generative image of a special person who walked among us and forged his way:

> The Master said: "The written word cannot do justice to speech, and speech cannot do justice to meaning."[44]
>
> "If this is the case, then is the meaning of the sages beyond our grasp?"
>
> The Master replied: "The sages constructed 'images' to make the most of their meaning, set up the hexagrams to convey as clearly as possible what is actual and what is contrived, wrote their judgments on the images and hexagrams in order to make the most of what they had to say, introduced the presumption of change and continuity as a way to make the most of any situation, and elaborated upon and embellished all this to do justice to their profundity."[45]

The cosmology as it is made explicit in the *Changes* provides the interpretive context not only for the classical Confucian canons but for the classical Daoist texts as well. The *Daodejing*, for example, encourages us to make sense of, discriminate, and valorize the otherwise dark and amorphous content of our experience as we are engaged in world-making:

> As for the process of way-making,
> It is ever so indefinite and vague.

42. Willard Peterson, "Making Connections: 'Commentary on the Attached Verbalizations' of the *Book of Changes*," *Harvard Journal of Asiatic Studies* 42, no. 1 (1982): 80–81.

43. See Ames, *Sourcebook*, 106: 聖人有以見天下之賾, 而擬諸其形容, 象其物宜, 是故謂之象.

44. The character *yi* 意 is translated variously as "concept," "thought/s," and "ideas." *Yi* is glossed in the *Shuowen* lexicon as "intended meaning, purpose" (*zhi* 志), reflecting its performative connotation. It is in this sense of "designing" that I understand it here.

45. 子曰"書不盡言, 言不盡意. 然則聖人之意, 其不可見乎." 子曰: "聖人立象以盡意, 設卦以盡情偽, 繫辭以盡其言, 變而通之以盡利, 鼓之舞之以盡神."

> Though vague and indefinite
> There are images within it.
> Though indefinite and vague,
> There are events within it.
> Though nebulous and dark,
> There are seminal concentrations of *qi* within it.[46]

Indeed, the *Daodejing* recounts how through this process of imaging a world into being, our cultural heroes as visionaries disciplined and stabilized the human experience, and perhaps even more importantly, they inspired it, drawing generation after generation toward their construal of what it means to be human:

> Seize the great image
> And the people of the world will repair to you.
> Repairing to you they steer clear of harm,
> And peace and security prevail for them.[47]

At the same time, because the *Daodejing* alerts us to the fact that "the greatest image has no ultimate shape,"[48] it also cautions us that any imaging of the world in the fullness of time is vulnerable to transformation and will gradually slip away on us:

> As for this "one"—
> Its surface is not dazzling
> Nor is its underside dark.
> Ever so tangled, it defies discrimination
> And reverts again to indeterminacy.
> This is what is called the form of the formless
> And the image of indeterminacy.[49]

The invention and ramification of images and metaphors is one of the fundamental ways through which a culture interprets its world. A

---

46. *Daodejing* 21: 道之為物, 唯恍唯惚. 忽兮恍兮, 其中有象; 恍兮忽兮, 其中有物. 窈兮冥兮, 其中有精.

47. *Daodejing* 35: 執大象, 天下往. 往而不害, 安平大.

48. *Daodejing* 41: 大象無形.

49. *Daodejing* 14: 一者, 其上不皦, 其下不昧. 繩繩不可名, 復歸於無物. 是謂無狀之狀, 無物之象.

third-century statement of this insight is to be found in the Wang Bi 王弼
commentary on the *Changes* entitled "Elucidating the Images" (*Mingxiang*
明象). In this discussion, Wang Bi attempts to parse the interpenetrating relationship obtaining among image (*xiang* 象), word (*yan* 言), and
meaning (*yi* 意), and in so doing provides us with an alternative to the
familiar notion of the literal and referential nature of language. Wang
Bi begins by reflecting upon the role of word and image in constituting
meaning, observing that

> an image expresses meaning; words clarify the image. To do full
> justice to meaning, nothing is as good as an image; to do full
> justice to an image, nothing is as good as words. Because words
> arise from images, we can explore the words as a window on
> the image. And because the image arises from meaning, we can
> explore the image as a window on meaning. Meaning is given full
> account with an image, and the image is articulated in words.
>
> Hence, words are whereby we clarify the image. In getting
> the image, we forget the words. The image is whereby we grasp
> the meaning. In getting the meaning, we forget the image. It
> is like the snare serving to capture the rabbit; in snaring the
> rabbit, we forget the snare. Or like the fish-trap serving to catch
> the fish; in catching the fish, we forget the trap. As such, words
> are the "snare" for the image. And the image is the "trap" for
> meaning. For this reason, holding on to the words is not getting
> the image; holding on to the image is not getting the meaning.[50]

Wang Bi concludes here by indicating both the heuristic function and
the limitations of words and images. We cannot catch rabbits and fish
without snares and traps, and we cannot capture meaning without
the effective deployment of words and images. Word and image are
triggers as well as repositories of meaning, but if they are interpreted
as mere repositories, they can hinder the holistic and dynamic process
of meaning-making. This is what the *Zhuangzi* means when it looks to

---

50. Wang Bi, "Mingxiang 明象" [Elucidating the images], *Zhouyi Lueli* [A summary
introduction to the *Book of Changes*] in the *Baibucongshu jicheng* 百部叢書集成 (Taipei:
Yiwen Publishing House, 1965), 10b–11b: 夫象者, 出意者也. 言者, 明象者也. 盡意莫
若象, 盡象莫若言. 言生於象, 故可尋言以觀象. 象生於意, 故可尋象以觀意. 意以象盡, 象
以言著. 故言者所以明象, 得象而忘言. 象者所以存意, 得意而忘象. 猶蹄者所以在兔, 得兔
而忘蹄; 筌者所以在魚, 得魚而忘筌也. 然則, 言者, 象之蹄也; 象者, 意之筌也. 是故存言
者, 非得象者也; 存象者, 非得意者也.

have a word with a person who in grasping the meaning has forgotten the words: "The reason for fish-traps is to catch fish, but having caught the fish, you forget the fish-trap. The reason for rabbit snares is to snare rabbits, but having caught the rabbit, you forget the snare. The reason for words is to capture meaning, but having grasped the meaning, you forget the words. Where can I find a person who has forgotten the words so that I can have a word with him?"[51] Imaging is analogical in the sense that it requires moving between a generalized situation made intelligible in word and image, and the meaning-productive detail of one's own particular circumstances. Imaging as such is collaborative and has performative force. Meaning is not simply given; it is reflexively appropriated and then projected and concretized. As such, while it is retrospectively appropriated, it is also generatively "made up" and "made one's own."

In the *Changes*, the meaning of a general situation is captured in an image, and the image is explained in words. The words constitute the most abstract level of discourse and, as such, have the least degree of meaning for one's own particular situation. Words, however, have the power to evoke an image, which in stirring one's imagination, enables one to bring one's particular situation into meaningful focus. What was abstract becomes increasingly concrete; what was broad in its generality becomes increasingly situationally and temporally specific; what was vague becomes increasingly focused and meaningful. By virtue of its stimulation, the image displaces the words, and as the image is explored as both a repository and stimulus of significance for one's own circumstances, the shape of the image begins to fade and thus gives way to meaning. In being deepened and made more determinate, and thus more meaningful for oneself, the image loses its more general character and becomes increasingly indistinct. And then the image retreats as the particular situation is suffused with meaning.

In thinking about the word-image-meaning circuit, we might take as an example sitting down on an afternoon to read *Pickwick Papers*, a recreation that would be anything but a passive affair. Dickens gives us carefully chosen words that bring a continuous flow of overlapping and stimulating images to mind, and he certainly provides us with a most meaningful experience that challenges our imagination and becomes increasingly our own. On reflection, the seriality of the installments of Dickens's travelogue is a fair suggestion of the phasal sequencing of

---

51. *Zhuangzi* 75/26/48–49: "莊子《外物》荃者所以在魚, 得魚而忘荃; 蹄者所以在兔, 得兔而忘蹄; 言者所以在意, 得意而忘言。吾安得忘言之人而與之言哉?"

word-image-meaning. And a reading of Dickens not only serves as a continuing source of inspiration but also contributes to the education of our imagination, and to the capacity we might accrue over time to become writers and image-makers ourselves.

Wang Bi's most important insight here is perhaps the fluidity and aspectual nature of the cyclical process of meaning-making that requires imaging and articulation while at the same time resisting any foundational claims among its several aspects. There is an inexhaustibly synergistic relationship obtaining among these levels of discourse that allows us to privilege each level in turn. Words and images in their stipulated forms are suggestive, but they are also equivocal in their application to particular times and situations. The meaning of a particular event, on the other hand, is distinct as an immediate experience, and yet in its particular detail, it is resistant to conceptual and explanatory clarity. Hence, in moving from words through images to meaning, the impoverished vagueness of generality that we often call "clarity" gives way to the rich vagueness of vital and transitory particularity.

Wang Bi's next step is to then turn the meaning-making circle in the alternative direction. Now, instead of images and words expressing meaning, meaning inscribes them. Meaning itself gives rise to new images and the words needed to express them, which in turn give rise to new meaning:

> Given that an image arises from the meaning, in holding on to the image, what you are holding on to is not really the image. Given that words arise from the image, in holding on to the words, what you are holding on to is not really the words. As such, to forget the image is to get the meaning; to forget the words is to get the image. Getting the meaning lies in forgetting the image; getting the image lies in forgetting the words.[52]

The intimacy of word, image, and meaning challenges any severe disjunction between determinacy and indeterminacy, between forming and functioning, between reality and appearance, between reasoning and imagination. Words as articulations of images do not identify and describe an independent reality, but both inscribe and take part in

---

52. Wang Bi, "Mingxiang 明象" [Elucidating the image]: 象生於意而存象焉，則所存者乃非其象也．言生於象而存言焉，則所存者乃非其言也．然則，忘象者，乃得意者也；忘言者，乃得象者也．得意在忘象，得象在忘言．

realizing it. That which is known and the act of realizing it come into being together. There is a porous line between meaningful experience, image as the presentation and inscription of meaning, and words as the language games that allow us to participate in experience.

Although Wang Bi is describing the content and structure of the *Changes* here, his insights really have a much broader compass in understanding the classical corpus. We might clarify his more theoretical commentary by looking at the way in which meaning is generated by the "turning" of productive images. In the case of the *Analects*, for example, the central "image" around which the text is constructed is the life of Confucius as "way-making" by "treading and thus making a path" until at age seventy he "could give heart-and-mind free rein without overstepping its boundaries." Indeed, the *Analects* over the centuries has functioned as an example of the image-word-meaning circuit where the images inspired by Confucius have in every generation generated both interlinear commentary and role models for meaningful lives.[53]

While remarking on the conversations remembered and compiled to constitute the *Analects*, it would be an oversight to fail to appreciate the middle chapters of this canonical text as an album of snapshots that depict in detail the image of Confucius as one particular human being living an exemplary life. The meaning that emerges from the words of the text is revealed through the reflexive act of appropriating and then recreating the image itself. The living image of this creative process is the source of meaning that is a bottomless stimulus for the continuing discussion and the commentaries that follow from these conversations. As the *Analects* in the fullness of time emerges to become a canonical text, generation after generation of self-confessed "Confucians" have continued to appeal to the words and to the conjured images in shaping the meaning of their own lives and what has become a persistent cultural identity.

Images carry meaning and continue this fluid process of meaning-making. We might follow Zhang Xianglong in taking the intelligible "words" of calligraphy as an example. In calligraphy, the meaning of the words retreat, and the expression of personal style becomes the performative configuring of an image ultimately revelatory of the artist as this particular person. The mood, times, joys and pain, and the singular place in the world of this particular artist are all resident in the shaping of the characters. In

---

53. *Analects* 1.4: 從心所欲, 不踰矩.

this sense, calligraphy is profoundly biographical. This notion of imagistic artistry as self-expression—"the outside of an inside"—is taken up by Stephen Owen in the distinction he insists upon between thinking of a poem as *poiesis*, or a "made artifact," and the Chinese *shi* 詩 (usually translated as "poem") as personal articulation. Owen insists that

> if we translate *shih* [*shi*] as "poem," it is merely for the sake of convenience. *Shih* is not a "poem"; *shih* is not a "thing made" like in the same way one makes a bed or a painting or a shoe. A *shih* can be worked on, polished, and crafted; but that has nothing to do with what a *shih* fundamentally "is." . . . *Shih* is not the "object" of its writer; it is the writer, the outside of an inside.[54]

We are always engaged in the project of organizing and bringing coherence to the world around us as our collective imaginaire. The imaging and naming of a meaningful world in our language games is nonreferential in the sense that the imaginative process itself is integral to the creation of both ourselves and our world. The processual nature of experience also means that any rational construal of experience as an image or as a name is always provisional and will inevitably be outrun by the process itself. It is this meaning that is conveyed in Zhuangzi's powerful image of the "tipping goblet words" (*zhiyan* 卮言) that fill up only to ultimately empty out whatever meaning has been poured into them. Again, it is the meaning we take away from the first chapter of the *Daodejing* as it insists that

> way-making that can be put into words is not really
> way-making
> And naming that would assign fixed reference to things is
> not really naming.[55]

---

54. Stephen Owen, *Readings in Chinese Literary Thought* (Cambridge, MA: Council on East Asian Studies, Harvard University Press, 1992), 27. My own response to Owen's reflection on *shi* here is that this same distinction is equally relevant to the expression of other cultural forms, and indeed to the art of living more broadly construed.

55. *Daodejing* 1: 道可道非常道, 名可名非常名.

Zhao Tingyang 趙汀陽

Figure 6.3. Zhao Tingyang.

Zhao Tingyang 趙汀陽 is a professor and member of the Chinese Academy of Social Sciences, and a senior fellow of Peking University Berggruen Research Center. In his *tianxia* system (All under Heaven), a theory of world order, Zhao tries to transcend Huntington's "clashes of civilizations" and advances an alternative to the Kantian conception of perpetual peace. He has published many books and articles primarily on metaphilosophy, ethics, and political philosophy. His best-known theories include *tianxia* as a philosophy of planetary order, the ontology of coexistence, human rights as credit rights, relational rationality, the metaphysics of *facta*, and the whirlpool theory of the formation of China. Two of his books translated by the Berggruen Institute are *All under Heaven: The* Tianxia *System for a Possible World Order* (2021) and *The Whirlpool That Produced China: Stag Hunting on the Central Plain* (2024).

Zhao Tingyang 趙汀陽: From a Metaphysics of "Things" to a Metaphysics of *Facta* (*shi* 事)

Zhao Tingyang in a series of recent articles hands down a stern indictment of the discipline of philosophy itself. There is nothing tentative or timid about the project Zhao has set out for himself. From a summary of some excerpts from his work we can take the weight and measure of his critique of traditional ontology and its capacity, or lack thereof, to deal with the human condition. For Zhao, "the human world can go wrong when misled by wrong ideas. . . . This is the reason for undertaking a reflexive critique of ontology as the deep structure of our understanding of the world. I will argue that philosophy has been derailed for quite some time by the 'metaphysics of things.' Consequently, a change in philosophy towards a 'metaphysics of *facta*' might be a useful way to rethink the problems of the world."[56]

For Zhao, "things" are merely the objects of knowledge while *facta* (*shi* 事) as "doings" are the objects of thinking itself that express human freedom, creativity, and historicity. It is only when "things" themselves become integral to "doing" in the sense of world-making that they take on their meaning and value. Zhao insists that philosophy to date has failed to provide us with an ontology that is compatible with and is of service to the world of everyday human experience. He has ruminated long and deeply over the past several decades on this metaphilosophical issue, formulating a revisionist ontology that is inspired by Chinese philosophy but that also has application for philosophy in its broadest compass. For Zhao, ontology as we have inherited it is for the most part commensurate with the world of the physical sciences and logic but does not provide suitable insight into the problems of human life. Most research into ontology has to do with how "things" (*wu* 物) exist, a problem that has little importance for the human lifeworld. That human beings exist is a given; it is the question of what can be made out of this human life experience that is the real issue.[57] In this respect, Zhao observes that

> although everything that human beings do takes place in a world of things, in fact they transcend the world of things, or we might say that they are traitors to necessity. It is precisely because all of their doings are miraculous that their life has meaning. . . . All the doings that have meaning and value are miraculous: labor is miraculous, freedom is miraculous, rights are miraculous, responsibility is miraculous, good fortune is miraculous, love is miraculous.[58]

---

56. Zhao Tingyang, "The Ontology of Co-existence: From *Cogito* to *Facio*," *Diogenes* 57, no. 4 (2012): 27.

57. 赵汀陽, 共在存在论: 人际与心际 [An ontology of coexistence: Shared relations and shared feelings] 《哲学研究》 [Philosophical research], 2009 年第 8期.

58. 赵汀阳: 《作为创世论的存在论》 [Ontology as world-making], 《哲学研究》 [Philosophical research] 2012年08期: 人所做的一切事情虽然发生在物的世界之中, 却是对物

For Zhao, it is because the subfield of metaphysics has reneged on the full explanation of a world of "things" that it had promised us that metaphysical philosophy itself has been deemed to be preoccupied with meaningless propositions and was rejected as a field of inquiry. Even so, the postmetaphysical philosophy that has followed in the wake of its demise has still failed to provide a necessary grounding for the human experience. To address this problem, Zhao offers his considered distinction between a metaphysics of "things" (*wu* 物) and what he terms a metaphysics of *facta*. For Zhao

> a *factum* is something done, and thus it carries intentionality. It is the *factum* that forces us to think because our life is made up of such *facta*. A *factum* by itself poses an immediate question to be answered and very often a problem to be solved. We are confronted with explaining why this and not that has been done, and we have to justify our reasons. In short, we do (in the sense of "we act"), and therefore we must be responsible for what is done. Our creation of the factual world, our world of life, is the primary ontological problem that cannot be evaded.[59]

In a later article, Zhao introduces what he calls an "ontological transposition" (*cunzailunhuanwei* 存在論換位) in which the world of things is transposed into a world of *facta*, in which the ontology of things is transposed into an ontology of events, and in which the ontological problem of "to be" is transposed into "doing."[60]

Zhao, recognizing as Heidegger does with his *Dasein* that persons and their being-in-the-world are to be understood in terms of their lived "facticity" rather than their "factuality," gives Heidegger credit for making a foray into a revisionist ontology. But Zhao then offers what is a fundamentally Confucian critique of Heidegger, claiming that Heidegger's focus is limited to the ontology of individual life stories while failing to contextualize such narratives within a relational human ecology. Persons far from being

---

的世界的超越，或者说是对必然性的背叛．正因为事情皆为奇迹，生活才有意义 . . . 一切具有意义和价值的事情都是奇迹: 劳动是奇迹，自由是奇迹，权利是奇迹，责任是奇迹，幸福是奇迹，爱情是奇迹．

59. Zhao Tingyang, "The Ontology of Co-existence," 28.

60. 赵汀阳:《作为创世论的存在论》．

individuals are constituted by and radically embedded in an unbounded manifold of human relations, and their lives are lived ethically, socially, and politically within these roles and relations.

In reflecting on the limits of traditional ontology and thus seeking to reinstate the wholeness of experience, Zhao challenges Descartes's *cogito* and its appeal to a radical subjectivity as its dualistic foundation for our epistemic consciousness. *Cogito* constructs an internal, self-sufficient world that cleaves a wide gap between the ego and everything it transcends. And it is for this reason that *cogito*, with no respect for the cosmos or nature's bounty and without any regard for the transcendent nature of external things, is simply occupied with the objective nature of the contents of its own thinking.[61]

Zhao takes "doing" in the world as his starting point and the persistent and irreducible quality of the human lived experience that allows him to bypass Descartes by formulating his own alternative maxim. Zhao argues that "the first characteristic of the world of human life is that being as human-being is immediately defined by doing . . . so that, in the world of life, the primacy of doing, *facio*, leads in consequence to a new metaphysical principle: *Facio ergo sum* (I do, therefore I am)."[62] Zhao's revisionist ontology gives *facio* primacy over *cogito*, the lifeworld over subjectivity, and "heart" over "mind," giving privilege to vital relationality. This leads to Zhao's insistence that in the ontology of human lives, there is a primacy of "coexistence" (*gongzai* 共在) over mere "existence" (*cunzai* 存在). Zhao observes:

> Whatever I do develops a relationship between others and myself in an open and ever-extending network that defines the world of life. Human relations are the invisible interfaces between hearts, laying out the destinies of possible lives. It is the others who in practice give license and support to what I do, and who recognise and reconfirm the meanings and values of what I do. Because of the necessary involvement of those others, the *facio* means not only the affirmation of my existence but also my coexistence with others.[63]

---

61. 《作为创世论的存在论》："我思"（cogito）构造了一个内在的自足世界，以悬隔之法驱逐了自我（ego）之外的一切超越者因此，"我思"不敬天地，不敬自然事物，不关注外在事物的超越性（transcendence），而只关注所思的内在客观性（objectivity）。

62. Zhao Tingyang, "The Ontology of Co-existence," 29.

63. Zhao Tingyang, "The Ontology of Co-existence," 32.

This priority of coexistence over existence begins from what I would describe as the Confucian conception of persons as irreducibly social and relationally constituted human "becomings," and it produces an entirely different set of ontological problems that spill over into ethics, and social and political philosophy as well. Zhao continues, arguing that

> the intentionality of the *facio*, the pursuit of heart, has to be achieved by means of cooperation with others and through their approval. This indicates that the *facio* generates the problem of relationship. Instead of the distinct individuals, it is the relations between them that define the ontological situation of the world of life, announcing an ontology of relations instead of an ontology of individuals. It is a change in the basic unit, as well as of the framework, of philosophical thinking. Hence relations, rather than individuals, must be reconsidered as the foundation of philosophy, as Confucianism did.

Zhao further clarifies this first-order ontology of relations by locating value as growth in the relations that constitute humans in their lifeworlds rather than being inherent in the individuals themselves. Zhao insists that, "according to this ontological grammar, a person does rather than is. No individual is good in himself; he is good only insofar as he is good to someone in a certain relationship. His presence as a good person is decided in the context of his relations with others. From this relationological point of view, it is relations that determine the existential situation and values of facts in the world of life."[64] Zhao allows that in the ordinary sense of these terms, "to be" and "what ought to be"—fact and value—stand independent of each other, like two parallel lines. One cannot be derived from the other. Hence, we have the problem of explaining how value arises in the first place. It is only in moving from "being" to "doing" that the "is" and the "ought" are compelled to converge. While being is being, when we actually do something, we must immediately confront the question of why we did this and not that. Since logic and the knowledge derived from its application can only deal with necessity and not with creativity, it cannot provide the answer. It is only because our doing transcends the world of things that we can look to it for an answer.

But the question arises: Since doing is always happening amid the confusion of creativity, how can "what is" in itself provide the answer to

---

64. Zhao Tingyang, "The Ontology of Co-existence," 33.

wherein the good lies? Zhao's response is that choosing one thing over another does not necessarily make what is chosen the better thing, but at the same time, it is more than just throwing the dice. Whether better or not, it is still the emergence of value. The "doing" has compelled "what is" to be valorized. But how can we then make the judgment that in what we have done therein resides the good? Since the answer to this question can only be found in the doing of things (*facio*), any and all possible justification must lie in the future unfolding of what is done. The justification is hidden in the futurity of doing, where either retribution or reward for our choices will provide us with our answer.

And for Zhao, this future is always a shared future. Although I am the grammatical subject in what I do, in the ontological sense, far from being the only person, other persons (and innumerable other persons) must be parties to what is done. With all of these people present at the same time, I cannot monopolize the future but must share it with others. Simply put, there is no future without others. This means that in my existing as myself, I certainly belong to me, but there is never a completely independent me as a bystander looking on at the world. It is only to the extent that I become a world-maker that I possess the world. And at the same time that I become a part of things, I become a possibility for the world.

The secret of success or failure in "doing" and "world-making" is hidden in the response to behavior. "Doing" triggers a line of responses and, in so doing, creates the world and its history. It is thus that responsiveness is a clue to the world of doings, and from this clue we can find the difference between order and chaos, between pain and joy, and so on. It is the response of others that will determine whether the "doing" will work. It is only with the agreement of others that things can come to fruition. A doing is only ontologically correct if and only if "no one is excluded," and thus only if it does not deprive any party of its future.[65]

What follows from the primacy of coexistence and our shared values as they grow in the relations that constitute our "doings" is Zhao's deep concern over what might be called the ideology of individualism. Zhao argues that this individualism has effectively been dehumanizing the lifeworld by depriving it of its happiness, observing that

> individualism has a serious side-effect in the estrangement of people from each other, especially through the affective separation of hearts. The claimed supremacy of the individual represents

---

65. 《作为创世论的存在论》.

a devaluation of virtues, and tacitly implies the devaluation of others. Even worse, individualism taken to its absolute limit implies even the negation of happiness, because happiness is not self-made but always depends on how the individual relates to others. No one can be happy by himself. Happiness is the noble gift of others, or the generous favour granted by others. A human being is always humanised through the human relations of reciprocal happiness-giving.[66]

One negative consequence following from the ontological error of individualism that would give individual persons priority over relations is an asymmetrical doctrine of human rights. In making such rights exclusive of obligations, it is paradoxical. That is, erstwhile unconditional individual rights and entitlements are given privilege over precisely those social obligations that persons must honor in order to guarantee these same individual rights for everyone, and in order to realize the social justice that these rights are meant to promise.

One concern I had on first reading Zhao's account of his alternative ontology was that, in his compelling argument for the limits of rationality, he seems to be willing to associate "mind" with the metaphysics of "things" and to reserve "heart" for the metaphysics of *facta*, thereby introducing a familiar Western dualism. But on the contrary, Zhao is offering us a sophisticated alternative to this dualism by defining his understanding of "heart" as inclusive of but not dominated by cognition. Zhao insists that

as an uncontrolled and disturbing trouble beyond the power of rationality, the problem of heart, a complex amalgam of spirit, values, faith and feelings, cannot be removed by rationality nor reduced to a matter of mind. On the contrary, heart is fundamental to mind and without it mind would be indifferent, inhuman and totally alienated from life. It is usually supposed that mind sees truth while heart recognises the good. But this does not mean a dualism. To separate mind and heart is a metaphysical as well as an epistemological error. The first truth is that truths will be nothing at all unless good for life. And the never-settled conflicts of the world may bring us to recognise that heart is prior to mind, just as the *facio* is prior to the *cogito*.[67]

---

66. Zhao Tingyang, "The Ontology of Co-existence," 36.

67. Zhao Tingyang, "The Ontology of Co-existence," 32.

What is clear to me from Zhao's holistic interpretation of "heart" and *facio* is that he is taking as his starting point the Confucian wholeness of experience. Zhao himself emphasizes the fundamentally empirical starting and ending point of Confucian philosophy in observing that,

> following Confucian realistic thinking, if something is considered most important in our lives, it must be justified by tangible and accessible evidence in the world of *hereness*, instead of through belief in a world of *thereness*. Confucianism trusts in what is done much more than in what is said, and even than in what is seen. It seems Confucianism is more reasonable in seeking the ontological principles of the human world in terms of the autonomy of the world of life.[68]

What makes Confucian philosophy more empirical than empiricism is that it is a *radical* empiricism. While growing out of the soil of an antique culture, Confucianism is rooted in an ontology of first-order, unbounded, constitutive, and vital relations that by definition would ascribe uniqueness to each and every event within it as constituting an always unique matrix of relations. There is no duplication. As such, this ontology is prospective and evolutionary in respecting the uniqueness of the omnipresent particular event as it emerges in a continuing present. Rather than advancing doctrines as universal principles or organizing experience around a taxonomy of natural kinds grounded in some notion of strict identity, Confucian philosophy proceeds from analogy with, and always provisional generalizations derived from, those *particular* historical instances of successful living. Confucius's signature neologism, "aspiring to consummate conduct in one's roles and relations" (*ren* 仁), for example, is not an appeal to some higher-order, antecedent principle or generic virtue but is rather a particular vision of living the exemplary human life aspired to through assiduous cultivation of one's relations with others as the ultimate source of meaning. As a generalization, *ren* emerges from the confluence of particular narratives that, in remembering the achievements of those who have gone before, can be of service to succeeding generations as a guiding source of value.

While thus appealing to a Confucian conception of experience, one of the most important contributions we find in Zhao's reflections on this alternative ontology is his ability to make productive correlations within the broad scope of world philosophy rather than limiting himself to the Chinese

---

68. Zhao Tingyang, "The Ontology of Co-existence," 30.

philosophical tradition alone. In discerning resonances between Confucian philosophy and the challenge to Cartesian rationalism and dualism advanced by the Italian philosopher Giambattista Vico, for example, Zhao is able to find both sameness and difference. Confucianism like Vico is radically historicist and empirical, but unlike Vico, it seeks an optimizing symbiosis from experience rather than some grander notion of truth. Zhao observes that

> the Confucian approach might remind us of that derived by Giambattista Vico for their similarity in their emphasis on the *factum*. But one of the differences between these two approaches is that Vico's *factum-verum* correlation is apparently a stronger principle than the Confucian approach in search of the *optimum* in the *factum*, the best of the possible lives. It is interesting that Chinese philosophy is much less ambitious in epistemology and is always satisfied with the best instead of with the truth.[69]

In his more recent publications, Zhao returns to this seminal project of bringing Chinese philosophy into the conversation in his formulation of a new ontology for world philosophy. In his doing so, I find important corroboration in the fact that Zhao offers us quite specifically what I take to be his own earlier version of what I am calling the ontological and zoe-tological distinction. Zhao begins by asking:

> How is an "existent" created? With respect to an entity that is self-conscious—such as a human society or a civilization—existence is no longer the natural existence of how something is as it is or *per se*, but the historical existence of historicity. For this reason, the question of "being" is changed to become equivalent to the question of "making or doing" (*zuo* 作). Making or doing is to go and create a history of existence, that is, it ensures that an entity becomes a historical entity that cannot be reduced to the ordinary concept of mere being.[70]

---

69. Zhao Tingyang, "The Ontology of Co-existence," 31.

70. Zhao Tingyang, 惠此中國: 作為一個神性概念的中國 [The making and becoming of China: Its way of historicity] (Beijing: Citic Press, 2016), 2: 一种存在是如何被创作的? 这意味着, 对于具有自觉意识的存在 (人类社会和文明) 而言, 存在不再是如其所示 (as it is) 的自然存在, 而是具有历史性的历史存在, 于是, "存在" (to be) 的问题转换为等价于 "因作 而在" (to be made to be) 的问题. "作" 就是去创造一种 "存在" 的历史, 也就是使一种存在

Zhao uses different terms such as "making" (*zuo* 作) and "doing" (*shi* 事) to capture what, in contrast with the classical Greek commitment to "being per se," he takes to be the history of a distinctively Chinese version of "ontology." Zhao avers that, "unlike Western thought, the starting point for Chinese thought is 'doings' (*shi* 事). Doing is not a thing but a dynamic relationship among things. Doing comes from acting. Therefore, it seeks its way in action."[71]

Zhao sees the distinction between the situated, relational, and dynamic understanding of this Chinese "ontology" and the Greek notion of self-sufficient "being" as a commitment that has had profound implications for the assumptions underlying Western and Chinese metaphysical thinking. He insists that

> the types of questions raised by Chinese and Western metaphysics differ, with both being matters of profound thought. In terms of the direction that such thought takes, Western philosophy is thinking that deals with necessity, while Chinese philosophy is thinking that deals with possibility. With respect to the structure of thought, Western philosophy provides a "dictionary" kind of explanation of the world, seeking to set up an accurate understanding of the limits of all things. In simple terms, it wants to make a determination of "what is what," with all concepts being footnotes to "being" or "is."[72]

For Zhao, this commitment in the history of Chinese philosophy to "doings" as opposed to "being" has required a very different role for the philosophical enterprise. Instead of the quest for certainty in trying to discover what necessarily and categorically *is*, Chinese "ontology" has been a dynamic process that takes advantage of the generosity of always newly

---

成为不可还原 (irreducible) 为一般存在概念的历史性存在. I am using with minor changes the translation of this book by Edmund Ryden, *The Whirlpool That Produced China: Stag Hunting on the Central Plain* (Albany: State University of New York Press, 2024).

71. Zhao Tingyang, 惠此中國 [The making and becoming of China], 147: 与西方思想不同, 中国思想的出发点是 "事." 事不是实体, 而实体之间的动态关系. 事发于行, 故因行求道.

72. Zhao Tingyang, 惠此中國 [The making and becoming of China], 147: 中西两种形而上学的问题各异, 但皆为深度思想. 在思想主旨上, 西方哲学是关于必然性的思想, 而中国哲学是关于可能性的思想. 在思想结构上, 西方哲学是对世界的 "字典式" 解释, 试图建立界定万物的决定理解, 简单的说, 就是断定 "什么是什么," 一切观念皆为 "在／是" (being/is) 的注脚.

emerging possibilities to make productive correlations within the context of vital relationships, and to thus expand upon their significance. Zhao observes that Chinese thought

> is an explanation of the "grammar" of the world, striving for a coordinated understanding of relationships—between heaven and humankind, humankind and things, or humans and humans—by means of which all "doings" are generated, with a special emphasis on the mutuality of relationships, and the compatibility of all things. Hence, the terms "persistence through change" (*biantong* 變通), "an optimizing harmony" (*he* 和), and "focusing the familiar" (*zhongyong* 中庸) referenced by the ancients are all insightfully generalized under the notion of "proper measure" (*du* 度) by Li Zehou 李澤厚. . . . In this sense, whatever gives rise to questioning is an opening up of possibilities: change, generation, the future, uncertainty, interaction, compatibility, and complementarity, and so on.[73]

Zhao in his reference to Li Zehou here is making the point that the familiar Chinese dyadic expressions appealed to in describing relations are not reporting on two originally separate elements of the world that are then being reconciled after the fact. Rather Li is referencing the first-order primacy of the relations themselves. This vital cosmic continuity is made explicit in the familiar mantra "the continuity between and inseparability of the human and the cosmic orders" (*tianrenheyi* 天人合一), where human beings are integral to their contextualizing cultural and natural worlds, and the human experience cannot occur save within this context. Li argues that, rather than aspiring to the uniting and conjoining of two separate domains, the emphasis is on the depth and quality (*du* 度) achieved in the already existing first-order and constitutive relationship that reveals two inseparable aspects of what is an always shared experience.[74]

---

73. Zhao Tingyang, 惠此中國 [The making and becoming of China], 147–148: 中国思想则是对世界的"语法式"解释, 力求对万事所生成的关系 (天与人, 人与物, 人与人) 的协调理解, 尤其重视关系的互相性或万事的合宜性, 即古人所谓"变通""和"或"中庸," 李泽厚精练地概括为对"度"的把. . . . 在这个意义上, 所有成问题的事情都是"可能性"的展开: 变化, 生长, 未来, 不确定性, 互动性, 合宜性, 互补 . . .

74. The one reservation I have had in my deep appreciation of Zhao's revised ontology is his interpretation of a kind of unilaterality in the *tian* and human relationship. Zhao states, 天道 . . . 是不可选择的标准, 如何在天道的限定条件下形成与之相配的人道, 此乃

From Zhao's appeal to the language of "makings" (*zuo* 作) and "doings" (*shi* 事) in capturing the dynamic and creative character of a specifically human historicity, it is then a short step for him to bring in the "Great Commentary" (*Dazhuan* 大傳) fascicle from the *Book of Changes* and scale up this notion of human growth to a cosmic level. Zhao takes the most basic language of "procreativity" (*shengsheng* 生生) itself—what I have called "zoetology"—to further define the kind of "ontology" that has real meaning for the human lifeworld as it unfolds within its cosmic context. Zhao contends that

> the primary question for the human way is that of generation and regeneration, and the first step herein is growth. This is the starting point for the evolutionary thread of Chinese thought. The "doing" (*shi* 事) of growth (*shengzhang* 生長) must seek what a thing relies on to be "deeply rooted and firmly planted" (*zhagen* 扎根) in its growth. Therefore, growth first of all requires putting down roots. The two metaphors of growth and putting down roots set out the path for Chinese thought.[75]

人之所思所慮 (The way of heaven is a nonnegotiable norm. What human beings think and reflect on is how to shape the human way and match that of heaven within the limiting conditions set by the way of heaven. Zhao Tingyang, 惠此中國 [The making and becoming of China], 149.

Elsewhere Zhao offers a similar reading of this *tian/ren* relationship: "The Confucian solution is to recognise the law of heaven as the higher principle while realistically recognising human-being's responsibility for the world of life, so that human-being has to define the values and worldviews for the world of life *only* in terms of humanity and human relations. Zhao Tingyang, "The Ontology of Co-existence," 31.

My own understanding is that the *tian/ren* relationship is not only first order but also collateral. It is the personal resolution (*cheng* 誠) needed to be cosmic co-creators with the heavens and the earth that makes the human being an essential player in the flourishing of our world. And it is only through deepening and achieving proper measure (*du* 度) in the correlative "human and cosmic" relationship (*tianrenheyi* 天人合一) as one of the collaborating three powers (*sancai* 三才)—the heavens, the earth, and the human being—that exemplary persons can make their profound contribution to cosmic meaning. Such clear resolution and the human sagacity that it produces is integral to the source from which the flourishing world order emerges, and as such, it adds additional momentum to the life force that guides the cosmos on its proper course.

75. Zhao Tingyang, 惠此中國 [The making and becoming of China], 148–149: . . . 人道問題首先正是 "生生," 而 "生生" 的第一步便是生长, 这正是中国思想演化线索的始发点. 生长之事, 必求生长之物 "深根固柢" 而使存在获得生长的依据, 因此生长首先要扎根. "生长"和 "扎根" 这两个隐喻表示了中国思想的行径.

Certainly "procreativity" (*shengsheng* 生生) is what is most basic, but as we have seen with Li Zehou's emphasis on achieving a "proper measure" (*du* 度), it is qualitatively much more than simply random growth. The very meaning of "life" (*sheng* 生) itself becomes normative as it seeks out the context and the conditions that will enable it to achieve its fullest measure of growth in meaning. Zhao in an article entitled explicitly as "Taking Ontology as Creatiology" invents his own neologism for this generative production of meaning as "world-making," calling it "creatiology" (*chuangshilun* 創世論). Summarizing his argument, he says that "since 'to be' and 'to do' are the same, and since 'doing' (*facio*) and 'creating' (*creo*) are the same, then ontology and creatiology are also the same."[76] Within the holography of classical Chinese cosmology, events are understood as foci within unbounded fields rather than as parts within wholes. As such everything is in anything, and as in a painting, each detail is ultimately implicated in the totality of the effect. This being the case, the fullest measure of growth as it is occasioned by procreativity is itself a holistic aesthetic achievement. Zhao insists that

> the "art" of growth is a kind of "ontology," and not one of the fine arts. Yet, this ontology of existence at the same time is made manifest as a testimonial to the aesthetic, prompting Confucius to say that life is "consummated by music" (*chengyuyue* 成于 樂). This would seem to imply that the metaphysics of growth can only ever be manifested in the phenomenal world. As such, growth is a form of rejoicing (*le* 樂). In the interpenetrating growth of the myriad things, this thriving becomes their source of rejoicing. This explains why among the six classics there are the *Odes* and *Music* that are directly related to aesthetics. "Music" (*yue* 樂) here is not limited to music as such but is used in the general sense of all aesthetic experience. There is a permeating musicality that moves in step with the rhythmical changes of the way of heaven that is the music of growth.[77]

---

76. 《作为创世论的存在论》: 存在 (to be) 和有为 (to do) 是同一的, 做事 (*facio*) 和创世 (*creo*) 是同一的, 所以, 存在论 (ontology) 与创世论 (creatiology) 是同一的.

77. Zhao Tingyang, 惠此中國 [The making and becoming of China], 149–150: 生长的 艺术 (Art) 是一种存在论, 而不是物象的艺术 (fine arts), 但生存的存在论也同时显示为美 学证据, 所以孔子说 "成于乐." 这似乎暗示着, 生长的形而上之道从总能够显形于形而下之 器, 于是, 生长是一种欢乐, 与生长相关之万物也成为欢乐之源. 由此可以理解为什么六经 中便有诗, 乐两经于美学经验直接相关. 乐并不限于音乐, 而泛指一切美学经验, 但贯穿着 音乐性, 于天道变化节奏同步便是生长之乐.

Zhao seems to be playing on the fact that in this classical language the same Chinese character pronounced differently is being used to mean both "rejoicing" (*le, yao* 樂) and "the playing of music" (*yue* 樂) as two seemingly different things. But perhaps we can use the distinction between sense and reference to close the distance between them. That the graph is referencing the same basic idea parsed differently should not be lost. The playing of music is vital and pervasive. It is an obvious source of shared enjoyment in the everyday events of a human life and is also elevated to punctuate the most important moments within it, accompanying both life and death. But it works the other way around as well. That is, shared enjoyment within relationships also confers on human life-forms their cadence and musicality, where a communicating community in the broadest sense of communication is a flourishing community. Again, we might observe that *le* is also cognate with "medicinal remedies" (*yao* 藥), suggesting that both the enjoyment of music and the music of enjoyment have therapeutic and restorative qualities as well.

RESPONSE

Zhao Tingyang like many contemporary Chinese scholars is keenly aware of a persistent and pernicious asymmetry in the way we continue to go about theorizing China through the lens of Western concepts and values. At the same time, they are cognizant of the seemingly purposeful opaqueness and obfuscation that sets China off as a self-contained and separate Chinatown of the world. Zhao has thus tasked both Chinese and Western scholars alike to "rethink China" (*chongsi Zhongguo* 重思中國).[78] For those on the outside, rethinking China is "thinking with China" by trying to understand China in light of its own historical experience, to try to take China on its own terms and, even where there is disagreement, to include a Chinese perspective in thinking through the issues that divide us. For inside China, it is "thinking with the world community," thereby making a concerted effort to articulate this same Chinese perspective clearly, to be more transparent and forthcoming in both its activities and purposes, and to accommodate the world's many different points of view as integral to its own self-understanding. As the alternative to zero-sum thinking among equal and independent nation-states, a new

---

78. Zhao Tingyang, 天下體系: 世界制度哲學導論 [The *tianxia* system: An introduction to the philosophy of world institution] (Beijing: People's University Press, 2011), 1.

planetary order that is both ecological and inclusive is envisioned by Zhao. In this model, any particular one both shapes and is shaped by its many others, without any particular one having privilege over the many. The new planetary order itself is thus the unsummed totality of all of the participating political entities with each entity construing the totality from its own particular perspective.

Zhao in his own words and using his own metaphors gives us a clear contrast that I think resonates with the distinction I am trying to make between ontological and zoetological thinking. Applying his neologism "creatiology" (*chuangshilun* 創世論) as his alternative to ontology, it is this "creatiological" or "world-making" understanding of Confucian philosophy that informs much of his other research and publications. If we recall the historicity he associates with the metaphysics of *facta* expressed as "doing," "acting," "making," and "creating" through a cluster of different terms (*facio, creo, zuo* 作, *shi* 事) and the metaphors of "setting the root" (*zhagen* 扎根) and "growing therefrom" (*shengzhang* 生長) that he deploys in expressing this way of thinking, we can see that it is the same dynamics of life and growth that informs the centripetal whirlpool metaphor he posits in answer to the question: Where did China come from? Indeed, Zhao's whirlpool theory of Chinese history can serve us as a concrete historical illustration of the more abstract philosophical reflections I have drawn from his several publications and rehearsed in this chapter.[79] In this theory, Zhao is forwarding a novel and compelling thesis on not only how we should understand China but also how, until recently, China has understood itself.

Over the past few decades, this question of "Where did China come from?"—that is, China as "All under Heaven" or *tianxia* 天下—has absorbed the thoughts of many of China's best historians and, more recently, of some of its philosophers as well. To this end, in interpreting the historical progression of the unbounded *tianxia* identity on the Central Plain of China, Zhao Tingyang has introduced what he terms a distinctively

---

79. Within Zhao Tingyang's substantial oeuvre, there two monographs cited earlier that give an account of his whirlpool theory of Chinese history: 惠此中國 [The making and becoming of China: Its way of historicity] and 天下的當代性: 世界秩序的實踐與想象 [A possible world of all-under-heaven system: The world order in the past and for the future]. The English translation of the former by Edmund Ryden is entitled *The Whirlpool That Produced China: Stag Hunting on the Central Plain* (2024), and the latter is *All under Heaven: The* Tianxia *System for a Possible World Order*, translated by Joseph E. Harroff (Oakland: University of California Press, 2021).

Chinese model of world order. For Zhao, this centripetal "whirlpool" process of identity formation has been driven by a series of interrelated "cultural attractors," with perhaps the most significant among them being the Chinese written characters, inspiring as they have the canonical texts that have perpetuated a shared cultural identity. These attractors have drawn the host of disparate populations on the Central Plain of China and its surrounding territories into a vortex, a whirlpool that during the Xia, Shang, and Zhou dynasties was already taking shape more than three thousand years ago, and that has continued in protean form down to the fall of the Qing dynasty in the early part of the twentieth century.

Zhao, as one of China's most distinguished intellectuals, provides a profoundly original philosophical as well as historical interpretation of China's story. In the spiritual world of China, its history and its canonical texts are drawn together as one, while at the same time these same classics and China's evolving history have set the standards against which each of them has been measured. In Zhao's efforts to interpret China's historicity philosophically, he touches on many questions in many relevant areas of knowledge. He references the discovery of the oracle bone script along with China's most recent century of exciting archaeological finds, in which the ancient silk and bamboo manuscripts are continuing to be recovered, and then moves on to the theorizing of China's history of thought and its sociology, politics, and economics.

Speaking of the realities of today, this continent called China is at once a state, a civilization, and a history. But in its temporality, the China that is a state, the China that is a civilization, and the China that is a history did not all happen simultaneously. Rather, these "Chinas" have happened in staggered stages that, in the end, have merged together to produce a vital and generative unity. What then, asks Zhao, are the causes, the forces, and the destiny that have coalesced to produce the one rich conception of China as, at once, a state, a civilization, and a history?

Zhao argues that the growth of China and Chinese culture was not due simply to the lures of expansionist behavior in the form of military conquest, nor merely to the interchange among the disparate civilizations that came to constitute it. Rather, such growth was the outcome of the fusion of the distinctive contributions made by the many different contenders for political control as they were constantly being pulled into the swirls and eddies of the whirlpool. He argues that once drawn into this whirlpool of growth and amalgamation the peoples surrounding the plains on all four sides competed to win the greatest material benefits and the greatest spiritual resources by shaping their ways of thinking and living around the evolving core spiritual culture of the Central Plain. For Zhao, the *tianxia* vision of world order was able to transform the various kinds of contention among the many cultures and peoples with their many different ways of life and forms of governance and achieve a degree of accommodation under a shared, syncretic, and evolving identity.

A fundamental issue engaged by Zhao is how the ontology of "becoming" and the vital eddies within the whirlpool became the method of China's evolution. And the primary question he seeks to answer is, How did this core culture of the Central Plain become such a virtually irresistible attraction to its peripheral populations to the extent that once a people with their territory was drawn into the whirlpool game, it was difficult if not impossible for them to withdraw? In thus interpreting the structure of China's historicity, Zhao invites the past to become present again and to thus engage with the contemporaneity of the present time.

Zhao Tingyang is a philosopher. In asking the question, "Where did China come from?" he begins from an ontological answer that he draws from the *Yijing* 易經 or *Book of Changes*. The fundamental explanation of existence itself is the unceasing process of procreation, of generation and regeneration. As the *Book of Changes* announces: "The greatest capacity of the cosmos is the production of life itself."[80] Zhao appeals to the archaeological scholarship of Xu Hong, whose notion of the "earliest China" (*zuizaodeZhongguo* 最早的中国) can serve as point of reference to establish the tentative trajectory of an inclusive and distinctively Chinese generative process of establishing and sustaining geopolitical order called *tianxia* 天下. The erstwhile beginnings and evolution of this conception of world order reach back into the mists of history before the Xia, Shang, and Zhou dynasties to what the prominent archaeologist Su Bingqi has called a "firmament full of constellations" (*mantianxingdou* 滿天星斗)—a description of the many different, independent, and unique civilizations, each with its own narrative integrity, that were spread out across the Chinese Central Plain and the four areas that surrounded it. In this earliest period, *tianxia* references an emerging, holistic world politics that, as an inside without an outside, is diverse without being fragmented by any notion of determinate and bounded nation-states. Cosmologically, and religiously too as a natural theology, *tianxia* is a process that, in its evolution, establishes a cultural center for the earth and, in so doing,

---

80. 天地之大德曰生.

sets an axis that sanctifies the human world in its veneration of the heavens and the earth.

Importantly Zhao's question is not "What is China?," which would suggest the search for some necessary, essential, and defining element to circumscribe this geographical and political entity. China in its original formulation is *tianxia*, an unbounded process of growth in world order. For Zhao, China is not a place but a "taking place"—a world-making out of a centripetal whirlpool that over time has taken the mere "variety" of the constellations of many different cultures and, on the basis of their vital, ecological interdependence, has transformed them into a shared syncretic "diversity" in which the differences that obtain among the many different peoples are activated to make a difference for the well-being of each other. Zhao, in reflecting on the emergence of this shared cultural and spiritual identity called China, dismisses the anachronistic language of the modern, particularly Western academy—terms such as nation-state, nationalism, dynastic succession, empire, and imperialism. Instead, he follows earlier philosophers such as Li Zehou 李澤厚 in asserting the intimate relationship if not the coincidence in ancient times among shamanism, political leadership, and the compilation of the historical record. It is this continuity among them that has led to the enduring cultural awareness and spirituality integral to the evolving Chinese *tianxia*.

Zhao selects his own metaphors. For Zhao, the economic and political motivational structure for the growth and continuity of China can best be described as a lengthy, continuous game—a "stag hunt" (*zhulu* 逐鹿) for political power—in which the issues, purposes, and very nature of the game are determined by the collective behavior of historical actors making rational choices directed at maximizing their own interests. In selecting this game metaphor, Zhao is alluding to a passage in Sima Qian's *Records of the Grand Historian* that observes that "the Qin empire having lost its stag, all of *tianxia* were on the hunt for it."[81] The game achieves its "focal point" or historical order from the most advantageous choices being made by the collective of players, and ultimately becomes their common history.

Zhao's second key metaphor is the centripetal whirlpool with its various cultural attractors exuding an irresistible force that draws the disparate populations into a game from which they neither want nor are able to extricate themselves. Certainly, features on the Central Plain such

---

81. 司马迁，《史记淮阴侯列传》秦失其鹿，天下共逐之.

as favorable terrain, climatic conditions, convenience in transportation, a concentration of wealth, and other material factors that usually conduce to civilization among human populations were an inspiration for would-be competitors to join the game. But Zhao argues it is the spiritual attractors that were the most powerful force in bringing together *tianxia* as an emerging political and cultural union out of difference.

First among these resources were the written Chinese characters, a development that wrested away the monopoly on history that had been owned by the political leaders through their shamanistic practices and made a shared historical narrative available as a unifying human resource. The written characters served as a sophisticated system for perpetuating a cultural corpus that, standing independent of the many spoken languages of the various peoples drawn in by it, could be read by all of them. At the Museum of Writing in Anyang that is situated in the middle of this same Central Plain, we see on display today a vast collection of the oracle bones that constitute the earliest extant record of this writing system. Remarkably, this sophisticated Shang dynasty script in its own time had already accumulated a vocabulary of over five thousand characters, a number that exceeds the normal literacy of an educated Chinese person today.

Zhao argues that this writing system was a technology of enchantment, a kind of magic, that enabled human beings to grasp the past, anticipate the future, and in so doing to transform time into their own self-awareness, self-narration, and historicity. This system established a legitimizing spiritual world the ownership of which gave political leaders an account of an authorized history and the capacity for knowledge production that could be used to organize the hearts and minds of the people. The written language was the powerful medium through which norms, laws, and institutions could be established, perpetuated, interpreted, and employed, and thus it carried with it a determinative force that far exceeded factors such as economic influence and military prowess. What galvanized the spiritual importance of this writing system itself was what it was used to convey: that is, the shared narration of the history and the values of a common lineage. The cultural corpus perpetuated through the compilation of the canonical texts provided a growing population with an evolving, collective spiritual identity, and the development of a common cosmology through which the human experience could be organized and explained. Indeed, within this spiritual world, these classics and the historical record were synergistically one, reinforcing and lending authority to each other. And even while the center of the whirlpool during different historical epochs would shift geographically from north to south and from east to west, the continuing spiritual center was this culture of the Central Plain.

One significant element in this worldview was the *tianxia* system with its mandate of *tian* (*tianming* 天命) developed during the Zhou dynasty that, being an unbounded and inclusive conception of world order, invited all players regardless of status or pedigree to take part in and compete for the control of the economic and political order. What it did too was to afford the winner of the stag hunt for *tianxia* with legitimacy by locating the new dynasty within a continuing natural and political theology, a single, exclusive lineage that dates back as far as the remotest traces of a continuing, glorious history. It was a shared history that garnered broad acceptance, and to which all deferred as it informed their life practices through a ritualized social grammar and a regimen of seasonal sacrifices to the ancestors. Again, this political theology was for any hegemon playing the game rationally justifiable as the strategy that exacted the lowest cost for legitimizing his claim, while at the same time paying him the highest economic, political, and spiritual dividends.

It is not until the Qin and Han dynasties with the establishment of China as a state within this all-inclusive world order that this earlier understanding of *tianxia* is revised. In thinking through what terminology best describes this new Chinese entity—empire, civilization, civilization-state, nation-state—Zhao makes the important point that its internal structure is a microcosm of the unbounded and inclusive notion of *tianxia* that had preceded it historically, and that it thus retains *tianxia* as its philosophical outlook. The gene of the original *tianxia* with its values of "being a match with heaven" (*peitian* 配天), of "no beyond" (*wuwai* 無外), and of "compatibility" (*xiehe* 協和) was the alternative to any kind of nationalism, where nationalism was a much later phenomenon that only emerged at the end of the Qing dynasty when a beleaguered China was set upon by imperialist powers that sought to dismember and consume it.

Tianxia as both a centrifugal and centripetal vortex provides a way of thinking about the constant and continuing cycle of amalgamation and interregnum that has been the dynamic calculus of China's dynastic narrative. It provides a vivid image of the ingesting spire of centripetal consolidation of "many becoming one" that defined the swelling centers of the great Han and Tang dynasties. And it also conveys the descent during interregnum periods such as Nanbeichao and the Southern Song into an excreting, centrifugal gyre in which the many were disgorged from the one. It is during these many occasions of disunity that the question of "How do we determine which among the several players is China?" becomes a point of deliberation. It also explains the hydraulics of the whirlpool when, most apparently during the Yuan and again the Qing dynasties, the Mongols and then the Manchus join the stag hunt for *tianxia* as initially "foreign" usurpers, only in the fullness of time to become integral to the genealogy of China itself. And in this process of identity formation, these dynasties swell the girth radially of a relatively stable center to include the outlying territories within the orbit of the *tianxia* domain.

Zhao in providing a profoundly original philosophical interpretation of China's own story at the same time insists that it has real relevance beyond the Chinese narrative itself. Indeed, Zhao's declared motivation for formulating his *tianxia* theory simply stated is for the benefit of a contemporary world community in search of a new planetary geopolitical order. Again, the fact that governance over the two thousand years of imperial China is almost equally divided between indigenous and "foreign" peoples does say something important about the diversity and inclusiveness of this history. And the familiar criticism that Zhao's advocacy of an all-inclusive world order masks the ambitions of Chinese hegemony simply because he expresses this goal with the Chinese term *tianxia* rather than "planetary order" quite simply misses this point.[82]

---

82. If we are going to read Zhao critically, we might perhaps worry that the story told is perhaps overly defensive and compensatory if not somewhat romantic. For example, his account of the civilizing of the Chinese experience glides perhaps too quickly over the costs of the war and carnage that was an always present factor. We need only to remember the juggernaut of Genghis Khan and the Mongol conquest during the thirteenth century in which it is estimated that over 10 percent of all of humanity perished. Again, apart from a utilitarian ethic in which rational actors in their own self-interest join the hunt, little is made of the importance of a Confucian family-centered ethic in the perpetuation of this living civilization that is captured in the prime moral imperative *xiao* 孝 or "family reverence." For such critical yet appreciative readings, see Sor-hoon Tan, "*Tianxia* and Global Distributive Justice," in Tianxia *in Comparative Perspectives: Alternative Models for a Possible Planetary Order*, ed. Roger T. Ames, Sor-hoon Tan, and Steven Y. H. Yang (Honolulu: University of Hawai'i Press, 2023), and Roger T. Ames, "The Confucian Concept of the Political, and 'Family Feeling' (*xiao* 孝) as Its Minimalist Morality," in *Formulating a Minimalist Ethic for a New Planetary Order: Alternative Cultural Perspectives*, ed. Roger T. Ames, Jin Young Lim, and Steven Y. H. Yang (Honolulu: University of Hawai'i Press, 2024).

When we reflect on Zhao's compelling account of "Where did China come from?" it is a Chinese "doing" and "making" that in a concrete way gives expression to Zhao's alternative ontology as "creatiology" (*chuang-shilun* 創世論) or "world-making." It is a story of how "setting the root" (*zhagen* 扎根) as a living civilization took place in China through the earliest practices and records of ancestral sacrifices, and how this shared and deepening cultural identity then continued to grow (*shengzhang* 生長) across the several millennia. The abstract language he uses, such as "coexistence" (*gongzai* 共在), "no outside" (*wuwai* 無外), "compatibility" (*xiehe* 協和), and "relational rationality" (*guanxilixing* 關係理性), comes alive as the underlying normative values that have perpetuated this long process of Chinese identity formation.

Again, Zhao's narrative of China's expansive growth provides us with insight into how to revise and historicize our understanding of some of the most basic terminologies that are appealed to in giving an account of an evolving Chinese culture. We might begin by citing Angus Graham, who would claim that different cultures produce different conceptual structures that best express their most important and enduring values. Graham avers "that people of another culture are somehow thinking in other categories is a familiar idea, almost a commonplace, but one very difficult to pin down as a topic for fruitful discussion."[83]

How then, stimulated by Zhao's historical account of *tianxia*, can we rethink the philosophical language we use to understand and explain China and its culture? Zhao's account of *tianxia* might prompt us to think of the China narrative itself as a composite and unsummed *dao* 道 or "world-making" by its cultural avatars as in each generation they have extended the central axis of a continuing and generative cultural lineage. As it observes in *Focusing the Familiar* (*Zhongyong* 中庸), "only those in the world of utmost resolve are able to separate out and braid together the many threads on the great loom of the world."[84] Again, if we want a fluid metaphor more in keeping with Zhao's whirlpool analogy, we might describe cultural China as the evolving confluence of many *dao*s across the millennia streaming together to become one: the *dao*s of Fu Xi and Shen Nong, of the Yellow Emperor, of Yao and Shun, of Wen and Wu, of Confucius and Mencius, of Dong Zhongshu, Zhu Xi, Wang Fuzhi, and so on, down to our own time and place. Importantly, these *dao*s are not

---

83. Graham, *Studies in Chinese Philosophy and Philosophical Literature*, 360.

84. *Zhongyong* 32: 唯天下至誠為能經綸天下之大經.

confined to some retrospectively determined orthodoxy but include those of all of the different populations and cultures that have been drawn into the whirlpool. And just as the "many as one" postulate is helpful in explaining the genealogical continuity, it also works the other way in emphasizing its multiplicity and diversity.

Another familiar Confucian expression that can be better understood by Zhao's account of the historical *tianxia* process is *he'erbutong* 和而不同, often translated into English as "the pursuit of harmony rather than sameness or uniformity." But such a simple translation does not do justice to Zhao's understanding of the *tianxia* game wherein rational choice among historical actors is the pursuit of maximum benefit at minimum cost. This being the case, the term *he* 和, conventionally translated as "harmony," is perhaps better understood in this context as beginning from the cultural differences that obtain among a truly diverse spectrum of peoples, and then ideally through inclusive patterns of deference in service to relational equity, to seek after an optimizing symbiosis. *He* thus understood is the assiduous effort to maximize the creative possibilities afforded by cultural difference to enrich the intergenerational transmission of an always evolving cultural identity and a shared political theology. The end game then is an achieved diversity.

Zhao offers an understanding of cultural identity that appeals to the creative "doings" as the distinguishing feature of humankind. Rather than a realist doctrine of truth and necessity, cultural identity emerges from the myriad of possibilities such doings engender. Culture, rather than being guided teleologically by some divine hand or transcendent purpose, is understood as a contrapuntal and open-ended responsiveness between human beings and their world. In this collaborative process, there is the opportunity for humankind to draw upon the available resources, to seek to elevate and refine them, and through this alliance to achieve a decidedly aesthetic and spiritual product. As such, the pursuit of such a superlative harmony in the flourishing and consummation of the human experience does much of the work that ontology's teleology offers as a desired end. This optimizing harmony, resourcing the historical past as its reservoir for analogy and projection, draws upon human resolve and imagination to forge an always new way forward. The human capacity for design, purpose, and direction assumed in this Confucian sense of harmony gives humankind a vital role in the evolution of an emergent and always provisional social, political, and ultimately cosmic order.

When we reflect upon the story Zhao tells of an emerging China, the cultural narrative is truly a distinctive one that can be recounted through these key philosophical concepts. More than most cultural traditions, there is a thick intergenerational continuity where the canonical past is still very much a part of the present as it is captured in the term *ru* 儒, conventionally translated as some variation on "Confucian." *Ru* is not to be understood as some potted and exclusive "Confucian" ideology but as the diverse and often disparate literati class of each succeeding generation responsible for inheriting, embodying, and perpetuating a high culture that, as a living tradition, must be reauthorized in every reiteration. And this same continuity is also expressed as *xiao* 孝 or "family reverence" as the prime moral imperative that grounds the traditional system of values. The character *xiao* 孝 that combines the graphs for "elders" (*lao* 老) and "offspring" (*zi* 子) reflects the assumption that the progenitors of each generation quite literally live on in their progeny, most obviously physically, but more importantly culturally and spiritually.

Tang Junyi like Zhao Tingyang draws upon the cosmology of the *Book of Changes* in characterizing this continuing process of cultural formation with the protean expression *yiduobufenguan* 一多不分觀, which we might translate as "one is many, many one."[85] This persistent feature of this cosmology as it is captured in its own expression, "continuity in change" (*biantong* 變通), provides us with yet another language for conceiving of the generative *tianxia* model of identity formation. Tang would insist that this postulate of "one is many, many one" is a distinctive and generic feature of the evolving formation of particular cultural identities that have implicated within them a boundless field of relations. Tang's postulate insists on the radical contextualism of all vital, relationally constituted orders within an ecology of "becoming," without the ecology privileging any particular one of them. Importantly, *yiduobufen* is another way of describing the doctrine of intrinsic, constitutive relationality that stands in stark contrast to a concept of external relations obtaining among discrete and independent things. These alternative understandings of relationality underlie the contrast that Zhao Tingyang explores in earnest between the gerundive process of "doing, making, creating" and the individuating and isolating function of "being." *Yiduobufen*, simply put, is the assumption that in the synergistic compositing of any "one," there is holographically

---

85. Tang Junyi, *Complete Works*, vol. 11,16–17.

implicated in it the contextualizing, unbounded, and unsummed "many." And further, that in this process of transformative syncretism (*hua* 化), one certainly changes the many, but the many also change the one, precluding the possibility of any one dominant order that would overwrite the particularity of the many. This *yiduobufen* proposition can be read in many different ways. If we use the achievement of cultural identity as an example, it restates in a different language the focus-field conception of cultures, where each of the continuing and continuous cultures, and each impulse in the life of each culture, has implicated within it the boundless "many" of its surrounds.

Far from being a rationalizing pattern of the many being disciplined by and assimilated into the one, Tang Junyi's *yiduobufen* postulate like *tianxia* asserts that identity formation in this process cosmology is effected collaboratively within the cultural ecology. What Tang means by this claim is that if we begin our reflection on the emergence of cosmic order from *tianxia* and the wholeness and inclusiveness of the lived experience, we can view this experience in terms of both its dynamic continuities and its manifold multiplicity, as both a ceaseless processual flow and as distinctive, consummatory events. This postulate is one more example of the mutual implication of binaries that characterizes all phenomena in the natural world—in this case, particularity and the totality, the subjective and objective, self and world. All unique focal identities are constituted by an unbounded field of more or less relevant relations that collaborate together to sponsor them, and they achieve their individuated identities as a function of the quality of coalescence they are able to achieve within these unique fields of relations. That is, moving from description to prescription, a dynamic reading of *tianxia* as *yiduobufen* is a summary of the way in which the opportunity is available for each entity to optimize the possibilities that honeycomb the relationships between it and its environing conditions. Importantly, any claim to the uniqueness and individuality of the particular, far from excluding its relations with other entities, is a function of the quality that it has been able to achieve within the unique configuration of these same relations.

Zhao's whirlpool model of understanding China as an inclusive *tianxia* certainly stimulates us to rethink some of the key philosophical vocabulary that can be drawn from the Chinese canonical texts to understand the sense of order dominant in this evolving cultural tradition. But perhaps in addition, it can have broader application in providing us with a different way of understanding the changing geopolitical configurations of our own time, and of anticipating their future possibilities. For example, can this centripetal whirlpool metaphor with the values of relational equity and achieved diversity be deployed to illuminate the possibilities and evaluate the emergent identities of the complex, syncretic histories of immigrant nations such as Australia, Canada, and the United States, with their own different versions of cultural hypergoods? Can this whirlpool model and its cultural attractors be invoked to help us understand the sometimes fraught but still noble vision of a European Union, a Europe that in our own time, with its own persistent and disintegrative Westphalian assumptions, is struggling to transform itself into a *tianxia* model of economic, political, and cultural order "with European characteristics"? Will a European Union emerge that as a political, social, and cultural order is no more than the unsummed totality of those specific particular orders that come to constitute it as it is construed from each of their different perspectives?

Sun Xiangchen 孫向晨

Figure 6.4. Sun Xiangchen.

Sun Xiangchen 孫向晨 is a professor at Fudan University, dean of the School of Philosophy, and director of the General Education Center. He was selected as a leading talent in social sciences (2020) and a leading talent in Shanghai (2019) under the National "Ten Thousand Talents Program." He has been a visiting scholar and visiting professor at many universities abroad, including Yale University, University of Chicago, Ecole Normale Supérieure, and the Free University of Berlin. Teaching projects that he has led or participated in have won the first prize of the National Teaching Achievement Award (2018) and the second prize of the National Teaching Achievement Award (2014). He has published many papers in top-tier journals such as *Chinese Social Science* and *Philosophical Research*, and his books and papers have won the Shanghai Philosophy and Social Science Outstanding Achievement Award. Two articles, "Dual Ontology: The Foundation for Shaping Modern China's Value Form" and "Modern Individual Rights and the 'Individual' in Confucian Traditions," were selected as "Top Ten Annual Recommendation Papers" by the Shanghai Association of Social Affairs in 2015 and 2017 respectively. An important recent monograph is his *On Family: The Individual and Devotion to Kin* (2019).

Sun Xiangchen 孫向晨: *Shengsheng* 生生 as "Being-between-the-Generations"

Comparative philosopher Sun Xiangchen, drawing largely upon Confucian and continental philosophies, has done much to establish "philosophy of family" as a new and, I would argue, a seminal turn in the global philosophical narrative. In so doing, Sun provides real insight into the centrality of "family reverence" (*xiao* 孝) as it has functioned as the prime moral imperative in the evolution of Confucian philosophy and culture.[86] In his work on Heidegger's *Dasein* or "being-in-the-world" (在世界之中存在), Sun sees himself perhaps overmodestly as clarifying, augmenting, and complementing Heidegger more than challenging him. By introducing the existential structure of "ceaseless procreation" (生生不息) as an alternative to Heidegger's own revisionist ontology, Sun is able to take advantage of insights into the human experience prominent in the family-centered and intergenerational Confucian tradition that are hidden if not missing in Heidegger's elaborations on *Dasein*.

Sun underscores the centrality of "procreating" (*shengsheng* 生生) in this early Confucian cosmology as it applies to the human experience by promoting his own novel genealogical interpretation of *Dasein* as an alter-

---

86. In this synopsis, I am summarizing Sun Xiangchen's ideas as they first appeared in an article entitled 生生: 在時代之中存在 [Procreativity: Being-between-the-generations] 哲學研究 [Philosophical research] 2018 年 9 期, 113–128, that have subsequently been expanded upon and included in his monograph 論家: 個體與親親 [On family: The individual and devotion to kin] (Shanghai: East China Normal University Press, 2019).

native to Heidegger's "being-in-the-world" that he calls "being-between-the-generations" (在世代之中存在). He sees his reading of this postulate *Dasein* as a way of supplementing Heidegger's formulation of it as "being-in-the-world" by compensating for temporal, relational, and historical aspects that have been underemphasized if not concealed or even overlooked. Certainly, temporality is there in Heidegger's *Being and Time* and in the *Da* of *Dasein* itself as "here" and "there" that is temporalized by including a "then." But Sun wants to bring further clarity and added emphasis to this temporality. To do so, he locates the emergence of "this person" (此身) and its "this being" (此在) within the family lineage of intergenerational kindred relations as the locus for the embodiment and transmission of a living cultural tradition. When *Dasein* is conflated with "world" and its generationality is overlooked, the *Mitsein* or "being-with" is obscured, and an isolated and individualistic *Dasein* stands out to be misconstrued as an independent subject.

We might note that in a cosmology made explicit in the *Book of Changes* where "change" (*yi* 易) is defined explicitly as "procreativity" (*sheng-sheng* 生生), radical temporality will not be denied.[87] Indeed, deep respect for change is built into the Chinese language itself. For example, even in the translating of Heidegger's "being-in-the-world" as 在世界之中存在, the Chinese-language binomial expression *shijie* 世界 that we translate as "world" is constructed by combining a diachronic, temporal aspect, *shi* 世 "worlding-as-intergenerational-temporal-succession," with a synchronic aspect, *jie* 界 "worlding-as-extending-spatial-boundaries." Expanding out further, the binomial *yuzhou* 宇宙 translated as "cosmos" combines a synchronic aspect, *yu* 宇 "cosmos-as-eaves-extending," and a diachronic aspect, *zhou* 宙 "cosmos-as-temporally-enduring." Importantly, each of these temporal and spatial terms is qualified by its correlative relationship with its paired other, and by the vitality of the process cosmology that serves as its interpretive context. The inseparability of time and place, of form and flow, becomes the cadence and musicality of the human experience in its pursuit of proper measure (*du* 度). Flow that cannot be separated from place becomes events "taking place," and form that cannot be separated from time becomes the rhythm of life.[88]

---

87. See Ames, *Sourcebook*, 103–104.

88. Interestingly, the English word "world" also has this emphasis on temporality. The proto-Germanic *weraldi* is a compound of *wer* "man" + *ald* "age," meaning "the age or era of man."

While Heidegger would place emphasis on the "encounter" (*begegnen*) that *Dasein* has with the "world," Sun wants to provide a more nuanced way in which the ideas of "being-with" and "world" are understood by informing them with the full semantic range of "generation" in its sense of both "growth" and of "family lineage." Rather than the tendency for *Dasein* to be construed as an isolated individual, the notion of "generation" brings to this idea a transitory in-betweenness in which the layers of *Dasein* from past generations are embodied in this human connector as it serves as a conduit to shape the *Dasein* of future generations.

For Sun, the limited emphasis on temporality and relationality in Heidegger is read as the influence of Heidegger's own Western philosophical narrative in which, going back to early Greek ontology, persons have persistently been interpreted as individual, self-sufficient, and independent "beings," and thus effectively as rootless originals. Such assumptions stand in stark contrast to the Confucian tradition in which there has been a sustained emphasis upon the intergenerational obligation persons have to the extended and continuing family lineage, with progenitors being perceived as living on in their progeny. While Heidegger in his own historical context is certainly a disruptive revolution against the self-sufficient subjectivity of Descartes, his frequent appeal to notions such as the "mineness" (*Jemeinigkeit*) of *Dasein* reflects a general absence of "rootedness" in the continuities of life that flow from this genealogical source.

Sun again introduces the idea of "body-in-the-world" as another Confucian alternative to the Heideggerian "being-in-the-world," where the character for the lived and social "body" (*shen* 身) is used as a designator for the concept of "self" or "myself." Sun makes much of the fact that this same character as it is found in the earliest oracle bone sources is a pictograph of a pregnant woman with a swollen belly ripe with child 身. The image of mother with child precludes any concept of persons as complete and self-sufficient subjects, and it is an indication that the perceived understanding of the embodied self is neither mother nor child taken separately but instead the intergenerational and constitutive relationship that obtains between them.[89] Again, the lived and social body (*shen*) that begins within family has both a social and an existential aspect. In the *Classic of Family Reverence* (*Xiaojing* 孝經) and echoed in other canonical texts, it states explicitly that "your physical person with its hair and skin is received from

---

89. Kwan, "Database," 西周中期 CHANT 246.

your parents."[90] Every "this body" (*cishen* 此身) is a tangible connection between self and parents. If we use the image of the family tree, the ancestral lineage is the pith and heartwood of the tree that provide its stable and enduring structure, while one's most immediate and intimate kinfolk (*qin* 親) are the continuing life process that is taking place in the outermost layer of sapwood. Every "this body" thus resides in the genealogical lineage that connects children-parents-ancestors and is thus the connector between the past and the future of humanity itself.

In Heidegger, "encountering the other" is understood as a function of "readiness-to-hand" (*Zuhandenheit*), and in Levinas it is being face-to-face with the Other. But with *Dasein* understood as "procreativity" (*shengsheng*) and thus as "being-between-the-generations," the original state of "being-with-others" does not happen as Heidegger and Levinas aver through tools or through an encounter with strangers respectively. Instead, it is grounded in the most primal and intimate human feelings. In *Focusing the Familiar* (*Zhongyong* 中庸) we are told that "aspiring to consummate conduct in your roles and relations (*ren* 仁) is becoming a person (*ren* 人), and devotion to your kinfolk is what is of greatest consequence."[91] The primal experience and original status of "being-with-others" emerges from one's most intimate relations—that is, the relationship between parents and children. It is thus that for Sun this expression "devotion to your kinfolk" or "family feeling" (*qinqin* 親親) carries with it a broad and deep "ontological" meaning for Confucian ethics. I put "ontology" in scare quotes here because as with Heidegger himself, Sun is using this term in a way that intends to subvert its original meaning.

Sun demonstrates that the meaning of "encounter" is integral to the etymology of the character *qin* 親 itself in its reference to both "intimacy" and "kinfolk." As explained in the *Shuowen* lexicon, the semantic element in the character *qin* 親 is *jian* 見, meaning "encountering." What *qin* thus means explicitly is the encountering of others as it is grounded in the intimacy, closeness, affinity, and love that is the substance of family relations. Such feelings are primal in defining the quality of the encounter and are

---

90. 身體髮膚受之父母.

91. *Zhongyong* 20: 仁者人也，親親為大. There is a resonant passage in *Mencius* 7B16: 孟子曰: "仁也者、人也. 合而言之，道也" (Mencius said: "Aspiring to consummate conduct in your roles and relations [*ren* 仁] is becoming a person [*ren* 人]; and when these two words—consummate conduct and your person—can be spoken together, you are walking the proper way").

then nominalized to reference the most immediate locus of such feelings, that is, a person's kinfolk. Sun describes this deep, ontological meaning of *qinqin* as the entry point and highest value in Confucian ethics and the way of "becoming human" for every *Dasein*. More primal and fundamental than virtue, the status of *qinqin* is seen by Sun as being comparable to *eros* in Greek philosophy and *agape* in Christianity. He underscores both the historical and the intergenerational importance of *qinqin* by citing the celebrated historian Wang Guowei 王國維 who, in reflecting on the transition of the "ritual and music culture" from the Zhou to the Shang dynasty, remarks that "all of their institutions were derivative of two values: deference to the worthy (*zunzun* 尊尊) and devotion to kin (*qinqin* 親親)."[92]

Given the ontological status of *qinqin* as primal human feelings, Sun argues that the other moral imperatives that define intergenerational family relations such as "family reverence" (*xiao* 孝) and "fraternal deference" (*ti* 悌) are themselves constructed out of this basic and primal human feeling and are then in turn the source of the other Confucian virtues: consummate conduct in roles and relations (*ren* 仁), a sense of what is optimally appropriate in those relations (*yi* 義), an achieved propriety in the lived roles of family and community (*li* 禮), and wisdom as it informs the quality of roles and relations (*zhi* 智). In ruminating on the absence in Heidegger of any explanation for the origins of ethics, Sun makes the argument that the perceived Confucian understanding of the source of ethics is made clear by a close reading of the *Mencius*. Sun cites Mencius, who looks precisely to these primal foundational feelings in the human experience as the watershed from which the values that structure the Confucian vision of the moral life flow:

> Mencius said: "What people are able to do without learning anything are their 'native capacities'; what they are able to realize without deliberation is their 'native wisdom.' There are no toddlers who are unaware that they love their parents, and as they grow up, there are none who are unaware of the respect they have for their elders. Affection for parents is an expression of consummate conduct (*ren*); respecting elders is an expression of a sense of optimal appropriateness (*yi*). For no other reason, such values have to be promoted throughout the world."[93]

---

92. See Wang Guowei's 《殷周制度论》.

93. *Mencius* 7A15: 孟子曰: "人之所不學而能者, 其良能也; 所不慮而知者, 其良知也. 孩提之童無不知愛其親者, 及其長也, 無不知敬其兄也. 親親、仁也, 敬長、義也, 無他, 達之天下也."

Sun gives a detailed account of the way in which "family reverence" (*xiao* 孝) that provides the existential structure for Confucian ethics is a higher-order sublimation of the more raw and primal *qinqin* feelings. He cites a passage from the "Zisizi" chapter of the *Complete Works of Master Zeng* (*Zengziquanshu*曾子全書), in which it states that "'family reverence' is the beginning of virtue," interpreting the genealogical sense of what is a "fetal beginning" (*shi* 始) as being the original structure of "generationness."[94] The components of the character *xiao* 孝 that combines "older generation" (*lao* 老) and "younger generation" (*zi* 子) express explicitly the underlying structure of "generationness." The character *xiao* references the continuity from one generation to the next while, at the same time, indicating the inseparability that obtains between them. Sun cites a verse from the *Book of Songs* that asks, "Who then can the fatherless rely upon; who then can the motherless depend upon?"[95] *Xiao* is the ontological structure of "being-between-the-generations."

While *xiao* locates persons between generations, for Sun *xiao* at a more macrocosmic level also carries with it an important cultural significance. He cites the *Mencius* that states "there are three ways of failing to observe family reverence, and to be without progeny is the most serious among them."[96] *Xiao* reflects awe for the continuity of life that, when in the absence of progeny, this continuity can be undone within a family lineage by the irrevocable termination of the seasonal ancestor sacrifices. But Sun interprets this passage as having consequences that go beyond responsibility for one's own personal family lineage in having reference to the continuing life of the culture itself. For Sun, *xiao* is a concept of sustained cultural transmission and inheritance that is much more than simple biological reproduction and continuity at the micro level.

Taking this microcosmic level one step further, while the relationship between the young and the old within the family might be seen as a private affair, Sun's argument is that primal *qinqin* feelings are the substance of a universalizable morality that transcends individual lives to locate all humanity in intimate relationships with others. It is *xiao* as the foundation and existential structure of Confucian ethics that is the source of the more specific, different modalities of virtuous action. Sun cites a passage from the *Analects* that uses the metaphor of rootedness to make this point explicitly: "As for family

---

94. 曾子全書《子思子》：孝，德之始也.

95. 詩經《蓼莪》：無父何怙、無母何恃.

96. *Mencius* 4A26: 不孝有三，無後為大.

reverence and fraternal deference, these are, I suspect, the root of becoming consummate in one's conduct (*ren* 仁)."[97] That *xiao* is the ground of other higher-level expressions of virtuous conduct is further elaborated upon in the *Mencius*, in which it states that "the realization of consummate conduct (*ren*) lies in serving one's parents and the realization of being optimally appropriate (*yi*) lies in deference to one's elder brothers. And the realization of living wisely (*zhi*) lies in holding resolutely to and never abandoning these two precepts."[98] The salient point being made here by Sun is that understanding *xiao* as the existential structure of Confucian ethics opens a hermeneutical space for such ethics to be taken as a first philosophy. He cites the *Analects* that reveals the radiality of this Confucian ethical philosophy as it begins here and goes there: "as a younger brother and son, be filial at home and, when going out, be deferential in the community."[99] What is personal, private, and particular can be "extrapolated" (*tuiji* 推及) from one's home to humanity itself. The *qinqin* intimate feelings that are expressed in the love for one's own parents are universalized as a moral consciousness that has no boundary. As it says in the *Classic of Family Reverence*, "For exemplary persons, their teaching family reverence is their way of showing respect for every father in the world, and their teaching fraternal deference is their way of showing respect for every older brother in the world."[100] And again in the *Mencius*, too, moral sentiments that begin at home are extended radially to be expressed as an unbounded cosmic morality: "Exemplary persons . . . expressing devotion to their kinsmen seek a consummatory relationship with the common people; seeking a consummatory relationship with the common people, they have a love for all things in general."[101]

In Sun Xiangchen's interpretation of the existential structure of *Dasein* as "being-between-the-generations," one of his most insightful contributions in this revisionist ontology is the reinstatement of family. He begins with a stern critique of Heidegger for the absence in his formulation of *Dasein* of any explicit reference to family. Indeed, the concept of family does not occur in *Being and Time*. Heidegger instead makes much of the ontological "homelessness" of human beings who, in their being separated and distanced

---

97. *Analects* 1.2: 孝弟也者, 其為仁之本與.

98. *Mencius* 4A27: 仁之實, 事親是也; 義之實, 從兄是也; 智之實, 知斯二者弗去是也.

99. *Analects* 1.5: 入則孝, 出則弟.

100. *Classic of Family Reverence* 13: 教以孝, 所以敬天下之為人父者也. 教以悌, 所以敬天下之為人兄者也.

101. *Mencius* 7A45: 君子 . . . 親親而仁民, 仁民而愛物.

from their own essential identities, live inauthentic lives. For Heidegger, such ontological homelessness is far more critical than any lack of a material residence or dwelling.

In the classical and modern Chinese language, both "family" and "home" are expressed by the same term *jia* 家, with the importance invested in family being primary. The graph *jia* 家 is composed of "roof" or "dwelling" (*mian* 宀) that occurs on the oracle bones as 介, and a "hairy pig" (*shi* 豕) that is written as 豕 in the oracle bone script. In combination then these two graphs become *jia* 家.[102] As with many Chinese terms, *jia* has a temporal and a spatial aspect. The pig represents the seasonal sacrifices to the ancestors as these practices are conducted within the space of the residence itself. Sun cites the late Qing scholar Wu Dacheng 吳大澂, who suggests that since the ordinary people did not have a special place for sacrifice, they would display the sacrificial animal in the home and conduct the sacrifice there.[103] It is this centrality of intergenerational ancestral sacrifices that gives priority to the family itself over the dwelling in which these ritual practices are conducted.

Sun's general critique of Heidegger's *Dasein* is that it seems to be too gross to serve as an ontological structure. "Being-with" or *Mitsein* does locate beings in the world, but as a conceptual framework, it is sorely lacking in any specificity or practicality or vitality. To the extent that "being-with" does have reference to context, it is little more than a thin and weak "they." Indeed, Sun sees "generationness" as the antidote to the "flatness, averageness, and anonymousness" of Heidegger's understanding of interpersonal relations. Buber with his "I and Thou" and Levinas with his "face-to-face" are responses that similarly attempt to go beyond Heidegger and, in their invoking immediacy, vitality, and responsibility, to bring the encounter with "Other" to life. But they like Heidegger locate and reflect on such relationships synchronically without sufficient attention to the diachronic aspect captured in Sun's notion of "generationness." The family as the ultimate source of social order is the locus of the vital "being-with," relating persons to their elders, to the members of their own generation, and to the younger generation that follows from them.

---

102. Kwan, "Database," 甲骨文合集 CHANT 2036, CHANT 1600A, and CHANT 3522 正 respectively.

103. There is an alternative explanation on the Kwan "Database" stating that *jia* 家 as it appears on the oracle bones means both "ancestral temple" (*zongmiao* 宗廟) and family lineage (*jiazu* 家族); later on in the bronze inscriptions it comes to reference the royal residence (*wangjia* 王家) and the court (*chaoting* 朝廷).

Heidegger's birth of *Dasein* as a being "thrown into the world" is thoroughly revised in Sun to become the notion of "being-born-into-family." The family provides the circle of life for *Dasein*, giving it a home and serving as the conveyor of generations (*chengshi* 承世). Family is certainly the primary social institution, but it is more, having ontological status as the structure of "being-with" that brings tangibility to "generationness." *Dasein* as being-born-into-family is further concretized as being *this* person being born into *this* family and *this* specific circle of intimate relations, where such family relations are the source and substance of personal authenticity.

With Heidegger's *Dasein* as being "thrown into the world," expressions such as idle talk (*Gerede*), curiosity (*Neugier*), and ambiguity (*Zweideutigkeit*) describe *Dasein*'s inauthentic role in the world. For Heidegger, the felt response of *Dasein* to its being "thrown into the world" is the feeling of uncertainty and anxiety that arises from a lack of subjective control. And with the personal experience of *Dasein* being pitted against the world, its authentic feeling is one of profound dread (*Grauen*). But for Sun, it is precisely the communicating family and its formative conventions that are the forum within which *Dasein* achieves its authentic personal identity. And it is the ordinary life in the family that carries the cultural genealogy as a continuing identity from generation to generation. For Sun, what Heidegger has missed utterly by ignoring being-born-into-family is enjoyment as a state of mind that emerges from being at home, a warm feeling that fills in the gap between *Dasein* and world. This being-born-into-family provides *Dasein* with the realization of its being-between-the-generations, and even though this locus is not of its own choosing, it serves as the context of care for all of the experiences that in sum make up a joyful life. Far from the dread and anxiety that would arise from a sense of having been thrown into the world, the world surrounding *Dasein* that it necessarily must confront is in fact one saturated with love and concern.

Sun takes the spirit of joy that comes from rejoicing in life itself as a central theme in the *Analects*. He cites a representative passage in which Confucius's favorite student Yan Hui, in spite of his poverty and his many hardships, is able to find real joy in life itself: "The Master said, 'An exceptional person, this Yan Hui! He has a bamboo bowl of rice to eat, a gourd of water to drink, and a dirty little hovel in which to live. Other people would not be able to endure his hardships, yet for Hui it has no effect on his enjoyment (*le* 樂). An exceptional person indeed, is this Yan Hui!' "[104] In Sun's best effort

---

104. *Analects* 6.11 子曰: "賢哉回也! 一簞食, 一瓢飲, 在陋巷. 人不堪其憂, 回也不改其樂. 賢哉回也!"

to understand and explain this sense of enjoyment (*le* 樂), he appeals to the Song dynasty Confucian commentators Cheng Yi 程頤 and Zhu Xi 朱熹, who both describe this feeling as a sense of primal satisfaction that comes with just being fully alive, a rejoicing in life itself that is more fundamental than good fortune or any particular accomplishment. Sun goes to the classical texts to further explicate this sense of rejoicing, arguing that there are two significant dimensions to it, one being a kind of religiousness and the other, morality.

The religious dimension of *le* 樂 comes with the rejoicing that attends a full coalescence between humanity and *tian* as humankind's natural and numinous context. As it says in the *Mencius*: "Is there any enjoyment greater than, with the myriad things of the world all implicated here in me, to turn personally inward and find resolution with all things?"[105] And in *Focusing the Familiar* (*Zhongyong*) that takes the possibilities of this correlative relationship between humanity and *tian* as its central axis, it elevates those who are able to become co-creators with the heavens and the earth rejoicing in thus forming a triad with them. It is "those who can assist in the transforming and nourishing activities of the heavens and earth . . . that can take their place as members of this triad."[106]

The second dimension of such enjoyment is moral. As it says in *Focusing the Familiar*, the rejoicing that is to be found in being-born-into-family is the very ground on which human beings walk as they pursue their journey through life:

> The proper way of exemplary persons is analogous to traveling a long way where you must set off from what is near at hand. It is analogous to climbing to the lofty heights where you must begin from the lowliest ground. The *Book of Songs* 164 says:
>> The loving relationship with wife and children
>> Is like the strumming of the zither and the lute.
>> In the harmonious relationship between older and younger brothers
>> There is an abundance of enjoyment and pleasure.
>> Be appropriate in your house and home
>> And bring joy to your wife and progeny.[107]

---

105. *Mencius* 7A4: 萬物皆備於我矣. 反身而誠, 樂莫大焉. 強恕而行, 求仁莫近焉."

106. *Focusing the Familiar* 22: 贊天地之化育 . . . 與天地參.

107. *Focusing the Familiar* 15: 君子之道, 辟如行遠必自邇, 辟如登高必自卑.《詩》曰: 妻子好合, 如鼓瑟琴; 兄弟既翕, 和樂且耽. 宜爾室家, 樂爾妻帑.

The journey is always from near to far, and the climb too is from low to high. The very notion of *zhongyong* as "focusing the familiar" in its sense of bringing focus and thus resolution to one's immediate family and communal roles and relations is rooted in family reverence (*xiao*), and it begins from a flourishing family life. At the same time, playing on the fact that in Chinese "enjoyment" (*le, yao*) and "music" (*yue*) are written with the same character 樂 pronounced differently, metaphorically the steep climb and the heights to be reached inspire the musicality to be achieved in elevating and enchanting what is ordinary and awaken the delight that is to be found in the deepening of the everyday. There is no destination on this shared journey but only "ends in view" as the road extends from generation to generation. And the rejoicing to be had on in the events experienced along the way is always better than the inn itself. Sun cites authorities such as philosophers Liang Shuming 梁漱溟 and Li Zehou 李澤厚 to make the argument that such enjoyment is much more than simply personal feelings; it is an ontologically grounded cultural disposition in the relationship between humanity and its world.

Sun Xiangchen then turns to the possible objection to *Dasein* being interpreted as "being-between-the-generations" as introducing a limitation on its freedom, and thus as a possible source of what Heidegger sees as inauthenticity in the human experience. Questioning the relevance of Heidegger's authenticity and inauthenticity distinction, Sun looks to the centrality of "learning" (*xue* 學) as the projective impetus for life and growth that defines the continuity from one generation to the next. Sun reflects on the fact that in the construction of the two characters "learning" (*xue* 學) and "family reverence" (*xiao* 孝) that both in different ways describe "being-between-the-generations," we find the same semantic component *zi* 子: "child, offspring, younger generation." This component gives a sense of "generationness" to the process of learning. Zhu Xi in his commentary on the *Analects* says that "the meaning of the term 'learning' (*xue*) is 'emulation.' "[108] And the object of this emulation for the younger progeny is the life experience of the former generations as this compounding wisdom is echoed down the ages to become the substance of the education of the present generation.

Heidegger reflects on the loneliness of *Dasein* as it sinks under the control of *das Man*, the anonymous other, the "everyone" who is no one. Even though Heidegger expounds on "being-as-having-been" (*Gewesensein*)

---

108. 學之为言效.

and the impact it exerts upon the world, he does not give any ontological status to learning as the mechanism through which this influence takes place. By contrast, Sun notes that in the Confucian tradition, the term "learning" itself is the embodying process of "teaching and learning" through which meaning is transmitted from one generation to the next. The *Shuowen* lexicon defines "teaching" (*jiao* 教) as "what is being practiced by the elders as it is emulated by those who follow."[109] In this sense persons, far from being independent existents, are the existential conduits who, being conditioned by the life experience of those who have come before, are the recipients in this gifting process of teaching and learning.

Sun references the immediate relationship between "family reverence" (*xiao*) and this teaching-and-learning-between-the-generations as it is described in the *Classic of Family Reverence*, where it identifies *xiao* as the first among the virtues and the very source and substance of education: "It is family reverence (*xiao*) that is the root of the virtues and is whence education itself is born."[110] The moral imperatives of "family reverence" (*xiao* 孝) and "fraternal deference" (*ti* 悌) are grounded in and sublimated out of the prereflective, natural, immediate, and intimate *qinqin* feelings, giving them their existential structure. These imperatives are then themselves extrapolated and generalized as the substance of Confucian moral education.

For Heidegger, *Dasein* is the self-projection of being that can be either authentic or inauthentic. But the Confucian *Dasein* transforms this self-projection into the relationship between self and other through teaching and learning, and locates *Dasein* in this projection as it is taking place between-the-generations. Teaching and learning are integral to the ontology of "being-between-the-generations." And the projection coming out of the past then conditions *Dasein* by transmitting and perpetuating the culture through the intergenerational process of teaching and emulation. Sun demonstrates how the link between teaching and family is captured specifically in the status of the teacher (*shi* 師) as "father" (*shifu* 師父), where the teacher has a key role as the agent of teaching and the exemplar of learning that provides the meaningful continuity between generations.

Sun Xiangchen takes the continuity of generationness itself as being the historicity of the existence of *Dasein* and sets up a contrast between this fulsome sense of historical consciousness and Heidegger's rather shallow appeal to the remanent tools of lost worlds. For Heidegger, tools from the past are

---

109. 上所施下所效也.

110. *Classic of Family Reverence* 1: 夫孝德之本也教之所由生也.

the history that remembers worlds that no longer exist and are what brings this distant and indirect history into *Dasein*. For the Confucian *Dasein*, it is a historical consciousness of human beings themselves rather than just their tools that is perpetuated directly through the process of transmission as it is revealed in the *Dasein* of being-between-the-generations. The living narrative of the preceding generation in all of its variances is impressed directly upon the *Dasein* of the succeeding generation, where generational differences are the form and substance of its historical consciousness. Sun points to the comprehensive history compiled by the Grand Historian Sima Qian 司馬遷 as the written record of the intergenerational continuities and changes that make up just such a historical consciousness.

For Heidegger, *Dasein* is itself a kind of temporal ecstasy that exists and is then gone, as the *Dasein* of the past ceases to exist in the world. Since change for *Dasein* is simply change in itself, it cannot produce any real historicity. Sun allows that Heidegger does make a gesture toward historicity in his notion of "a handing down of a heritage," but given the existential structure of his *Dasein*, there does not seem to be a space for this inheritance. On Sun's reading, any real historicity for *Dasein* must be a consciousness of change in its own existence as it is disclosed by differences within the continuities of generations, and thus can only be revealed in the historical consciousness of being-between-the-generations.

In any case, the real emphasis in Heidegger is on the various possibilities of the authentic *Dasein* that can be projected against the oppressiveness of daily averageness (*Durchschnittlichkeit*). For the Confucian *Dasein*, generationness is inherited by, inherent in, and can only be realized as aspects of *Dasein*. This process of inheritance and transmission requires the condition of being-between-the-generations. Heidegger puts much emphasis upon the authentic *Dasein* achieving separation from the daily average, but in being an empty self, it seems to be lacking in the resources needed to achieve this transcendence. It is only when *Dasein* can draw upon the ample sustenance available from being-between-the-generations that it has the strength to accomplish this overcoming of mediocrity. It is because "being-as-body" (*shen* 身) is itself generative that generationness serves as the ground and precondition for creativity.

Sun is aware of a certain kind of conservativeness that comes with the historicity of being-between-the-generations, but he observes that succeeding generations are not required to simply maintain and repeat what has come before. Indeed, even though *Dasein*'s historicity is a structural a priori that must be confronted and responded to, *Dasein* is not compelled to conform to this legacy. The historical inheritance is better regarded as a substantial gift rather than remnants and shards, and in the dialogue *Dasein* in a continuing present has with its past, this gift can provide it with new possibilities for shaping its future. And indeed, there is in *Dasein* a resolve directed toward its own future. This positive locus of *Dasein* as an intermediary that transmits the achievements of the past for the enrichment of future generations is captured for Sun in a passage from the *Record of Rites* (*Liji* 禮記): "The engraver of the bronzes inscribed his own name, and with this inscription setting forth and praising the many virtues of his ancestors, it shed light upon these ancestors for the benefit of generations yet to come."[111] Sun further argues that the understanding of *Dasein* and its relationship to its own death and the death of others is very different when we move from Heidegger to being-between-the-generations. Heidegger wants to make use of death to lay emphasis on the possibilities for *Dasein*'s projection of life into a finite future. For Heidegger, an adequate understanding of *Dasein*'s inevitable death is important as revealing of its totality and finitude, where this being-toward-death has a profound effect on its existential consciousness and its entire existence. But its death is neither an object nor an experience for *Dasein*. In encountering its death as the end of its life, *Dasein* no longer exists.

With respect to the death of others, Sun cites Heidegger, who describes the deceased as having been "torn away from those who have 'remained behind' (*den 'Hinterbliebenen*), and is an object of 'concern' in the ways of funeral rites, interment, and the cult of graves."[112] Heidegger allows that the death of the other is not final in the sense that the other is still with *Dasein* in some way, but that is all. He does not develop this insight, but simply concludes that in our "being-with," we do not have an authentic experience of the other's demise. What Heidegger ignores here with respect to the death of the other has profound significance for *Dasein* within the structure of being-between-the-generations and has deep roots in Chinese culture.

Allowing that *Dasein* can neither experience its own death or the demise of others, this does not mean that the death of the other and especially the death of our parents does not come without profound significance for the

---

111. See the *Concordance to the* Liji 26.23/133/8: 《禮記》銘者, 自名也. 自名以稱揚其先祖之美, 而明著之後世者也.

112. Martin Heidegger, *Being and Time*, trans. John Macquarrie and Edward Robinson (Oxford: Basil Blackwell, 1962), 282.

way in which we live and feel. This significance of the death of the other is integral to the existential structure of being-between-the-generations, where this vital importance is expressed in the key role that funeral services for parents have for their offspring. As the *Mencius* observes, "Simply taking care of parents in life does not amount to any great deed; it is only in the solemn obsequies conducted in the funeral and sacrificial services that great things are done."[113] Sun sees the very existential structure of being-between-the-generations as beginning in *qinqin* as the primal intimate feelings expressed as devotion to kinfolk and then reaching its end in the funeral services held for deceased parents.

Sun Xiangchen reminds us that "family reverence" (*xiao* 孝) provides the existential structure for being-between-the-generations, and that *Mitsein* as the being-with-family-members after their death is maintained through the centrality of funeral and sacrificial ritual practices. As it says in the *Analects* with respect to the members of the preceding generation, "While they are living, serve them according to the observances of ritual propriety; when they have passed, bury them and sacrifice to them according to the observances of ritual propriety."[114] It is through such family-centered ritual practices that the names of intimate persons are perpetuated and kept alive. Looking at "being-with" from the perspective of those who have passed gives additional meaning to the *Analects* passage, which declares that "exemplary persons (*junzi*) hate the thought of ending their days without having established a name."[115] The added implication here would be that exemplary persons hate the thought of their name not being mentioned after their death because it is the life of their name that allows them to continue to exist between generations. While ritual and sacrificial practices (*liji* 禮祭) might appear to be overly elaborate and formal, Sun reminds us of the centrality of the association that an inclusive "appropriateness" and "meaningfulness" (*yi* 義) has with these practices as the substance and continuity of being-between-the-generations.

Sun cites the canonical texts that define "sacrifice" explicitly in terms of continuing to care for and revere those who are gone: "Sacrifice is the means of seeking to nourish them and to perpetuate family reverence."[116] Again, in

---

113. *Mencius* 4B13: 養生者不足以當大事, 惟送死可以當大事.

114. *Analects* 2.5: 生事之以禮; 死葬之以禮, 祭之以禮.

115. *Analects* 15.20: 君子疾沒世而名不稱焉.

116. See the *Concordance to the* Liji 26.2/130/1:《禮記》祭者, 所以追養繼孝也.

Focusing the Familiar it gives instructions to the living on the proper disposition to assume in carrying out these generational duties: "Serving their dead as though they were still living and serving those long departed as though they are still here—this is family reverence at its best."[117] What is pervasive in these texts that report on the role of ritual practices and sacrifices is the sense that in this being-between-the-generations structure, the relationship between the living and the dead is itself very much alive. Sun cites the *Record of Rites*: "The day of the sacrifice: On entering the chamber, he seems to be sure that he can see the deceased where the tablet is placed. Having carried out the various services, in departing the chamber, he with solemnity is sure that he can hear the sounds of the deceased moving about. And having departed the chamber, listening one more time, with deep feeling he is sure he can hear the departed sighing audibly."[118] Sun continues with this same chapter of the *Record of Rites* in which he explores the vital and intimate relationship that connects humanity to the world of the spirits and ghosts of the ancestors that is then captured in the language of a kind of shared spirituality (*shen* 神) pervasive in the space between-the-generations: "All living things must die, and in their dying 'return' (*gui* 歸) to the earth. This is why they are said to be 'ghosts' (*gui* 鬼). Their flesh and bones molder away beneath the ground and disintegrating become the earth of the field. But their *qi* carries on above to become brightness. The rising vapors and odors produce a feeling of desolation. This is what is quintessential in all things and is a manifestation of their spirituality."[119]

In such passages we see the inseparability of life and death in a continuing cycle. Confucius himself reflects at length on this living relationship between humanity and the spiritual world. And from what he says we can gather that for him, it is sacrifice between-the-generations that makes the spirits present and brings them together with their progeny in this spiritual relationship: "The expression 'sacrifice as though present' is taken to mean 'sacrifice to the spirits as though they are present.' But the Master said: 'If I myself do not participate in the sacrifice, it is as though I have not

---

117. *Focusing the Familiar* 19: 事死如事生, 事亡如事存, 孝之至也.

118. See the *Concordance to the* Liji 25.3/123/30:《禮記》: 祭之日: 入室, 僾然必有見乎其位, 周還出戶, 肅然必有聞乎其容聲, 出戶而聽, 愾然必有聞乎其嘆息之聲.

119. See the *Concordance to the* Liji 25.25/126/8:《禮記》: 眾生必死, 死必歸土: 此之謂鬼. 骨肉斃於下, 陰為野土; 其氣發揚於上, 為昭明, 焄蒿, 淒愴, 此百物之精也, 神之著也." There is a play on the paronomastic relationship between the characters for "returning" (*gui* 歸) and "ghost" (*gui* 鬼) that are similar in pronunciation.

sacrificed at all.' "[120] Sun argues that it is through these sacrificial practices that *Dasein* can return to its ancestors and to its source of life, and through its bodily and personal participation captured in the term *shen* 身, *Dasein* can reaffirm this continuity and express its reverence. He cites the *Record of Rites*: "Exemplary persons returning to their ancestors and to their source of life do not forget how it is that they came into existence. This is how they express their reverence, convey their feelings, and expend all of their energies in carrying out this service. They would not dare to do anything less."[121] Since this body has been gifted to one from one's parents, the death of the parents and one's own death in which one's body is returned to those who have come before have continuity. As it states in the *Record of Rites*: "As for my person, it is a body handed down from my parents. In attending to this legacy from my parents, how could I dare but be reverent?"[122] The feelings of solemn veneration and sincerity that are occasioned by these sacrifices are internalized to consolidate and galvanize the virtues of *Dasein*, and they constitute the existential structure of being-between-the-generations. And such feelings are deeply rooted and primordial: "It is because all things are rooted in *tian* and human beings are again rooted in their ancestors that this sacrifice is in accord with the high gods. In carrying out the *jiao* sacrifices, there is a deep expression of gratitude to this rootedness and a return to the source of life."[123]

These ancestral sacrifices have deep cultural meaning in securing the values that bring stability to the human experience, connecting one's own personal experience to the cosmic moral order. Master Zeng, the paragon of family reverence in the Confucian canons, remarks on the profound influence sacrifices have in the moral education of the people: "Master Zeng said: 'When one is circumspect in funerary services and continues the sacrifices to the distant ancestors, moral excellence among the common people will thrive.' "[124] It is "family reverence" (*xiao*) that provides the existential structure of *Dasein* being-between-the-generations. First, as it states

---

120. *Analects* 3.12: 祭如在, 祭神如神在. 子曰: "吾不與祭, 如不祭."

121. See the *Concordance to the* Liji 25.30/126/21: 《禮記》: 君子反古復始, 不忘其所由生也, 是以致其敬, 發其情, 竭力從事, 以報其親, 不敢弗盡也."

122. See the *Concordance to the* Liji 25.35/127/20:《禮記》: 身也者, 父母之遺體也. 行父母之遺體, 敢不敬乎?

123. See the *Concordance to the* Liji 11.20/71/2:《禮記》: 萬物本乎天, 人本乎祖, 此所以配上帝也. 郊之祭也, 大報本反始也.

124. *Analects* 1.9: 曾子曰: 慎終追遠, 民德歸厚矣.

explicitly in *Focusing the Familiar*, family reverence continues the way of life and the values of those who have come before: "Family reverence means being good at continuing the purposes of one's predecessors and maintaining their ways."[125] The highest expression of family reverence certainly demands much from human beings in their own personal cultivation and in their contribution to a continuing living tradition. As its states in the *Classic of Family Reverence*: "Distinguishing yourself and walking the proper way (*dao*) in the world; raising your name high for posterity and thereby bringing esteem to your father and mother—it is in these things that family reverence finds its consummation."[126]

Such reverence is the celebration of one's own life as it embodies and continues the culture inherited from one's parents and from the highest ancestors. Family reverence begins from respect for one's own person as what is closest at hand, extends such concern to the care for one's family and kin, and then culminates in dedicating one's service to one's ruler and to posterity. In this same passage, King Wen—that is, King "Culture" (*wen* 文)—is singled out as the moral exemplar and historical source from which succeeding generations draw their inspiration and to whom, with the cultural dividends they are able to accrue, they can make appropriate return: "In the 'Greater Odes' section of the *Book of Songs* it says: 'How can you fail to remember your ancestor, King Wen? You must cultivate yourself and extend his virtuosity.' "[127] If we want to capture the implied meaning of this same passage as it serves Sun's understanding of *Dasein* as "being-between-the-generations," we could translate it alternatively as "How can you fail to embody the culture of your ancestors? You must cultivate yourself and extend the reach and influence of their virtuosity."

RESPONSE

Sun Xiangchen provides us with a classic example of the method of comparative cultural hermeneutics and the explanatory force he is able to muster by its effective application. In Sun's efforts to highlight important, unannounced assumptions that are defining of the Chinese and Western philosophical narratives, he first lays emphasis upon the

---

125. *Focusing the Familiar* 19: 夫孝者: 善繼人之志, 善述人之事者也.

126. *Classic of Family Reverence* 1: 立身行道, 揚名於後世, 以顯父母, 孝之終也.

127. *Classic of Family Reverence* 1 cites the *Book of Songs* 235: 《大雅》云: "無念爾祖, 聿脩厥德."

intergenerational transmission of family-centered cultural values as the signature of the classical Confucian texts and then brings Confucian philosophy into engagement with Heidegger's understanding of *Dasein*, or "being there." In his detailed comparison, Sun continues to use the term "ontology," but like Heidegger, he is reinterpreting "being" as a way of subverting substance ontology and, in so doing, is trying to establish a new understanding of what is most basic in the human experience. Sun is highly appreciative of Heidegger's substantial attempt to overcome the traditional, entrenched ontological assumptions that have persisted within the Western philosophical narrative from its origins in classical Greek philosophy. At the same time, in his revisionist Confucian reading of *Dasein* as "being-between-the-generations," he is able go beyond Heidegger's Western limits by creating a much-expanded hermeneutical circle that includes the processual sensibilities of Confucian zoetological thinking. Sun not only temporalizes *Dasein* in a way that is insufficiently in evidence in Heidegger, but he also contextualizes and humanizes *Dasein* by locating it within the warmth of vital and continuing family relations. Again, Sun argues for the important role of somaticity in the transmission of a living cultural tradition, and how *Dasein* as "being-between-the-generations" serves as a conduit for "emulation" and embodiment in the "teaching and learning" that is the substance of the Chinese civilization. Like Heidegger, death is an important theme in Sun's reconstruction, but for him the discussion focuses on how ancestral sacrifices have served to galvanize familial institutions as the medium through which a living civilization is embodied and transmitted from one generation to the next.

What I would like to add to Sun's novel and compelling elaboration on Heidegger's *Dasein* is further discussion on two related themes that he draws upon from classical Confucian philosophy, (1) the centrality of "family reverence" (*xiao* 孝) as the prime moral imperative in this continuing civilization, and (2) the way in which "family reverence" is rooted historically and philosophically in the seasonal practices of ancestral sacrifices (*jisi* 祭祀). Indeed, the dynamics of *xiao*, conventionally translated as "filial piety," that has a key role in effecting social, political, and cosmic order through the intergenerational embodiment and transmission of a living culture has too often been dismissed in the commentarial literature as a prime example of hierarchical and oppressive power relations. Given that Confucian philosophy has so often failed to live up to its own premises, this is certainly a legitimate historical concern. But it is also too simple, and does not do justice to the phenomenon. Again, there is from the highest antiquity the singular importance that ancestral sacrifices has had in setting the root from which the Confucian civilization would continue to grow. These ancestral sacrifices were the occasion for the evolving institutionalization of ritualized living in family and community (*li* 禮) that, lifting human life out of its animality, served to aestheticize the human experience. Again, the development of the written language that codified ritual practices around a robust cluster of terms now used to express the Confucian vision of the moral life is closely associated with these same sacrificial performances.

What I want to do in my response to Sun Xiangchen is to provide the backstory that will enable the reader to appreciate more fully Sun's presentation of Confucian philosophy's importantly different "ontology" or first philosophy. To begin with, *xiao* 孝 as the prime moral imperative in this continuing Confucian tradition has conventionally been rendered into English as "filial piety," but Henry Rosemont and I in our translation of the *Classic of Family Reverence* (*Xiaojing* 孝經) have chosen to translate it as "family reverence." What recommends "family reverence" as a translation over filial piety is that, in degree, it disassociates *xiao* from the duty to God implied by "piety" and from the notion of unilateral obedience that would follow from it. "Family reverence" is collateral, with the elder generation receiving appropriate deference from their younger members within their family lineages, and the younger generation deriving sustained pleasure from deferring to and emulating those elders who in their own embodiment of the tradition have given both meaning and substance to the lives of those who come after them. The term "family reverence" at the same time retains the sacred connotations that are certainly at play in the ritualized culture as it evolved around ancestral sacrifices.

As Sun Xiangchen has pointed out, the collaterality of "familial reverence" (*xiao* 孝) is captured in the composition of the character itself, constituted as it is by the combination of the graph for "elders" (*lao* 老) and that for "offspring, son, daughter, child, youth" (*zi* 子). As a term, *xiao* expresses quite explicitly Sun's reinterpretation of *Dasein* from "being-in-the-world" to "being-between-the-generations." Indeed, *xiao* has immediate reference to our lived experience within the narrative of succeeding generations as we remember our own parents and grandparents, and as we attend to our own children and grandchildren. *Xiao* quite literally describes and makes normative the lived roles and relationships that constitute the communities of elders and young people across successive generations, both in the thick relations that obtain between the present generation and those generations that have gone before, and in the responsibility the present generation must acknowledge for those yet to come. *Xiao* references the continuing process of physical and cultural embodiment from one generation to the next, the inseparability of grandparents and grandchildren, of fathers and daughters, of progenitors and progeny, and underscores the fact that such familial roles can only be learned and lived together. As with terms such as "consummate persons/conduct" (*ren* 仁) that resist any simple formulaic understanding, *xiao* too requires us to access and to build upon our own existential sense of what it means to live our specific and usually hierarchical roles as they evolve over a lifetime within this family and this community.

When we examine the earliest form of the character for "elders" (*lao* 老) as it appears on the oracle bones, we find that it depicts an old person with long, disheveled hair, leaning on a walking stick 𠂤, bringing immediately to mind the indelible photographs of Albert Einstein with his dandelion hair.[128] In the small seal script this same graph for "elders" becomes stylized as 耂, anticipating its present graphic form as 老. In comparing this character for "elders" (*lao*) with the earliest instance we have of the character for "family reverence" (*xiao*) itself as it is found on the later bronzes 𢾑, we discover that the image of a "young person" (*zi* 子) has quite literally taken the place of the walking stick as the support upon which the elders can lean, thereby constituting this *xiao* character as "elders" being supported by their "young."[129] While *xiao* certainly references the respect, aid, and comfort that succeeding older generations can enjoy from the progeny that come after them, the complement flows in the other direction as well. That is, *xiao* is also the vital process whereby the members of the younger generation are transformed into and become an always novel yet persistent embodied variant of those elders to whom they have deferred. The older generation is a reservoir of culture from whom the succeeding generation can draw sustenance and meaning, and in so doing, this younger generation provides their progenitors with a conduit that allows them to live on both in the bodies and in the lived, cultural experience of a continuing lineage. This then is how this key term "family reverence" (*xiao*) is able to convey Sun's interpretation of *Dasein* as "being-between-the-generations" in its vital, physical, cultural, and existential sense.

---

128. Kwan, "Database," 甲骨文合集 CHANT 0039A.

129. Kwan, "Database," 西周晚期 CHANT 3937.

We might elaborate upon Sun's appeal to how *xiao* expresses the sense of rootedness in the patterns of moral education and growth that follow from it. In the *Classic of Family Reverence*, Confucius begins by elevating *xiao* to be Confucian philosophy's highest moral imperative, declaring that this "way of family reverence" is the very substance of morality and education: "It is family reverence (*xiao*) that is the root of moral virtuosity (*de*), and whence education (*jiao*) itself is born."[130] The image of *xiao* as the root of the Confucian project in its aspiring to consummatory conduct in one's roles and relations (*ren* 仁) is made explicit in one familiar passage from the *Analects*: "Exemplary persons (*junzi*) concentrate their efforts on the root, for the root having been properly set, the vision of the moral life (*dao*) emerges therefrom. As for family reverence (*xiao*) and fraternal deference (*ti*), these are, I suspect, the root of becoming consummate in one's roles and relations (*ren*)."[131]

What then does it mean to take the practical activities of revering family members (*xiao* 孝) and of deferring appropriately to elders (*ti* 弟) to be the root (*ben* 本) of becoming consummate in one's roles and relations (*ren* 仁)? Indeed, much commentarial ink has been spilled on trying to argue against the explicit claim found in this passage that "family reverence" (*xiao*) is the "root" of "consummate conduct" (*ren*). Zhu Xi 朱熹 himself in his commentary on the *Analects* worries over this same issue and endorses the interpretation of his philosophical predecessors, the Cheng brothers 二程, who go to great lengths in challenging this reading. The Cheng brothers in their commentary insist that since *ren* is integral to "human nature" itself, it must be prior to *xiao*, and that *xiao* rather than serving as a resource to actually "become" *ren* only provides us with a forum in which to "practice" *ren*.[132] To this end, they introduce a distinction between "practicing *ren*" (*xingren* 行仁) and "becoming *ren*" (*weiren* 為仁), ascribing the former to *xiao*. *Xiao* for the Cheng brothers must be the fruit of consummatory conduct rather than its root.

But the claim in the *Analects* that *ren* is actually "rooted" in "family reverence" can be argued for in many different ways. To begin with, there are few persons consummate or otherwise who are not constituted by and grow themselves in their family relations. Hence, the distinction between "family reverence" (*xiao*) and consummate conduct (*ren*) as

---

130. *Classic of Family Reverence* 1: 子曰：夫孝，德之本也，教之所由生也。

131. *Analects* 1.2: 君子務本, 本立而道生. 孝弟也者, 其為仁之本與.

132. See the discussion in Ames, *Confucian Role Ethics*, 88–90.

these terms describe "human becomings" is aspectual rather than being analytic or exclusive and are simply referencing two ways of looking at the same vital process.

Again, the alternative graphic form of the character *ren* 仁 itself found on the bamboo strips recovered in a recent archaeological find is often characterized in the scholarly literature as "the representation of *ren* as the inseparability of lived body and heartmind" (*shenxinheyideren* 身心合一的仁). In fact, this alternative graphic form of *ren* is composed of a woman's pregnant body *shen* ▇ with the graph "heartmind" (*xin* 心) beneath it, expressing the "twoness" of *ren* in perhaps its most profound familial sense.[133] Clearly, any conception of family must begin from woman with child, and thus, as this graphic form would suggest, any notion of consummatory moral conduct must have its entry point in those family relations in which we learn to love by being loved. In Confucian philosophy, the "natural propensities" (*xing* 性) that serve as a Confucian alternative to some fixed, essential, and universal understanding of "human nature" are at birth a vital matrix of prosocial relations constitutive of infants within the narratives of family and community: that is, in their vital roles as sons and daughters, nieces and nephews, cousins and playmates. These relations once activated serve as the locus for their lifelong project of cultivating themselves as morally competent persons.

"Family reverence" (*xiao*) certainly entails deference to elders. Confucius repeatedly insists on the importance of compliance when the young are serving their elders in family and community, and on a sense of duty in carrying out official responsibilities at court. He makes clear the continuing weight and substance of deferential conduct throughout one's life when in the *Analects* he says: "Those today who are filial are considered so because they are able to provide for their parents. But even dogs and horses are given that much care. If you do not respect your parents, what is the difference?"[134] While Confucius is surely claiming that such patterns of interpersonal behavior are necessary for family flourishing and societal harmony, he is equally guiding his protégés toward living the life of deference as a path of spiritual cultivation in which appropriate conduct expressed through a reverential attitude toward family elders and, by extension, to the ancestors and cultural heroes, is an opportunity for personal elevation and refinement.

---

133. Kwan, "Database," 西周中期 CHANT 246.

134. *Analects* 2.7: 今之孝者, 是謂能養. 至於犬馬, 皆能有養; 不敬, 何以別乎?

It is important to note that in promoting the family as the pervasive model of order, the Confucian worldview does not accept that hierarchical social institutions are necessarily pernicious, or that simple egalitarianism should have an uncritical value. In respect of a perceived tension between equality and hierarchy, three points of clarification on the idea of deference are needed. First, concerning hierarchy, we must resist any simplistic equation between family reverence (*xiao*) and blind obedience. Family reverence focused on the bottom-up deference children owe their elders must be distinguished clearly from paterfamilias that we associate with Roman law as the juridical *patria potestas* or power and privilege of the father. Indeed, there are times when being truly filial within the family, like being a loyal minister at court, requires courageous remonstrance (*jian* 諫) rather than automatic compliance. And indeed, with this doctrine of *xiao*, initiating such remonstrance is not perceived as a possibility or an option one might choose to exercise but as a stern if not sacred obligation one owes to one's seniors. Even with respect to one's own person, there is also a space for "self-remonstrating." Built into the vital, relational "two-ness" of consummate persons/conduct (*ren* 仁) as it is rooted in *xiao*, is the cultivation of a critical self-awareness and a sense of shame that would provide a perspective from which to critique one's own roles as they are lived within family and community.

The *Classic of Family Reverence* is a conversation between Confucius and Master Zeng, who in the fullness of time is to become the paragon of family reverence in the Confucian tradition. Master Zeng, having benefited from a full fourteen chapters of the Master's instructions on *xiao*, asks the Master explicitly if strict obedience is the substance of family reverence: "Master Zeng said, 'Parental love (*ai*), reverence and respect (*jing*), seeing to the well-being of one's parents, and raising one's name (*ming*) high for posterity—on these topics I have received your instructions. I would presume to ask whether children can be deemed filial (*xiao*) by obeying every command of their father.' "[135] Confucius responds to Master Zeng's query with a disappointed impatience, making the argument that such an uncritical attitude of automatic compliance with the dictates of one's elders, far from being the substance of family reverence, can on the contrary be a source of gross immorality in conduct. An exasperated Confucius complains

---

135. *Classic of Family Reverence* 15: 曾子曰: "若夫慈愛、恭敬、安親、揚名, 則聞命矣. 敢問子從父之令, 可謂孝乎?"

"What on earth are you saying? What on earth are you saying?" said the Master." . . . If confronted by reprehensible behavior on his father's part, a son has no choice but to remonstrate with his father, and if confronted by reprehensible behavior on his ruler's part, a minister has no choice but to remonstrate with his ruler. Hence, remonstrance is the only response to immorality. How could simply obeying the commands of one's father be deemed filial?"[136]

Indeed, the *Xunzi* as a later Confucian text takes on this same issue of automatic compliance, and devotes an entire chapter to multiple stories providing examples of how blind obedience to the older generation, far from constituting family reverence, offends against this very same value by consistently producing dire consequences.[137]

A second point to be made here in clarifying the meaning of deference entailed by family reverence is that the locus of one's immediate family is only its beginning. *Xiao* must become a pattern of reverential conduct that, with unrelenting attention, is extended out from family to include all members of the community and polity, and ultimately even to nature itself. Given that morality, simply put, is growth in relations, deference has a profoundly vital function as a necessary condition for such growth. Within the human experience, *xiao* is nothing less than the motive force that drives the intergenerational transmission and extension of the living cultural tradition itself.

In the first chapter of the *Classic of Family Reverence*, it declares that "family reverence begins in service to your parents, continues in service to your lord, and culminates in distinguishing yourself in the world."[138] Again, in the chapter entitled the "Three Powers," *xiao* has cosmic reference, correlating the relationships that obtain among the heavens, the earth, and the human world within this *xiao* moral imperative. It is because these three powers are mutually implicated in each other that such cosmic relations, providing as they do a context for the human experience, have themselves a moral aspect. The human institutions of

---

136. *Classic of Family Reverence* 15: 子曰: "是何言與! 是何言與! . . . 當不義, 則子不可以不爭於父, 臣不可以不爭於君. 故當不義則爭之. 從父之令, 又焉得為孝乎!"

137. See *Xunzi* chapter 29.

138. *Classic of Family Reverence* 1: 夫孝始於事親, 中於事君, 終於立身.

family and state are isomorphic with the cosmic order, with state and cosmos being perceived as simulacra of family flourishing:

> "Incredible—the profundity of family reverence!" declared Master Zeng. "Indeed," said the Master. "Family reverence is the constancy of the heavenly cycles, the appropriate responsiveness (*yi*) of the earth, and the proper conduct of the people. It is the constant workings of the heavens and the earth that the people model themselves upon. Taking the illumination (*ming*) of the heavens as their model and making the most of the earth's resources, they bring the empire into accord (*shun*). This is the reason that education can be effective without being severe, and political administration can maintain proper order without being harsh."[139]

As Sun Xiangchen has argued, the transformative power of education exploits the cognate relationship between the characters for "education" (*jiao* 教) and "family reverence" (*xiao* 孝). As we have seen, the graph for "family reverence" (*xiao* 孝) itself is constituted by "elder" (*lao* 老) and "younger" (*zi* 子). The graph for "education" (*jiao* 教) then adds to *xiao* 孝 the "branch" radical (*zhi* 攴) as we find on the oracle bones 𣀔 that, according to commentators, references the teacher's rod used as a prop for counting and calculating numbers.[140] Importantly the character *jiao* underscores the centrality of familial reverence in the actual content and goals of proper education, while the cognate relationship *jiao* has with "emulating" (*xiao* 效) emphasizes the modeling role that the elder generation has for its progeny. As Sun Xiangchen has observed, the *Shuowen* lexicon captures these associations in defining *jiao* as "what is being practiced by the elders as it is emulated by those who follow."[141]

The third point to be made regarding *xiao* and deference is that this notion of *xiao* can be appealed to in important measure to reconcile the tension between hierarchy and equality. *Xiao* construes the

---

139. *Classic of Family Reverence* 7: 曾子曰: "甚哉! 孝之大也." 子曰: "夫孝、天之經也, 地之義也, 民之行也. 天地之經而民是則之, 則天之明, 因地之利, 以順天下. 是以其教不肅而成, 其政不嚴而治.

140. Kwan, "Database," 甲骨文合集 CHANT 3233.

141. 上所施下所效也.

evolving relations that obtain among infant, adult person, grandparent, and ancestor not in an egalitarian way but in terms of the affordances provided by the relational equity among these roles that *xiao* as patterns of deference requires. Relational equity begins from respect for the uniqueness of each person and each stage they have achieved in the shared human narrative, where the infant having her glass of milk to strengthen her bones is analogous to grandpa having his glass of wine to guarantee a good night's sleep. Further, such affordances allow for the inclusion of real differences at every level of growth and, in providing a space for the complexity of the human experience, are ultimately the source of an achieved diversity.

The opening chapter of the *Classic of Family Reverence* provides us with the familiar pattern found consistently in the Confucian literature of rootedness and radial progression from a determinate center to an unbounded extreme. This circle expands outward from protecting one's own immediate physicality to the heights of distinguishing oneself as a model for the generations: "Your physical person with its hair and skin are received from your parents. Vigilance in not allowing anything to do injury to your person is where family reverence begins. Distinguishing yourself and walking the proper way (*dao*) in the world; raising your name high for posterity and thereby bringing esteem to your father and mother—it is in these things that family reverence finds its consummation."[142] Family reverence begins with respect shown to your own embodied person as what is closest at hand, extends radially with concern shown in caring for your family and kin, and then culminates in dedicated service to your ruler and to posterity. Of course, this progression in personal cultivation is symbiotic rather than sequential, with each level of achievement being implicated in the others.

Again, with respect to the theme of rootedness, this first tenet of familial reverence for persons to protect the body that has been entrusted to them by their parents and ancestors places the solemn responsibility on them to return this body to their progenitors intact. An abbreviated form of the character for body (*ti* 體) that is now used as the simplified version in Chinese and Japanese is *ti* 体, combining the graphs for "person" (*ren* 人) and the ideograph for "root, trunk" (*ben* 本). Our lexical sources discourage the claim that 体 is an abbreviated form

---

142. *Chinese Classic of Family Reverence* 1: 身體髮膚, 受之父母, 不敢毀傷, 孝之始也. 立身行道, 揚名於後世, 以顯父母, 孝之終也. 夫孝, 始於事親, 中於事君, 終於立身.

of 體 and, in reading the character 体 as *ben* rather than *ti*, interpret it as referencing a "stout fellow." Even so, this association between the two graphic forms can at least provide us with a useful heuristic. The first and hugely significant factor we must consider in the process of cultivating a personal identity is the extent to which the structures of our understanding are "rooted" in (*ti* 体) and shaped by the fact of the ongoing internalizing and "embodying" (*ti* 體) processes of our always "discursive" bodies with their visceral connection to the world.

Confucian role ethics in substance is perpetuated through family lineages that have complex political, economic, and religious functions. There are two cognate characters that are integral to the dynamics of "family reverence" (*xiao*) in the intergenerational transmission of the continuities of the family lineage: *ti* 體 ("embodying," "body," "forming and shaping," "category," "class") and *li* 禮 ("achieving propriety in one's roles and relations," "ritual"). Without the formal and determinate dimension provided by embodied living (*ti* 體) and by the social grammar afforded by meaningful roles and relations (*li* 禮), there is a very real question as to whether the significant refinement that is aspired to through such embodied life-forms would even be possible. Put simply, determinate forms in their many different variations—body, ritual, language, the institutions of family and ancestral reverence, and so on—are a necessary condition for cultural refinement.

But while the charge in this tradition to keep the body intact is certainly referring to a person's own carnal physicality, it also lends itself to an important broader, cultural reading. That is, each succeeding generation has the responsibility for inheriting and maintaining the "corpus" of culture that it comes to embody, as whole and alive. The "lived body" (*ti* 體) and its "embodied living" (*li* 禮) is the narrative site of the conveyance and the continuing enhancement of the culture through which a living civilization is perpetuated: that is, the persistence of its language, its mores and values, its religious rituals, its aesthetics of cooking, song, and dance, and so on.

At a genealogical level, our bodies and the process of human procreativity lead to the birthing of distinctive and unique persons from those who have come before. And the "embodied knowing" and "living on" that is taking place in this process is not meant merely rhetorically. Even more obvious and significant than the transmission of physical likenesses are the continuities of the cultural tradition itself: its language, institutions, and values. Within this ongoing, overlapping process of intergenerational embodiment, the earlier progenitors literally persist in this continuing process as they are transmuted into their progeny. That is, while persons emerge to become specifically who they are as unique individuals, the parents, grandparents, and ancestors of such persons continue to live on in them, most obviously in their physical appearance but also in terms of how they think, feel, and live their lives. And the eventful process continues as both they and their progeny live on in their later descendants. We have proposed a focus-field language as a way of thinking about the relationship between particulars and the totality. This foregrounding and backgrounding of particular and totality seems immediately relevant to a genealogical holography in which the entire field of the physical and cultural experience is implicated in the moment-by-moment narrative of each person.

In the Confucian tradition, the body is understood as an inheritance from a family lineage and as a vital current in a genealogical stream that reaches back to the remotest ancestors. The body infused as it is with culture brings with it a sense of continuity, contribution, belonging, and importantly a sense of felt worth as precisely those feelings that most immediately inspire our religious sensibilities. The *Record of Rites* gives an account of this process: "The Master said: 'Among those things born of the heavens and nurtured by the earth, nothing is grander than the human being. For the parents to give birth to one's whole person, and for one to return this person to them intact is what can be called family reverence (*xiao*). And avoiding the desecration of your body and disgrace to your person is what can be called keeping your person whole.'"[143] To show respect for our own bodies—both the physical body and its function as the locus of the cultural corpus that our family lineage has bequeathed to us—is to show reverence for the ancestors embodied therein and for the relationship we have with them. Alternatively, to disrespect our bodies by treating them lightly is to be doubly shameless: we first fail to acknowledge our debt to our family lineage, and further, we bring shame instead of honor upon those who have come before. What is significant in this reflection on our embodied persons is that physically, socially, and religiously, our bodies are a specific matrix of nested relations that are a collaboration between our own persons and the extended web of our many familial, social, cultural, and natural rela-

---

143. *A Concordance to the* Liji 25.36/128/6: 夫子曰: 天之所生, 地之所養, 無人為大. 父母全而生之, 子全而歸之, 可謂孝矣. 不虧其體, 不辱其身, 可謂全矣.

tions. Nobody and no "body"—not the vital, the carnal, nor the discursive body—does anything by itself.

There is an important scene recounted in the *Analects* in which Master Zeng as the paragon of family reverence is on his deathbed surrounded by his students, and he expresses to them a deep sense of relief in having come to the end of his life with his body still intact:

> Master Zeng was ill, and summoned his students to him, saying, "Look at my feet! Look at my hands!
> The *Book of Songs* says:
> Fearful! Trembling!
> As if peering over a deep abyss,
> As if walking across thin ice.
> It is only from this moment hence that I can at last know relief, my young friends."[144]

This passage is usually and quite properly interpreted as Master Zeng expressing profound relief that he has been able to live his life without issue to a point where he can now anticipate returning his carnal body to his ancestors. But the first chapter of the *Classic of Family Reverence* provides us with important commentary on this exchange between the dying Master Zeng and his students that might prompt us to read something more into his concern for his body. The *Classic of Family Reverence* certainly does declare that "your physical person—literally, 'your vital and discursive body' (*shenti* 身體)—with its hair and skin are received from your parents." But as I have suggested, when the text goes on to assert that "vigilance in not allowing anything to do injury to your person is where family reverence begins," it perhaps lends itself to an understanding of "body" in a broader cultural sense. I would argue that Confucius in elaborating upon the importance of "family reverence" (*xiao*) here is not simply referencing respect for the carnal body but is also alluding to the function that the body has as the site of intergenerational cultural transmission—that is, the "vital body" and the "discursive body" too. Confucius defines the substance of education as the serious responsibility of each generation to transmit the culture in its fullness and without diminution to the generations that follow. In so

---

144. *Analects* 8.3, *Book of Songs* 195: 曾子有疾, 召門弟子曰: "啟予足! 啟予手!《詩》云 戰戰兢兢, 如臨深淵, 如履薄冰. 而今而後, 吾知免夫! 小子!

doing, he reinforces his claim in this same chapter that *xiao* is indeed "the root of human virtuosity (*de*), and whence education (*jiao*) itself is born." Thus, keeping the cultural "body" intact is the process of embodying the tradition fully, drawing upon it creatively as a resource for distinguishing oneself in the world, and adding dividends to this compounding resource by establishing a name for oneself and one's family that will be remembered by posterity. In this way, the evolving corpus of the cultural tradition—the civilization itself—is continued in each person, embodied in each succeeding generation, and thus perpetuated for the benefit of those who follow.

In this Confucian tradition, the intergenerational transmission of civilization is the responsibility of two different but related conceptions of "family" (*jia* 家). There is the continuing civilizing function of the *daotong* 道統 or "orthodox way" embodied as it is in the elite social stratum of "the literati family lineage" or *rujia* 儒家. And then more broadly, but certainly informed by the orthodox way of the literati lineage, there is the inclusive *xiaodao* 孝道 or "way of family reverence" that guides the lives of everyone within their extended family lineages or *jiazu* 家族. For a family to be without progeny is not only a failure to continue the blood lineage but also a failure to produce the human conduits necessary for the transmission of the living cultural tradition. It is certainly an offense against a person's parents for whom the continuity of sacrificial offerings will be broken, but it is also a transgression against the collective ancestors who were the distant founders and transmitters of the civilization itself. Given that Confucian morality is nothing other than "procreativity" (*shengsheng*) as continuing growth in one's relationships, to lack the progeny needed to attend to one's ancestors in this broadest cultural sense can and has often been construed as an acute moral lapse.[145]

---

145. That family reverence (*xiao*) requires having progeny has and continues to be read as an exclusionary Confucian imperative that precludes alternative preferences and lifestyles. An alternative interpretation would argue that although this pattern might serve as a general precept, at the same time the relations between persons and world are too complex for such a simple answer. It would insist that the Confucian values of inclusiveness, relational equity, and an optimizing symbiosis as the source of diversity override such a conservative view. Indeed, the commitment to getting the most out of the creative possibilities of the human experience would require that, in order to be true to its own premises, Confucian social and political values be progressive and accommodating of an always evolving understanding of persons, family, and community.

Kinship as the root of human relations is defined by the moral imperatives of "family reverence" (*xiao* 孝) and "fraternal deference" (*ti* 悌), and as Sun Xiangchen has pointed out, primal "family feeling" (*qinqin* 親親) is the ultimate and underlying source of the second order cluster of terms that define the Confucian vision of the moral life. Friendship as the way of extending this pattern of kinship relations to include non-relatives is pursued through an ethic of "putting oneself in the place of others" (*shu* 恕), "commitment and resolve" (*cheng* 誠), "doing one's utmost" (*zhong* 忠), and "making good on one's word" (*xin* 信).[146] All such ethical values are aspired to as the way of reconciling the tensions among and promoting the accommodations made within the specific personal relationships of family members and community.

There is a primacy afforded vital relationality that is exemplified by the centrality given to family reverence (*xiao*) as the prime moral imperative. If *religare* as the Latin root of "religious" does mean "binding tightly" (as reflected in its cognates such as "ligament," "obligation," "league," and "ally")—then we can see that "family reverence" (*xiao*) so described has a profoundly religious import as well, referencing as it does those familial, communal, and ancestral bonds that together constitute a resilient and enduring social fabric.[147] And it is this profoundly religious sense of "binding tightly"—that is, the strengthening of family and communal bonds—that we would appeal to in interpreting the Master's autobiographically revealing response when Zilu asks him what he would most like to do: "I would like to bring peace and contentment to the aged, to share relationships of trust and confidence with friends, and to love and protect the young."[148]

---

146. See for example *Analects* 1.4 and 1.8. There is an ambiguity in the expression "associates and friends" (*pengyou* 朋友) as it is used in the documents of the Western Zhou and Spring and Autumn period where these texts do not distinguish nonrelated friends from agnatic male relatives—that is, paternal relatives such as brothers, uncles, nephews, cousins, and so on. Some scholars have argued that *pengyou* becomes a term commonly and specifically used to denote nonkin friends only in the Warring States period. See Yiqun Zhou, *Festival, Feasts, and Gender Relations in Ancient China and Greece*, 110–111 and 137–139.

147. Sarah F. Hoyt, "The Etymology of Religion," *Journal of the American Oriental Society* 32, no. 2 (1912): 126–129, provides some interesting textual evidence for this very old and sometimes disputed etymology.

148. *Analects* 5.26: 子曰: "老者安之, 朋友信之, 少者懷之."

Sun Xiangchen traces this Confucian family-centered religiousness back to the institution of ancestral sacrifices. On the oracle bones the character for "ancestral sacrifice" (*ji* 祭) is written as 𦥔 and on the bronzes as ▨,[149] where in both cases the characters are a pictograph of a hand grasping sacrificial meat with the several dots representing drops of blood that serve as an offering to the spirits. The later addition of *shi* 示 on the bronzes is an image of the sacrificial tablet of the ancestors or spirits to whom the offering is being made. Animal sacrifice is fundamental in this Confucian "zoetology" or "art of living" in that the solemn liberating of the life of the venerated sacrificial animal and the sharing of the meat both with the ancestors and the living community are themselves the sanctification and celebration of life itself. It would seem that such regularized discursive practices are replete with personal, social, political, and religious meaning. The centrality of ancestors in the sacrifices, for example, speaks to the continuity of a shared genealogical identity at every level, providing an occasion for the human and spiritual worlds to commune. The importance of this custom is reflected in the fact that the complex writing system itself with the five thousand characters recovered from the oracle bones dating back to the Shang dynasty had its origins in these same practices and, once developed, was then used in the compilation of the canonical texts that set the root for the continuing growth of a literate civilization. As pointed out by historian Zhou Yiqun, a full 20 percent of the *Book of Songs* is devoted to remembering such ancestral sacrifices and the banquets as part of the ceremony that followed them.[150]

The *Analects* in describing the priorities needed for effective governance, ascribes importance to four areas of responsibility: the common people, food, mourning, and sacrifice.[151] Again it states that Confucius "would not kowtow on receiving gifts from friends, even those as lavish as a horse or a carriage, with the sole exception of sacrificial meat."[152] The responsibility of continuing sacrificial practices to ancestors has high value in an aristocratic tradition that takes "family reverence" (*xiao* 孝) as it is expressed through intergenerational transmission of the

---

149. Kwan, "Database," CHANT 甲骨文編 and 春秋晚期 CHANT 245.

150. Zhou Yiqun, *Festivals, Feasts, and Gender Relations in Ancient China and Greece*, 104.

151. *Analects* 20.1: 民、食、喪、祭.

152. *Analects* 10.21: 朋友之饋, 雖車馬, 非祭肉, 不拜.

cultural legacy as its prime moral imperative. Throughout the Confucian texts sacrifice, as a sign of deference to and respect for both ancestors and the cultural heroes who have come before, is taken as an integral aspect of the "ritual propriety" (*li* 禮) that undergirds the continuity of the civilization itself. The graphs for other key philosophical terms are derived from these sacrifices. "Optimizing appropriateness" (*yi* 義), for example, is constituted by a sacrificial sheep (*yang* 羊) and the dagger-ax (*ge* 戈) that is used to dispatch and bleed the sheep for the ceremony. Again the same character *yi* is itself cognate with *yi* 儀 as meaning ceremonial decorum, as well as with the animal of a pure color that has been reared specifically for the sacrifice (*xi* 犧).

From earliest times, sacrifice was a communal affair that through the formal exercise of ritual propriety reflected the proper social hierarchies and protocols. There is a continuity between the role of the ritual priest, the first in the descent group, and the head of state as they reside in the same person. In an extended passage in *Focusing the Familiar*, Confucius rehearses a detailed account of how such practices were used by the former sage-kings to establish and reinforce a structure of deference and refinement within the community, and to promote a religious sense of worth and belonging among their peoples:

> The Master said: "King Wu and the Duke of Zhou—there indeed were two thoroughly filial exemplars (*xiao*)! Family reverence (*xiao*) means being good at continuing the purposes of one's predecessors and at maintaining their ways. In the proper season, they made repairs to the ancestral temple, laid out the sacrificial vessels of their ancestors, exhibited the robes used in funerary observances, and sacrificed from the newly harvested crops. They used ritual propriety (*li*) in the ancestral hall as their way of arranging the tablets of the departed generations appropriately on the left and right sides of the temple; they deferred to the titles of office as their way of recognizing degrees of nobility; they used the sequence of the services as their way of distinguishing those most worthy; they used the drinking pledges in which inferiors toast superiors as their way of reaching down to include the lowliest, and they took into consideration the color of the hair as their way of seating participants according to their seniority. Taking up the places of their forbearers, carrying out their ritual observances

(*li*), playing their music (*yue*), showing respect to those whom they esteemed, extending their affection to those of whom they were fond, serving the dead as though they were living, and serving those who are long departed as though they were still here—this then is family reverence in its highest form.[153]

This same important passage concludes by echoing the claim in the *Analects* that those who really know how to explain the most venerated of these sacrifices could rule the empire as though it were a bauble in their hand: "Ritual observances performed in the ancestral temple are ways of making sacrifices to one's forbearers. For those who have a clear understanding of the sacrificial observances to the heavens and the earth, and of the meaning of the Grand *di* sacrifice and the autumnal *chang* sacrifice performed in the ancestral temple, the governing of the empire is as easy as turning something over in the palm of their hand."[154]

153. *Focusing the Familiar* 19: 子曰: "武王、周公, 其達孝矣乎! 夫孝者: 善繼人之志, 善述人之事者也. 春、秋修其祖廟, 陳其宗器, 設其裳衣, 薦其時食. 宗廟之禮, 所以序昭穆也; 序爵, 所以辨貴賤也; 序事, 所以辨賢也; 旅酬下為上, 所以逮賤也; 燕毛, 所以序齒也. 踐其位, 行其禮, 奏其樂, 敬其所尊, 愛其所親, 事死如事生, 事亡如事存, 孝之至也."

154. *Analects* 3.11: "宗廟之禮, 所以祀乎其先也. 明乎郊社之禮、禘嘗之義, 治國其如示諸掌乎!"

Epilogue

In my best effort to bring the distinction between ontological and zoeto-logical thinking as two alternative first philosophies into clearer focus, there is an important caveat that I hasten to make. This distinction must not be construed as a simple, "either/or" comparison of Chinese and Western thinking. The classical Greek causal ontology that we can trace back at least to Parmenides has certainly had a formative and persistent impact on the evolution of mainstream Western philosophy and culture, but at the same time, there are many examples of zoetological thinking in the countercurrents within the Western narrative itself. There is the pragmatic if not expedient logic of political survival formulated by Niccolò Machiavelli; the "new science" and its emphasis on rhetoric, history, and a philosophy of the imagination posited by the anti-Cartesian humanist Giambattista Vico; the identification of God with nature (*Deus sive Natura*) that was the signature of Baruch Spinoza's pantheism; the transition from poetics to the engraving of images by the antinomian William Blake; the transcendentalism of Romantic figures such as William Wordsworth and Samuel Taylor Coleridge; the deference paid to Ralph Waldo Emerson as the hero of William James and John Dewey, who both took him to be a precursor of their own philosophical pragmatism; to name but a few.[1]

Even more significant than this counterculture, however, is the fact that in the second half of the nineteenth century, a seismic shift occurs within the Western philosophical narrative itself that takes substance ontology with all of

---

1. For an interesting argument for cross-cultural influences on the emergence of zoeto-logical thinking within British culture, see Yu Liu's *From Chinese Cosmology to English Romanticism: The Intricate Journey of a Monistic Idea* (Columbia: University of South Carolina Press, 2023). See also Martin Powers, *China and England: The Preindustrial Struggle for Justice in Word and Image* (London: Routledge, 2020).

its implications as the specific target of its denunciation. Taking Nietzsche's proclamation that "God is dead" as a signpost in this Western turn toward zoetological thinking, I would argue that many if not most of the various movements that have defined Western philosophy in the twentieth and twenty-first centuries have been a sustained attempt to extricate themselves from this old and now deemed fallacious way of thinking.

In the twentieth and twenty-first centuries, following in the wake of this full-blown revolution taking place in the Western philosophical narrative, various forms of process thinking have emerged to declare themselves a devastating if not a fatal critique of ontological thinking. When William James published his Lowell lectures as a monograph entitled *Pragmatism* that launched pragmatism as a philosophical movement, he wrote to his brother Henry, declaring, "I shouldn't be surprised if ten years hence it should be rated as 'epoch-making' . . . something quite like the protestant revolution."[2] In this unfolding and yet unfinished story, process philosophy has set a new direction in philosophical thinking that is committed to inoculating our cultural self-understanding against what it takes to have been a long-term chronic illness—that is, the metaphysical quest for a permanent and unchanging "substance" (*on*) and ontology's promise of an epistemology of truth and certainty.

Indeed, the revolution that has taken place within the Western philosophical community might be fairly described in the following terms. This intellectual insurrection is an attempt to set aside substance ontology and the metaphysics of a transcendent universalism that issues from it, to cast off the logic of the changeless that attends such universalist assumptions, and to repudiate the dualistic binaries that follow from an assumed ontological disparity between reality and appearance. Such an internal critique continues to be waged within professional Western philosophy under the many banners of process philosophy (hermeneutics, poststructuralism, postmodernism, existentialism, pragmatism, neo-Marxism, deconstructionism, feminist philosophy, and so on), taking as their shared target what Robert Solomon has called "the transcendental pretense" in its many iterations: universalism, idealism, rationalism, foundationalism, objectivism, formalism, logocentrism, essentialism, the master narrative, ontotheological thinking, "the myth of the given," and so on. Philosophers today are intent on disavowing these familiar reductionistic "isms" that have emerged over time as

---

2. William James, *The Correspondence of William James* (Charlottesville: University of Virginia Press, 1994), vol. 3, 339.

putatively novel choices on the merry-go-round of systematic philosophy. In the place of a discredited Cartesian rationalism that in its quest for objective certainty privileges the precision of clear and distinct ideas, new vocabularies of process, change, particularity, metaphor, creative advance, and indeed of productive vagueness have come increasingly into vogue. Simply put, an important direction in contemporary Western philosophy is the attempt to think process and to cultivate the practical wisdom needed for philosophy to be relevant to an always changing world order. The problem such a sea change in thinking faces, of course, has been that ontology's causal thinking, appealing as it does to something foundational in the human experience, is thoroughly entrenched in the syntax and semantics of the Indo-European languages. Even as we attempt to "speak" zoetology, these same languages continue to betray our best efforts to escape what persists as our own recalcitrant common sense.

In addition to Nietzsche's requiem for God, we might take Charles Darwin as another of the many markers in the zoetological turn of the Western philosophical narrative. Daniel Dennett in his *Darwin's Dangerous Idea* is categorical in his estimation of the power of Darwin's theory of evolution, not only for the discipline of philosophy but both constructively and deconstructively, for Western culture in the broadest possible terms. Dennett, laying his cards on the table, announces:

> If I were to give an award for the single best idea anyone has ever had, I'd give it to Darwin, ahead of Newton and Einstein and everyone else. In a single stroke, the idea of evolution by natural selection unifies the realm of life, meaning, and purpose with the realm of space and time, cause and effect, mechanism and physical law. But it is not just a wonderful scientific idea. It is a dangerous idea. . . . There are many more magnificent ideas that are also jeopardized it seems, by Darwin's idea, and they, too, may need protection.[3]

In the wake of Darwin's own great cultural revolution, Whitehead diagnoses what he calls "the fallacy of misplaced concreteness" to be an error in reasoning that is committed when the formally abstracted is taken

---

3. Daniel C. Dennett, *Darwin's Dangerous Idea: Evolution and the Meanings of Life* (New York: Simon & Schuster, 1995), 21–22.

to be what is real and concrete.[4] For Whitehead, such theorizing is fatally reductionistic, ignoring the genuine connectivity and transitivity of such "things" that animate them in the transactional events of our ordinary experience. This fallacy of misplaced concreteness is to regard abstracted entities presumed to have a simple location as being what is concrete while, at the same time, ignoring the vital and processual transitivity that attends all things in our experience of them.[5] Whitehead rehearses the history of this "fatal virus" that, under the spell of ontological thinking, has inhibited our understanding of the intrinsic, constitutive, and productive nature of relatedness. In his stern critique of the great men of our philosophical story whom he deems as having indeed misplaced concreteness, he accuses Epicurus, Plato, and Aristotle as being "unaware of the perils of abstraction" that render knowledge closed and complete.[6]

For the same Whitehead, the concept of the discrete individual is a prime and powerful example of the fallacy of misplaced concreteness said in different terms: that is, what Whitehead calls the fallacy of simple location. Simple location is the familiar and yet fallacious claim that isolating, decontextualizing, and analyzing things as simple particulars is the best way to understand the content of our experience. Allowing that persons experience each other within the narratives of events that in sum constitute our shared lives together, Whitehead is insisting that we treat persons as interpenetrating "events" rather than standing outside each other as discrete "things."

The paralogism of what Whitehead is calling alternatively the fallacies of misplaced concreteness and of simple location is in fact the same complaint being directed at the discipline of philosophy earlier by John Dewey. Dewey regards an uncritical commitment to transcendentalism in any of its various forms to be one bit of faulty reasoning so persistently exercised by the philosophical elite that he dubbed this particular *déformation profesionnelle* "*the* philosophical fallacy." Dewey's important assertion here is that, at least for the Western narrative, "the most pervasive fallacy of philosophical thinking" has been the error of ignoring the historical, developmental, and contextualizing aspects of experience—the unbounded, reflexive, and processual nature of experience itself. The methodological problem as he saw

---

4. For Whitehead's fallacy of "misplaced concreteness," see Whitehead, *Process and Reality*, 7, 18, 20.

5. Whitehead in *Process and Reality*, 137, observes: "This presupposition of individual independence is what I have elsewhere called, the 'fallacy of simple location.'"

6. Whitehead, *Modes of Thought*, 58.

it is "the abstracting of some one element from the organism which gives it meaning, and setting it up as absolute," and then proceeding to revere this one element "as the cause and ground of all reality and knowledge."[7] Simply put, *the* philosophical fallacy (or we might substitute *the* ontological fallacy) is committed whenever some outcome of a process is presumed to be antecedent to that process—and to be the foundational cause of it. Such a problem arises from the causal thinking that has given us the many variations of a "One-behind-the-many" systematic metaphysics.

Dewey would argue that *the* philosophical fallacy has arisen as a persistent error in thinking because as a tradition we have been habituated to look for knowledge in all the wrong places. Dewey, in describing this entrenched fallacy and an alternative to it, avers that "there are, indeed, but two alternative courses. We must either find the appropriate objects and organs of knowledge in the mutual interactions of changing things, or else, we *must* seek them in some transcendent and supernal region. The human mind, deliberately as it were, exhausted the logic of the changeless, the final and the transcendent, before it essayed adventure on the pathless wastes of generation and transformation."[8] What has been put at risk in philosophy's endorsing *the* philosophical fallacy as a way of thinking is of no small consequence. As we have seen, such ontological thinking threatens the notion of process itself—development, education, creativity, particularity, temporality, history, growth, progress, and so on. Whitehead argues that such causal thinking eclipses "life" as the real hopes, fears, joys, sorrows, ideas, and attitudes of flesh-and-blood human beings. For Dewey too, the human being is a social achievement, an adaptive success made possible through the applications of social intelligence. Given the reality of change, this success is always provisional, leaving us as incomplete creatures with the always new challenge of contingent circumstances. And yet this success is progressive and programmatic. "We *use* our past experiences to construct new and better ones in the future."[9]

Immediately relevant to this monograph is the fact that, in the wake of professional philosophy's rejection of ontological thinking, this ongoing reconfiguration of the discipline anticipates the growing importance of Chinese philosophy as it emerges in the twenty-first century to influence new directions that are occurring in world philosophy. In fact, we can parse

---

7. Dewey, *Early Works*, vol. 1, 162.

8. Dewey, *Essential Dewey*, vol. 1, 41.

9. Dewey, *Middle Works*, vol. 12, 134.

the trajectory of the influence of German philosophy in twentieth-century China as it has moved from Kant to Hegel, on to the phenomenology of Husserl, and most recently, to Wittgenstein and particularly, to Heidegger. The movement begins early in the twentieth century in an appeal to German philosophy as a standard of rigorous thinking that, by comparing and contrasting it with Chinese philosophy, might lend Chinese philosophy legitimacy. A century later, more recent movements in German philosophy that have been liberated from their ontological assumptions have become a resource that, through real engagement with Chinese philosophy, are serving to enrich China's own indigenous philosophical sensibilities. The good news for comparative philosophy is that these recent developments in mainstream Anglo-European philosophy are themselves giving rise to an interpretive vocabulary that promises a more productive engagement with a Chinese philosophical tradition that has never denied the reality of change. A case in point is the research efforts of the several Chinese comparative philosophers rehearsed in the last chapter of this monograph. These contemporary avatars of Chinese philosophy are good examples of how the Heideggerian critique of traditional Western ontology in particular can open up a hermeneutical space that reveals and allows further reflection upon the zoetological sensibilities inherent in traditional Chinese philosophy.

Classical Chinese cosmology, like Whitehead and Dewey, subscribes to the mantra "the only kind of creativity is situated co-creativity." And, inspired by the critiques of Whitehead and Dewey, a sustained reflection on the fact that classical ontology has little relevance for Chinese assumptions about cosmic order can pay us important philosophical dividends. The pervasive Chinese assumption about the always emergent nature of order in all of its forms speaks to the more basic question of why Chinese philosophy might at this particular historical moment provide us with a salutary intervention in the Western philosophical narrative. That is, in this classical Chinese worldview there is an alternative nuanced and sophisticated zoetological way of thinking about cosmology that can join the internal critique of transcendentalism taking place within the discipline of philosophy itself. As I have argued in this monograph, comparative cultural hermeneutics, in setting a contrast between ontological and zoetological thinking, provides us with a method for a deepening appreciation of both narratives. Chinese philosophy certainly benefits by being challenged by values that undergird liberal democracy such as autonomy, equality, personal choice, rationality, individual rights, and so on. By the same token, the newly emerging Western versions of process philosophy as they mature within their own philosophical culture can, with profit, draw both substance and critique from a Chinese tradition that has been committed to various forms of process philosophy since the beginning of its recorded history.

A second important caveat I would want to make regarding the distinction between ontological and zoetological thinking is that even though post-Darwinian Western philosophy has rejected substance ontology as a fallacious mode of thinking and, for a century now and counting, has pivoted decidedly in a zoetological direction, the earlier ontological detour did in fact produce many great things. Just to cite a few examples, there are the industrial and then technological revolutions inspired by modern science; the emancipation of human beings from theocracy by the promotion of humanistic values; the sustained liberating movements on behalf of class, gender, and racial equality; the promotion of the values of liberal democracy grounded in a doctrine of universal human rights; the transparency and rigor that comes with the Enlightenment celebration of reason; the struggle for the emancipation of humanity not only from caste and class privilege but from dogma in all of its forms. And there is much more. Again, while following the trajectory of world philosophy in giving primacy to zoetological thinking, we must at the same time allow that many of the commitments to rigor in ontological thinking such as rational argument, formal definition, objective description, categorical organization, taxonomical classification, and so on, when treated more modestly as functional techniques rather than as *the* one and only path to apodictic knowledge, continue to be an important resource for disciplining the human experience and providing it with consistency and precision.

Where then is world philosophy today? Up until a generation or two ago, the self-understanding of the mainstream professional discipline has been that philosophy is exclusively an Anglo-analytic, Continental, and perhaps in its highest form, a German undertaking. Ironically perhaps, this claim has been as true in Tokyo, Seoul, Beijing, and Delhi as it has been in Frankfurt, London, and Boston. But the tide is changing. Perhaps responding to the sea change in the economic and political order of the world, non-Western philosophy in many different forms has been moving in from the periphery, especially South Asian, East Asian, and Latin American philosophical traditions. While to declare that economically and politically there is a changing world order might be proclaiming the obvious, I would argue that this same trajectory now in an intellectual guise is less noticeable and perhaps only incipient, but it is also true within the changing composition of world philosophy.

Bibliography

Allen, R. E. *Plato's* Euthyphro *and the Earlier Theory of Forms*. London: Routledge, 1970.

Ames, Roger T. *A Conceptual Lexicon for Classical Confucian Philosophy*. Albany: State University of New York Press, 2022.

———. "The Confucian Concept of the Political, and 'Family Feeling' (*xiao* 孝) as Its Minimalist Morality." In *Formulating a Minimalist Ethic for a New Planetary Order: Alternative Cultural Perspectives*, edited by Roger T. Ames, Jin Young Lim, and Steven Y. H. Yang. Honolulu: University of Hawai'i Press, 2024.

———. *Confucian Role Ethics: A Vocabulary*. Albany: State University of New York, 2020 [rpt.].

———. *Human Becomings: Theorizing Persons for Confucian Role Ethics*. Albany: State University of New York Press, 2021.

———. "The Meaning of Body in Classical Chinese Philosophy." In *The Self as Body in Asian Theory and Practice*, edited by Roger T. Ames, Wimal Dissanayake, and Thomas P. Kasulis. Albany: State University of New York Press.

———. "Reconstructing A. C. Graham's Reading of *Mencius* on *Xing* 性: A Coda to 'The Background of the Mencian Theory of Human Nature' (1967)." In *Having a Word with Angus Graham: At Twenty-Five Years into His Immortality*, edited by Carine Defoort and Roger T. Ames. Albany: State University of New York Press, 2018.

———. *A Sourcebook in Classical Confucian Philosophy*. Albany: State University of New York Press, 2023.

———. "What Ever Happened to Wisdom? Confucian Philosophy of Process and 'Human Becomings.'" In *Star Gazing, Fire Phasing, and Healing in China: Essays in Honor of Nathan Sivin*, ed. Michael Nylan, Henry Rosemont Jr., and Li Waiyee, special issue of *Asia Major*, 3rd series, 21, part 1 (2008).

Ames, Roger T., and David L. Hall, trans. *Daodejing: Making This Life Significant*. New York: Ballantine, 2003.

Ames, Roger T., and Peter D. Hershock, eds. *Value and Values: Economics and Justice in an Age of Global Interdependence*. Honolulu: University of Hawai'i Press, 2015.

Angle, Stephen C. *Sagehood: The Contemporary Significance of Neo-Confucian Philosophy*. New York: Oxford, 2009.

Aristotle. *The Complete Works of Aristotle: The Revised Oxford Translation*. Edited by Jonathan Barnes Princeton: Princeton University Press, 1984.

Austin, J. L. *Philosophical Papers*, Oxford: Oxford University Press, 1961.

Behuniak, Jim. Book Review. Slingerland, Edward. *Mind and Body in Early China: Beyond Orientalism and the Myth of Holism*. Dao: A Journal in Comparative Philosophy 18, no. 2 (2019).

———. Response to Edward Slingerland. *Dao: A Journal in Comparative Philosophy* 18, no. 3 (2019).

Burnet, John. *Early Greek Philosophy*. London: Adam and Charles Black, 1920.

Chan, Wing-tsit. *A Source Book in Chinese Philosophy*. Princeton: Princeton University Press, 1963.

Chang, Wejen. "Classical Chinese Jurisprudence and the Development of the Chinese Legal System." *Tsinghua China Law Review* 2, no. 2 (Spring 2010).

Chen, Lai 陳來. 《竹帛 "五行" 與簡帛研究》 [Research on the five phases from silk and bamboo manuscripts]. Beijing: Sanlian, 2009.

Clippinger, John Henry. *A Crowd of One: The Future of Individual Identity*. New York: Public Affairs, 2007.

Coutinho, Steve. *Zhuangzi and Early Chinese Philosophy: Vagueness, Transformation and Paradox*. Aldershot, UK: Ashgate, 2004.

Culliney, John L., and David Jones. *The Fractal Self: Science, Philosophy, and the Evolution of Human Cooperation*. Honolulu: University of Hawai'i Press, 2007.

Dennerline, Jerry. *Qian Mu and the World of Seven Mansions*. New Haven: Yale University Press, 1988.

Dennett, Daniel C. *Darwin's Dangerous Idea: Evolution and the Meanings of Life*. New York: Simon & Schuster, 1995.

Dewey, John. *The Early Works, 1892–98*, 5 vols. Edited by Jo Ann Boydston. Carbondale, IL: Southern Illinois University Press, 1971.

———. *The Essential Dewey*, vol. 1. Edited by Larry Hickman and Thomas Alexander. Bloomington: Indiana University Press, 1998.

———. *Experience and Nature*. Mineola, NY: Dover, 2000.

———. *The Later Works of John Dewey, 1925–53*. Edited by Jo Ann Boydston. Carbondale: Southern Illinois University Press, 1985.

———. *The Middle Works of John Dewey, 1899–1924*. Edited by Jo Ann Boydston. Carbondale: Southern Illinois University Press, 1977.

———. *The Moral Writings of John Dewey*. Edited by James Gouinlock. New York: Prometheus Books, 2002.

Douven, Igor. "Peirce on Abduction." "Abduction." In *The Stanford Encyclopedia of Philosophy* (Spring 2011 edition), edited by Edward N. Zalta. https://plato.stanford.edu/archives/sum2021/entries/abduction/.

Emmett, Dorothy. *Rules, Roles and Relations*. London: Macmillan, 1967.

Farquhar, Judith. *Knowing Practice: The Clinical Encounter of Chinese Medicine.* Boulder: Westview Press, 1994.

Fei, Xiaotong. *From the Soil: The Foundations of Chinese Society.* A translation of *Xiangtu Zhongguo* 鄉土中國 by Gary G. Hamilton and Wang Zheng. Berkeley: University of California Press, 1992.

Gadamer, Hans-Georg. *Truth and Method*, 2nd ed. Translated by Joel Weinsheimer and Donald G. Marshall. New York: Crossroad, 1997.

Gernet, Jacques. *China and the Christian Impact: A Conflict of Cultures.* Translated by J. Lloyd. Cambridge: Cambridge University Press, 1985.

Goldin, Paul R. "The Myth That China Has No Creation Myth." *Monumenta Serica* 56, no. 1 (2008).

Graham, A. C. *Disputers of the Tao.* La Salle, IL: Open Court, 1989.

———. *Later Mohist Logic, Ethics and Science.* Hong Kong: Chinese University Press, 1978.

———. "Replies." In *Chinese Texts and Philosophical Contexts: Essays Dedicated to Angus C. Graham*, edited by Henry Rosemont Jr. La Salle, IL: Open Court, 1991.

———. *Studies in Chinese Philosophy and Philosophical Literature.* Albany: State University of New York Press, 1990.

Guo, Qiyong 郭齊勇. 儒家倫理爭鳴集: 以親親互隱為中心 [Debates on Confucian ethics: The mutual concealment among family members]. Wuhan: Jiaoyuchubanshe, 2004.

Hadot, Pierre. *What Is Ancient Philosophy?* Translated by Michael Chase. Cambridge, MA: Belknap Press of Harvard University, 2002.

Hall, David L. *Eros and Irony: A Prelude to Philosophical Anarchism.* Albany: State University of New York Press, 1982.

———. Review of John Berthrong, *Concerning Creativity: A Comparison of Whitehead, Neville, and Chu His.* Albany: State University of New York Press, 1998. *American Journal of Theology and Philosophy* 20, no. 3 (September 1999).

Hall, David L., and Roger T. Ames. *Anticipating China: Thinking Through the Narratives of Chinese and Western Culture.* Albany: State University of New York Press, 1995.

———. *Thinking from the Han: Self, Truth, and Transcendence in Chinese and Western Culture.* Albany: State University of New York Press, 1998.

———. *Thinking Through Confucius.* Albany: State University of New York Press, 1987.

Hegel, G. W. F. *The Encyclopedia Logic.* Indianapolis: Hackett, 1991.

Hershock, Peter D. *Valuing Diversity: Buddhist Reflection on Realizing a More Equitable Global Future.* Albany: State University of New York Press, 2012.

Hoyt, Sarah F. "The Etymology of Religion." *Journal of the American Oriental Society* 32, no. 2 (1912).

Hu, Qiguang 胡奇光. *Zhongguoxiaoxueshi* 中國小學史 [A history of Chinese philology]. Shanghai: Shanghai People's Press, 2005.

James, William. *The Correspondence of William James*. Charlottesville: University of Virginia Press, 1994.

———. *A Pluralistic Universe*. New York: Longmans, Green, 1912.

———. *Varieties of Religious Experience: A Study in Human Nature*. New York: Penguin, 1981.

———. *The Works of William James*, Vol. 1: *Pragmatism*. Edited by Frederick H. Burkhardt. Cambridge, MA: Harvard University Press, 1975.

———. *The Works of William James*, Vol. 3: *Essays in Radical Pragmatism*. Edited by Frederick H. Burkhardt. Cambridge, MA: Harvard University Press, 1976.

Johnson, Mark. *The Body in the Mind: The Bodily Basis of Meaning, Imagination, and Reason*. Chicago: University of Chicago Press, 1987.

Jullien, François. *The Book of Beginnings*. New Haven: Yale University Press, 2016.

Keightley, David N. "Shang Divination and Metaphysics." *Philosophy East and West* 38, no. 4 (October 1988).

Kwan, Tze-wan 關子尹. "Multi-function Character Database," 2014. http://humanum.arts.cuhk.edu.hk/Lexis/lexi-mf/.

Laks, André, and Glenn Most. *The Concept of Presocratic Philosophy: Its Origin, Development and Significance*. Princeton: Princeton University Press, 2018.

Laozi. *Lao Tzu: Tao Te Ching*. Translated by D. C. Lau. London: Penguin Books, 1963.

Lau, D. C., and Chen Fong Ching. *A Concordance to the* Hanshiwaizhuan. Hong Kong: Commercial Press, 1992.

———. *A Concordance to the* Huainanzi. Hong Kong: Commercial Press, 1992.

———. *A Concordance to the* Liji. Hong Kong: Commercial Press, 1992.

Legge, James, trans. *The Chinese Classics*, 5 vols. Hong Kong: University of Hong Kong Press, 1960 [rpt.].

Leibniz, Gottfried Wilhelm. *Writings on China*. Translated by Daniel J. Cook and Henry Rosemont, Jr. La Salle, IL: Open Court, 1994.

Liu, Lydia H. *Translingual Practice: Literature, National Culture, and Translated Modernity—China, 1900–1937*. Stanford: Stanford University Press, 1995.

Liu, Yu. *From Chinese Cosmology to English Romanticism: The Intricate Journey of a Monistic Idea*. Columbia: University of South Carolina Press, 2023.

Lloyd, Geoffrey, and Nathan Sivin. *The Way and the Word: Science and Medicine in Early China and Greece*. New Haven: Yale University Press, 2002.

Makeham, John. *Name and Actuality in Early Chinese Thought*. Albany: State University of New York Press, 1994.

Malpas, Jeff. "Hans-Georg Gadamer." In *The Stanford Encyclopedia of Philosophy* (Fall 2018 edition), edited by Edward N. Zalta. https://plato.stanford.edu/archives/fall2018/entries/gadamer/.

May, Larry. *Sharing Responsibility*. Chicago: University of Chicago Press, 1992.

Mill, J. S. *On Liberty in Focus*. Edited by John Gray and G. W. Smith. London: Routledge, 1991.

———. *A System of Logic, Ratiocinative and Inductive; Being a Connected View of the Principles of Evidence and the Methods of Scientific Investigation*, 8th ed. London: Longmans, Green, 1930.

Mote, Frederick. *Intellectual Foundations of China*. New York: McGraw-Hill, 1989.

Needham, Joseph. *Science and Civilisation in China*, vol. 2. Cambridge: Cambridge University Press, 1956.

Nietzsche, Friedrich. *Beyond Good and Evil*. Translated by W. Kaufmann. New York: Vintage, 1966.

Norman, J., and T. Mei. "The Austroasiatics in Ancient South China: Some Lexical Evidence." *Monumenta Serica* 32 (1976).

Nuyen, A. T. "Confucian Role Ethics." *Comparative and Continental Philosophy* 4, no. 1 (2012).

Nylan, Michael. "*Yin-yang*, Five Phases, and *Qi*." In *China's Early Empires: A Reappraisal*, edited by Michael Nylan and Michael Loewe. Cambridge: Cambridge University Press, 2010.

Okin, Susan Moller. *Justice, Gender, and the Family*. New York: Basic Books, 1989.

O'Neill, Timothy Michael. *Ideography and Chinese Language Theory: A History*. Berlin: Walter de Gruyter, 2016.

Ovid. *The Metamorphoses*. Translated by Allen Mandelbaum. New York: Everyman's Library, 2013.

Owen, Stephen. *Readings in Chinese Literary Thought*. Cambridge: Council on East Asian Studies, Harvard University Press, 1992.

Palmer, John. *Parmenides and Presocratic Philosophy*. Oxford: Oxford University Press, 2009.

Pang, Pu 龐樸. "Yizhong youji de yuzhou shengcheng tushi: Jieshao Chujian Taiyi shengshui" 一種有機的宇宙成圖式: 介紹楚簡《太一生水》 [An organic schematization of the universe: An introduction to the Chu bamboo slips "Taiyishengshui"]. *Daojia wenhua yanjiu* 道家文化研究 17 (1999).

Papineau, David. "Naturalism." In *The Stanford Encyclopedia of Philosophy* (Fall 2023 edition), edited by Edward N. Zalta and Uri Nodelman. https://plato.stanford.edu/archives/fall2023/entries/naturalism/.

Peerenboom, R. P. "Beyond Naturalism: A Reconstruction of Daoist Environmental Ethics." In *Environmental Philosophy in Asian Traditions of Thought*, edited by J. Baird Callicott and James McRae. Albany: State University of New York Press, 2014.

Peters, F. E. *Greek Philosophical Terms: A Historical Lexicon*. New York: New York University Press, 1967.

Peterson, Willard. "Making Connections: 'Commentary on the Attached Verbalizations' of the *Book of Changes*." *Harvard Journal of Asiatic Studies* 42, no. 1 (1982).

Plato. *The Being of the Beautiful: Plato's* Theaetetus, Sophist, *and* Statesman. Translated by Seth Bernardete. Chicago: University of Chicago Press, 1984.

———. *The Last Days of Socrates*. Translated by Hugh Tredennick and Harold Tarrant. London: Penguin, 2003.

———. *The Republic*. Edited by G. R. F. Ferrari, translated by Tom Griffith. Cambridge: Cambridge University Press, 2000.

———. The Symposium *and* The Phaedrus: *Plato's Erotic Dialogues*. Translated by William S. Cobb. Albany: State University of New York Press, 1993.

———. *Timaeus*. In *Timaeus and Critias*. Translated by Robin Waterfield, introduction by Andrew Gregory. Oxford: Oxford University Press, 2008.

Powers, Martin. *China and England: The Preindustrial Struggle for Justice in Word and Image*. London: Routledge, 2020.

Psillos, Stathis. "Abduction: Between Conceptual Richness and Computational Complexity." In *Abduction and Induction: Essays on their Relation and Integration*, edited by A. K. Kakas and P. Flach. Dordrecht: Kluwer, 2000.

Puett, Michael. *To Become a God: Cosmology, Sacrifice, and Self-Divinization in Early China*. Cambridge: Harvard University Asia Center, 2002.

Putnam, Hilary. *The Many Faces of Realism*. La Salle, IL: Open Court, 1987.

———. *Realism with a Human Face*. Cambridge, MA: Harvard University Press, 1990.

Rorty, Richard. "Philosophy and the Hybridization of Culture." In *Educations and Their Purposes: A Conversation among Cultures*, edited by Roger T. Ames and Peter D. Hershock. Honolulu, University of Hawai'i Press, 2007.

Said, Edward W. *Orientalism*. New York: Pantheon Books, 1978.

Sandel, Michael. *Liberalism and the Limits of Justice*. Cambridge: Cambridge University Press, 1982.

Schleiermacher, Friedrich D. E. *The Christian Faith*. Edited by H. R. Mackintosh and J. S. Stewart. London: T & T Clark, 1999.

Schlipp, Paul. *The Philosophy of Alfred North Whitehead*. New York: Tudor, 1941.

Shaughnessy, Edward L., trans. *I Ching: The Classic of Changes*. New York: Ballantine, 1997.

Shields, Christopher. *Aristotle*. New York: Routledge, 2007.

Shusterman, Richard. *Body Consciousness: A Philosophy of Mindfulness and Somaesthetics*. Cambridge: Cambridge University Press, 2008.

Skrbina, David. *Panpsychism in the West*. Cambridge, MA: MIT Press, 2005.

Sivin, Nathan. Foreword to Manfred Porkert, *The Theoretical Foundations of Chinese Medicine*. Cambridge, MA: MIT Press.

———. *Medicine, Philosophy and Religion in Ancient China: Researches and Reflections*. Aldershot, UK: Variorum, 1995.

Slingerland, Edward. "Body and Mind in Early China: An Integrated Humanities–Science Approach," *Journal of the American Academy of Religions* 81, no. 1 (2013).

———. *Mind and Body in Early China: Beyond Orientalism and the Myth of Holism.* Oxford: Oxford University Press, 2019.

———. Response to Jim Behuniak. *Dao: A Journal in Comparative Philosophy* 18, no. 3 (2019).

Smiley, Marion. *Moral Responsibility and the Boundaries of Community.* Chicago: University of Chicago Press, 1992.

Sommer, Deborah. "Boundaries of the *Ti* Body." In *Star Gazing, Fire Phasing, and Healing in China: Essays in Honor of Nathan Sivin*, ed. Michael Nylan, Henry Rosemont Jr., and Li Waiyee, special issue of *Asia Major*, 3rd series, 21, part 1 (2008).

Steele, Dave Ramsey, ed. *Genius in Their Own Words: The Intellectual Journeys of Seven Great 20th-Century Thinkers.* Chicago: Open Court, 2002.

Sun, Bin. *Sun Bin: The Art of Warfare: A Translation of the Classic Chinese Work of Philosophy and Strategy.* Translated by D. C. Lau and Roger T. Ames. Albany: State University of New York Press, 2003.

Sun, Xiangchen 孫向晨. 論家: 個體與親親 [On family: The individual and devotion to kin]. Shanghai: East China Normal University Press, 2019.

———. 生生: 在時代之中存在 [Procreativity: Being-between-the-generations] 哲學研究 [Philosophical research] no. 9 (2018).

Tan, Sor-hoon. *Confucian Democracy: A Deweyan Reconstruction.* Albany: State University of New York Press, 2003.

———. "*Tianxia* and Global Distributive Justice." In Tianxia *in Comparative Perspectives: Alternative Models for a Possible Planetary Order*, edited by Roger T. Ames, Sor-hoon Tan, and Steven Y. H. Yang. Honolulu: University of Hawai'i Press, 2023.

Tang, Junyi 唐君毅. *Complete Works* 唐君毅全集. Taipei: Xuesheng shuju, 1991.

Taylor, Charles. *The Language Animal: The Full Shape of the Human Linguistic Capacity.* Cambridge, MA: Harvard University Press, 2016.

———. *Sources of the Self: The Making of the Modern Identity*, Cambridge MA: Harvard University Press, 1989.

Tiles, Mary. "Idols of the Market Place: Knowledge and Language." Unpublished manuscript, n.d.

———. "Images of Reason in Western Culture." In *Alternative Rationalities*, edited by Eliot Deutsch. Honolulu: Society for Asian and Comparative Philosophy Monograph, 1992.

Tu, Wei-ming. *Centrality and Commonality: An Essay on Confucian Religiousness.* Albany: State University of New York Press, 1989.

Vattimo, Gianni. *After Christianity.* New York: Columbia University Press, 2002.

Wang Bi 王弼. "Mingxiang 明象" [Elucidating the images]. *Zhouyi Lueli* [A summary introduction to the *Book of Changes*] in the *Baibucongshu jicheng* 百部叢書集成, Taipei: Yiwen Publishing House, 1965.

Weissman, David. *A Social Ontology*. New Haven: Yale University Press, 2000.

Whitehead, A. N. *Modes of Thought*. New York: Free Press, 1938.

———. *Process and Reality: An Essay in Cosmology*, corrected 2nd ed. Edited by Donald Sherburne. New York: Free Press, 1979.

Wolgast, Elizabeth H. *The Grammar of Justice*. Ithaca, NY: Cornell University Press, 1987.

Wong, David. "Cultivating the Self in Concert with Others." In *Dao Companion to the Analects*, edited by Amy Olberding. Dordrecht: Springer, 2014.

———. "If We Are Not by Ourselves, If We Are Not Strangers." In *Polishing the Chinese Mirror: Essays in Honor of Henry Rosemont, Jr.*, edited by Marthe Chandler and Ronnie Littlejohn. New York: Global, 2008.

———. "Relational and Autonomous Selves." *Journal of Chinese Philosophy* 34, no. 4 (December 2004).

Yu, Jiyuan. *The Ethics of Confucius and Aristotle: Mirrors of Virtue*. New York: Routledge, 2007.

———. *The Structure of Being in Aristotle's* Metaphysics. Dordrecht: Kluwer Academic, 2003.

Zhang, Longxi. "Translating Cultures: China and the West." In *Chinese Thought in a Global Context: A Dialogue between Chinese and Western Philosophical Approaches*, edited by Karl-Heinz Pohl. Leiden: Brill, 1999.

Zhang, Xianglong 張祥龍. 概念化思維與象思維 [Conceptualizing thinking and imagistic thinking]. 杭州師範大學學報 [Journal of Hangzhou Normal University] no. 5 (September 2008).

Zhang, Yanhua. *Transforming Emotions with Chinese Medicine: An Ethnographic Account from Contemporary China*. Albany: State University of New York Press, 2007.

Zhao, Tingyang 赵汀阳. 作为创世论的存在论 [Creatiology as ontology]. 哲学研究 [Philosophical research] no. 8 (2012).

———. 惠此中國: 作為一個神性概念的中國 [The making and becoming of China: Its way of historicity]. Beijing: Citic Press, 2016; *The Whirlpool That Produced China: Stag Hunting on the Central Plain*. Translated by Edmund Ryden. Albany: State University of New York Press, 2024.

———.《作为创世论的存在论》 [Ontology as world-making].《哲学研究》 [Philosophical research] no. 8 (2012).

———. "The Ontology of Co-existence: From *Cogito* to *Facio*." *Diogenes* 57, no. 4 (2012).

———. 天下體系: 世界制度哲學導論 [The *tianxia* system: An introduction to the philosophy of world institution]. Beijing: People's University Press, 2011; *All under Heaven: The* Tianxia *System for a Possible World Order*. Translated by Joseph E. Harroff. Oakland: University of California Press, 2021.

———. 共在存在论: 人际与心际 [An ontology of coexistence: Shared relations and shared feelings].《哲学研究》 [Philosophical research] no. 8 (2009).

Zheng, Kai 鄭開. *The Metaphysics of Philosophical Daoism*. Translated by Hanliang Ruan. New York: Routledge, 2021.

———. 試論孟子心性論哲學的理論結構 [On the theoretical structure of Mencius's philosophy of *xinxing* theory]. 國際儒學 [International Confucianism] 1, no. 2 (2021).

———. 中國哲學語境中的本體論與形而上學 [Ontology and metaphysics within the context of Chinese philosophy]. 哲學研究 [Philosophical research] no. 1 (2008).

Zhou, Yiqun. *Festival, Feasts, and Gender Relations in Ancient China and Greece*. New York: Cambridge University Press, 2010.

Zhuangzi 莊子. Harvard-Yenching Institute Sinological Index Series, Supp. 20. Peking: Harvard Yenching Institute, 1947.

Ziporyn, Brook. "Vast Continuity versus the One: Thoughts on *Daodejing* 42, *Taiyishengshui*, and the Legacy of Roger T. Ames." In *Appreciating the China Difference: Engaging Roger T. Ames on Methods, Issues, and Roles*, edited by James Behuniak. Albany: State University of New York Press, 2018.

Index